VISUAL AND MULTIMEDIA INFORMATION MANAGEMENT

IFIP - The International Federation for Information Processing

IFIP was founded in 1960 under the auspices of UNESCO, following the First World Computer Congress held in Paris the previous year. An umbrella organization for societies working in information processing, IFIP's aim is two-fold: to support information processing within its member countries and to encourage technology transfer to developing nations. As its mission statement clearly states,

IFIP's mission is to be the leading, truly international, apolitical organization which encourages and assists in the development, exploitation and application of information technology for the benefit of all people.

IFIP is a non-profitmaking organization, run almost solely by 2500 volunteers. It operates through a number of technical committees, which organize events and publications. IFIP's events range from an international congress to local seminars, but the most important are:

- The IFIP World Computer Congress, held every second year;
- open conferences;
- working conferences.

The flagship event is the IFIP World Computer Congress, at which both invited and contributed papers are presented. Contributed papers are rigorously refereed and the rejection rate is high.

As with the Congress, participation in the open conferences is open to all and papers may be invited or submitted. Again, submitted papers are stringently refereed.

The working conferences are structured differently. They are usually run by a working group and attendance is small and by invitation only. Their purpose is to create an atmosphere conducive to innovation and development. Refereeing is less rigorous and papers are subjected to extensive group discussion.

Publications arising from IFIP events vary. The papers presented at the IFIP World Computer Congress and at open conferences are published as conference proceedings, while the results of the working conferences are often published as collections of selected and edited papers.

Any national society whose primary activity is in information may apply to become a full member of IFIP, although full membership is restricted to one society per country. Full members are entitled to vote at the annual General Assembly, National societies preferring a less committed involvement may apply for associate or corresponding membership. Associate members enjoy the same benefits as full members, but without voting rights. Corresponding members are not represented in IFIP bodies. Affiliated membership is open to non-national societies, and individual and honorary membership schemes are also offered.

VISUAL AND MULTIMEDIA INFORMATION MANAGEMENT

IFIP TC2 / WG2.6
Sixth Working Conference on Visual Database Systems
May 29–31, 2002, Brisbane, Australia

Edited by

Xiaofang Zhou
University of Queensland
Australia

Pearl Pu
Swiss Institute of Technology in Lausanne (EPFL)
Switzerland

SPRINGER SCIENCE+BUSINESS MEDIA, LLC

Library of Congress Cataloging-in-Publication Data

IFIP TC2/WG2.6 Working Conference on Visual Database Systems (6th : 2002 : Brisbane, Qld.)
Visual and multimedia information management : IFIP TC2/WG2.6 sixth Working Conference on Visual Database Systems, May 29-31, 2002, Brisbane, Australia / edited by Xiaofang Zhou, Pearl Pu.
p. cm. — (International Federation for Information Processing ; 88)
Includes bibliographical references and index.
ISBN 978-1-4757-6935-7 ISBN 978-0-387-35592-4 (eBook)
DOI 10.1007/978-0-387-35592-4
1. Database management—Congresses. 2. Image processing—Congresses. I. Zhou, Xiaofang. II. Pu, Pearl. III. Title. IV. International Federation for Information Processing (Series) ; 88.

QA76.9.D3 I1665 2002
006.4'2—dc21 2002021860

Table of Contents

Preface

The papers in this volume were presented at the 6th IFIP 2.6 Working Conference on Visual Database Systems (VDB6), which was held in Brisbane, Australia from 29-31 May 2002. Previous conferences on Visual Database Systems have been held in Tokyo in 1989, Budapest in 1991, Lausanne in 1995, L'Aquila, Italy in 1998 and Fukuoka, Japan in 2000.

The nature of data managed by modern database systems has drastically changed over the last decade, moving from text, images, sound and video to compositions of those media to realize advanced multimedia applications. Visual representations are used extensively within recent user interfaces and are essential mechanisms for accessing data through database systems. The IFIP WG2.6 Visual Database Systems conference series provides a forum to present the latest research results, new technology development and new applications in the area of visual data management, visual interfaces to query databases and visual interface to interpret information retrieved from database systems. This year VDB6 received 46 submissions from 11 countries and regions. Each paper has been carefully reviewed by at least three members of the international program committee. This volume includes nineteen papers selected by the program committee from regular submissions, five papers selected from a special track on multimedia information retrieval organised by Dr. Qing Li (City University of Hong Kong) and Dr. Ji-Rong Wen (Microsoft Research, China). It also includes three keynote speech papers presented at VDB6 by leading experts in spatial and multimedia information management, Professor Hans-Jörg Schek of ETH Zürich, Dr. Dave Abel of CSIRO Australia and Dr. Hongjian Zhang of Microsoft Research China. An invited paper by Lory Molesky and Jayant Sharma of Oracle to reflect recent industry trends in visual database systems is also included.

The conference received generous financial support from the VLDB Australian Conference Fund, the University of Queensland (School of Information Technology and Electrical Engineering), and Queensland University of Technology (School of Information Systems). We are grateful to Professor Maria Orlowska (the General Chair of VDB6), Dr. Phoebe Chen (the Local Organisation Chair), Ms. Kathleen

Williams (the Conference Secretary), Mr. Sham Prasher, and Ms. Maureen Shields for their great effort in supporting and organising this conference. We would also like to thank the VDB Steering Committee members, Professor Stefano Spaccapietra and Professor Tiziana Catarci for their continuous support and close involvement in organising VDB6, without which it is not possible to have such a successful conference.

Finally, we would like to take this opportunity to thank all Program Committee members and external reviewers for their expertise and help in evaluating papers.

Xiaofang Zhou and Pearl Pu
VDB6 Program Committee Co-Chairs

General Chair
Maria Orlowska, *University of Queensland, Australia*

Program Co-Chairs
Xiaofang Zhou, *University of Queensland, Australia*
Pearl Pu, *Swiss Institute of Technology, Lausanne, Switzerland*

Steering Committee of VDB Conferences
Stefano Spaccapietra, *Swiss Federal Institute of Technology Switzerland*
Tiziana Catarci, *University of Roma La Sapienza, Italy*

Program Committee Members

Karl Aberer	*EPFL, Switzerland*
Masatoshi Arikawa	*University of Tokyo, Japan*
Dominique Brodbeck	*Macrofocus, Switzerland*
Tiziana Catarci	*Universita' degli Studi di Roma, Italy*
Sang K. Cha	*Seoul National University, Korea*
Elisabeth Chang	*University of New Castle, Australia*
Phoebe Chen	*Queensland University of Technology, Australia*
Ed H. Chi	*Xerox PARC, USA*
Wesley Chu	*UCLA, USA*
Isabel Cruz	*University of Illinois at Chicago, USA*
Umesh Dayal	*HP, USA*
Leila De Floriani	*University of Genova, Italy*
Peter Eades	*University of Sydney, Australia*
Max Egenhofer	*University of Maine, USA*
Martin Erwig	*Oregon State University, USA*
Eddy Flerackers	*Limburgs Universitair Centrum, Belgium*
Oscar Firschein	*Stanford University, USA*
Carol Goble	*University of Manchester, UK*
Amarnath Gupta	*University of California San Diego, USA*
Jesse Jin	*University of Sydney, Australia*
Yahiko Kambayashi	*Kyoto University, Japan*
Daniel Keim	*University of Constance and ATT Labs, Germany*
Masaru Kitsuregawa	*Tokyo University, Japan*

Additional Reviewers

Houman Alborzi, *University of Maryland,USA*
Serafino Cicerone, *Univ. of L'Aquila, Italy*
Philippe Cudre-Mauroux, *EPFL, Switzerland*
Anwitaman Datta, *EPFL, Switzerland*
Leila de Floriani, *University of Genova, Italy*
Marlon Dumas, *Queensland University of Technology, Australia*
Tim Dwyer, *University of Sydney, Australia*
David Edmond, *Queensland University of Technology, Australia*
James Farrugia, *University of Maine, USA*
Luc Girardin, *Macrofocus GmbH, Switzerland*
Tony Griffiths, *University of Manchester, UK*
Gisli R. Hjaltason, *RightOrder, Inc., USA*
Jinyu Hou, *University of Southern Queensland, Australia*
Kimberly James, *Worcester Polytechnic Institute, USA*
Victor Liu, UCLA, USA
Paola Magillo, *University of Genova, Italy*
Anirban Mondal, *National University of Singapore, Singapore*
Laura Papaleo, *University of Genova, Italy*
Paulo Pinheiro da Silva, *University of Manchester, UK*
Magdalena Punceva, *EPFL, Switzerland*
Atsuhiro Takasu, *National Institute of Informatics, Japan*
Masashi Toyoda, *university of Tokyo, Japan*
Yukari Shirota, *Gakushuin University, Japan*
Aya Soffer, *IBM Research Lab in Haifa*
Jie Wu, *EPFL, Switzerland*
Qinhhua Zou, *UCLA, USA*

HYPERDATABASES

Infrastructure for the Information Space

Hans-J. Schek, Heiko Schuldt, and Roger Weber
Database Research Group, Institute of Information Systems
ETH Zentrum, CH–8092 Zurich, Switzerland
Email: {schek,schuldt,weber}@inf.ethz.ch

Abstract The amount of stored information is exploding while, at the same time, tools for accessing relevant information are rather under-developed. Usually, all users have a pre-defined view on a global information space and have to access data by the same primitive means. However, a more convenient solution from a user's point of view considers her/his individual context and interests by mapping the global information space to a personal one. Yet, the organization and personalization of information spaces induces a set of tightly related problems: First, user interfaces have to present personalized information in a user-friendly way and have to be enriched by sophisticated, context-sensitive navigation techniques. Second, the personal information space has to be organized automatically, by exploiting similarities between multimedia documents. Third, in order to allow the user to influence the automatic organization of her/his information space, relevance feedback techniques for multimedia similarity search have to be provided. Finally, taken into account that information is replicated at several sources and is subject to modification, sophisticated coordination mechanisms have to guarantee consistent views on the global information space. In this paper, we introduce the vision of *hyperdatabases* as the core infrastructure to support these requirements in a holistic way. Moreover, we present the ETHWorld project and its sub-projects in which we apply hyperdatabase concepts for managing and organizing the information space of a virtual campus.

Keywords: Information Spaces, Information Space Organization, Personalization, Multimedia Similarity Search, Relevance Feedback, Consistency, Process Management.

1. INTRODUCTION

The amount of stored information is exploding as a consequence of the immense progress in computer and communication technology during the last decades. However, tools for accessing relevant information and processing globally distributed information in a convenient manner are under-developed. For instance, consider the information space spanned by an intranet or a digital library. Nowadays, every user has the same view on this global information space (neglecting authorized sub-spaces) and has to access data by the same primitive means, e.g., with a keyword-based search engine or a manually maintained bookmark list. However, each user has a different context and is only interested in a small part of the entire information space. Therefore, search and navigation tools should not operate on the global information space. Rather, they should map the global information space to personal information spaces tailored to the needs of the users and should operate only within these much smaller spaces. Navigation within a personal space must go beyond the simple principle of hyper links, e.g., we need tools that support orientation, context sensitive navigation, and visualization of (dynamic) sub spaces. Furthermore, most search tools are specialized for textual information only. Although these methods can be adapted to multimedia documents, their retrieval quality is far from being satisfactory. To search for images, as one important multimedia type, it is often not sufficient to index images just with annotations or meta data (file name, URL). Advanced search techniques like content-based retrieval exist, but their performance characteristics are often not acceptable as they disallow for interactive search. Finally, entering queries is often a difficult task as the users have to have some common understanding about how the search engine works. We envision the usage of relevance feedback as an easy-to-use methodology to refine queries.

Another key problem with distributed information spaces, as they occur in intranets or digital libraries, is consistency of data stored at several places in the space. For instance, consider a query with some keyword x evaluated with a search engine. Since the search engine computed its indexes based on recently downloaded copies of the original data, a document d only means that it contained at some point in time the keyword x. In many situations, this retrieval quality is sufficient but it is unacceptable for applications requiring precise results. Google, as one major search engine on the web, rebuilds its indexes in 30 days and uses them for another 30 days (Google, 2002). As a consequence, the version of the document used for the index may be up to 60 days old and documents updated or created in the last few days can not be found. Analogously, replicated information in the information space has to be kept consistent. For instance, an overview page with all current projects of an university should reflect the data provided by each research group. However, since the research groups may change their project data at any point in time, and often without notifying related authorities, the overview page will soon contain outdated data and becomes quickly useless. Consequently, the future infrastructure for a global information space has to provide some consistency guarantees (Pu et al., 2001). The owner of an information space must be able to define rules how information from several sources has to be propagated to several destinations involving information extraction, aggregation, transformation and data integration. To this end, processes for the propagation of information have to be defined and to be linked to events necessitating coordination activities, i.e., a process is automatically executed whenever necessary. The processes then correspond to the activities required to provide the desired consistency guarantees.

We have studied the above problems, i.e., advanced search and navigation, and consistency, within the ETHWorld project. ETHWorld was established by ETH Zurich to create a virtual campus where students, assistants, professors, researches inside and outside ETH, and guests can meet, chat, discuss, exchange information, or work together. ETH Zurich consists of many engineering oriented research institutes and therefore spans a very large information space. This inevitably necessitates the support for individual, personalized views on the global information space. Moreover, due to the vast amount and variety of multimedia documents that are generated in every-day's research and teaching activities, sophisticated support for efficient and effective search is needed in order to make use of this plethora of information. However, the independence of all research groups prohibits the centralized organization and management of data. Yet, the infrastructure for information space organization has to consider the execution of appropriate processes in a largely distributed system to nevertheless provide certain consistency guarantees.

Our solution consists of three main actions:

- Improved Human-Computer interaction to visualize and navigate in the information space and to refine queries by means of relevance feedback,
- Advanced document retrieval with interactive response times, and
- Development of an open infrastructure that allows to guarantee consistency within the information space.

The glue to all these different aspects and the basic underpinning of the infrastructure for information space organization is the concept of *hyperdatabases* (Schek et al., 2000). In short, a hyperdatabase provides database functionality, but at a much higher level of abstraction than traditional database systems, i.e., at the level of information components instead of data objects.

The remainder of this paper is organized as follows. In Section 2, the concept of hyperdatabases is introduced. Then, the main activities towards the ETHWorld architecture for information space organization are presented in a top-down approach. First, we introduce the interface aspects associated with the presentation of information spaces. (Section 3). Then, the support for multimedia similarity search with focus on image retrieval and relevance feedback is presented (Section 4). In Section 5, we discuss the realization of process-based coordination and sketch the overall architecture of the ETHWorld infrastructure. Section 6 finally concludes.

2. THE HYPERDATABASE CONCEPT

When relational database systems have been introduced twenty years ago, they have been considered as infrastructure and main platform for development of data-intensive applications. Data independence was considered to be a breakthrough: programmers were freed from low-level details, e.g., how to access shared data efficiently and correctly, given concurrent access. But by now, the prerequisites for application development have changed dramatically. For instance, communication has become fairly cheap. Consequently, the role of database concepts must be re-visited and newly determined. Undoubtedly, the database system plays an important role. However, it has degenerated to a storage manager to a large extent, far away from the applications. More and more researchers are making these observations and start to question the role of databases for future distributed information systems (Brodie, 1999, Stonebraker et al., 1999) and, as a consequence, for the organization of information spaces. In what follows, we provide our personal view on this future infrastructure and identify its building blocks which together allow for the coherent and consistent management and organization of information spaces.

2.1. What is a Hyperdatabase?

A first rough definition is: A Hyperdatabase (HDB) is a database over databases (Schek et al., 2000). It administers objects that are composed of objects and transactions that are composed of transactions. Hence, an HDB is a database, the primitives of which are again databases. In a more general setting we say that an HDB administers distributed components in a networked environment and provides a kind of higher order "data independence". Now we must strive for immunity of application programs not only against changes in storage and access structure, but also against changes in location, implementation, workload, the number of replica of software components and their services. What is the difference between a DB and an HDB? In a nutshell we say: a DB is a platform for clients concurrently accessing shared data. We need data definition, data manipulation, and transactions at the interface. The DB under the cover performs query optimization, correctness for parallel access, recovery, persistence, load balancing, availability. Similarly, an HDB is a platform for clients, concurrently accessing shared application services (c.f. Figure 1(a)). As opposed to shared data in a DB, in an HDB we have shared components and services. At the interface of an HDB we need component and service definition and description, service customization, transactional processes encompassing multiple service invocations. The HDB, under the cover, performs optimization of client requests, routing, scheduling, parallelization, correctness of concurrent accesses, flexible failure treatment, providing guaranteed termination (i.e., a generalized form of atomicity), availability, flexible recovery, and scalability.

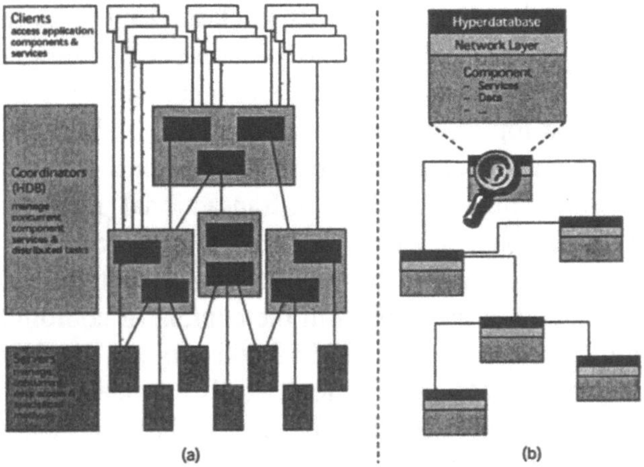

Figure 1. Service composition in a HDB (a) and distributed HDB implementation (b)

2.2. Hyperdatabases and Information Spaces

In addition to the general characteristics of hyperdatabases, special features are required to support the goal of organizing and maintaining complex and even dynamic information spaces. Essentially, organizing an information space means providing a coherent, integrated, and consistent view on a vast amount of information that is produced, stored, and even updated by distributed components within a networked environment. The most crucial requirement of an information space is to provide users with information with the following quality of service characteristics. Information has to be

- relevant, i.e., must be subjective, time- and location dependent
- reliable, i.e., has to be correct, consistent, and certified
- available to everybody, i.e., each user may have her/his personal view
- available everywhere, i.e., (individual) information spaces are continuously maintained and kept up-to-date; even mobile users connecting occasionally and from different locations are always served with fresh data.

When comparing a DB and an HDB in the context of information space organization and management, the provision of efficient access to objects has to be considered. A database applies indexing techniques to data records. An HDB, however, has to run dedicated services like feature extractions to derive information about information sources. In addition, since these information sources as well as the services that have to be applied to them are physically distributed, a core functionality of an HDB for the information space is coordination. This means that the HDB has to keep track of changes, to continuously propagate these changes, and to derive and update particular views of the overall information space. As a consequence, HDB functionality is implemented in a distributed way on top of existing components by adding an HDB layer (c.f. Figure 1(b)) rather than being realized by an additional centralized, monolithic component. Following the analogy of transactional processes being the HDB abstraction of database transactions, a HDB as coordinator has to run such transactional processes and to guarantee their correct termination.

A concrete application of an HDB is in the context of coordinating multimedia information components in the ETHWorld project. The HDB's task is to observe information sources and to automatically execute a sequence of services (e.g., for extracting color and shape features and for term extraction from text). These features are required to maintain an index allowing for sophisticated search techniques within the information space. Hence, the HDB is the infrastructure that, under the cover, provides users with quality of service guarantees for the information she/he wants to access. In addition, the processes controlled by the HDB also account for the fact that information is aggregated in the way this is required for individual information spaces.

3. DYNAMIC COLLABORATIVE INFORMATION SPACES

The goal of the ETHWorld sub-project *All4u–Dynamic Collaborative Information Spaces* is the development of a tool for navigation, organization and orientation in the personal information space of a user in ETHWorld. By its definition, All4u requires an infrastructure that maintains documents distributed over a large number of peers. This *infostructure* must be able to integrate data from several sources to gather a global view, to propagate and map this view to the users, to cache information of/for mobile clients, to grant or deny access to documents, to keep track of changes at the data and meta data level, and to enforce consistency in case of replication. All4u further demands for specialized components which support users in shaping and visualizing their personal information space, in searching documents context and content sensitive, and in keeping track of activities, of context changes and of the workspace of users.

From our perspective, the concept of hyperdatabase perfectly suits these requirements (cf. Figure 2). A hyperdatabase would offer a simple way to add and administer specialized components. The services provided by these components can be combined to form application aware processes with specific execution guarantees (recovery, exception handling, alternative executions, consistency, concurrency control, etc.). Commonly, such processes are trigge-

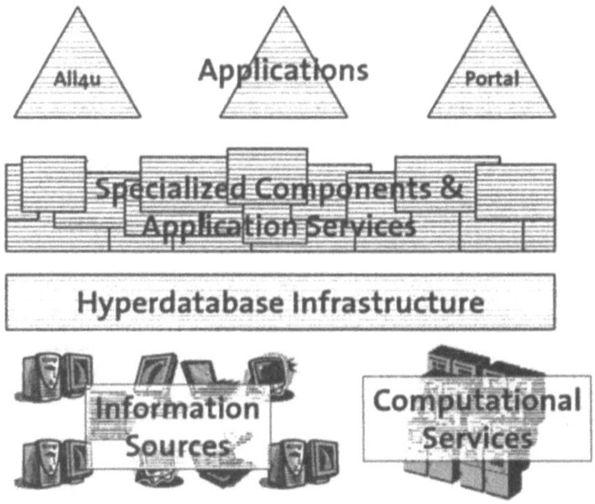

Figure 2. Architecture for a global information space as proposed for ETHWorld.

red by events like insertion, update, or connect/disconnect. Computationally expensive tasks like content and context aware similarity search may easily be scaled out to a cluster of workstations (computational services). We see All4u as a top-level application which interacts with the users of ETHWorld. It is built on top of specialized components which, in turn, are based on a global, distributed, and consistent infrastructure: a hyperdatabase.

In what follows, we shed some light on the main ideas of All4u and its architecture. The information model in All4u, depicted in Figure 3, consists of three layers: i.) a global information space subsuming all information made available by a peer, ii.) a personal information space which is tailored to the needs of a user in his/her current context, and iii.) the visualization of interaction with the personal information space.

On the bottom level, we define the global information space of ETHWorld as a bag containing documents from diverse, distributed sources like local file systems, e-mail accounts, news archives, intranet, and the Internet. Usually, these sources are distinctly separated from each other and for each source type one needs a different tool to organize, search, or maintain its documents. In our vision, the borders between information sources will diminish and all documents can be administered with a single application. Every participant of ETHWorld can share his/her information with any other user, group of users or with all users (much like with peer-to-peer file sharing system). This level is automatically maintained by background processes that are attached to events on the sources (e.g. insertion of a new document).

The global information space contains far too much data for an individual user. This quickly leads to loss of orientation and degenerated retrieval quality

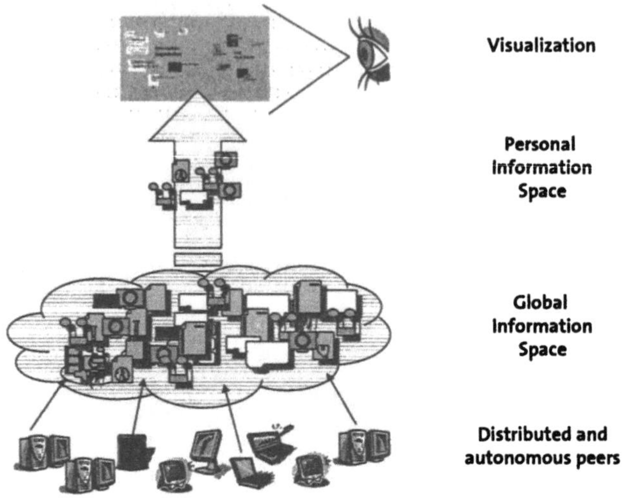

Figure 3. From global to personal information space.

when searching for documents. At the intermediate level of All4u, we preprocess the global information space and tailor it to the needs of the user in his/her current context. The result is a *personal information space* which can be arbitrarily manipulated by the user. Any change to a personal information space is appropriately propagated to the global information space and, transitively, to the personal information spaces of other users. In All4u, the user's context is dependent on his/her current task, his/her focus, his/her relations to other users (membership in groups, friends), and the history of documents visited and actions performed in the past. Basically, we apply filters to map the global information space to a personal one. The filters are based on "hard-wired" associations (this e-mail comes with this document), on hierarchy information at the sources (all documents in the same folder), on retrieval results on data or meta data (all documents containing the keywords "info space"), on content similarity (all documents similar to this one), and on recommendations of others (all documents my friends like). In our architecture, specialized components capture the contexts of users and use them to adjust the mapping from global to personal information space. Further components are able to efficiently select those documents from the global information space which pass the filters, i.e. which form the current personal information space.

Finally, on the top level, we have to visualize the personal information space and we need to provide proper navigation methods. With respect to layouting, we apply standard techniques like Fisheye Views, Cone Trees (Robertson et al., 1991), Hyperbolic Trees (Lamping et al., 1995), and methods for clustering high-dimensional feature representations of documents like, for instance,

FastMap (Faloutsos and Lin, 1995) or Self-Organizing Maps (Kohonen, 2001). Layouting is based on a number of criteria which are chosen according to the current context of the user (analogue to the one used for filtering). Whenever possible, documents are depicted by thumbnails together with some highlighted key words. As a second dimension, we apply different emphasizing methods to further distinguish the documents in the personal information space. For instance, we can vary the size of the document representation, its coloring, its transparency attribute, or, if the thumbnails of documents overlap, its visibility (i.e. z-position). We can apply the same criteria for emphasizing the documents as for layouting them. However, best results are achieved if layout criteria and emphasis criteria are orthogonal. Visualization is supported by enhanced client applications (e.g. applets) and dedicated server components. Interaction is modeled as a foreground process on top of the services for All4u.

4. INTERACTIVE SIMILARITY SEARCH IN LARGE ENVIRONMENTS

In All4u, we use context and content aware filters to map the global information space to a personal one. For instance, given a current working document and the user's context, what are the relevant documents in the global space? The similarity to the working document and how well a document fits to the context determine the relevance of a document. Based on the similarity scores, we can cluster documents and layout them such that similar documents are grouped together. To allow such interactive exploration of the global information space, the infrastructure of All4u must provide efficient and effective document search methods. Some of these components are provided by the related project *ISIS–Interactive SImilarity Search* (ISIS, 2002). Its goals are to i.) identify and build effective content descriptors for various document types, to ii.) develop efficient search methods that allow for complex similarity retrieval, and to iii.) build easy-to-use and powerful relevance feedback methods to support query formulation. The functionality is again provided by specialized components and by background processes. The processes enforce consistency after changes on any of the information source. For instance, the `InsertDocument` process (c.f. Figure 4) is triggered whenever a document is inserted somewhere.

4.1. Effective Content Descriptors

Firstly, the problem is to define and extract a compact representation for the content of multimedia documents. Most of the research in this field has concentrated on extracting descriptors from the raw data, e.g. words from a text document, color or texture feature from an image, or frequency histograms from audio. However, in a distributed and highly linked environment like in

All4u, the content of a document is not only defined by its physical representation (text, image data, audio, etc.) but also by its "neighborhood" which defines the context of the document. With multimedia document types like image, video, and audio, the context may even play the dominant role. For instance, by analyzing only image data or audio data, it is hardly possible to detect who is depicted by the image or who is singing. However, given the neighboring documents of the image or audio clip, we might derive this information more easily.

Secondly, we have to classify these descriptors under various aspects like retrieval quality, search efficiency, and storage overhead. Commonly, there is a trade off between search efficiency and retrieval quality. In interactive search scenarios, the first steps of a search are often aiming at finding the "right query". Thus, efficiency is more important than effectiveness. During later steps, however, effectiveness plays the dominant role as users wish to retrieve all relevant documents. Hence, given the quality characteristics of features, we may dynamically choose features depending on whether efficiency or effectiveness is important.

4.2. Efficient Search Methods for Effective Similarity Retrieval

In the past, search engines fot multimedia content often deployed only the simplest descriptors in order to be sufficiently fast. For instance, a widely used search technique for images is keyword based, and the URL (or ALT-attribute) of the image defines the textual description of the content. Although the search is very efficient, the retrieval quality is in almost all cases unsatisfactory. On the other hand, effective image retrieval systems deploy very complex descriptors which are not efficient enough for interactive search in large environments.

Our goal in ISIS is to find a sufficient trade-off between search efficiency and retrieval effectiveness. Our core search technique, the so-called vector approximation file (VA-File), already allows for interactive searching for similar images in image databases with millions of images (Weber et al., 1998; Boehm et al., 2001a). It is based on high-dimensional content-descriptors (e.g. color distribution, texture, and shape) and performs a nearest neighbor search to identify similar objects for a given a set of samples.

Retrieval for multimedia documents, however, mostly involves the usage of different types of descriptor representations, e.g. visual descriptors, keywords, or linkage information. Our goal is to develop a suite of index structures and search algorithms that enable queries using any combination of descriptors and that guarantees efficient and effective retrieval.

4.3. Relevance Feedback

Searching for documents is not a single step process. Rather, the query is reformulated and adapted many times before the result contains a sufficient number of relevant documents. While query refinement is relatively easy with text documents, it is very difficult for other document types like, for instance, images, especially if the retrieval measure is based on content descriptors (like color histogram). If an initial query with a sample image does not return a sufficient result, a user cannot just alter the image in some way. Rather, he needs support from the system. The so-called relevance feedback component refines a query given a result set and user judgments like "I like this image" and "I do not like this image". This step is repeated until the query yields a sufficient result.

Our aim is to identify the best methods and to improve current feedback techniques. Thereby, we address two orthogonal problems: i.) how can we get sufficient feedback information from the user, and ii.) how can this information be exploited to refine the query. Another interesting aspect is how to integrate relevance feedback techniques into the search algorithms. In the literature, a large number of feedback techniques have been proposed. But not all of them are useful as they impose high retrieval costs. We aim at the development of good feedback technique that leads to queries for which efficient search algorithms are available (Boehm et al., 2001b; Weber and Boehm, 2000).

Finally, we see relevance feedback and query refinement as an interactive process running in our hyperdatabase environment. Specialized components take care of capturing, analyzing and storing user feedback, and re-query the database with improved similarity search. Due to interactivity, these processes must be very efficient to be accepted by the user. The main problem is again to find a good trade-off between effective feedback models and efficient ones.

5. COORDINATION OF MULTIMEDIA INFORMATION

In this section, we present the hyperdatabase concepts for process execution and thus for the coordination of multimedia information sources. We also briefly introduce the architecture of the OSIRIS system we have built for coordination in ETHWorld.

5.1. Guaranteeing Consistency within the Global Information Space

In large-scale, distributed information systems spanning a global information space, information is usually replicated at several sites and derived information, e.g., the VA-File, is generated and maintained so as to provide efficient access to the information space. Obviously, changes in the source documents have to be automatically propagated to their replicas and to derived data in order to guarantee a consistent view on the global information space. The propagation of these changes now requires that i.) changes of documents are observed and ii.) that a well-defined sequence of services, called *process* is executed. Similarly, processes not only encapsulate the necessary services for guaranteeing consistency but they rather allow for distributed applications within the information space such as complex similarity queries which require the extraction of features, the consideration of relevance feedback, and finally the presentation of information. While the services being the single computational steps of processes are well in place, the infrastructure to seamlessly glue these services together is needed. To this end, hyperdatabase concepts are applied to allow for process description, execution, and monitoring as well as to provide certain execution guarantees for processes even in the presence of failures (Leymann, 1995), and concurrency (Schuldt et al., 1999).

5.2. OSIRIS: Distributed Platform for Process Support

Processes play a central role in the management of the global information space. When implementing a hyperdatabase as infrastructure for process support, various crucial requirements stemming from the dynamic characteristics of large-scale information spaces have to be considered. The most important of these requirements is scalability, both in terms of the number of users and in the number of services and information sources to be considered. Significantly growing numbers of concurrent users should not have impact on the performance of the overall system. The same holds for number of information sources and thus for the number of processes to execute in order to enforce consistency. Other requirements are stemming from the fact that services may be dynamically added to the system. In the presence of several semantically equivalent services, the infrastructure has to apply sophisticated load balancing techniques to equally distribute the workload among the components providing these services. Finally, the inherent heterogeneity and the autonomy of the systems being part of the global information space have to be considered.

For all these reasons, relying on a centralized implementation for process support would have severe impacts on scalability and the overall performance and hence would not support the aforementioned requirements. Rather, hyperdatabase functionality has to be distributed and parallelized. The *OSIRIS – Open Service Infrastructure for Reliable and Integrated process Support* (OSIRIS, 2002) system that is currently being implemented as part of the ETH-World infrastructure (Schuler et al., 2001) accounts for all these constraints. Following the model of transactional process management for execution guarantees (Schuldt et al., 2002), OSIRIS comes along with a kernel part in which

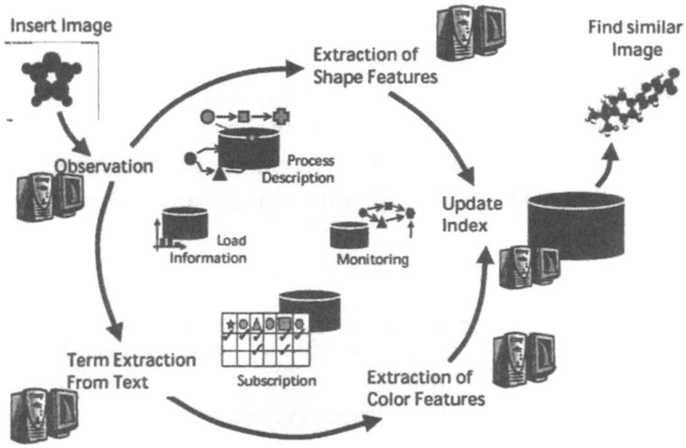

Figure 4. OSIRIS: Distributed Process Support Infrastructure in the ETHWorld Application

process models and the current system configuration is managed (which components exist, which services they provide). This kernel also maintains statistics about the load of all components and the currently running processes. Process execution, however, is realized in a completely distributed way in that the necessary information to locally drive the execution of a process is distributed to all components. This information contains, for instance, the service that has to be invoked after a local service is terminated (as being specified in the process models) and the load of all components providing this particular service. When components dynamically join or leave the system, and when the load of components significantly change, all components being affected of these changes are informed. As a consequence, the infrastructure is able to adjust dynamically to changing environments.

In Figure 4, the OSIRIS infrastructure for the `InsertDocument` process is depicted: process execution is triggered by the components providing the services of the process (outer circle) while meta information required for process execution is collected by the kernel components (within the circle) and distributed to the corresponding components of the outer circle.

6. CONCLUSIONS

In this paper, we have discussed the various requirements for an infrastructure aiming at organizing and managing the global information spaces. The core of the infrastructure is formed by a set of services and a hyperdatabase which allows for the seamless combination of these services into a coherent whole. This infrastructure supports similarity search of multimedia documents and sophisticated relevance feedback techniques. In addition, it provides support for processes realizing complex applications within the information space and guaranteeing a consistent view on the overall information space.

We have presented the ETHWorld project with its sub-projects All4u, ISIS, and OSIRIS in which we have successfully applied hyperdatabase concepts for the organization and management of the information space of a virtual campus.

REFERENCES

Boehm, K., Mlivoncic, M., Schek, H.-J., and Weber, R. (2001a). Fast Evaluation Techniques for Complex Similarity Queries. In *Proc. of 27th Int. Conf. on Very Large Data Bases (VLDB'01)*, pages 211–220, Rome, Italy.

Boehm, K., Mlivoncic, M., and Weber, R. (2001b). Quality-Aware and Load-Sensitive Planning of Image Similarity Queries. In *Proceedings of the 17th International Conference on Data Engineering (ICDE'01)*, pages 401–410, Heidelberg, Germany. IEEE Computer Society Press.

Brodie, M. (1999). Que Sera, Sera: The Coincidental Confluence of Economics, Business, and Collaborative Computing. In *Proc. of the 15th Int. Conf. on Data Engineering (ICDE'99)*, pages 2–3, Sydney, Australia.

ISIS (2002). `http://www.isis.ethz.ch`

Faloutsos, C. and Lin, K.-I. (1995). FastMap: A Fast Algorithm for Indexing, Data-Mining and Visualization of Traditional and Multimedia Datasets. In *Proceedings of ACM SIGMOD*, pages 163–174, San Jose, California, USA.

Google (2002). `http://www.google.com`.

Kohonen, T. (2001). *Self-Organizing Maps*, volume 30 of *Springer Series in Information Sciences*. Springer-Verlag, third edition.

Lamping, J., Rao, R., and Pirolli, P. (1995). A Focus+Context Technique Based on Hyperbolic Geometry for Visualizing Large Hierarchies. In *Proceedings of the ACM Conference on Human Factors in Computing Systems (CHI'95)*, pages 401–408, Denver, Colorado, USA.

Leymann, F. (1995). Supporting Business Transactions via Partial Backward Recovery in Workflow Management Systems. In *Proceedings of BTW'95*, pages 51–70, Dresden, Germany. Springer Verlag.

OSIRIS (2002). `http://www.osiris.ethz.ch`

Pu, C., Schwan, K., and Walpole, J. (2001). Infosphere Project: System Support for Information Flow Applications. *SIGMOD Record*, 30(1):25–34.

Robertson, G., Mackinlay, J., and Card, S. (1991). Cone Trees: Animated 3D Visualizations of Hierarchical Information. In *Proceedings of the ACM Conference on Human Factors in Computing Systems (CHI'91)*, pages 189–194.

Schek, H.-J., Boehm, K., Grabs, T., Roehm, U., Schuldt, H., and Weber, R. (2000). Hyperdatabases. In *Proceedings of the 1st International Conference on Web Information Systems Engineering (WISE'00)*, pages 14–23, Hong Kong, China. IEEE Computer Society Press.

Schuldt, H., Alonso, G., Beeri, C., and Schek, H.-J. (2002). Atomicity and Isolation for Transactional Processes. *ACM Transactions on Database Systems*, 27(1). To appear.

Schuldt, H., Alonso, G., and Schek, H.-J. (1999). Concurrency Control and Recovery in Transactional Process Management. In *Proceedings of the 18th ACM Symposium on Principles* *of Database Systems (PODS'99)*, pages 316–326, Philadelphia, Pennsylvania, USA. ACM Press.

Schuler, C., Schuldt, H., and Schek, H.-J. (2001). Supporting Reliable Transactional Business Processes by Publish/Subscribe Techniques. In *Proceedings of the 2nd International Workshop on Technologies for E–Services (TES'01)*, pages 118–131, Rome, Italy. Springer LNCS, Vol. 2193.

Stonebraker, M., Carey, M., and Hellerstein, J. (1999). Seminar Talk: A Sketch of Regres. http://db.cs.berkeley.edu/postmodern/stonebraker-final.ppt.

Weber, R. and Boehm, K. (2000). Trading Quality for Time with Nearest Neighbor Search. In *Proc. of the 7th Int. Conf. on Extending Database Technology (EDBT'00)*, pages 21–35, Konstanz, Germany.

Weber, R., Schek, H.-J., and Blott, S. (1998). A Quantitative Analysis and Performance Study for Similarity-Search Methods in High-Dimensional Spaces. In *Proceedings of 24rd International Conference on Very Large Data Bases (VLDB'98)*, pages 194–205, New York City, USA. Morgan Kaufmann.

BIOGRAPHIES

Hans–J. Schek received the M.Sc. degree in mathematics and the Ph.D. degree in civil engineering from University of Stuttgart, West Germany, in 1968 and 1972, respectively. He is currently a Professor of Computer Science at the Swiss Federal Institute of Technology (ETH) Zurich, Switzerland, where he is the head of the Database Research Group. From 1983 to 1988 he was a Professor of Computer Science at the Technical University of Darmstadt, West Germany, where he led the DASDBS project. Between 1972 and 1983 he was with the IBM Heidelberg Scientific Center, where he started the AIM database research project in 1978.

Heiko Schuldt studied computer science in Karlsruhe, Germany and Grenoble, France. He received the M.Sc. degree in 1996 from the University of Karlsruhe and the Ph.D. degree in 2001 from the Swiss Federal Institute of Technology (ETH) Zurich. He is currently a senior research associate in the Database Research Group of Prof. Hans-J. Schek at ETH Zurich.

Roger Weber received the M.Sc. degree in 1996 and the Ph.D. degree in 2001 from the Swiss Federal Institute of Technology (ETH) Zurich. He is currently a senior research associate in the Database Research Group of Prof. Hans-J. Schek at ETH Zurich.

FEDERATED INFORMATION SYSTEMS FOR COMMUNITIES

David J. Abel
CSIRO Mathematical and Information Sciences
GPO Box 664, Canberra, ACT 2601, Australia
Dave.abel@csiro.au

1. EXTENDED ABSTRACT

One of the more exciting opportunities enabled by the Internet is sharing of data and software within communities of interest. The early waves of exploitation have provided faster and easier communication, through email and through Web publishing of research results, research materials (including data and software), news and general information. For individual researchers, this has enabled access to a richer set of resources and fostered cooperation within specialist groups. A strengthening trend is for individuals or institutions to share resources (both data and software) through Web services. To search for available information on a gene, for example, a biotechnology researcher can now access a remote genomic database, rather than incur the costs of maintaining her own local database. This paper envisages the establishment of collections of Web services, by a community of interest and for the community of interest. Technically, this form of Federated Information System poses the usual problems of size (the number of services present) and heterogeneity in the services. Although recent advances in the area give some confidence that large-scale, highly-heterogeneous networks of Web services are within reach, the social aspects of establishing shared resources require reconsideration of some fundamental elements of architectural design. This paper examines some informations systems research issues in design of federated information systems for large communities of interest.

In this paper, we will use as case studies three representative communities of interest. We will use our experience in design and implementation to observe and generalize some common elements that are influential in the design of information systems. These communities are an association of local government authorities in Sydney , the astronomical research community, and a consortium of Australian human health research institutions. Information systems developed or under development are the Sydney Information Highway, the Virtual Observatory and the Australian Health Research Network, respectively. These consortia are essentially defined by common goals and an acceptance of benefits, to the members and to their stakeholders, from a collective effort.

These common goals are generally loose, rather than able to be defined in terms of a crisp set of objectives or common processes. For example, an astronomer will develop greater insight into a stellar object by fusing data from many sources. Fusing the data will typically require intelligent selection of data sources, analysis and visualization tools, rather than following a well-defined process. While some standard processes can be established, often the network acts as a resource collection, enabling many processes, many of which are combined on a once-off basis.

The success of the community's efforts is vitally dependant on achieving a critical mass of resources within a reasonable time. The extent and vigour of participation by an individual member depends on the benefits to the member, peer-group and stakeholder expectations on contributions, continuing competition between members, and the costs of participation. This leads to a social structure of the community as a loose federation, with weak centralised coordination and management. This contrasts a social structure in which a central unit is mandated to establish the resource (including metadata), perform integration and establish standards.

Together these factors suggest that the well-known methodologies for establishing the resource collection and achieving interoperability have limited applicability. Approaches based on a global schema, process models and comprehensive standards are all highly problematical. Three clusters of issues are particularly interesting.

Firstly, there is the issue of describing services in a highly-heterogeneous collection. The importance of minimizing the barriers to participation leads to the desirability of allowing a member to contribute a service 'as is, where is', rather than extending existing capabilities or migrating to a new, standards-compliant environment. It is also intuitively undesirable to inhibit a member from offering capabilities that are special in some way. The technical challenge is then to accommodate differing capabilities in data sources, in terms of selection operators, both in description of the services and in any command language. A further open question is in the modelling of applications, such as statistical routines in the Australian Health Research Network.

Secondly, data integration across services has some complexities. In our case studies, it appears infeasible to capture a global schema, because it would be very large indeed and because the set of services will be very dynamic. Rather it is more likely that the activities of the members of the community will lead to publication of collections of purpose-specific views materialising sets of objects of interest. In some cases, linkages across data sources will be facilitated by common keys for objects (such as the astronomical designations of the International Astronomical Union), or by standardized representations of values in some domains (such as the coordinate systems of geospatial information systems). In other cases, linkages will need to be by joins, using both the common relational operators and externally-defined join relations. Tools to discover views and means of publishing them in usable ways will be particularly valuable. The local-as-view schema definition approach will be an important element.

Finally, there is the question of effective use of the large-scale resource that could be assembled collectively by the community. In addition to the data sources, there could be software and high-performance computing systems. Resource discovery, task planning (including optimization) and task execution are topics likely to reward re-consideration of the current techniques.

BIOGRAPHY

Dave Abel has contributed to the fields of spatial access methods, spatial databases and multidatabase systems. He is currently Chief Scientist in CSIRO. His current work centres on Web services.

RELEVANCE FEEDBACK IN CBIR

Hongjiang Zhang, Zhong Su
Microsoft Research Asia

Abstract: A new focus in content-based image retrieval (CBIR) research is applying *relevance feedback* originally developed for text document retrieval, to improve the retrieval performance. This effort tries to bridge the gap between low-level image features and high-level semantic contents of images as this gap is the bottleneck of CBIR. We consider relevance feedback in CBIR a small sample-learning process in sparse image feature space. Almost all of the previously proposed methods fall well into such framework. In this paper, we present a brief overview of the current state-of-the-art of this topic, and present a framework of integrated relevance feedback and semantic learning in CBIR.

Key words: Relevance Feedback, Content-based image retrieval (CBIR), Machine Learning

1. INTRODUCTION

Having been actively researched on in the last decade [1][13][21], content-based image retrieval (CBIR) attempts to automate the process of indexing in image database. CBIR approaches work with descriptions based on inherent properties of images, such as colour, texture and shape. However, despite all the research efforts, the retrieval accuracy of today's CBIR algorithms is still very limited. Apart from many other difficulties, the bottleneck is the gap between low-level image features and semantic image contents. This problem stems from the fact that visual similarity measures, such as color histograms, in general do not necessarily match *semantics* of images human *subjectivity*. To make the problem even worse, people often have different semantic interpretations of the same image.

Even the same person may have different perception about the same image at different times. To address this bottleneck, interactive relevance feedback techniques have been proposed. The key idea is that we should incorporate human perception subjectivity into the retrieval process and provide users opportunities to *evaluate* retrieval results and automatically *refine* queries on the basis of those evaluations. In the last few years, this research topic has become the focus in CBIR research community.

Relevance feedback, originally developed for textual document retrieval [18], is a supervised active learning technique used to improve the effectiveness of information systems. The main idea is to use positive and negative examples from the user to improve system performance. For a given query, the system first retrieves a list of ranked images according to a predefined similarity metrics. Then, the user marks the retrieved images as relevant (positive examples) to the query or not (negative examples). The system will refine the query based on the feedback and retrieves a new list of images and presents to user. Hence, the key issue in relevance feedback is how to incorporate positive and negative examples to refine the query and/or to adjust the similarity measure.

It is very interesting to notice that relevance feedback techniques in document retrieval were studied rather limitedly, it becomes the most active research topic in the last three years after being introduced into CBIR community. The chief fact contributed to this phenomenon is that the retrieval accuracy of general CBIR algorithm is so low that directly apply the relevance feedback framework developed for textual document retrieval is able to improve the accuracy significantly [3][20][26][27][28].

In this paper, we first survey the current state-of-the-art of CBIR relevance feedback research in terms of their natures and limitations. We then present a framework of integrated relevance feedback that support active learning, automated annotation with semantic propagation and cross-modality query expansion. In this framework, while the user is interacting with the system by providing feedbacks in a query session, a progressive learning process is activated to propagate the keyword annotation from the labelled images to un-labelled images as the system refines the retrieval. In addition, a cross-modality query expansion scheme is implemented to improve the retrieval performances significantly either a query is initiated with a keyword or an example image.

2. RELEVANCE FEEDBACK IN CBIR—A REVIEW

There are many issues in relevance feedback approaches to CBIR, such as learning schemes, feature selection, index structure and scalability.

Instead of giving an exhaustive survey of each published relevance feedback algorithms for CBIR in term of their advantages and limitations, we focus our discussions with the consideration that relevance feedback in CBIR is a machine learning problem and extend our survey in detail in respect to learning and search natures of each algorithm. To give some background, we first provide an overview of classic relevance feedback approaches to document retrieval.

2.1 Classic Relevance Feedback Algorithms

The early relevant feedback schemes for ICBR were mainly adopted from those developed for classical textual document retrieval. These approaches can be classified into two approaches: query point movement (query refinement) and re-weighting (similarity measure refinement) [1]. Both of them were developed based on vector model, the most popular models used in information retrieval [22].

The query point movement method essentially tries to improve the estimate of the "ideal query point" by moving it towards good examples point and away from bad example points. The frequently used technique to iteratively improve this estimation is the Rocchio's formula given below for sets of relevant documents D'_R and non-relevant documents D'_N given by the user [18].

$$Q' = \alpha Q + \beta\left(\frac{1}{N_{R'}} \sum_{i \in D'_R} D_i\right) - \gamma\left(\frac{1}{N_{N'}} \sum_{i \in D'_N} D_i\right) \tag{1}$$

where α, β, and γ are suitable constants; $N_{R'}$ and $N_{N'}$ are the number of documents in D'_R and D'_N respectively. This technique is implemented in the MARS system [19]. Experiments show that retrieval performance can be improved considerably by using such relevance feedback approaches.

The basic idea behind the re-weighting method is to enhance the importance of the dimensions of a feature that help in retrieving the relevant images and reduce the importance of those dimensions that hinder this process. The MARS system implemented a slight refinement to the re-weighting method called the standard deviation method [19].

Recently, more computationally robust methods that perform global feature optimization have been proposed. The MindReader retrieval system designed by Ishikawa et al. [10] formulates a minimization problem on the parameter estimating process. Unlike traditional retrieval systems whose distance function can be represented by ellipses aligned with the coordinate axis, the MindReader system proposed a distance function that is not necessarily aligned with the coordinate axis. Therefore, it allows for correlations between attributes in addition to different weights on each component. A further improvement over this approach is given in [20]. In their CBIR system, it not only formulates the optimization problem but also takes into account the multi-level image model.

2.2 Visual Features vs. Semantics

All the approaches described in Section 2.1 perform relevance feedback at the low-level feature vector level by basically replacing keywords with features when adopting the vector model developed for document retrieval. While these approaches do improve the performance of ICBR, there are severe limitations. The inherent problem is that the low-level features are often not as powerful in representing complete semantic content of images as keywords in representing text documents. Furthermore, users often pay more attention to the semantic content (or a certain object/region) of an image than to the background and other, the feedback images may be similar only partially in semantic content, but may vary largely in low-level features. Hence, using low-level features alone may not be effective in representing users' feedbacks and in describing their intentions.

There have been efforts on incorporating semantics in relevance feedback for image retrieval. The framework proposed in [13] attempted to embed semantic information into a low-level feature based image retrieval process using a correlation matrix. In this effective framework, semantic relevance between image clusters is learnt from user's feedback and used to improve the retrieval performance. In other word, the framework maintains the strengths of feature-based image retrieval while incorporating learning and annotation in the relevance feedback processes.

The FourEye system by Minka and Picard[19] and the *PicHunter* system by Cox, *et al* [3] made use of hidden annotation through learning process. However, they excluded the possibility of benefiting from good annotations, which may lead to a very slow convergence.

As to be presented in Section 3 and 4, our proposed framework integrates both semantics and low-level features into the relevance feedback process in a new way. Only when the semantic information is not available, our method is reduced to one of the previously described low-level feedback approaches as a special case.

2.3 With vs. Without Memory

Another disadvantage in the classic relevance feedback approaches, such as [19], [20], is that the captured knowledge in the relevance feedback processes in one query session is not memorized to continuously improve the retrieval. That is, even with a same query, a user will have to go through the same, often tedious, feedback process to obtain the same result, despite the fact the user has given the same query and feedbacks before. Strictly speaking, there is no learning or only limited learning in such systems as there is no knowledge accumulation across different query sessions. To overcome these limitations, another school of ideas is to using learning approaches to memorize users' subjectivities in relevance feedback process. The challenge in this approach is how to memorize knowledge learned and how to handle the inconsistency of content subjectivities across difference users and/or across different query sessions of the same user.

The framework proposed in [13] was the attempt to explicitly memorize learned semantic information to improve CBIR performance. In this effective framework, users' subjectivities in the form of semantic relevance between image clusters is learnt from user's feedback and memorized in a correlation matrix. Experiments have shown that this new framework effective utilizes the knowledge learnt from previous queries to reduce the number of iterations in following queries. Annotation-based approaches, such as [14], are ones with explicit.

2.4 Learning vs. Classification

Relevance can be considered as a leaning problem— a user provides feedback examples from the retrieval result of a query and system learns from such examples to refine retrieval results. According to Mitchell's [31] definition, machine learning is concerned with the question of how to construct computer programs that automatically improve with experience. In this view, any task that could be improved with respect to certain performance measure based on some experience can be considered the machine-learning task. In CBIR, relevance feedback is a task to improve the retrieval performance and the *experience* here is user's providing feedback examples. Almost all of the previous state-of-the-art relevance feedback methods for CBIR are classic machine-learning methods, such as decision tree learning [32], artificial neural networks [33], Bayesian learning [3][28], kernel based learning [30] and etc. However, as users are usually reluctant to provide a large number of feedback examples, the number of training samples is very small, typically less than ten in each round of feedback session. On the contrary, feature dimensions in CBIR systems are usually high. Hence, the crucial issue in performing relevance feedback in CBIR systems is how to learn from *small training samples in a very high dimension feature space*. This fact makes many learning methods, such as decision tree learning and artificial neural networks, not suitable for CBIR.

The original query-movement method represented by the Rocchio's formula and re-weighting method [19][21] are both simple learning methods. Compared with other learning methods, Bayesian learning shows its advantages in CBIR task. Many works have been done in this field [3][26][28] and achieved remarkable performances. Naïve Bayesian [15]; Optimized Bayesian classification [28]; Bayesian inference network and Monte-Carlo methods [3], almost all aspects of Bayesian learning have been touched in researching for effective relevance feedback schemes for CBIR. Vasconcelos and Lippman [28] treated feature distribution as a Gaussian mixture and used Bayesian inference for learning during feedback iterations in a query session. Under their feature distribution model, regional matching can be supported. The potential problems of their methods are computing efficiency and complex data model that leads to too many parameters need to be estimated with very limited samples. Cox et al. [3] used Bayesian framework to do target search by attempting to minimize number of feedback iterations by entropy estimation.

Some researchers consider relevance feedback process in CBIR as a pattern recognition or classification problem. Under such consideration, the positive and negative examples provided by user can be treated as training examples and a classifier could be trained. Then, such classifier can separate all data set into relevant and irrelevant groups. It seemed that many existing pattern recognition tools could be adopted for this task and many kinds of classifiers have been experimented, such as linear classifier [34], nearest-neighbour classifier [35], Bayesian classifier [27], support vector machines(SVM) [30], and so on. In this category, the most popular algorithm is represented by [30] where SVM classifier is trained to divide the positive and negative examples. Then such SVM classifier will classify all images in database into two groups: relevant and irrelevant groups to a given query.

Here we will not enumerate pervious works. Rather, we focus on the discussion whether or not it is reasonable to treat relevance feedback process in CBIR as a pattern recognition problem. In a typical pattern recognition case, there usually is a clear class structure. In other words, each item in a data set belongs to one or a number of clearly defined classes. The classification algorithm usually has very clear goal: to separate different classes as much as possible in whole data set. However, the case of content based image retrieval is different from such typical cases. In most cases, there is no pre-defined class structure. Even if there is a pre-defined class structure, it is still often difficult to determine an image item belong to which category. This is due to human subjectivities and inconsistence in human perception. Hence, the classification often lacks no clear goal. From application point of view, such classification-based methods may improve the retrieval performance in some constrained contexts; but they will be limited when applied to general purpose image databases.

2.5 Category Search vs. Target Search

Actually, this topic is not directly related with feedback. The issue here is what a user needs when using a CBIR system. User may look for similar images or a particular image. Before Cox et al. [3] presented the idea of *target search*, *category search* was the only search style in CBIR system. In category search, user provides the sample image and wants to find those images similar in contents with the sample. Under relevance feedback framework, user can make the relevance judgement to iteratively refine the retrieval performance. User can provide binary judgement of positive and negative examples [27][28]. Single judgement also been widely used where only positive examples are considered [10][26]. Some systems provide more complex interactive methods where relevance and irrelevance degree are to be considered [20]. Different level represents different degree of how relevant or irrelevant of the image comparing with the query image.

Target search [3] is another kind of scenario. Under such scenario, a user looks for a particular target image and the positive examples he provides in one retrieval session are those closer to the target image he wants. The work by Cox, et al, was the first one presented such idea, in which Bayesian inference was applied to answer the question. However, a number of practical problems need to be considered under such search style. First, which image is closer to the target is a challenging question for user to answer. Second, similar in image contents may be far away from each other in a feature space. Hence, it may be mission impossible for relevance feedback to solve the target search problem.

3. OUR PROPOSED FRAMEWORK

As discussed in the last section, the most crucial issues in relevance feedback of CBIR systems are the following. 1) How to learn effectively from small sets of feedback samples; 2) How to accumulate knowledge learned from feedback; 3) How to integrate low-level visual and high-level semantic features in query and feedbacks. An effective relevance feedback system should provide effective solutions to address these three issues, in addition many others.

In addition, there typically are two different modes of user interactions involved in image retrieval systems. In one case, the user types in a list of keywords representing the semantic contents of the desired images. In the other case, the user provides a set of examples images as the input and the retrieval system will try to retrieve other similar images. In most image retrieval systems, these two modes of interaction are mutually exclusive. We argue that combining these two approaches and allow them to benefit from each other yields a great deal of advantage in terms of both retrieval accuracy and ease of use of the system.

To address all of above-mentioned four issues, we have proposed a CBIR framework with integrated relevance feedback and query expansion, in which the semantic-based index and relevance feedback are seamlessly integrated with those based on low-level feature vectors. Figure 1 illustrates the proposed framework. As illustrated, the proposed relevance feedback framework consists of a semantic network which links images to semantic annotations in a database, a similarity measure that integrating both semantic features and image features, and a machine learning algorithm to iteratively update the semantic network and to improve the system's performance over time.

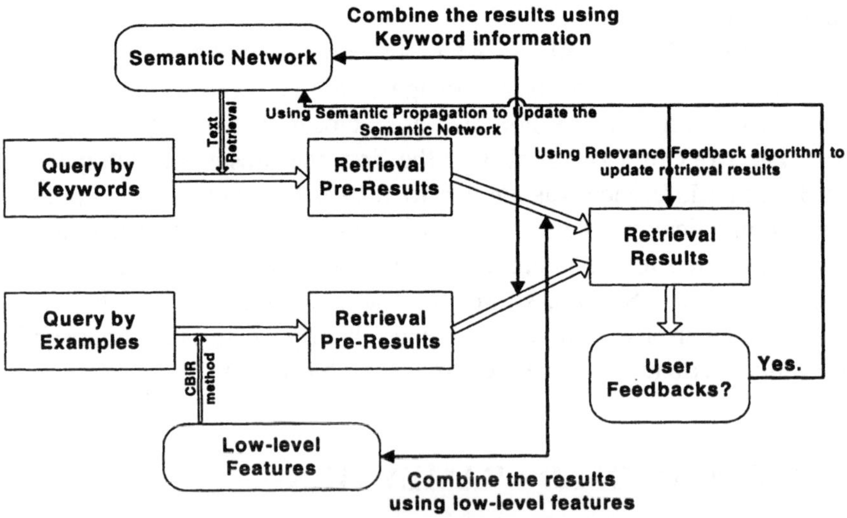

Figure 1. The Proposed Framework of Integrated Relevance Feedback and Query Expansion.

The framework supports both query by keyword and query by image example through semantic network and low-level feature indexing. Cross-modality query expansion is supported. That is, the retrieved images based on keyword search are considered as the positive examples, based on which the query is expanded by features of these images. In this way, the system extends a keyword-based query into feature-based queries to expand the search range. For query by image example, similar procedure takes effect to extend the retrieval from feature space to semantic space. In this way, user input information is utilized as much as possible to improve the retrieval performance. More importantly, there is a progressive learning process to propagate the keyword annotations from the labelled images to un-labelled ones during the feedback. In this way, more and more images are implicitly labelled by keywords by the semantic propagation process. In addition to supporting keyword search, this annotation propagation process also the retrieval system accumulated users' feedback information so that it will be improve performance of future retrieval requests.

The proposed framework has an integrated relevance feedback scheme in which both low-level feature based and high-level semantic feedback are performed. We define a unified metric function G to measure the relevance between query $Q^{'}$ and any image j within an image database in terms of both semantic and low-level feature content, where $Q^{'}$ includes the original query and users' feedback information.

$$G(j,Q^{'}) = \alpha \cdot sim_k(j,Q^{'}) + (1-\alpha) \cdot sim_f(j,Q^{'}) \tag{2}$$

where $\alpha \in [0,1]$ is the weight of the semantic relevance in the overall similarity measurement which can be specified by users. The larger α is, the more important the semantic relevance will play in the overall similarity measurement. $sim_f(j,Q^{'})$ and $sim_k(j,Q^{'})$ are the low-level feature similarity and semantic similarity between image j and $Q^{'}$, respectively.

The semantic network is a two-layered structure. The top layer is represented by a set of keywords having links to the images in the database. Weights are assigned to each individual link, as shown pictorially in

Figure 2. The degree of relevance of the keywords to the associated images' semantic content is represented as the weight on each link. This layer is what we need in keyword relevance feedback and will be updated during the semantic propagation. Bottom layer is a keyword thesaurus to construct the connection between different keywords.

Semantic based relevance feedback is performed in keyword vector space. Each dimension is represented by a specific keyword. For each image, there are corresponding text descriptors composing by a text feature vector. The vector can be obtained by manual labelling or assigned according to its URL, filename, ALT text, hyperlinks and surrounding text if the image is downloaded from website, more keywords can be assigned. Of course, if no keyword information to the image, the corresponding feature vector is set to null. The semantic propagation method is used to annotate such image during user's feedback iteration, which will be described in later session.

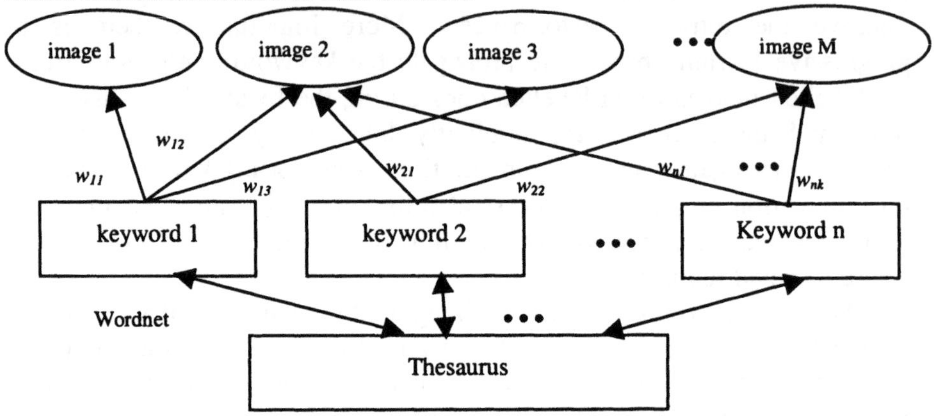

Figure 2. Semantic Network.

4. PROBABLISTIC PROPAGATION SCHEME

As illustrated in Figure 2, the more images are annotated (correctly), the better the system retrieval performance will be. However, the reality is human labelling of images is tedious and expensive, hence not a feasible solution, which was what motivated CBIR research fifteen years ago. To address this issue, a probabilistic progressive keyword propagation scheme is proposed in our framework to automatically annotate images in the databases in the relevance feedback process utilizing based a small percentage of annotated images.

We assume that initially only a few images in a database have been manual labelled with keywords and the retrieval is performed mainly based on low-level features. As stated before, the initial keywords annotation can be from web through the crawler when the images are from the Web, or labelled by humans. While the user is interacting with the system by providing feedbacks in a query session, a progressive learning process is activated to propagate the keyword annotation from the labelled images to un-labelled images so that more and more images are implicitly labelled by keywords. In this way, the semantic network is updated in which the keywords with a majority of user consensus will emerge as the dominant representation of the semantic content of their associated images. As more queries are inputted into the system, the system is able to expand its vocabulary. Also, through the propagation process, the keywords that represent the actual semantic content of each image will receive a large weight.

There are two major issues in keyword propagation: which images and which keyword(s) should be propagated during a query session.

To answer the first question, a probability model, based on Bayesian learning, is proposed. We assume that, (1) all positive examples in one retrieval session belong to the same semantic class with common semantic object(s) or meaning(s); and (2) the features from the same semantic class follows the Gaussian or Mixture Gaussian distributions. Therefore, all positive feedbacks in a query session are used to calculate and update the parameters of the corresponding semantic Gaussian classes. Then, the probability of each image in the database belonging to such semantic class is calculated. The common keywords in positive examples are propagated to the images with very high probability belonging to this class.

As we can see, the propagation framework uses the same procedure as the feedback algorithm in low-level features. The only difference is that for low-level feature feedbacks, the calculated probability is used for the ranking of an image in retrieval candidate list, while here it is used to determine if an image should be in the propagation candidate list.

Same as the feedback algorithm in low-level feature space, $p(c_i)$, can be calculated [26]. Then the propagation candidate set S is obtained as follows:

$$S = \{c_1, \ldots, c_k\}, \text{ where } p(c_i) > \psi \qquad (3)$$

ψ is a constant threshold which can be estimated by the training process. The weight associates with the propagated keyword i and the image m $w_{im} = p(c_m)$. More complex distribution model, for example Mixture Gaussian, may be used in this propagation framework. However, because the user's feedback examples in practice are often very few, complex models will leads into much more parameter estimation errors as there are more parameters to be estimated.

Also, to determine which keyword(s) should be propagated when an image is associated with multiple keywords, a region-based approach is evolved. Unlabelled images to be propagated are firstly segmented into regions. By analysing the feature distribution of the segmented regions, a probability association between each segmented regions and annotated keywords is set up for labelled images by region-based relevance feedback approach. Then, each keyword of labelled image was assigned to one or several regions of the image with certain probabilities. The region-based feedback framework we used is described in [11]. It is also a probabilistic feedback approach. Currently, all common keywords will be propagated to the candidate list.

5. EXPERIMENTAL RESULTS

The image set we used is the Corel Image Gallery. 10,000 images of 79 semantic categories are selected to calculate the performance statistics. 200 random selected images compose the test query set. Whether a retrieved image is correct or incorrect is judged according to the ground truth. Three types of colour features and three types of texture features are used in our system. Feedback process is running as follows: Given a query example from the test set, a different test image of the same category as the query is used in each round of feedback iteration as the positive example for updating the Gaussian parameters. For negative feedback process, the first two irrelevant images are assigned as negative examples. The accuracy is defined as:

$$Accuracy = \frac{\text{relevant images retrieved in top } N \text{ returns}}{N} \quad (1)$$

Several experiments have been performed as follows. First, our Bayesian feedback scheme is compared with previous feedback approaches presented by Nuno [28] and Rui [20][21]. This comparison is done in the same feature space. **Error! Reference source not found.** shows that the accuracy of our Bayesian feedback method becomes higher than the other two methods after two feedback iterations. This demonstrates that the incorporated Bayesian estimation with the Gaussian parameter-updating scheme is able to improve retrieval effectively.

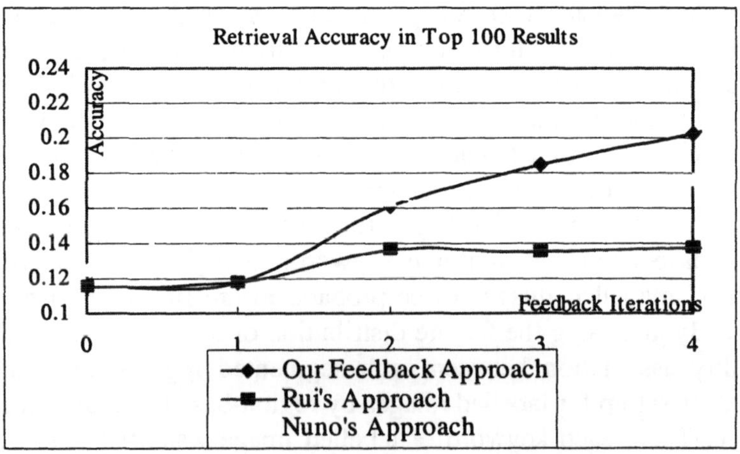

Figure 3: Retrieval accuracy for top 100 results in original feature space.

To demonstrate the performance of the semantic propagation, we design the following experiment. We have annotated the 200 images in the query set by its category names. So, only one keyword is associated to one query image and other images in database have no keyword annotations. During the test, each query image was used twice. Then we compared the retrieval performance as shown in Figure 4. It is seen that for feedback with propagation, the retrieval accuracy is much higher than the original one without it. This is because, without propagation, the system has no 'memory'. Every time when user re-submits the same query, user has to start from the very low accuracy. However, when a system has propagation ability, latter user can utilize the accumulated knowledge from previous feedback iterations. In other words, system has the leaning ability and will be smarter with more users' interactions.

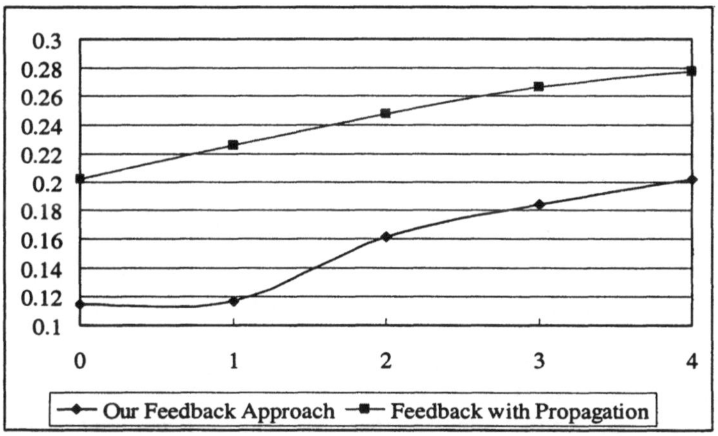

Figure 4: Retrieval accuracy for top 100 results performance between feedback without propagation and feedback with propagation scheme.

6. CONCLUSION

In this paper, we present the framework design of our image retrieval system which is build based on relevance feedback and probabilistic keyword propagation. Our method utilizes both semantic and low-level feature properties of every feedback image in refine the retrieval, while in the meantime, learning semantic annotations of each image. While the user is interacting with the system by providing feedbacks in a query session, a progressive learning process is activated to propagate the keyword annotation from the labelled images to un-labelled images so that more and more images are implicitly labelled by keywords at certain probabilities. In this way, more and more images are implicitly labelled by keywords by the semantic propagation process. Thus, such process will improve the retrieval performance in future, either query by image examples or by keywords. This new framework makes the image retrieval system to be superior over either the classical CBIR or text-based systems.

REFERENCES

[1] Buckley, C., and Salton, G. "Optimization of Relevance Feedback Weights," in Proc of SIGIR'95.

[2] Chandrasekaran, S. et al. "An Eigenspace Update Algorithm for Image Analysis". CVGIP: Graphical models and image processing journal, 1997.

[3] Cox, I. J., Minka, T. P., Papathomas, T. V. and Yianilos, P. N. "The Bayesian Image Retrieval System, PicHunter: Theory, Implementation, and Psychophysical Experiments" IEEE Transactions on Image Processing -- special issue on digital libraries, 2000.

[4] Deng, Y., Manjunath, B. S. and Shin, H., "Color Image Segmentation", in Proc. IEEE Computer Society Conference on Computer Vision and Pattern Recognition, CVPR '99, Fort Collins, CO, vol.2, pp.446-51, June 1999.

[5] Diamantaras, I., and Kung, S.Y. "Principal Component Neural Networks, Theory and Applications" John Wiley & Sons. Inc. 1996

[6] Duda, R. O., and Hart, P. E. (1973). "Pattern Classification and Scene analysis." New York: John Wiley & Sons.

[7] Faloutsos, C. and Lin, K., "Fastmap: A Fast Algorithm for Indexing, Data-mining and Visualization of Traditional and Multimedia " In Proc. of SIGMOD, pages 163-174, 1995.

[8] Flickner, M. et al. "Query by Image and Video Content: The QBIC system." Computer. Vol 28, pp23-32, 1995

[9] Fukunaga, K., "Introduction to Statistical Pattern Recognition" 2nd Edition, Academic Press 1990

[10] Ishikawa, Y., Subramanya R., and Faloutsos, C., "Mindreader: Query Databases Through Multiple Examples," In Proc. of the 24th VLDB Conference, (New York), 1998.

[11] Jing, F., Zhang, B., Lin, F., Ma, W. and Zhang, H. "A Novel Region-Based Image Retrieval Method Using Relevance Feedback", 3rd Intl Workshop on Multimedia Information Retrieval (MIR 2001), Ottawa, Canada, October 5, 2001.

[12] Kirby, M. and Sirovich, L. "Application of the Karhunen-Loeve procedure for the characterization of human faces", In IEEE Transactions on Pattern Analysis and Machine Intelligence, vol. 12, no. 1, pp. 103-108, January 1990.

[13] Lee, C., Ma, W. Y., and Zhang, H. J. "Information Embedding Based on user's relevance Feedback for Image Retrieval," Technical Report HP Labs, 1998.

[14] Lu, Y., Hu, C., Zhu, X., Zhang, H. and Yang, Q. "A Unified Framework for Semantics and Feature Based Relevance Feedback in Image Retrieval Systems", The 8th ACM Multimedia International Conference, November 2000, Los Angeles, CA.

[15] Meilhac, C. and Nastar, C. "Relevance Feedback and Category Search in Image Databases", IEEE International Conference on Multimedia Computing and Systems, Italy, 1999.

[16] Ng, R. and Sedighian, A.. "Evaluating Multi-dimensional Indexing Structures for Images Transformed by Principal Component Analysis". Proc. SPIE Storage and Retrieval for Image and Video Databases, 1996.

[17] Brunelli, R. and Mich, O. "Image Retrieval by Examples". IEEE Trans. On Multimedia. Vol. 2. No. 3, September 2000.

[18] Rocchio, Jr., J. J.(1971). Relevance Feedback in Information Retrieval. In *The SMART Retrieval System: Experiments in Automatic Document Processing* (Salton, G. eds) pp313-323. Prentice-Hall.

[19] Minka, T. and Picard, R. "Interactive Learning using a 'Society of Models'", Pattern Recognition, 30(4), 1997.

[20] Rui, Y., Huang, T. S., and Mehrotra, S. "Content-Based Image Retrieval with Relevance Feedback in MARS," in Proc. IEEE Int. Conf. on Image proc., 1997.

[21] Rui, Y., and Huang, T. S. "A Novel Relevance Feedback Technique in Image Retrieval," ACM Multimedia, 1999.

[22] Salton, G., and McGill, M. J. "Introduction to Modern Information Retrieval," McGraw-Hill Book Company, 1983.

[23] Shaw, W. M. "Term-Relevance Computation and Perfect Retrieval Performance," Information processing and Management.

[24] Sheikholeslami, G., Chang, W. and Zhang, A. "Semantic Clustering and Querying on Heterogeneous Features for Visual Data." 6th ACM International Multimedia Conference, Bristol, UK, September 1998.

[25] Stone, H. S. and Li, C. S. "Image Matching by Means of Intensity and Texture matching in the Fourier domain," in Proc. IEEE Int. Conf. Image Processing. Santa Barbara. CA. Oct 1997.

[26] Su, Z., Li, S., Zhang, H. "Extraction of Feature Subspaces for Content-Based Retrieval Using Relevance Feedback" ACM Multimedia 2001, Ottawa Canada

[27] Su, Z., Zhang, H and Ma, S. "Relevant Feedback using a Bayesian Classifier in Content-Based Image Retrieval" SPIE Electronic Imaging 2001, January 2001, San Jose, CA

[28] Vasconcelos, N., and Lippman, A. "Learning from User Feedback in Image Retrieval Systems" NIPS'99, Denver, Colorado, 1999.

[29] Zhu, L. and Zhang, A. "Supporting Multi-example Image Queries in Image Databases" IEEE International Conference on Multimedia and Expo, July, New York City, NY.

[30] Tong S. and Chang E. "Support Vector Machine Active Leaning for Image Retrieval" ACM Multimedia 2001, Ottawa, Canada.

[31] Mitchell. T. "Machine Learning". McCraw Hill, 1997

[32] MacArthur, S.D.; Brodley, C.E.; Shyu, C.-R. "Relevance feedback decision trees in content-based image retrieval" IEEE Workshop on Content-based Access of Image and Video Libraries, 2000. Page(s): 68 -72

[33] Laaksonen, J. Koskela, M. and Oja, E, "PicSOM: Self-Organizing Maps for Content-Based Image Retrieval", Proceedings of International Joint Conference on NN, July,1999.

[34] Wu, Y. Tian, Q. and Huang, T.S, "Discriminant EM algorithm with Application to Image Retrieval", IEEE CVPR , South Carolina, 2000.

[35] Wu, P. and Manjunath, B. S., "Adaptive Nearest Neighbour Search for Relevance Feedback in Large Image Database", ACM Multimedia conference, Ottawa, Canada, 2001.

AN OVERVIEW OF ORACLE CHART BUILDER AND MAPVIEWER

Lory Molesky and Jayant Sharma
Oracle Corporation
lory.molesky@oracle.com, jayant.sharma@oracle.com

Abstract: Oracle Chart Builder is a real-time Java charting API. It enables more effective communication and analysis of information for business graphics and performance applications. MapViewer is a programmable tool for rendering maps using spatial data managed by Oracle Spatial. MapViewer provides tools that hide the complexity of spatial data queries and cartographic rendering, while providing customizable options for more advanced users. This paper presents an overview of data visualization features in the 9*i* Application Server product from Oracle.

Key words: Charting, map display, Oracle 9*i* Application Server, visualization

1. INTRODUCTION

Web-based and other applications benefit from the ability to visualize data. For example, a brokerage firm may host a stock trading web site that displays charts for market data and fundamental data. A web hosting company may provide users with various charts displaying web statistics. A business intelligence application may display average household income for U.S. census blocks in a given region of the country.

However, enterprises face serious challenges when building applications that visualize data. These challenges include:

- **Interactive Visualization and Visualizing High-Bandwidth Feeds**
  Interactive charting applications must provide real-time response, otherwise users will become impatient and go elsewhere. High-bandwidth data feeds—where thousands of charts must be updated frequently—such as real-time market data feeds or constantly changing system load conditions, require short batch cycle times.
- **Displaying Time-Related Data**
  Displaying time-related charts is difficult, because data sets are often defined over numerous frequencies and contain different numbers of observations over time. Automating this task is important, because so much data is time-related.
- **Integrating Map Display with Business Graphics and Reports**
  Much business information has an implicit location component. Displaying it on a map, therefore, is an effective means of communicating this information. The viewer can also quickly grasp spatial relationships (such as proximity) between relevant business entities that would not be explicit in a tabular report or chart.

Chart Builder generates charts in a fraction of a second, and provides extensive support for time series data. One unique and powerful feature of Chart Builder is support for automatic time scaling, which maximizes the readability of the time axis. With Chart Builder, developers do not need to explicitly define time axis labels. This enables the generation of a wide range of charts without custom programming.

MapViewer generates thematic maps from data (spatial and non-spatial) and metadata stored in an Oracle database server. One form of thematic map allows the placement of charts (pie, bar, line, or area) on a map. For example, one can display quarterly sales by region, or gross sales for each major product category by store location.

This paper presents an overview of the above features that are part of the Oracle 9*i* Application Server (9*i*AS). The remainder of this paper is structured as follows. Sections 2 and 3 describe Chart Builder, while MapViewer is presented in Sections 4 and 5. Section 6 give one example of integrating Chart Builder and MapViewer. Finally Section 7 summarizes the functionality and benefits of visualization components in 9*i*AS.

2. CHART BUILDER FEATURES

Chart Builder supports numerous variations on all popular chart types. Chart Builder's intelligent default settings allow developers to easily create charts with just a few method calls. Developers can customize virtually any chart attribute.

2.1 Chart Timeseries data

Because the need to chart time series data is so common, Chart Builder provides extensive support in this area. Chart Builder automatically scales time axis labels to maximize the readability of the chart. Developers supply only the data set (in the form of date/value pairs). All axis labels, including the choice of labels for the time axis, are automatically derived by Chart Builder's internal algorithms.

For example, consider the case where the time axis is defined by daily dates. When only a few days (10) are provided, each day is labeled. Supplying more days (in this case 60) results in labeling full month names. The labeling of hours and minutes is also supported.

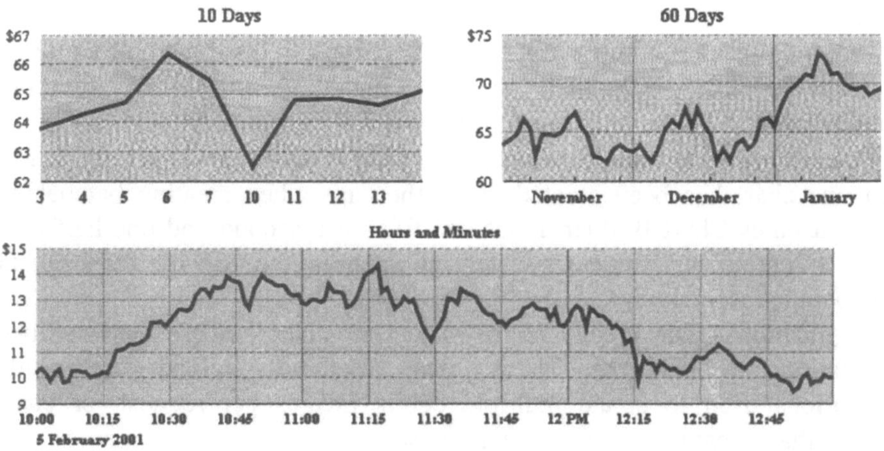

2.2 Deploy charts in multiple languages

Chart Builder generates axis labels using the language specified by the current Java Locale setting of the application. In addition, developers can customize the format of numerical axis labels by choosing from various numerical and currency formats.

2.3 Generate Images in GIF, WBMP, and JPG Formats

Chart Builder uses the Java `BufferedImage` class to create in-memory raster images. Developers can create chart images in GIF and WBMP formats by passing the buffered image to the standard encoding routines included with Chart Builder. GIF is the recommended file format for web sites, while the WBMP format is ideal for wireless devices. Developers can also encode charts using JPG encoders included with Java. However, this format is not recommended because it was designed for photographs.

2.4 Create charts in under a second

Chart Builder creates charts for typical data sets in a fraction of a second—including data sets containing hundreds of points. The following description refers to performance measurements of the time (in seconds) taken to create a single line chart containing either 10, 100, 500, or 1000 points, in both cold and warm start scenarios. These performance measurements were taken on a modest laptop (300 MHz Pentium III, with 128 megabytes of memory, running Windows NT).

The cold start scenario measures the time taken to create a chart under the least favorable caching conditions—when charting methods are not cached in memory.

Under cold start conditions, it takes Chart Builder less than half a second to create the raster image of a line chart containing 100 points, and about three-quarters of a second to chart 1000 points.

Warm start performance measures the time taken to create charts after at least one chart has been created, as is the case when creating batches of charts. It takes Chart Builder about one fifth of a second and one half of a second to create an in-memory raster and generate the GIF file for 100 and 1000 points, respectively.

Applications that create more than one chart—where performance expectations follow the warm start scenario—include server-side applications used to create multiple charts images per request, or chart services that remain active between requests.

3. CHART BUILDER DEPLOYMENT

DEPLOY INTERACTIVE CHARTS

Chart Builder supports interactive charts in Java applications and applets, JavaServer Pages (JSP), and pure HTML contexts. Chart Builder provides mechanisms to detect events, such as mouse clicks, mouse entry, and mouse exit within a chart element (chart elements are individual pie slices, individual bars, etc.). Support for these methods is tailored to the runtime context (support for JSP environments is discussed in a separate section):

- **Java Applications and Applets Contexts**
  Chart Builder provides access to the Java event model, enabling users to

detect mouse events on individual chart elements. This model gives developers complete flexibility to associate actions with chart events.

- **HTML Contexts**
  In an HTML context, interactive charts are provided by chart image maps. Chart image maps are automatically generated by Chart Builder, and associate mouse events on a chart with various actions. For example, entry into a bar can trigger a data drill down using image replacement, a link to a URL, or both. Both client-side and server-side image maps are supported.

The next example illustrates an interactive chart that could be implemented in either a Java application, a Java applet, or HTML. The

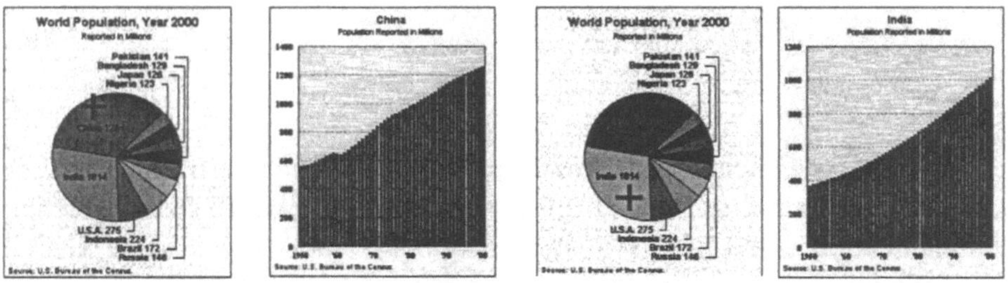

example detects cursor entry into any pie slice, highlights the slice, and displays a bar chart next to the pie chart that provides detail about the pie slice.

Placing the cursor in the slice labeled *China* highlights the *China* pie slice, and triggers the display of the *China* bar chart; if the cursor is moved to the slice labeled *India,* the *India* pie slice is highlighted, and the *China* bar chart is replaced by the *India* bar chart.

This technique, side-by-side images triggered by mouse overs, illustrates one of the many ways in which Chart Builder facillitates the development of effective user interfaces.

DEPLOY CHARTS IN JSP ENVIRONMENTS

JavaServer Page (JSP) technology is attractive because it allows enterprises to provide dynamic web content. Chart Builder's speed and image generation capabilities makes real-time response possible for JSP applications that embed charts.

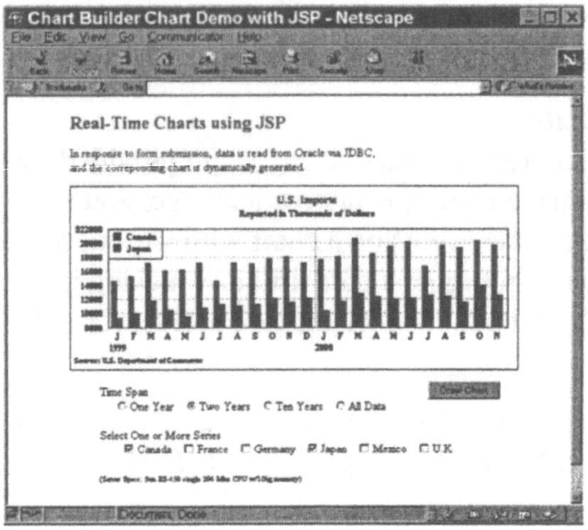

In summary Oracle Chart Builder provides a Java class library that lets you easily generate charts to display your data. It enables more effective communication and analysis of information for applications using charts. The following sections provide an overview of 9iAS MapViewer and its integration with Chart Builder.

4. OVERVIEW OF ORACLE 9*i*AS MAPVIEWER

The Oracle9i Application Server MapViewer (or simply, MapViewer) is a programmable tool for rendering maps using spatial data managed by Oracle Spatial. It can be deployed in a platform-independent manner and is designed to integrate with map-rendering applications.
MapViewer includes three main components:

- A rendering engine (Java class library) that provides cartographic rendering capabilities
- An XML API that provides a programmable interface to MapViewer
- A map definition tool that can be used to manage the metadata in a spatial database

The rendering engine connects to the Oracle database through JDBC. It also loads the map definitions, styling rules, and symbology from the database, and applies them to the retrieved spatial data.

The XML API provides a convenient interface for high-level application developers, for submitting a MapRequest to the mid-tier MapViewer and handling its MapResponse. The map definition tool simplifies the process of creating and managing map, theme, and symbology information in the back-end database.

The primary benefit of MapViewer is its integration with Oracle Spatial. It is not a full-featured web map or spatial application server.

4.1 Basic Flow of Action

With MapViewer, the basic flow of action involves two steps:

1. The client requests a map, passing in the map name, data source, center location, map size, and optionally other data to be plotted on top of a map.

2. The server returns the map image (or a URL for the image) and the minimum bounding rectangle (MBR) of the map.

4.2 MapViewer Concepts

When an application uses MapViewer, it applies specific styles (such as colors and patterns) to specific themes (that is, collections of spatial features, such as cities, rivers, and highways) to render a map (such as a GIF image for display on a Web page). For example, the application might display a map in which state parks appear in green and restaurants are marked by red star. A map typically has several themes representing political or physical entities, or both. For example, a map might show national and state boundaries, cities, mountain ranges, rivers, and historic sites. When the map is rendered, each theme represents a layer in the complete image.

5. DEFINING STYLES, THEMES, AND MAPS

MapViewer lets users define maps, styles, and themes, including the rules for applying one or more styles to each theme. These maps, styles, themes, and associated rules are stored in the database in map definition tables under the Oracle Spatial (MDSYS) system schema, and they are visible to users through metadata views. A set of basic styles is inserted automatically when MapViewer is installed. The set of styles, themes, and maps that users can access is determined by metadata views (USER_SDO_STYLES, USER_SDO_THEMES, and USER_SDO_MAPS) collectively referred to as a user's mapping profile. Users can manage styles, themes, and maps with the Map Definition Tool.

5.1 Styles

A style is a visual attribute that can be used to represent a spatial feature. The basic map symbols and legends for representing point, line, and area features are defined and stored as individual styles. Each style has a unique name and defines one or more graphical elements in an XML syntax.
Each style is of one of the following types:

- **Color**: a color for the fill or the stroke (border), or both.
- **Marker**: a shape with a specified fill and stroke color, or an image.
- **Line**: a line style (width, color, end style, join style) and optionally a center line, edges, and hashmark. Lines are often used for linear features.
- **Area**: a color or texture, and optionally a stroke color. Areas are often used for polygonal features such as counties and census tracts.
- **Text**: a font specification (size and family) and optionally highlighting (bold, italic) and a foreground color.
- **Advanced**: a composite used primarily for thematic mapping..

5.2 Themes

A theme is a visual representation of a particular data layer. Each theme is associated with a specific spatial geometry layer, that is, with a column of type MDSYS.SDO_GEOMETRY in a table or view. For example, a theme named US_States might be associated with the STATE_SHAPE spatial geometry column in a STATES table.

All the themes for a database user are stored in that user's USER_SDO_THEMES view.

5.2.1 Styling Rules

Each theme is associated with one or more styling rules. The styling rules for each theme are expressed using an XML syntax, such as in Example 5.2.1 for an Airport theme.

Example 5.2.1 XML Definition of Styling Rules for an Airport Theme

```
<?xml version="1.0" standalone="yes"?>
```

```
<styling_rules>
  <rule>
    <features style="c.black gray">
    runway_number &gt; 1
    </features>
    <label column="name" style="t.airport name">
      1
    </label>
  </rule>
  <rule>
    <features style="m.airplane">
    runway_number = 1
    </features>
  </rule>
</styling_rules>
```

Each styling rule has a required <features> element and an optional <label>element. The <features> element specifies which rows in the base table or view will be selected based on its attribute value, and the style to be used for those selected features. The <label> element specifies whether or not to annotate the selected feature, and if so, which column in the base table or view to use for text labels.

In Example 5.2.1, there are two styling rules associated with the Airport theme:

- The first rule specifies that only those rows (features) that satisfy the condition runway_number > 1 (that is, runway number greater then 1) will be selected, and these will be rendered using the style named c.black gray. Any valid SQL WHERE clause conditions can be used as value of the <features> element, which provides flexibility in labeling and annotation. If no value is supplied, no WHERE clause condition is applied. For example, if the definition had been the following (that is, omitting the runway_number > 1 condition):

```
<?xml version="1.0" standalone="yes"?>
<styling_rules>
  <rule>
    <features style="c.black gray"/>
    <label column="name" style="t.airport name">
      1
    </label>
  </rule>
</styling_rules>
```

then all airport features would be selected and would be rendered using the Color style named c.black gray.

The first rule also has a <label> element, which specifies that the NAME column in the base table or view will be used to annotate each airport using the text style t.airport name. The value of the label element is used to determine whether the feature will be annotated or not. If the value is greater than zero, the feature will be annotated. In this case, because the value is 1, all the features specified by the <features> element will be annotated, using the values in the NAME column. If the value is less than or equal to zero, that feature will not be annotated.

- The second rule, which applies to those airports with only one runway, does not have a <label> element, thus preventing all such airports from being annotated. In addition, the features that satisfy the second rule will be rendered using a different style as specified in its <features> element.

5.2.2 Thematic Mapping

Thematic mapping refers to the drawing of spatial features based on their attribute values. For example, a Counties theme can be drawn using colors with different hues that map directly with the population density of each county.

To achieve thematic mapping, specify Advanced styles in the styling rules associated with a theme. You must specify attribute columns in the base table or view whose values will be used to determine exactly how a feature will be rendered thematically. Example 5.2.2 is the XML definition for an Earthquakes theme.

Example 2-2 XML Definition of Styling Rules for an Earthquakes Theme

```
<?xml version="1.0" standalone="yes"?>
<styling_rules theme_type="nature">
  <rule column="RICHTER_SCALE">
    <features style="v.earthquakes">
    </features>
  </rule>
</styling_rules>
```

Note that the theme in Example 5.2.2 has only one rule. The <rule> element includes an attribute named column that does not appear in the Airport theme in Example 5.2.1. The column attribute specifies one or more columns (comma-separated) that provide the attribute values needed for thematic mapping. The style specified for the features element is named v.earthquakes, and it is an Advanced style.

Another part of this definition of the Earthquakes theme referred to in Example 5.2.2 specifies the base table that contains the data to be rendered. This table must contain a column named RICHTER_SCALE in addition to a column (of type MDSYS.SDO_GEOMETRY) for the spatial data. The RICHTER_SCALE column must be of type NUMBER. To understand why, look at the definition of the Advanced style definition in Example 5.2.3.

Example 5.2.3 Advanced Style Definition for Earthquakes Theme

```
<?xml version="1.0" ?>
<AdvancedStyle>
  <VariableMarkerStyle
    basemarker="m.circle" startsize="7" increment="4" >
     <Buckets>
         <RangedBucket seq="0" label="4 or less" high="4" />
         <RangedBucket seq="1" label="4-5" low="4" high="5" />
         <RangedBucket seq="2" label="5-6" low="5" high="6" />
         <RangedBucket seq="3" label="6-7" low="6" high="7" />
         <RangedBucket seq="4"  label="7 and up" low="7" />
     </Buckets>
  </VariableMarkerStyle>
</AdvancedStyle>
```

This style specifies that the marker named m.circle is used to indicate the location of an earthquake. The size of the marker depends on the numeric value of the RICHTER_SCALE column for that row, as specified by the <Buckets> ... </Buckets> tag. In this example there are five buckets, each covering a predetermined range of values. For example, if an earthquake is of magnitude 5.7 on the Richter scale, the marker size will be 15 pixels (7 + 4 + 4), because the value 5.7 falls in the third bucket (5 - 6) and the starting marker size is 7 pixels (startsize="7") with an increment of 4 for each range (increment="4").

5.3 Maps

Maps are collections of themes with their scale ranges. A map is a stack of themes rendered on top of each other. A map also has an associated coordinate system that all themes in the map must share. For example, if the map coordinate system is 8307 (a Spatial Reference System Identifier defined by Oracle Spatial which indentifies Longitude / Latitude (WGS 84), a common system used for GPS devices), all layers in the map must have geometries defined using that coordinate system.

Maps are created by specifying a base map name or by using the programming interface to add themes, and then rendering the map into a window. The order in which the themes are added determines the order in which they are rendered, with the last specified theme on top, so be sure you know which themes you want in the background and foreground.

All base map names and definitions for a database user are stored in that user's USER_SDO_MAPS view. The DEFINITION column in the USER_SDO_MAPS view contains an XML description of a map. Example 5.3.1 shows a map definition.

Example 5.3.1 Map Definition

```
<?xml version="1.0" ?>
<map_definition>
<theme name="theme_us_states" min_scale="10" max_scale="0" />
<theme name="theme_us_parks" min_scale="5" max_scale="0" />
<theme name="theme_us_highways" min_scale="5" max_scale="0" />
<theme name="theme_us_streets" min_scale="0.05" max_scale="0"
/>
</map_definiton>
```

A map is made up of themes, each of which has a scale range within which it is displayed. Referring to Example 5.3.1, the theme named theme_us_streets is not displayed unless the map request is for a level of detail within the specified scale range.

The display order of themes is the same as their order in the map definition. In Example 5.3.1, the theme_us_states theme is rendered first, then theme_us_parks, then theme_us_highways, and finally (if the current scale is within its specified range) theme_us_streets.

5.4 Displaying Charts on Maps

Displaying charts at particular location on a background requires associating a chart type with a set of point geometries. A subtype of the Advanced Style defines the chart type and presentation. A corresponding theme associates the location with the data required for generating charts at those locations.

An example of an Advanced Style for defining a Pie Chart is:

```
<?xml version="1.0" ?>
<AdvancedStyle>
    <PieChartStyle pieradius="10">
        <PieSlice name="LOWINCOME"   color="#ff0000" />
        <PieSlice name="MEDINCOME"   color="#ffff00" />
        <PieSlice name="HIGHINCOME"   color="#008888" />
    </PieChartStyle>
```

```
</AdvancedStyle>
```

while the corresponding theme definition is:

```
Styling rule =
<styling_rules theme_type="advanced">
  <rule column="LOWINCOME,MEDINCOME,HIGHINCOME" >
     <features style="C.REDBORDER">  </features>
          <label column="KEY" style="V.PIECHART2"> 1 </label>
  </rule>
</styling_rules>
```

```
Base table name = CADEMO1 (it has columns named KEY,
LOWINCOME, MEDINCOME, HIGHINCOME)
```

```
Geometry column name = LOCATION (is a column of type
MDSYS.SDO_GEOMETRY in CADEMO1)
```

The following figure shows a sample map generated when using the above theme in its definition.

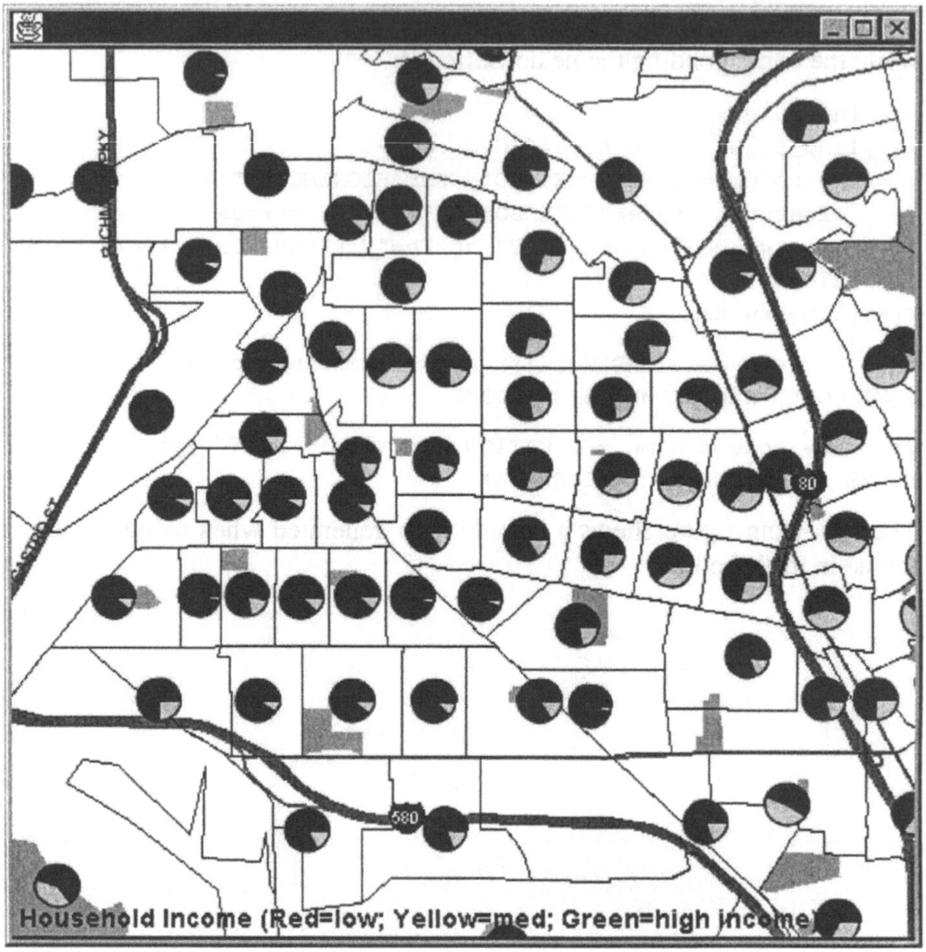

Figure 5.1: Sample map showing use of Chart Builder with MapViewer.

6. CONCLUSIONS

Oracle Chart Builder and MapViewer provide a Java class library and servlet that let you easily generate charts and maps to display your data. They enable more effective communication and analysis of information for applications using charts and maps. Their primary benefit is tight integration with the Oracle internet platform, that is, the 9*i* data and application servers and their application development and deployment infrastructure.

SOM-BASED K-NEAREST NEIGHBORS SEARCH IN LARGE IMAGE DATABASES

Zaher AGHBARI
Graduate School of Information Science and Elec. Eng., Kyushu University, Japan
zaher@is.kyushu-u.ac.jp

Kun-Seok OH
College of Engineering, Chosun University, Korea
okseok38@hotmail.com

Yaokai FENG
Graduate School of Information Science and Elec. Eng., Kyushu University, Japan
fengyk@db.is.kyushu-u.ac.jp

akifumi MAKINOUCHI
Graduate School of Information Science and Elec. Eng., Kyushu University, Japan
akifumi@is.kyushu-u.ac.jp

Abstract We address the problem of K-Nearest Neighbors (KNN) search in large image databases. Our approach is to cluster the database of n points (i.e. images) using a self-organizing map algorithm. Then, we map each cluster into a point in one-dimensional distance space. From these mapped points, we construct a simple, compact and yet fast index structure, called *array-index*. Unlike most indexes of KNN algorithms that require storage space exponential in dimensions, the *array-index* requires a storage space that is linear in the number of generated clusters. Due to the simplicity and compactness of the *array-index*, the experiments show that our method outperforms other well know methods.

1. INTRODUCTION

A wide range of database applications requires the ability to answer queries based on similarity. In a database of n points, given a query point $\mathbf{q}$ (a d-dimensional vector), we want to return the K points in the database that are most similar to $\mathbf{q}$. Those K points are called the K-Nearest Neighbors (KNN) to $\mathbf{q}$. Finding KNN points is one of the most expensive operations in high-dimensional databases, such as image databases [1], time series databases [2], data mining [3], etc. However, KNN search is an essential requirement to most of these applications.

In this paper, we propose a new KNN search approach based on clustering the image data and then using the representative vectors of these clusters to build a simple, compact and yet efficient index structure. First, using a wavelet transform method, we extract the color feature of each image in the database; thus, mapping an image into a point in a high-dimensional feature space. Then, these high-dimensional points are clustered based on their similarity using a self-organizing map (SOM) algorithm. Each formed cluster C_i is represented by a d-dimensional vector $\mathbf{m}_i$, called *codebook vector* (CBV), where d is the dimensionality of the input points.

From among the CBVs, a reference point $\mathbf{R}$ is selected, then the distance $D(\mathbf{m}_i, \mathbf{R})$ between each $\mathbf{m}_i$ and $\mathbf{R}$ is computed. Using $\mathbf{R}$ and the computed distances, we map the CBVs of the clusters into a 1-dimensional distance space in which the mapped clusters are ordered based on their similarity to $\mathbf{R}$. Since the number of clusters N_C is very small as compared to the number of images N_I in the database, we can use a simple sorted array structure, called *array-index*, to index these clusters. Using a simple sorted array structure allows us to find the most similar C_i, called a *winner node* (WN), to a given $\mathbf{q}$ using the fast binary search algorithm whose complexity is $O(logN_C)$. As a result, fast KNN search in large image databases is achieved.

The rest of this paper, is organized as follows: Section 2 describes some of the related work. Section 3 discusses how to generate and cluster the data, then build the *array-index*. In Section 4, we present the KNN search algorithm. The experiments are discussed in Section 5. Finally, we conclude the paper in Section 6.

2. RELATED WORK

The problem of finding the exact, or approximate, KNN points in a database to a given query point has been addressed by a large number of works. Most of these works have provided good solutions for the low-dimensionality case, but for the high-dimensionality case there have been very little progress. The following are some examples of the related work.

Multi-dimensional index structures, such as the R*-tree [4] is known to perform well as compared to many other multi-dimensional index structures. However, performance of the R*-tree degrades as dimensionality increases [9]. Newly proposed trees such as the X-tree [5] improves performance over that of the R*-tree by extending the overflown nodes into super nodes. Another new index, called the A-tree [10], improves performance in high-dimensional space by storing virtual bounding rectangles instead of the actual MBRs.

Other methods apply "dimensionality reduction" techniques on the data points before inserting them into the trees. The QBIC system [11] of IBM uses a bounding method to map the high-dimensional color histograms of images into points in a 3-dimensional space and then organizes those points by an R*-tree. Chakrabarti et. al. [12] utilizes the Principle Component Analysis method to reduce the dimensions of the locally correlated clusters, then each locally correlated cluster is indexed by a hybrid tree. The resulting hybrid trees are then joined by a global index. However, this system requires expensive preprocessing of the data to find the correlated clusters and reduce the dimensions.

Some other algorithms are proposed to return exact KNN answer points, others return approximate KNN answer points. Roussopoulos et. al. [14] proposed an algorithm that starts at the root of the tree and performs a depth-first traversal to find the exact KNN points. Berchtold et. al [7] proposed a different approach that precomputes the result of any nearest neighbor search that corresponds to a computation of a voronoi cell of each data point. Then, they use an X-tree to store the voronoi cells. Other approaches, such as the works proposed by Kleinberg [8] and by Brin [15], have settled for approximate KNN in return of better performance. Although finding approximate KNN answer points to a given query point is of use in some applications, finding exact KNN answer points is our goal in this paper.

3. BUILDING THE INDEX

One of the goals of this paper is to build a simple, compact and yet fast index structure for our image database. Hence, the core of our new approach is to reduce the size of the index structure in order to speed up the KNN search. The size-reduction of the index structure is achieved by, first, clustering the data points (i.e. images) and, then, indexing the clusters rather than the data points themselves, as explained below.

3.1. Wavelet Transformation

We are using a Haar wavelet transform to decompose images into several frequency bands and then compute a feature vector from these bands. As a result of using the Haar wavelet transform, the generated feature vectors are compact since we can use only a few coefficients to sufficiently represent the image color content. Moreover, the Haar wavelet basis is the simplest wavelet basis, in terms of implementation, and the fastest to compute [16].

3.2. SOM-Based Clustering

According to [17], the SOM is unsupervised neural network that maps high-dimensional input data $\Re^n$ onto a usually two-dimensional output space while preserving the topological relations (similarities) between the data items. The SOM consists of nodes (neurons) arranged in a two-dimensional rectangular or hexagonal grid. A *codebook vector* (CBV) $\mathbf{m_i} \in \Re^n$ is associated with every node i. An input vector $\mathbf{x} \in \Re^n$ is compared with the $\mathbf{m_i}$, and the best-matching-node (BMN), which has the smallest Euclidean distance $D(\mathbf{x}, \mathbf{m_i})$, see Equation 1, is selected. The input is thus mapped onto the location of the selected BMN.

$$D(\mathbf{x}, \mathbf{m_i}) = \left(\sum^{N_d} (\mathbf{x} - \mathbf{m_i})^2 \right)^{1/2} \tag{1}$$

Where, N_d is the dimensionality of the input vectors. The CBV $\mathbf{m_c}$ of the BMN is adopted to match the input vector. That is done by moving $\mathbf{m_c}$ towards $\mathbf{x}$ by a certain fraction of the distance $D(\mathbf{x}, \mathbf{m_c})$. Moreover, the CBVs of nodes in the neighborhood of the BMN are moved towards $\mathbf{x}$, but to a lesser extent than the CBV of the BMN. This learning process finally leads to a topologically-ordered mapping of the input vectors. That means the similarity between data points and between clusters are represented in the map. The CBV of a node (cluster) is quite representative of all points within the node. In this paper, we will use the terms node and cluster alternatively.

3.3. Cluster Mapping

After generating the clusters by a SOM, we propose to index the clusters' CBVs instead of the data points themselves. As a result, our index structure is not only simple, but also compact. The most convenient data structure that can efficiently accommodate such a small number of clusters is a sorted array, called *array-index*. The idea is to map the clusters' CBVs from the 2-dimensional SOM grid into a 1-dimensional distance space, as discussed below.

3.3.1 Reference Point Selection. For the image database that we used in our experiments, we found that selecting a reference node $\mathbf{R}$ at the center of all nodes in the SOM grid (called, center $\mathbf{R}$) leads to a slightly faster search time than selecting a reference node at the edge of all nodes in the SOM grid (called, edge $\mathbf{R}$). That is because a center $\mathbf{R}$ leads to a more sparse mapping (less overlapping between clusters); thus, for a given query $\mathbf{q}$ the search space decreases.

3.3.2 Distance Computation. After selecting **R**, we compute the Euclidean distance $D(\mathbf{R}, \mathbf{m_i})$ between $\mathbf{m_i}$ of each CBV and **R**. By computing these distances, we actually map the CBVs into a one-dimensional distance space as illustrated in Figure 1. Such mapping is necessary for the following reasons:

(1.) Arranging the CBVs in a 1-dimensional distance space enables us to use the fast binary search algorithms to find a certain cluster in $O(logN_C)$ time, where N_C is the number of clusters.

(2.) During clustering, the SOM cannot position all similar clusters next to each other in the grid due to its geometry; therefore, mapping those clusters into a 1-dimensional distance space corrects clusters' layout by bringing together similar clusters next to each other. However, clusters that are equidistant from **R**, although not necessarily similar, are placed next to each other in the 1-dimensional space. These equidistant clusters are pruned during the KNN search as we will explain in Section 4.

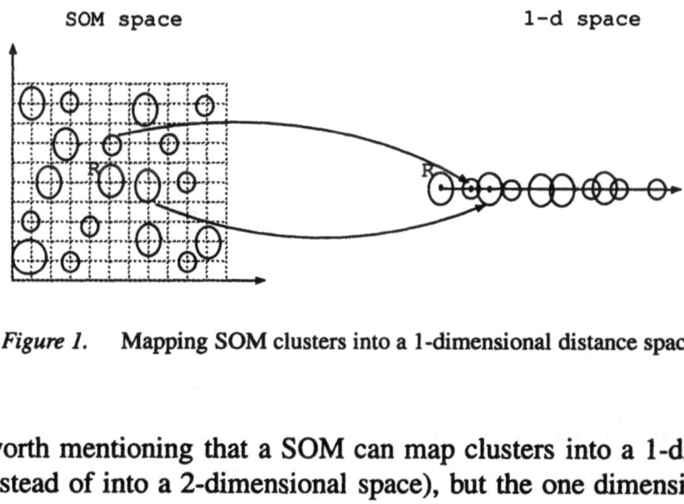

Figure 1. Mapping SOM clusters into a 1-dimensional distance space.

It is worth mentioning that a SOM can map clusters into a 1-dimensional space (instead of into a 2-dimensional space), but the one dimensional space will have the same problem of the 2-dimensional space where similar clusters can not be positioned next to each other. Thus, a remapping is necessary.

3.3.3 ***array-index* Construction.** The computed distances $D(\mathbf{R}, \mathbf{m_i})$ are inserted into the *array-index*. Along with each distance, a pointer to the best-matching-list (BML) of the corresponding cluster is set. The BML of cluster C_i is a list of images associated the C_i. Also, for every C_i, we compute its radius r_i that reflect the size of C_i (see Section 4.1 for a formal definition of r_i). The constructed *array-index* is very small in size since it only contains three fields (distance, pointer, radius) for every generated cluster. Therefore, the *array-index* can be updated, resized or rebuilt with a very small overhead that is compromised by the fast search time it provides.

Most KNN algorithms either require a storage space exponential in dimension, or require a query time not much better than a linear scan [8]. In our method, the size of the *array-index* does not depend on the dimensions of data, but it requires a storage space that is linear in the number of clusters, as opposed to dimensions.

4. K-NEAREST NEIGHBORS SEARCH

Given a query image **q**, we want to retrieve the exact KNN images. Our KNN search algorithm starts by finding the *winner node* (WN), which is a node with the most similar CBV to **q**, on the *array-index*. Then, as shown in Figure 2, the algorithm continues the search for similar clusters on both the left and right directions of the WN. During the search, dissimilar clusters are pruned based on some pruning condition (see Equation 4). Based on an ending condition (see Equation 5), the search ends when all KNN images are retrieved and further checking of new clusters does not result in new KNN answer images. Before, discussing the details of our KNN search algorithm, we introduce the pruning and ending conditions.

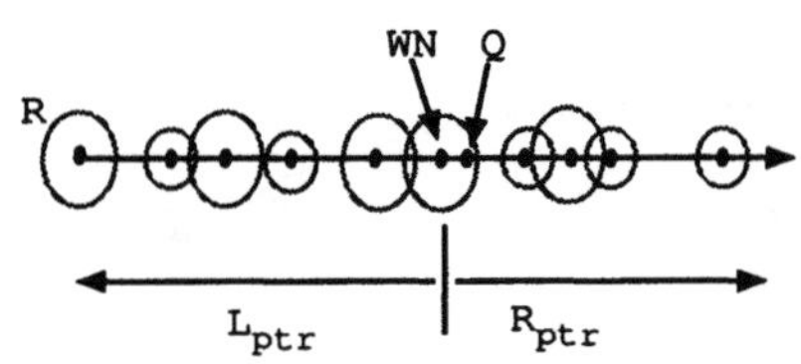

Figure 2. Searching to the left and right of the winner node (WN).

4.1. Conditions for KNN Search

To achieve efficient computation of the exact KNN answer points (i.e. images), our KNN search algorithm requires conditions on which pruning dissimilar clusters and ending the KNN search are based. Let r_i be the radius of cluster C_i and r_{max} be the largest radius among the radii of all clusters. Formally,

Definition 1 *Let P be a set of points in C_i, then, radius r_i is the largest distance between the CBV $\mathbf{m}_i$ of C_i and any point $p \in P$.*

$$r_i = \{D(\mathbf{m}_i, p) | p, \acute{p} \in P : p \neq \acute{p} : D(\mathbf{m}_i, p) \geq D(\mathbf{m}_i, \acute{p})\} \tag{2}$$

Definition 2 *Let S be a set of radii of all clusters, then r_{max} is the maximum radius in S.*

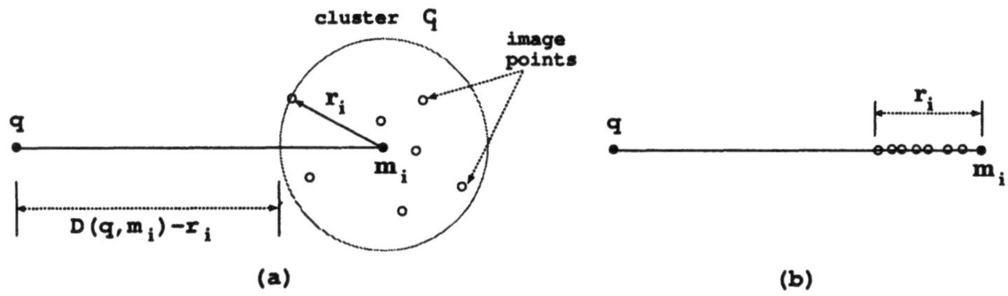

Figure 3. (a) An illustration of a radius of a cluster, (b) the image points on the 1-dimensional distance space.

$$r_{max} = max\{r_i | r_i \in S\} \tag{3}$$

Figure 3 shows the mapping of image points, which are associated with cluster C_i, onto the 1-dimensional distance space based on their Euclidean distances from $\mathbf{m}_i$. Clearly, image points that are equidistant from $\mathbf{m}_i$ are mapped to the same position on the 1-dimensional distance space.

4.1.1 Pruning Condition. Let D^c_{knn} be the current largest distance in the KNN list. Hence, cluster C_i is pruned if the distance between $\mathbf{q}$ and the closest point in C_i to $\mathbf{q}$ is greater than D^c_{knn} (see Figure 3.a). Formally,

Condition 1 *During the KNN search, cluster C_i is pruned if the following condition holds true:*

$$|D(\mathbf{q}, \mathbf{m}_i)| - r_i > D^c_{knn} \tag{4}$$

To assure that our pruning condition does not miss any qualifying clusters, we need to prove that cluster C_i is pruned only if the distance D^c_{knn} is less than, or equal to, the distance between $\mathbf{q}$ and any point in C_i. Formally, we need to prove:

Lemma 1 $D^c_{knn} \leq D(\mathbf{q}, \mathbf{p})$, *where $\mathbf{p} \in P$, and P is a set of all image points in the pruned C_i.*

Proof: By Definition 1, r_i is the largest distance $D(\mathbf{m}_i, \mathbf{p})$, where $\mathbf{p} \in P$ and P is a set of all points in the pruned C_i. Refer to Figure 3, if $\mathbf{p}$ is on the circumference of C_i, then $\mathbf{p}$ is at distance r_i from $\mathbf{m}_i$; thus, $|D(\mathbf{q}, \mathbf{m}_i)| - r_i = D(\mathbf{q}, \mathbf{p})$. Otherwise, if $\mathbf{p}$ is inside the perimeter of C_i, then $\mathbf{p}$ is at a distance less than r_i from $\mathbf{m}_i$; thus, $|D(\mathbf{q}, \mathbf{m}_i)| - r_i < D(\mathbf{q}, \mathbf{p})$. And, since

$|D(\mathbf{q}, \mathbf{m}_i)| - r_i > D^c_{knn}$ (see Equation 4), we conclude that $D^c_{knn} \leq D(\mathbf{q}, \mathbf{p})$. Proof is Complete.

4.1.2 Ending Condition. Most of the previous KNN search algorithms, such as [14], traverses the whole index structure, except for the pruned branches; as a result, a large number of nodes are accessed. Therefore, we need to determine a condition on which the KNN search ends as soon as the exact KNN answer points are retrieved without the need to traverse the whole index structure.

To guarantee that no qualifying image points are missed, the search should not end if there exist a cluster overlapping D^c_{knn} because there might be an image point, in the overlapped portion of the cluster, whose distance from $\mathbf{q}$ is smaller than D^c_{knn}. That is we need to check all clusters whose $\mathbf{m}_j$ are in the vicinity of D^c_{knn} point up to r_{max} (that is $D^c_{knn} + r_{max}$) because r_{max} specifies the position of the farthest possible $\mathbf{m}_j$ of C_j that might be overlapping with D^c_{knn}. Formally, we state the ending condition of the KNN search as follows:

Condition 2 *The KNN search ends when the following condition holds true in both the left and right directions:*

$$D^c_{knn} + r_{max} < |D(\mathbf{q}, \mathbf{m}_i)| \qquad (5)$$

Let the largest distance in the final KNN list be D^f_{knn}. To guarantee that the KNN search stops without missing any qualifying image points, we need to prove that D^f_{knn} is less than, or equal to, the distance between $\mathbf{q}$ and any image point in the set of all unchecked clusters. Formally, we need to prove that:

Lemma 2 $D^f_{knn} \leq D(\mathbf{q}, \mathbf{u})$, *where,* $\mathbf{u}$ *is a point such that* $\mathbf{u} \in U$ *and* U *is a set of all unchecked clusters.*

Proof: By Definition 2, r_{max} is the maximum radius among the radii of all clusters. For any unchecked cluster that is overlapping with D^c_{knn}, we find $r_{max} \geq max\{||D(\mathbf{q}, \mathbf{m}_i)| - D^c_{knn}|\}$, where $\mathbf{m}_i$ is the CBV of an unchecked cluster. That means, by checking all clusters whose $D(\mathbf{q}, \mathbf{m}_i)$ is less than, or equal to, $D^c_{knn} + r_{max}$ we can guarantees that no other cluster $C_j \in U$ has an image point $\mathbf{u}$ with $D(\mathbf{q}, \mathbf{u})$ less than D^c_{knn}. Therefore, D^f_{knn} is less than, or equal to, the distance between $\mathbf{q}$ and any image point $\mathbf{u}$ in the set of unchecked clusters. Proof is complete.

4.2. KNN Search of *array-index*

Let's first explain some of the routines and notations in the *KNN_Search* algorithm, which is shown below. The *KNN_list* keeps the distances of, and pointers to, the K most similar images to $\mathbf{q}$. The *update_KNN_list*(C_{ptr}) routine computes the distances between $\mathbf{q}$ and each of the image points associated with the cluster pointed at by C_{ptr} and updates the *KNN_list* according to the computed distances. Lptr and Rptr are pointers used to traverse the *array-index* toward the left and the right of WN, respectively.

Algorithm: *KNN_Search*
Input: query image $\mathbf{q}$ and the *array-index*
Output: *KNN_list* of images
1. WNptr = *find_WN*(q)
2. *update_KNN_list*(WNptr)
3. Lptr = Rptr = WNptr
4. *KnnFound* = FALSE
5. *LeftSearchEnded* = *RightSearchEnded* = FALSE
6. *TraverseLeft* = *TraverseRight* = TRUE
7. While(NOT *KnnFound*)
8.   If (NOT *LeftSearchEnded* AND *TraverseLeft*)
9.   compute $|D_L(\mathbf{q}, \mathbf{m}_{Lptr--})|$
10.   If ($D^f_{knn} + r_{max} < D_L - r_{Lptr}$) *LeftSearchEnded* = TRUE and go to step 12
11.   If ($D_L - r_{Lptr} > D^c_{knn}$) prune C_{Lptr} and go to step 8
12.   If (NOT *RightSearchEnded* AND *TraverseRight*)
13.   compute $|D_R(\mathbf{q}, \mathbf{m}_{Rptr++})|$
14.   If ($D^f_{knn} + r_{max} < D_R - r_{Rptr}$) *RightSearchEnded* = TRUE and go to step 16
15.   If ($D_R - r_{Rptr} > D^c_{knn}$) prune C_{Rptr} and go to step 12
16.   *TraverseLeft* = *TraverseRight* = TRUE
17.   If (*LeftSearchEnded* AND *RightSearchEnded*) *KnnFound* = TRUE
18.   Else If (NOT *LeftSearchEnded* AND NOT *RightSearchEnded*)
19.   If ($D_L < D_R$) *update_KNN_list*(C_{Lptr}); *TraverseLeft* = FALSE
20.   Else *update_KNN_list*(C_{Rptr}); *TraverseRight* = FALSE
21.   Else If (*LeftSearchEnded* AND NOT*RightSearchEnded*) *update_KNN_list*(C_{Rptr})
22.   Else If (NOT *LeftSearchEnded* AND *RightSearchEnded*) *update_KNN_list*(C_{Lptr})
23. return *KNN_list*

The first essential step in the *KNN_Search* is to find WN, which is a cluster whose CBV is the most similar to $\mathbf{q}$, as in line 1. In line 2, the *KNN_list* is updated with the image points associated with the WN. Line 3 initializes Lptr and Rptr to the value of the pointer that points to WN. Lines 4-6 defines boolean variables used to control the ending of a search, pruning of dissimilar clusters, and traversal to the left and right of the WN. The search for KNN points is contained in the loop between lines 7-23. Lines 8-11 traverse the *array-index* towards the left of WN. The distance between $\mathbf{q}$ and the $\mathbf{m}_{Lptr}$ of the next unvisited cluster to the left of WN is computed, as shown in line 9. Then, in line 10, the ending condition for the left traversal is checked and the left traversal is ended if the condition holds true. Otherwise, if the left traversal is not ended, the currently visited cluster is checked against the pruning condition, if it holds true, the currently visited cluster is pruned and the algorithm advances to the next unvisited cluster in left direction. The right traversal (lines 12-15) is similar to that of the left traversal.

Lines 16-17 check if both traversal directions (left and right) have been ended. If so, the search ends and the *KNN_Search* algorithm returns the *KNN_list*. In lines 18-20, if the left traversal and right traversal have not been ended, then the *KNN_list* is updated with one of the two currently visited cluster (the one with the smaller distance from **q**), then the traversal in the opposite direction is blocked temporarily, so that the next iteration of the algorithm fetches the next cluster in the direction of the currently visited *closer* cluster (the one with the smaller distance) and keeps the currently visited *farther* cluster for the next comparison. Line 21 handles the case when the left traversal is ended and the search is advancing only in the right direction, thus, the *KNN_Search* algorithm updates the *KNN_list* with the next qualifying cluster on the right direction. Similarly, in lines 22, the search only advances in the left direction. In line 23, the *KNN_list* is returned with the exact KNN answer points.

5. EXPERIMENTS

We performed our experiments on collected images from publicly available image databases; H^2 Soft [18] and Stanford University [19]. The size of the collected image database is 40,000 artificial and natural images that span the following categories: landscapes, animals, buildings, people, plants, CG, etc. The image size is fixed at 128×128 pixels. We performed the experiments on an EPSON DIRECT PC (RAM: 128 Mbytes and CPU: Celeron 700 MHz) with a FreeBSD4.2 OS.

We extracted the color feature of each image using the Haar wavelets (see Section 3.1). The color space used in this paper is the YIQ color space since it exploits certain characteristics of the human eye, where Y carries luminance information and I and Q carry color information and some luminance information. The color feature for each image is represented by a d-dimensional vector. To demonstrate the efficiency of our KNN search algorithm, we generated 3 databases with different dimensionalities: 3, 12, and 48 dimensions by applying a 7-level, 5-level, and 3-level decomposition, respectively, of the Haar wavelet transform on the image data.

From each database (3, 12, and 48 dimensions), we generated different test data sets 1K, 5K, 10K, 20k, 30k, 40k vectors, where k = 1000. Each of these data sets was clustered by a SOM, as explained in Section 3.2. As shown in Table 1, we specified two map sizes (numbers of SOM nodes) for each data set: 'fixed map size' and 'adaptive map size'.

Fixed and Adaptive Map Sizes: The fixed and adaptive map sizes of each set reflect the maximum number of possible clusters and are used as parameters for the SOM. Hence, for each data set we generated two sets of clusters.

Table 1. Map sizes ('fixed' and 'adaptive') of each data set.

Data set	Map size	
	fixed map size	adaptive map size
1000	20 × 20	30 × 30
5000	30 × 30	70 × 70
10000	30 × 30	100 × 100
20000	30 × 30	130 × 130
30000	30 × 30	170 × 170
40000	30 × 30	200 × 200

The number of nodes of the 'fixed map size' is small as compared to the cardinality of (number of images in) the database; thus, the number of generated clusters is almost equal to the specified number of nodes. On the other hand, for the 'adaptive map size', the number of specified nodes is equal to the number of images in the corresponding data set; thus, clustering the data generated empty nodes (nodes containing no images). As illustrated in Figure 4, the number of generated clusters in the 'adaptive map size' is adaptive to the size of the database (the number of clusters increases as the size of the database increases), where the number of generated clusters is decided by the SOM algorithm based on the features of input database. Also, we notice that the 12-dimensional data sets have lower number of empty nodes than those of the 3-dimensional and 48-dimensional data sets. That is because the data sets in the 12-dimensional space are more sparse, hence occupies more clusters. On the other hand, the data sets in 3-dimensional space suffers from high degree of detail loss leading to large number of false similarities and bigger, but fewer, clusters. Also, in the 48-dimensional space, there is more overlap between image vectors due to the 'dimensionality curse' leading to less number of clusters as compared to the 12-dimensional clusters.

Search Efficiency: To analyze the effect of dimensionality on the KNN search time, we measured the search time of data sets of different sizes and different dimensionalities, as shown in Figure 5. First, we randomly selected 10 images from the database and issued a query to retrieve the KNN (where, K=1 and K=100) answer images for each of the different sizes and different dimensionalities. The search times shown in Figure 5.a and 5.b are the average of 10 queries. We notice that for both K=1 and K=100 the 12-dimensional data sets have lower KNN search time than the 3-dimensional and 48-dimensional data sets especially when the size of the data sets increases ($\geq$ 10000). That is because the 12-dimensional data is more sparse, thus occupying more clusters; as a consequence, when a query is issued only a fewer number of clusters is needed to be accessed to retrieve the KNN images as compared to the other dimensionalities.

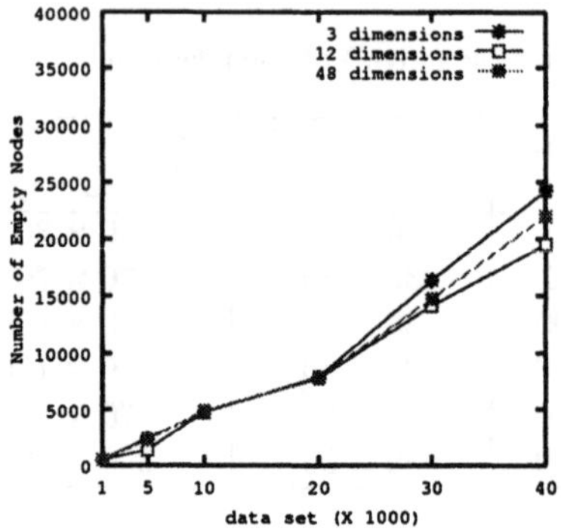

Figure 4. The number of empty nodes in the three databases: 3-dim DB, 12-dim DB, and 48-dim DB.

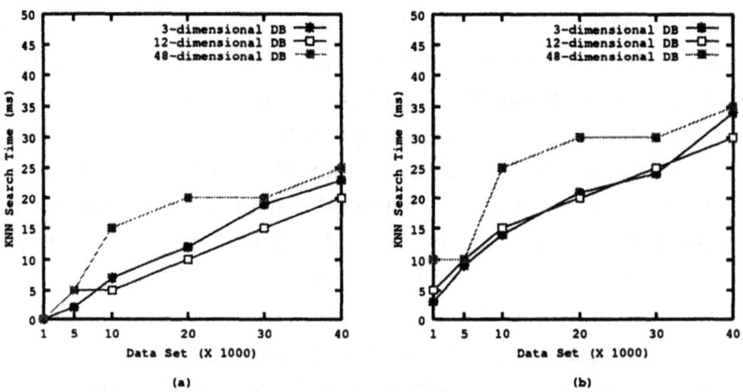

Figure 5. Average KNN search time versus database size when (a) K = 1, and (b) K = 100.

To prove the above reasoning, we measured the percentage of visited non-empty (associated with one or more images) clusters accessed to retrieve the KNN images to a given query (see Figure 6). We notice that, for both cases K=1 and K=100, the percentage of visited nodes of the 12-dimensional data is lower than those of the 3-dimensional and 48 dimensional data especially for data sets $\geq$ 10000 images.

To analyze the dynamics of the *array-index* method, first, we clustered a small data set, which is 5000 image, using the 'fixed map size' (30 $\times$ 30) as a parameter for the SOM algorithm and measured the KNN search time. Then, as shown in Figure 7, we increased the size of the database to 10000, 20000, 30000, and 40000 images and measured the KNN search time at each database size. The test shown in Figure 7 is for a database with 48 dimensions and K=1. We notice, for the 'fixed map size', as the database size increases the KNN

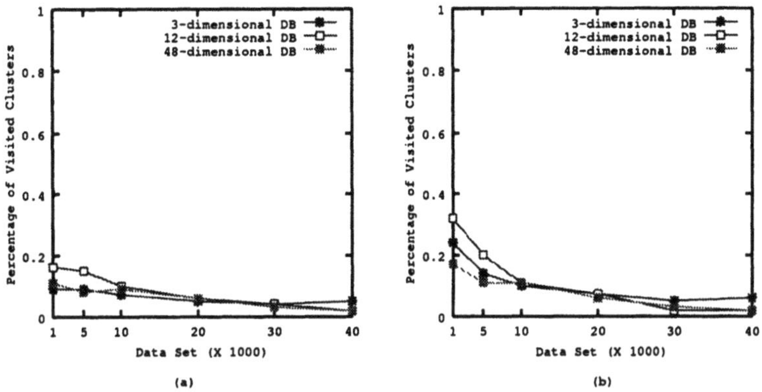

Figure 6. The percentage of the accessed database (visited nodes) versus database size when (a) K = 1, and (b) K = 100.

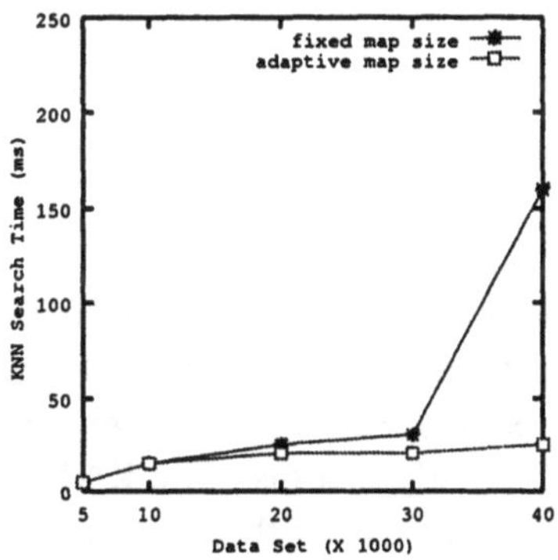

Figure 7. Comparison between the 'fixed map size' and 'adaptive map size' to show the dynamic extent of the array-index method (dimensions = 48, and K = 1).

search time increase slightly up to the database size of 30000, and beyond that size the KNN search time shoots up with great increases. The reason is that beyond the database size of 30000 images the size of clusters become very big (containing large number of images); thus, the number of false alarms for a given query increase greatly in the clusters leading to many distance computations to remove those false alarms and hence increases the KNN search time. Thus, we conclude that beyond the database size of 30000 the system should recluster the database with an increase in the map size (number of clusters). As a comparison, in Figure 7, we show the KNN search time of the same data sets but with different number of clusters (using the 'adaptive map size', see Table 1).

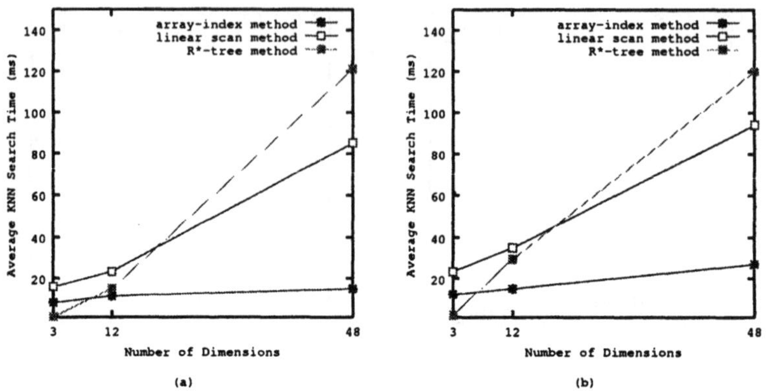

Figure 8. Comparison between the array-index method and a linear scan method in terms of KNN search time versus number of dimensions: (a) for K = 1, and (b) for K = 100.

Comparative Study: According to [8], most KNN search algorithms, require a search time not much better than a linear scan. We compared the *array-index* method with other well known methods (R*-tree and linear scanning), which serve as a stick-yard to evaluate our method, in terms of KNN search time. Figure 8 shows the comparison between the three methods for K=1 and K=100 using a database of size 20000 images. Obviously, the *array-index* method outperforms the other two methods, R*-tree and linear scanning, particularly, at high-dimensionalities ($\geq 12 dimensions$), which are the bottlenecks for most KNN search algorithms. The KNN search time of the linear scanning methods increases linearly with the number of dimensions and the search time of the R*-tree increases exponentially with the number of dimensions. On the other hand, the *array-index* method shows more robustness to the number of dimensions since the KNN search time only increases slightly as the dimensionality increases. Clearly, the *array-index* method reduces the search space greatly due to its simple and compact structure.

6. CONCLUSION

We presented a simple and efficient method, called *array-index*, to retrieve exact *K*-nearest neighbors for a given query. The *array-index* method is based on clustering the data and then indexing the clusters' representative vectors instead of the data points themselves; thus, reducing the size of the index structure. Although, we clustered the database using a SOM algorithm, the *array-index* method will works well with any clustering technique. The compactness and the ordering of clusters in the *array-index* are the main reasons behind the fast KNN search time as compared to other known methods. The compactness of the *array-index* enabled us to put the whole index structure in memory leading to an elimination of I/O cost, and the ordering of clusters based on their distances from a reference point helped reducing the percentage of accessed database necessary to determine the exact KNN answer images.

REFERENCES

[1] P.Korn, N.Sidiropoulos, C.Faloutsos, E.Siegel, Z.Protopapas. *Fast and Effective Retrieval of Medical Tumor Shapes*. IEEE Trans. on Knowledge and Data Engineering, Vol.10, No.6. Nov/Dec 1998.

[2] E.Keogh, K.Chakrabarti, S.Mehrotra, M.Pazzani. *Locally Adaptive Dimensionality Reduction for Indexing Large Time Series Databases*. ACM SIGMOD, 2001.

[3] C.Faloutsos and K.Lin. *A Fast Algorithm for Indexing, Data-Mining and Visualization of Traditional and Multimedia Datasets*. ACM SIGMOD, May 1995.

[4] N.Beckmann, H.Kriegel, R.Schneider, B.Seeger. *R*-tree: An Efficient and Robust Access Method for Points and Rectangles*. ACM SIGMOD, pp. 322-331, May 1990.

[5] S.Berchtold, D.Keim, H.P.Kriegel. The X-tree: An Index Structure for High-Dimensional Data. VLDB 1996.

[6] S.Berchtold, C.Bohm, D.Keim, H.P.Kriegel. A Cost Model for Nearest Neighbor Search in High-Dimensional Data Spaces. ACM SIGACT-SIGMOD-SIGART, 1997.

[7] S.Berchtold, B.Ertl, D.Keim, H.P.Kriegel, T.Seidl. *Fast Nearest Neighbor Search in High-Dimensional Space*. Int'l conf. on Data Eng. (ICDE), 1998.

[8] J.M.Kleinberg. *Two Algorithms for Nearest Neighbor Search in High Dimensions*. 29th ACM Symposium on Theory of Computing, 1997.

[9] C.Faloutsos. *Searching Multimedia Databases By Content*. Kluwer Academic Publishers, Boston, USA, 1996.

[10] Y.Sakurai, M.Yoshikawa, S.Uemura. *The A-tree: An Index Structure for High-Dimensional Spaces Using Relative Approximation*. VLDB 2000.

[11] M. Flickner, H. Sawhney, W. Niblack, J. Ashley, Q. Huang, B. Dom, M. Gorkani, J. Hafner, D, Lee, D. Perkovic, D. Steele, P. Yanker. *Query by Image and Video Content: The QBIC System*. IEEE, Sept. 1995.

[12] K.Chakrabarti, S.Mehrotra. *Local Dimensionality Reduction: A New Approach to Indexing High Dimensional Space*. 26th VLDB, Egypt, 2000.

[13] C.Faloutsos, M.Ranganathan, Yannis Manolopoulos. *Fast Subsequence Matching in Time-Series Databases*. ACM SIGMOD, 1994.

[14] N.Roussopoulos, S.Kelley, F.Vincent. *Nearest Neighbor Queries*. ACM SIGMOD, 1995.

[15] S.Brin. *Near Neighbor Search in Large Metric Spaces*. VLDB 1995.

[16] A.Natsev, R.Rastogi, K.Shim. *WALRUS: A Similarity Retrieval Algorithm for Image Databases*. SIGMOD record, vol.28, no.2, pp.395-406, Philadelphia, PA, 1999.

[17] T.Kohonen. *Self-Organizing Maps*. Springer-Verlag, 1997. 2nd extended edition.

[18] H^2soft, http://www.h2soft.co.jp.

[19] Stanford University, http://www-DB.Stanford.EDU/IMAGE/.

... [illegible] ... leading to an elimination of I/O cost and the ordering of clusters based on their distances from a reference point [illegible] ... of [illegible] ... the exact KNN answer [illegible].

REFERENCES

[1] [illegible]

[2] [illegible]

[3] [illegible]

[4] [illegible]

[5] [illegible]

[6] [illegible]

[7] [illegible]

[8] [illegible]

[9] [illegible]

[10] [illegible]

[11] [illegible]

[12] [illegible]

[13] [illegible]

[14] [illegible]

[15] [illegible]

[16] [illegible]

[17] [illegible]

[18] [illegible]

[19] [illegible]

PARTIAL IMAGE RETRIEVAL USING COLOR REGIONS AND SPATIAL RELATIONSHIPS

Yunyun Cao*, Yoshitomo Yaginuma**, Masao Sakauchi*

*Sakauchi Lab, the 3rd Department
Institute of Industrial Science
University of Tokyo
4-6-1 Komaba, Meguro-ku, Tokyo 153-8505, Japan
{cao, sakauchi}@sak.iis.u-tokyo.ac.jp

***National Institute of Multimedia Education*
2-12 Wakaba, Nihama-ku
261-0014, Chiba, Japan
yaginuma@nime.ac.jp

Abstract In this paper, we present a novel approach to retrieve images that contain the query image as a part regardless of the size and position the query image appears. Images in Database are segmented in advance, for each major region obtained, a composite measurement of color, area percentage and position are stored as the feature. While retrieving, the query image is also first segmented, and then the major regions' colors, their area ratios and spatial relationships are generated for narrowing the searching space. The utilization of multiple regions alleviates the influence of inaccurate segmentation, the pre-segmentation of images in database allows indexing of features of color regions and enables the fast retrieving. The experiment shows the advantages and weakness of the proposed method.

Keywords: Partial image retrieval, color region, segmentation, spatial relationship

1. INTRODUCTION

In recent years, with the dramatic improvements in computer technology and the advent of World-Wide Web, there has been a rapid increase of the size of digital image collections. However, we can not access to or make use of the information unless it is organized so as to allow efficient browsing, searching and retrieval. Many researchers and institutions are currently involved in providing tools and methods to efficiently manage pictorial digital libraries.

Up to now, a great deal of effort has been made on global measurement of image similarity (Cinque et al., 1999) (Flickner et al., 1995) (Yi et al., 1999) (Smith et al., 1999) (Shih et al., 2000) (Smith et al., 1997) (Li et al., 2000), some of them deal with color regions. However, it is not conducive to building systems that retrieve images which are semantically related to a given query image. Semantic image similarity, which is what the Content-Based Image Retrieval (CBIR) users expect and demand, often follows only from partial match between images as shown in Figure 1, in which the two images are semantically relative since they contain the same announcer.

Figure 1 Semantically related images

What seems to be lacking, however, is the research on partial image retrieval. Only in recently few years, some attentions are paid on it (Cohen, 1999) (Kim et al., 2000) (Moghaddam et al., 1999). However, the current research status is still far away from perfect. Most of them focus on the local feature defining and matching, neglecting the problem of "interactive-time" which is very important while the volume of image database is large.

In this paper, we will present a novel approach for partial image retrieval, which pre-segment the images in database, allowing the indexing of features of color regions and enabling the fast retrieval for query image by utilizing a combination of multiple color regions to calculate the similarity.

The rest of this paper is organized as follows: Section 2 introduces the retrieval method in detail, including the image segmentation, the features stored in database and used for retrieval, and the searching process. In Section 3 experimental results are reported, and advantages and weakness of the proposed method are discussed. Finally Section 4 presents conclusions and our future work.

2. PROPOSED METHOD

In this section, we propose a novel partial image retrieval method which utilizes color regions' color, area percentage and their spatial relationships for retrieval. In this method, all images are segmented into regions in advance. For each region, certain features are extracted and indexed for later retrieval. While given a query image, the query image is also segmented first, and the corresponding features of major regions are extracted and combined for local measurements similarity calculation (Figure 2).

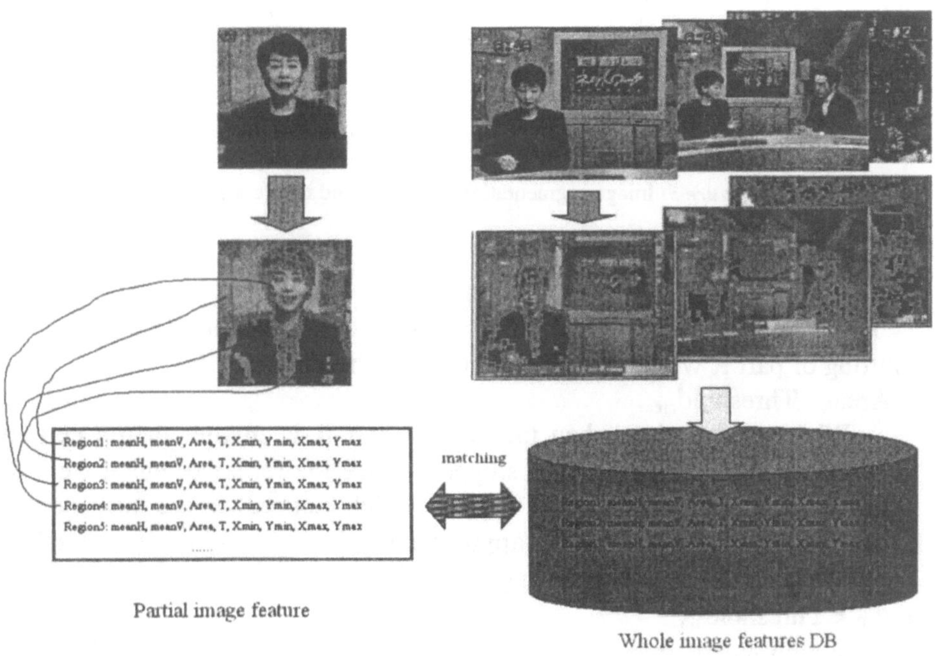

Figure 2 **Partial image retrieval with color regions and spatial relationships**

2.1 Image segmentation

An improved split_and_merge method is developed for image segmentation, which can segment an image into regions with certain colors and texture patterns.

Split

The image is at first split into four parts recursively --- NW, NE, SW, SE parts (Figure 3(a)).

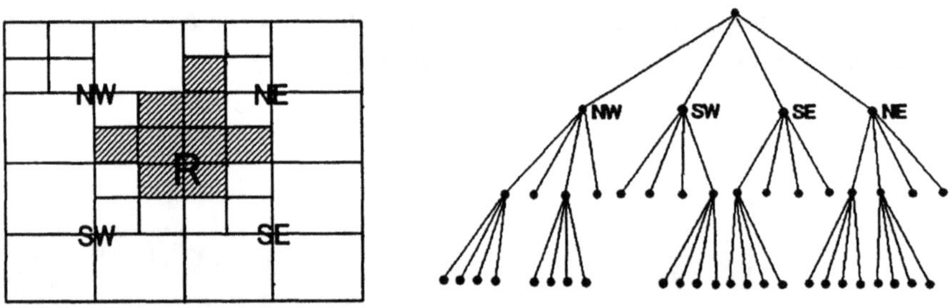

(a) Example of splitting (b) Structure of the quad tree

Figure 3 Image segmentation with split and merge method

Let $mean_R$ be the average color of part R, σ_R be the deviation. The splitting of part R would be stopped in any of the three cases:

1. $Area_R < Threshold_{area}$,

   Which means that when the area of part R is smaller than a certain value, the splitting should be stopped. Since the retrieval which we will discuss later utilizes multiple regions which can reduce the influence of inaccurate segmentation, an appropriate value for $Area_R$ can be taken with a trade-off between the segment accuracy and cost.

2. $\sigma_R < Threshold_\sigma$,

   Which means that if the color in part **R** is almost the same, then this part does not need to be split further.

3. For two consecutive levels of splitting,

   $\sigma_R \approx \sigma_{NW} \approx \sigma_{NE} \approx \sigma_{SE} \approx \sigma_{SW}$ and

   $mean_R \approx mean_{NW} \approx mean_{NE} \approx mean_{SE} \approx mean_{SW}$

Which means that the part **R** may be a region which has a certain color or texture pattern. With this condition, a texture region would not be split into small ones.

The result of the split is represented as a quad tree (Figure 3 (b)), in which the leaf nodes mean the final parts which do not need to be split further.

<u>**Merge**</u>

After the image has been split into a set of sub-regions, the next work is merging the neighboring ones which have similar colors into a larger region.

Figure 4 illustrates some examples of segmentation results.

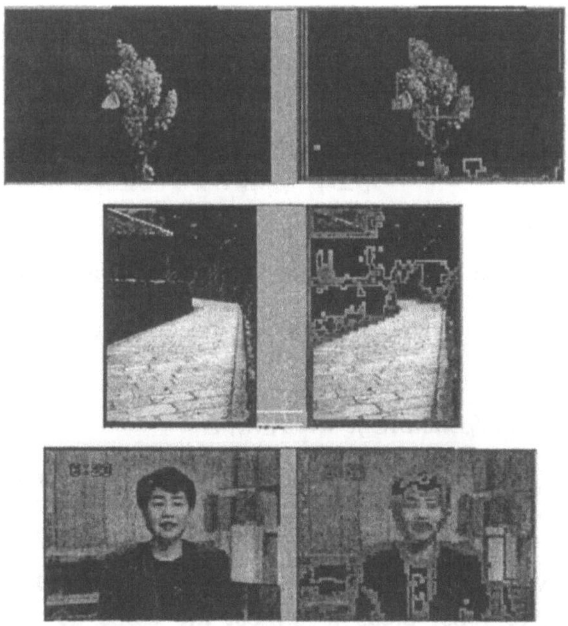

Figure 4 Examples of image segmentation

2.2 Features for retrieval

As we have mentioned at the beginning of Section 2, for each image in Database, the features of its major regions are extracted and stored for later retrieval. Considering the retrieval requirements as well as the costs, we set the number of major regions as 30. For each region, a composite feature of color, area percentage, and position is extracted. The feature vector is described as:

$$(imgID, meanH, meanV, meanC, Area, T, Xmin, Ymin, Xmax, Ymax)$$

Where *imgID* denotes the ID number of the image which contains the region.
meanH denotes the mean value of Hue of this region.
meanV denotes the mean value of Value of this region.
meanC denotes the mean value of Chroma of this region.
Area indicates the percentage of this region's area to the whole image.
T denotes this image's position on time axis. It is used in case the image is a frame in a video/image sequence.
Xmin, Ymin, Xmax, Ymax indicate the coordinates of the minimum bounding rectangle of this region relative to the top-left vertex of the image, for the whole image they are (0, 0, 1, 1).

For retrieval, the query image is also segmented. However, only main regions (according to the area size) are utilized for retrieval. Suppose that we use the top N regions, the features of them are described as:

$$(meanH_i, meanV_i, meanC_i, Area_i, T_i, Xmin_i, Ymin_i, Xmax_i, Ymax_i), \quad i = 1, \ldots, N$$

Where $Area_i >= Area_{i+1}$

For the query image, the features used for retrieval are described as:

a. Color feature

It is described as:

$$(meanH_i, meanV_i, meanC_i), \; i = 1, \ldots, N$$

The Euclidean distance is utilized as its distance measurement D_c.

b. Area ratio

It is obviously that even the size of an object changed, the ratio of the corresponding regions' areas is almost the same as it appears in the original image. Therefore the ratio of region areas can be used as a feature, which is invariant to image size. Since we have obtained a feature element *Area,* which means percentage of a segmented region's area to the area of the whole image, The feature **Area ratio** is described as:

$$\left(\frac{Area_1}{Area_2}, \frac{Area_2}{Area_3}, \ldots, \frac{Area_i}{Area_{i+1}}, \ldots, \frac{Area_{N-1}}{Area_N}\right)$$

c. Spatial relationships of the major segmented regions

Some researchers have worked on retrieving images on spatial relationships (Kim et al., 1999) (Venkat, 1998). We considered and briefly investigated various techniques for spatial representation and matching, including the elastic spring models and graph matching. But in the end, considering the spatial information available in our work --- the minimal bounding rectangle of segmented regions, we opted for a much simpler formulation based on the consistency of arrangement of vertex in x and y axis, as illustrated in Figure 5.

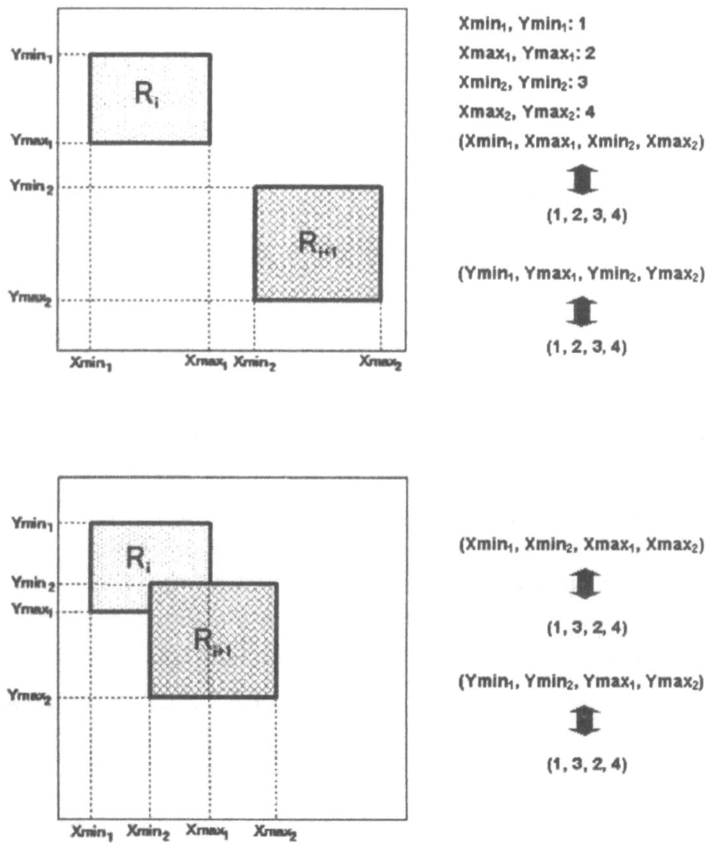

Figure 5 Representation of spatial relationship between two regions

Let (Xmin, Ymin), (Xmax, Ymax) be the top-left and bottom-right vertex of the minimal bounding rectangle of a region. For two regions R_i and R_{i+1} as shown in Figure 5, assign labels 1, 2, 3, 4 to $Xmin_1$, $Xmax_1$, $Xmin_2$, $Xmax_2$ respectively. Sorting the $Xmin_1$, $Xmax_1$, $Xmin_2$, $Xmax_2$, the sequence of the corresponding labels becomes the x-axis spatial relationship of R_i and R_{i+1}. The y-axis spatial relationships can be obtained similarly.

For example, for Figure 5 (a), the spatial relationship of R_i and R_{i+1} is represented as (1, 2, 3, 4) for x-axis, (1, 2, 3, 4) for y-axis, and for Figure 5 (b), it is represented as (1, 3, 2, 4) for x-axis, (1, 3, 2, 4) for y-axis.

Let $(l_{x1}, l_{x2}, l_{x3}, l_{x4})$, $(l_{y1}, l_{y2}, l_{y3}, l_{y4})$ refer to the x-axis, y-axis spatial relationships between a pair of regions, respectively. The distance between two pairs of regions is calculated with the following equation:

$$D_s = \sqrt{\sum_{i=1}^{4}(l_{xi} - l_{xi}')^2 + \sum_{i=1}^{4}(l_{yi} - l_{yi}')^2}$$

For example, the distance between Figure 5 (a) and Figure 5 (b) is:

$$\sqrt{0+1+1+0+0+1+1+0} = 2$$

Therefore, the spatial relationship of the query image can be described as:

$$\{(l_{xi1}, l_{xi2}, l_{xi3}, l_{xi4}\ l_{yi1}, l_{yi2}, l_{yi3}, l_{yi4}) \mid i=1, \ldots, N-1\}$$

For each i, $(l_{xi1}, l_{xi2}, l_{xi3}, l_{xi4}\ l_{yi1}, l_{yi2}, l_{yi3}, l_{yi4})$ denotes the spatial relationship between region R_i and R_{i+1}.

2.3 Retrieval with combination of multiple color regions

Assuming that the query image is segmented into N major regions: $\{R_1, R_2, \ldots, R_N\}$, from these N regions, three kinds of features discussed in Section 2.2 can be obtained.

On the other hand, for each image in the Database, features of top 30 segmented exclusive regions are available. They are represented as:

$$(imgID', meanH'_j, meanV'_j, meanC'_j, Area'_j, T'_j, Xmin'_j, Ymin'_j, Xmax'_j, Ymax'_j),\quad j = 1, \ldots, 30$$

Where $Area'_j >= Area'_{j+1}$

An image which contains a region set of $\{R'_1, R'_2, \ldots, R'_N\}$ is considered the final candidate, if it satisfies the following conditions:

a. $D_c(R_i, R'_i) < Threshold_c,\ i=1, \ldots, N$

Which means that the colors of corresponding regions should be identical.

b. $\left|\frac{Area_i}{Area_{i+1}} - \frac{Area_i}{Area_{i+1}}\right| < Threshold_A,\ i=1, \ldots, N-1$

Which means that the area ratios of the corresponding region pairs should be identical.

c. $D_s\ ((R_i, R_{i+1}), (R'_i, R'_{i+1})) < Threshold_s,\ i=1, \ldots, N-1$

Which means that the spatial relationships of the corresponding region pairs should be identical.

At first, the largest region R_1 is searched according to its color feature, a result set of $\{(imgID_i,\ region_{i1},\ D_{ci1})\}$is obtained. then it's the turn of the second largest region R_2, it is not necessary to search the whole feature space now. For each $(imgID_i,\ region_i,\ D_{ci})$ in the result set, check the 30 regions in image $imgID_i$, if there does not exist a corresponding R'_2 which satisfies the three conditions, then delete the $(imgID_i,\ region_{i1},\ D_{ci1})$ from the result set, else the result set becomes $\{(imgID_i,\ region_{i1},\ region_{i2}, D_{ci1+}\ D_{ci2})\}$. Repeat the process until the last region R_N is processed.

The region-based partial image retrieval is processed serially region by region. At each step, the searching space is narrowed according to the three conditions discussed above.

3. EXPERIMENTAL RESULTS

For experiments, we constructed an image database of 11000 images, in which 3300 images with size of 192x128 are from Tesmic System, and 7200 images with size of 162x120 are extracted at the rate of 1 frame per second from two hours videos of NHK news. The remaining 500 images are extracted from a driving shot of urban scene. Although the three types of images have different size and qualities, our method can handle them as the same.

Figure 6 and Figure 7 show two examples of retrieved results.

It can be seen from the figures that the proposed method can retrieve images containing the query object with varying size and locations.

The results show that for an object with special color regions (Figure 6(a)), the method works well, however, for an object with common color regions, e.g., in Figure 7(a), the announcer wears a suit of a very popular color, the approach failed to generate a good precision and recall.

(a) Query image

(b) Examples of true results

(c) Examples of false results

Figure 6 Results of partial image retrieval (1)

(a) Query image

(b) Examples of true results

(c) Examples of false results

Figure 7 Results of partial image retrieval (2)

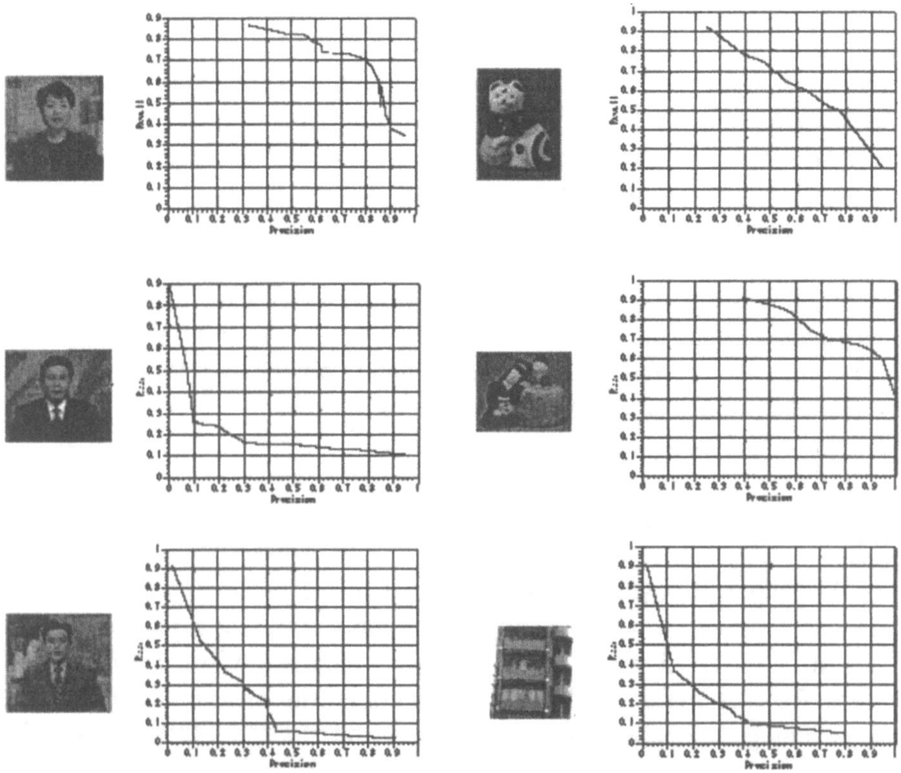

Figure 8 Precision-recall relations for corresponding objects

Here we use *precision* and *recall* for further evaluation. They are defined as:

$$Precision = \frac{|A \cap B|}{|B|}$$

$$Recall = \frac{|A \cap B|}{|A|}$$

Where A is the set of all *relevant* images, which contains the query image as a part, B is the set of retrieved images resulting from the query.

From the definition we can know that *precision* is the ratio of the number of relevant images retrieved to the total number of images retrieved. Perfect *precision* (100%) means that all retrieved images are relevant. *Recall* is the ratio of the number of relevant images retrieved to the total number of relevant images. Perfect *recall*(100%) can be obtained by retrieving the entire collection, but the *precision* will be poor. Generally there is a trade-off between *precision* and *recall*.

Figure 8 illustrates *precision-recall* relations for retrieving some objects. The horizontal axis indicates the *precision* and the vertical axis indicates the *recall*. From these results, we can also obtain the same conclusion which we observed from Figure 6 and Figure 7 --- this method can work well for objects with special or rich color regions, but is weak for objects which only have popular colors, such as simple black or gray.

The experiment was processed on a PC with CPU of 1G, memory of 384M, and the program was written with Visual C++. The average time of retrieving one image is about 50 seconds, which we thought is an acceptable cost compared with the cost of (Cohen, 1999) --- the time of per query-image comparison is about 0.1 seconds which is obviously a high cost while the volume of database grows to thousands of images.

4. CONCLUSIONS AND FUTURE WORK

In this paper, a novel method for partial image retrieval was proposed, which can retrieve images that contain the query image as a part regardless of the size and position. Images in image database were segmented in advance, for each major region obtained, a composite measurement of color, area percentage and position was extracted and stored as the feature. The pre-segmentation and the simple features allows the indexing of features of color regions and enables the fast retrieval. While retrieving, the query image was also first segmented, and then the major regions' colors, their area ratios and spatial relationships were generated for narrowing the searching space. Since the color feature is used as main feature, the proposed method can work well for objects with special or rich color regions, but is weak for objects which only have popular colors, such as simple black or gray, as shown in our experiment.

Our future work includes adding new features such as shape features to enhance the precision, and utilizing a high dimensional index structure to accelerate the retrieving process.

REFERENCES

Cinque L., Levialdi S., et al. (1999) Color-Based Image Retrieval Using Spatial-Chromatic Histograms, *Proc. of Int. Conf. on Multimedia Computing and Systems Volume II*

Cohen S. (1999) Finding Color and Shape Patterns in Images, *Stanford University Technical Report STAN- CS-TR-99-1620*

Flickner M., Sawhney H., et al. (1995) Query by Image and Video Content: The QBIC System, *IEEE Computer, Vol. 28, No. 9*

Kim B. and Um K. (1999) 2D+ String: A Spatial Metadata to Reason Topological and Directional Relationships, *Proc. of the 11th International Conference on Scientific and Statistical Database Management*

Kim T-Y and H. Han J. H. (2000) Partial Image Matching by Measures From Connected Color Regions, *Proc. of IEEE International Conference on Multimedia and Expo, pp. 367-370*

Li J., Wang J. Z. and Wiederhold G. (2000) IRM: Integrated Region Matching for Image Retrieval, *Proc. of the 8th ACM International Conference on Multimedia*

Moghaddam B., Biermann H. and Margaritis D. (1999) Defining Image Content with Multiple Regions-of-Interest, *Proc. of IEEE Workshop on Content-based Access of Image and Video Libraries (CBAIVL'99)*

Shih T. K., Wang C-S., Chang A. Y., and Kao C-H (2000) Indexing and Retrieval Scheme of the Image Database Based on Color and Spatial Relations, *Proc. of IEEE International Conference on Multimedia and Expo, pp. 129-132*

Smith J. R. and Chang S. F. (1999) Single Color Extraction and Image Query, *Proc. of IEEE International Conference on Image Processing*

Smith J. R. and Chang S. F. (1997) Querying By Color Regions Using the VisualSEEK Content-Based Visual Query System, *Intelligent Multimedia Information Retrieval. AAAI Press, Menlo Park, CA, pp. 23-41*

Venkat N. G. (1998) $\Theta\Re$String: A Geometry-Based Representation for Efficient and Effective Retrieval of Images by Spatial Similarity, *IEEE Trans. on Knowledge and Data Engineering, Vol. 10, No. 3, pp. 504-509*

Yi T. and William I. G. (1999) Spatial Color Indexing: A Novel Approach for Content-Based Image Retrieval, *Proc. of the IEEE International Conference on Multimedia Computing and Systems Volume I*

BIOGRAPHIES

Yunyun Cao received the B. Eng. Degree in Computer Application in 1987 and the M. Eng. Degree in Computer Organization and Architecture in 1990 from Tianjin University, and Ph.D degree in Information and Communication Engineering from the University of Tokyo in 2001. She is now an associate professor, School of Science, Tianjin University and a poster doctor, Institute of Industrial Science, University of Tokyo. She is a member of IEEE, ACM and IEICE(Japan). Her research interests include multimedia database, multimedia systems, image processing and understanding.

Yoshitomo Yaginuma received the B.Eng. degree in Phys. Instr. in 1988, and the M. Sci. degree in Physics in 1990, both from the University of Tokyo. He is now an associate professor, National Institute of Media Education. He is a member of Information Processing Society of Japan. His research interests include data structure, multimedia database and database acquisition

Masao Sakauchi is the Director general and a professor, Institute of Industrial Science, Univ. of Tokyo. He received the B.Sci. degree in Electrical Engineering from the Univ. of Tokyo in 1969 and the M S and Ph D degrees in Electronics Engineering from the Univ. of Tokyo in 1971 and 1975, respectively. He has acted as, General chairman of 4 International

Conferences and Workshops, Including the IEEE International Workshop on Machine Vision and Machine Intelligence (1987), IAPR and IEEE International Conference on Document Analysis and Recognition (ICDAR '93) (1993), International Symposium on Multimedia Mediation Systems(2000), Program Chairman of 3 International Conferences, Including IEEE International Conference of Multimedia Processing and Systems (IEEE Multimedia 96) (1996), ITSC 99 (1999), and Organizing and Program committee member of Many International conferences. He also served as Chairman of the technical committee on Machine Vision and Machine Intelligence, IEEE IE society (1985-1992), Associate editor of IEEE Multimedia Magazine, (1993-99) IEEE trans. on Industrial Electronics. (1984-1992), Editor in chief of Transactions on Information and Systems of Institute of Electronics, Information and Communication Engineers (IEICE) in Japan. (1989-1991), Chairman of three technical committees on Image Engineering of IEICE of Japan, and, Institute of Television Engineers of Japan (1987-1993). He wrote over 340 refereed papers in the research fields of multimedia databases, multimedia systems, image processing and understanding, spatial data structures, and geographical information systems and fault tolerant computing. He is now the project leader of two big research project on Multimedia Mediation Systems and ITS.

HIGH-DIMENSIONAL IMAGE INDEXING BASED ON ADAPTIVE PARTITIONING AND VECTOR APPROXIMATION

Guang-Ho Cha
Department of Multimedia Engineering, Tongmyong University of Information Technology, Busan 608-711, South Korea.
ghcha@tit.ac.kr

Abstract: In this paper, we propose the *LPC⁺-file* for efficient indexing of high-dimensional image data. With the proliferation of multimedia data, there is an increasing need to support the indexing and retrieval of high-dimensional image data. Recently, we developed the LPC-file (Cha et al. 2002) for indexing high-dimensional data based on vector approximation. The LPC-file gives good performance especially when the dataset is uniformly distributed. However, compared with for the uniformly distributed dataset, its performance degrades when the dataset is clustered. Real image datasets are often strongly clustered and the dimensions of the feature vectors are usually correlated. We improve the performance of the LPC-file for the strongly clustered image dataset. The *basic idea* is to adaptively partition the data space to find subspaces with high-density clusters and to assign more bits to them to increase the discriminatory power of the vector approximation. An empirical evaluation shows that the LPC⁺-file results in significant performance improvements for real image datasets strongly clustered.

Key words: LPC⁺-file, high-dimensional indexing, similarity search, nearest neighbor search, multimedia database

1. INTRODUCTION

Image databases often represent the image objects as vectors of d numeridc features, and access them via the feature vectors and similarity measures. Feature vectors can be viewed as points in a d-dimensional vector space and the similarity measure can be viewed as a measure of distance within that space. An important problem in such a system is to find the *k* most similar images to a given sample image. This problem is typically solved by first mapping the sample image to its corresponding feature vector and then finding the *k* nearest neighbors (NNs) of the vector. The basic issue then is how to efficiently find the *k* NNs.

For applications where the vectors have low or medium dimensionalities (e.g., less than 10), existing multidimensional indexing methods (MIMs), such as the R*-tree (Beckmann et al. 1990), the X-tree (Berchtold et al. 1996), the HG-tree (Cha & Chung 1998), and the SR-tree (Katayama & Satoh 1997), can be usefully employed to solve the problem. So far, however, there is no effective solution to this problem for the applications in which the vectors have high dimensionalities, say over 100. In fact, for a high dimensionality, in theory or in practice, the performance of existing MIMs degenerates to being worse than that of the brute-force sequential scan that compares the query object to each data object (Arya et al. 1998) (Indyk & Motwani 1998) (Kushilevitz et al. 1998) (Weber et al. 1998). So the main issue is to overcome the *curse of dimensionality* (Niblack et al. 1993) – a phenomenon that the performance of indexing methods degrades drastically as the dimensionality increases. With this urgent need, recently, we developed a new vector approximation-based indexing method called the *LPC* (*Local Polar Coordinate*)*-file* for the *k*-nearest neighbor (*k*-NN) search. The LPC-file significantly improves the search performance for large collections of high-dimensional vectors compared with the sequential scan and the VA-file (Weber et al. 1998). Although the LPC-file provides significant improvements compared with current techniques, it suffers the performance degradation when the dataset is highly clustered because it employs the simple space partitioning and the uniform bit allocation strategy for the partitioned cells. These strategies are appropriate for only uniform datasets. However, real image datasets are not uniformly distributed but highly clustered and skewed. In this paper, we discuss the problem to efficiently index high-dimensional image datasets.

2. RELATED WORK

Various approaches have been tried for the *k*-NN search in database systems. Intuitively, it is natural to use MIMs to speed up the *k*-NN search because objects are often represented by points in a multidimensional data space. However, most MIMs are defeated by the high dimensionality. MIMs work by partitioning the data space, clustering data according to partitions, and using the partitions to prune the search space for queries. Unfortunately, while MIMs generally perform well at low dimensional data spaces, their performance degrades drastically as the dimensionality increases. It is very unlikely that existing MIMs can prune some search space in high-dimesional data spaces. Because of the sparsity of the data space caused by the high dimensionality, the distance $k\text{-}NN^{dist}(q)$ between the query point q and its k-th NN may become far larger than the length of each dimension of the data space. As a result, the sphere $k\text{-}NN^{sphere}(q)$ with center q and radius $k\text{-}NN^{dist}(q)$ may intersect every partition in the data space, and thus the k-NN search may visit every partition (node) in an index. Motivated by the disadvantages of the state-of-the-art MIMs for high-dimensional data spaces, more recently, other kinds of approaches have been investigated to overcome the dimensionality curse. They are classified into four categories:

- Dimensionality reduction approach,
- Approximate nearest neighbor approach,
- Multiple space-filling curves approach,
- Vector approximation-based approach.

The dimensionality reduction approaches (Chakrabarti & Mehrotra 2000) (Kanth et al. 1998) (Lin et al. 1994) first condense most of information in a dataset to a few dimensions by applying the Singular Value Decomposition, the Discrete Cosine Transform or the Discrete Wavelet Transform. The data in the few condensed dimensions are then indexed to support fast retrieval. While the methods based on the DR approach provide a solution to the dimensionality curse, they have several drawbacks: (1) Dimensionality reduction is inevitably accompanied by the loss of precision of query results; (2) They are not readily applicable to dynamic databases because the transform has to be computed *a priori* on the entire data set and the computation is expensive; (3) The dimensionality may be still so high even after it is reduced that the MIMs cannot be used for the dataset.

The idea behind the approximate nearest neighbor (ANN) approaches (Arya et al. 1998) (Indym & Motwani 1998) (Kushilevitz et al. 1998) is to retrieve k ANNs faster within a given error bound ε instead of retrieving exact k NNs. Given a query point q and a distance error $\varepsilon > 0$, a point p is a $(1 + \varepsilon)$-*approximate nearest neighbor* of q such that for any other database point p',

$$\| q - p \| \leq (1 + \varepsilon) \| q - p' \|.$$

The multiple space-filling curves approach [14, 17] is also a kind of approximate approach in the sense that it gives up some accuracy of query results. This approach orders the d-dimensional space in many ways, with a set of space-filling curves such as Hilbert curves, each constituting a mapping from $R^d \rightarrow R^1$. This mapping gives a linear ordering of all points in the data set. Therefore, when a query point is mapped to the space-filling curve, one can perform a range search for nearby points along the curve to find near neighbors in the data space. However, due to the nature of the $R^d \rightarrow R^1$ mapping, some near neighbors of the query point may be mapped far apart along a single curve. To make sure that these points are not overlooked, multiple space-filling curves are used, based on different mappings from $R^d \rightarrow R^1$. The set of candidate nearest neighbors is formed from the union of sets of points in small neighborhoods (ranges) from all of the curves.

Although this approach improves the performance of the k-NN search, it is possible that some near-neighbors may be omitted during a search. To improve the chances of finding all k NNs, more space-filling curves have to be used or a larger neighborhood on each curve has to be scanned. However, they diminish the benefits of the approximate approach since both of these methods increase the size of the candidate set.

The vector approximation approach overcomes the dimensionality curse by filtering the feature vectors so that only a small fraction of them must be visited during a search. Among the approaches that aim at overcoming the dimensionality curse, this approach is the only one that outputs the *exact k* NNs. The VA-file (Weber et al. 1998) and the LPC-file (Cha et al. 2002) are classified into this category. The VA-file divides the data space into 2^b rectangular cells where b denotes the total number of bits specified by the user. Each cell has a bit representation of length b which approximates the data points that fall into a cell. The VA-file itself is simply an array of these bit vector approximations of data points.

The k-NN search in a VA-file consists of two phases. In the first phase, the set of all vector approximations is scanned sequentially and lower bound d_{min} and upper bound d_{max} on the distance of each cell to the query vector are computed. In this phase, if an approximation is encountered such that its d_{min} exceeds the k-th smallest upper bound found so far, the corresponding vector can be eliminated safely since k better candidates already exist. At the end of this phase, the vectors with the smallest bounds are found to be the *candidates* for k NNs of the query. In the second phase, the algorithm refines the candidate set by visiting real vectors themselves in the increasing order of d_{min}. This phase ends when an approximation is encountered whose d_{min} exceeds or equals the k-th actual NN distance in the answer set, and the final k nearest vectors in the answer set are the search result.

The LPC-file aims at improving the filtering power of the vector approximation with a minimum number of additional bits. The LPC-file partitions the vector space into hyper-square cells and approximates vectors using the *polar coordinates* on the partitioned cells. The approximation $\boldsymbol{a}$ for a vector $\boldsymbol{p}$ in the LPC-file is generated as follows. The first step is to assign the same number of bits b to each dimension and to divide the whole data space into 2^{bd} cells, where d is the number of dimensions. Thus the length of each side of a cell is the same. Typically b is a small integer between 4 and 8

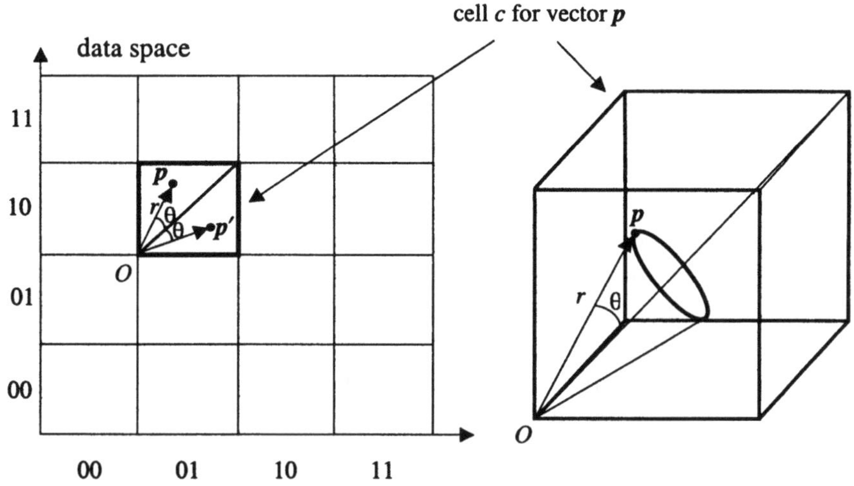

(a) 2-dimensional space (b) 3-dimensional space

Figure 1. Vector ***p*** and its approximation in the LPC-file

depending on the dimensionality and the data distribution. The cell is simply represented by the concatenation of the binary bit patterns for each dimension in turn. Figure 1(a) shows an example in a 2-dimensional space: the cell c is represented by the sequence of bits (01 10) where $d = 2$ and $b = 2$.

The second step is to represent the vector $\boldsymbol{p}$ using the polar coordinates (r, θ) within the cell in which $\boldsymbol{p}$ lies. As illustrated in Figure 1(a), the local origin O of each cell is determined as the lower left corner of the cell. The distance r of the polar coordinate is computed by the distance between the local origin O and the vector $\boldsymbol{p}$. The angle θ is computed by the angle between the vector $\boldsymbol{p}$ and the diagonal from the local origin to the opposite corner. As a result of this approximation, the vector $\boldsymbol{p}$ is represented by the triplet $\boldsymbol{a} = < c, r, \theta >$, where c, r, θ denote the approximation cell, the distance and the angle of $\boldsymbol{p}$ based on the local origin O, respectively. The compactness of the LPC-file vector approximation improves the search performance.

3. LPC$^+$-FILE FOR IMAGE DATA

The current vector approximation approach has an implicit assumption that it is very unlikely that several points lie in the same cell since the number of cells 2^{bd} is far larger than the size of a database, where b is the number of bits assigned to each dimension and d is the dimensionality. Actually, the vector approximation approach benefits from the *sparseness* of the data space as opposed to the partitioning or clustering methods (i.e., the traditional MIMs). However, if the data points are highly clustered, the probability that a certain cell includes several points increases, and therefore those vectors may use the same approximation. This means that the discriminatory power of the approximation decreases and thus candidates are less eliminated, and ultimately more disk accesses occur during the search.

Figures 2 and 3 show the vector selectivity comparison between random and real image datasets during the filtering and the refinement phases of the vector approximation approach, respectively. The vector selectivity is a good performance estimator because the performance of the k-NN search depends largely on the number of disk blocks visited and it is affected by the vector selectivity. The first phase vector selectivity means the ratio of candidates not eliminated after the first filtering phase to the total number of vectors. The second phase vector selectivity is the ratio of real vectors visited to the total number of vectors. In Figure 2, the x-axis represents the datasets and query types used in the experiment and the y-axis represents the percentage of remaining vectors after the filtering phase (i.e., the first phase vector selectivity). The cluster query means that the query vector is selected from the real image dataset itself, and the random query means that the query vector is selected randomly. In the experiment, we used 13,724 256-dimensional images of U.S. stamps and photos: Stamps often come in series (e.g., states, birds, flowers) with common colors and related designs, and the U.S. Post Office has often used similar colors for many long-running stamps. As a result, this real image dataset shows *strongly clustered distribution.* The random dataset used in the experiment also consists of 256-dimensional 13,724 random vectors. For the random dataset, 1,000 random 10-NN queries were posed, and for the real image dataset, 1,000 random 10-NN queries and 1,000 cluster 10-NN queries were posed, and their results were averaged.

In the case of the LPC-file in Fig. 2(a), the experimental result shows that, after the first phase filtering, the number of remaining vectors for a real image dataset is 2.66 to 4.68 times more than that for a random dataset. Similarly, in the case of the VA-file in Fig. 2(b), after the first phase filtering, the number of remaining vectors for a real image dataset is 2.34 to 16.57 times more than that for a random dataset. These mean that, compared with the random dataset, for the clustered dataset, the filtering power of the current vector approximation approach decreases drastically.

For the second refinement phase, in the case of the LPC-file as shown in Fig. 3, the number of real vectors visited for a real image dataset is 2.43 to 6.49 times more than that for a random dataset. In the VA-file, the number of real vectors visited for a real image dataset is 2.02 to 76.67 times more than that for a random dataset. These mean that the I/O cost occurred during the k-NN search for the clustered dataset is much higher than that for the random dataset.

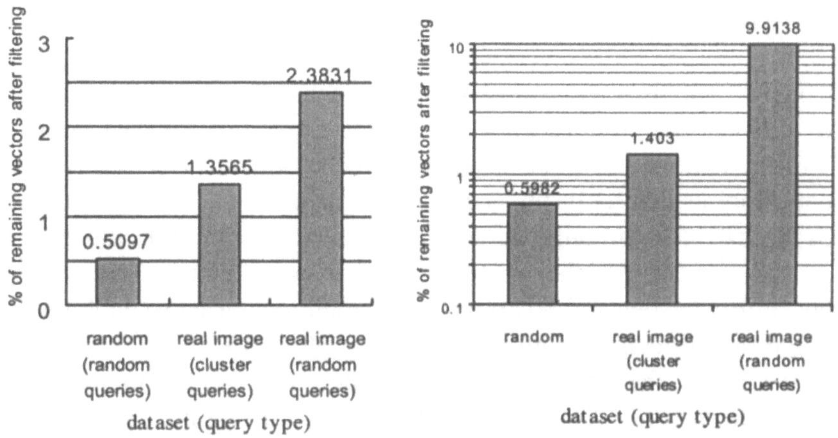

(a) LPC-file (b) VA-file

Figure 2. Selectivity comparison between random and real image datasets in the first phase (filtering)

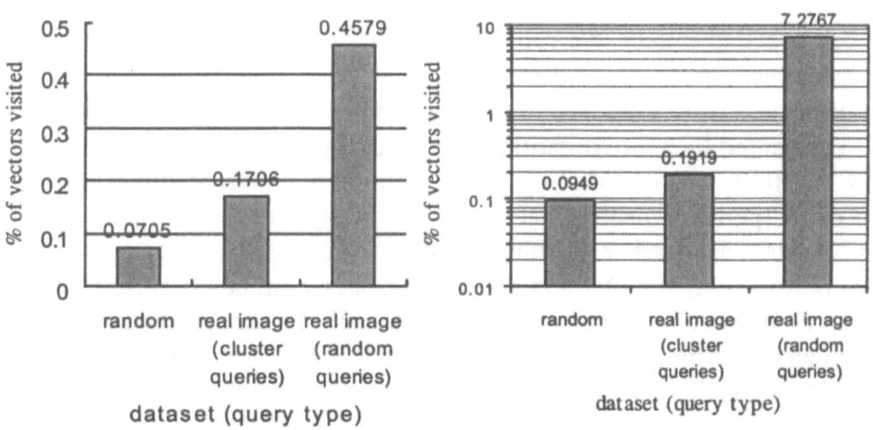

(a) LPC-file (b) VA-file

Figure 3. Selectivity comparison between random and real image datasets in the second phase (refinement)

This performance degeneration for the clustered dataset is a common problem of the current vector approximation approach. The reason for the performance degeneration is because bits are uniformly allocated to each partitioned cell while the data distribution is not uniform and the density of each cell varies greatly. The way to overcome this problem is to adaptively assign bits to each cell according to the data statistics of the cell. This is the focus of the LPC$^+$-file.

3.1 Adaptive Partitioning of Data Space

The LPC$^+$-file uses a *density-based* approach to determine the number of bits to allocate to a cell. To approximate the density of the data points, the LPC$^+$-file partitions the data space into hyper-square *cells* and finds the number of points that lie inside each cell of the partition. To accomplish this, like in the LPC-file, initially we assign b bits equally to each dimension j, $j \in \{1, \ldots, d\}$, and divide the whole data space into 2^{bd} cells, where d is the number of dimensions and b is typically a small integer between 4 and 8 depending on the dimensionality and the data distribution. Since each cell has the same volume, the number of points inside it can be used to approximate the density of the cell. The vast majority of the partitions are empty since the number of partitions 2^{bd} is much larger than the number of points in a dataset. In addition, for a real image dataset, most points lie inside some partitions due to the high clustering property of the image dataset.

The *selectivity* of a cell is defined to be the fraction of data points in the cell to the total data points. We call a cell c *dense* if the selectivity of c is greater than τ, where the *density threshold* τ is an input parameter. Otherwise, the cell is called *sparse*. We call a dense cell a *cluster* and call the points that lie inside the sparse cells *outliers*.

Once the sparse cells are found, the outliers lying inside the sparse cell are represented by approximation $<c, r, \theta>$, where c, r and θ are the same as the LPC-file's. The cell c of the initial outliers is represented by the bit pattern of the partition itself. That is, the initial outliers are represented by bd bits. Clusters are further partitioned into 2^d sub-cells until the points inside them become outliers. Outliers generated from a common partition share the bit representation of the partition. Thus, the cell of each outlier is represented by the common bit patterns of the partition to which the cell belongs and its own d bits for the cell it belongs to. In other words, the outliers generated from a common partition are represented by only d bits and the common bit pattern is shared among outliers. In effect, this greatly reduces the number of bits to represent the cell, and therefore the I/O cost for reading approximations can be reduced. Figure 4 shows the number of disk accesses for reading the approximation files for the LPC$^+$-file, the LPC-file, and the VA-file from the same experiments described above. In other words, this illustrates the I/O cost for the first phase of the k-NN search in the vector approximation approach. During the experiment, the size of a page used was 4 KB. The number of disk accesses of the LPC$^+$-file is almost a half of those of the LPC-file and the VA-file. This means that, for the LPC$^+$-file, the number of bits used to represent the cell approximation is a half of those of the LPC-file and the VA-file.

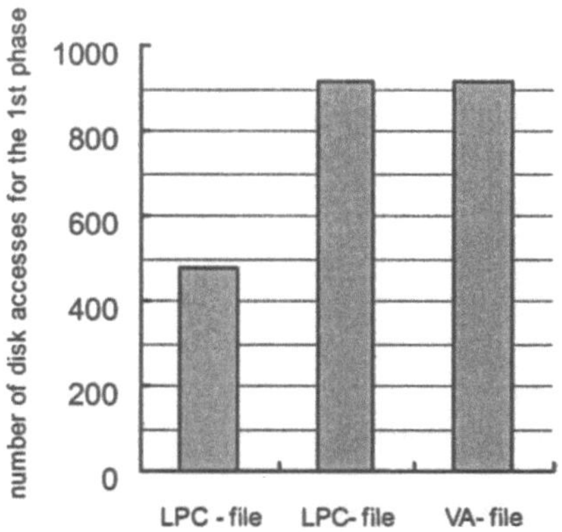

Figure 4. Comparison of the number of disk accesses during the first phase of the search

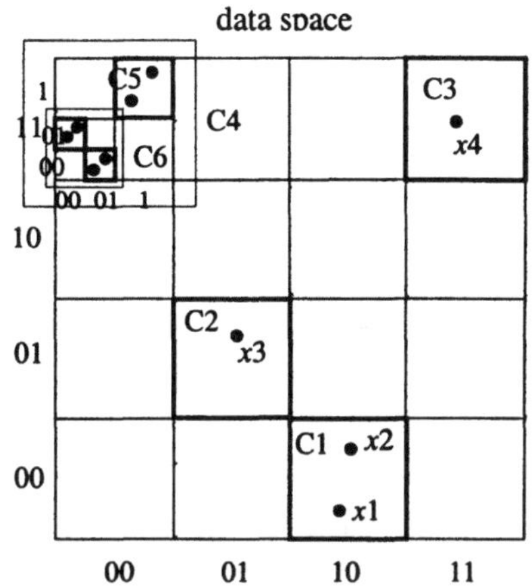

Figure 5. LPC$^+$-file's non-uniform partition of the data space

Example 1: We assume that the dimensionality is 2, the number of bits initially assigned to each dimension is 2, and the density threshold τ is $2/N$, where N is the total number of points in a database. In Figure 5, the two-dimensional space has been initially partitioned by 4×4 cells by using 2 bits per dimension. Outliers, i.e., data points fallen into a cell c_i whose selectivity is less than or equal to τ, are approximated by $<c_i, r, \theta>$. Points $x1$, $x2$, $x3$, and $x4$ are approximated by the cell c_i in which they lie and their polar coordinates in c_i. Clusters, i.e., the cells whose selectivity is greater than τ, e.g., cell C4, are further divided into 2^2 sub-cells. The cell C4 is subdivided into 4 cells and the points in cell C5 are approximated by $<c_5, r, \theta>$. The cell C6 is further divided into smaller cells and finally all points are approximated. The cell representations of the cells C1, C2, and C3 are (10 00), (01 01), and (11 11), respectively. The points in the cell C5 have the cell representation of (1 1) and a common cell representation (00 11). The two cells within the cell C6 have the cell representations (0 1) and (1 0), respectively, with a common cell representation (000 110) for C6. Since the real image data tend to cluster in certain cells, in fact, there are many points that share a common cell representation. This reduces the cost of disk I/O as shown in Figure 4.

3.2 Algorithm

The adaptive partitioning algorithm first starts partitioning the data space with b bits per dimension. From this initial partitioning, outliers and clusters are determined, and the cells of the outliers are represented by bd bits. The clusters are further partitioned to find appropriate number of bits to represent them and subsequent outliers are found and approximated. The following algorithm performs the partitioning of a cluster. The function **MakeOutliers** collects outliers on a given level and approximates them by using the LPC-file approximation.

Algorithm Partition(dataset S, dataset_size s, split_dimension j, split_location l_j, global_cell c_g, local_cell c_l)

```
// S: dataset of a cluster to split
// s: size of dataset S
// j: dimension to split
// d: dimensionality of the data space
// l_j: location to split in the dimension j.
// S_1, S_2: two datasets split from S based on j and l_j.
// size(S_1), size(S_2): number of points in S_1 and S_2, respectively
// c_g: initial global cell for dataset S
// c_l: a local cell partitioned from c_g. Initially, c_g is the same as c_l.
// n: density threshold τ· total number of points in a dataset
{
1. Divide the dataset S into two subsets S_1 and S_2 based on the split dimension j and
   the split location l_j.
2. If (size(S_1) > 0) {
     If (j < d) {
       2.1  Determine a new split location l_{j+1} based on the local cell c_l and new
            split dimension j+1.
       2.2  Adjust the local cell c_l based on the split.
       2.3  Invoke Partition(S_1, size(S_1), j+1, l_{j+1}, c_g, c_l).
     }
     Else {
       If (size(S_1) < n)
          Invoke MakeOutliers(S_1, size(S_1), c_g).
       Else {
          2.1 Determine a new split location l_1 based on the local cell c_l and the
              first dimension 1.
          2.2 Invoke Partition(S_1, size(S_1), 1, l_1, c_l, c_l).
       }
     }
   }
3. If (size(S_2) > 0) {
     If (j < d) {
       3.1 Determine a new split location l_{j+1} based on the local cell c_l and the
           new split dimension j+1.
       3.2 Adjust the local cell c_l based on the split.
       3.2 Invoke Partition(S_2, size(S_2), j+1, l_{j+1}, c_g, c_l).
     }
     Else {
       If (size(S_1) < n)
          Invoke MakeOutliers(S_2, size(S_2), c_g).
       Else {
          3.1 Determine a new split location l_1 based on the local cell c_l and the
              first dimension 1.
          3.2 Invoke Partition(S_2, size(S_2), 1, l_1, c_l, c_l).
       }
     }
   }
}
```

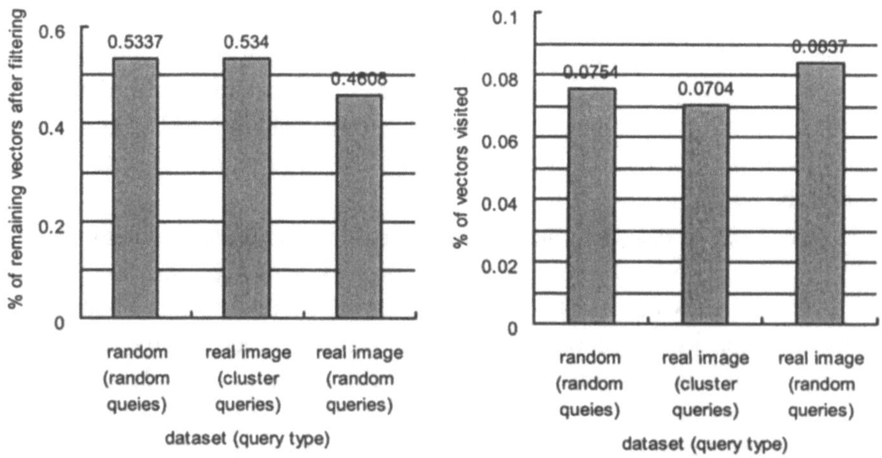

(a) first phase (b) second phase

Figure 6. Selectivity performance of the LPC$^+$-file

4. PERFORMANCE EVALUATION

For the experimental evaluation, we used 13,724 256-dimensional image histogram data set described in Section 3. In all experiments, the Euclidean distance metric L_2 was used, and the number of nearest neighbors to return was always ten, i.e., $k = 10$. The page size used in the experiment was 4 KB. 1,000 random and 1000 cluster 10-NN queries were processed and the results were averaged. The initial number of bits per dimension of the approximation cell used was 6. The density threshold τ used was 0.001.

Figure 6 compares the vector selectivity of the LPC$^+$-file for random and real image datasets during the first and the second phases. The x-axis represents the datasets and query types used in the experiment. The y-axis in Figure 6(a) represents the percentage of remaining vectors (i.e., the vector selectivity) after the first phase and the y-axis in Figure 6(b) represents the percentage of real vectors visited during the second phase. Compare the results of Figure 6 with those of Figures 2 and 3. For the LPC$^+$-file, the number of remaining vectors in the first phase of the search on the real dataset is less than or nearly equal to that on the random dataset. Observing Figures 2 and 3 for the VA-file and the LPC-file, for the real image dataset, the number of remaining vectors after the first phase is 2.34 to 16.57 times larger than that for the random dataset. In the second phase, for the real image dataset, the LPC$^+$-file visits less real vectors than for the random dataset when the cluster 10-NN queries were posed, and visits only 0.0083% more real vectors (actually, the number of vectors read more is 2.79) than for the random dataset when the random 10-NN queries were posed. On the other hand, for the VA-file and the LPC-file, on the real image dataset, the number of vectors visited during the second phase is 2.02 to 76.77 times larger than that on the random dataset. Summarizing this result, the performance of the LPC$^+$-file never degrades even though the dataset is strongly clustered as opposed to the VA-file and the LPC-file.

Figure 7 illustrates the average number of disk accesses during the second phase for 10-NN queries. Note that the disk access pattern is sequential in the first phase, whereas that is random in the second phase. Thus disk accesses occurred in the second phase have greater effects on the search performance than those in the first phase. In Figure 4, we already showed the average number of disk accesses of the LPC$^+$-file, the LPC-file and the VA-file during the first phase. It shows that the number of disk accesses of the LPC$^+$-file is almost a half of those of the LPC-file and the VA-file in the first phase. Observing the result of Figure 7, for the LPC$^+$-file, the increase of the number of disk accesses due to the search in the real image dataset is tiny. For cluster queries to a real image dataset, the number of disk accesses is nearly the same as that for a random dataset. For random queries to a real image dataset, in fact, only 2.79 more accesses on the average were performed. On the other hand, for the VA-file and the LPC-file, the increase of the number of disk accesses is significant for the real image dataset, especially for the VA-file. Note that the performance of the LPC$^+$-file on the real dataset is far superior to those of the LPC-file and the VA-file.

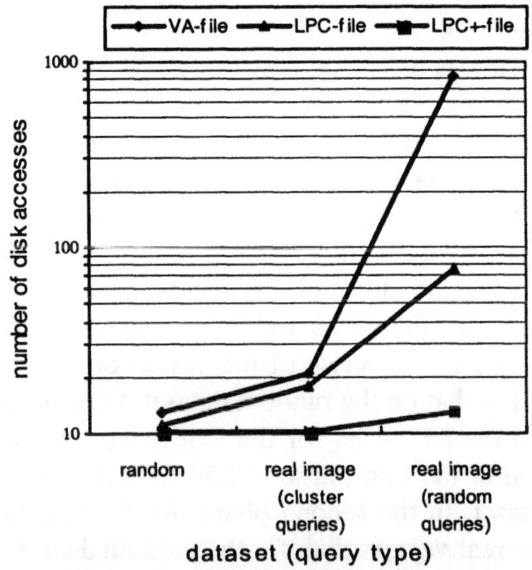

Figure 7. Average number of disk accesses during the second phase

5. CONCLUSIONS

In this paper, we proposed a new approximation-based high-dimensional indexing method called the LPC$^+$-file for clustered image datasets. We stated and discussed the problems associated with the current vector approximation approach for high-dimensional indexing. The current vector approximation approach such as the VA-file and the LPC-file assumes that it is very unlikely that several points lie in the same partition cell, applies a simple space partitioning technique, and employs a uniform bit allocation strategy for the cell representation. However, these assumption and strategies are appropriate only for uniformly distributed datasets, whereas real image datasets are often strongly clustered.

The LPC$^+$-file uses a density-based approach to determine the number of bits to allocate to a cell. The goal of the LPC$^+$-file is to improve the discriminatory (i.e., filtering) power of the vector approximation with the minimum number of bits. The essential idea of the LPC$^+$-file is to assign more bits to vectors in dense regions and less bits to vectors in sparse regions. Moreover, the LPC$^+$-file saves bits to represent the vector approximation by sharing the common bit pattern of the cell on which vectors lie together. The LPC$^+$-file achieves significantly better approximations of the vectors with smaller number of bits, and therefore improves the search performance in clustered high-dimensional image datasets.

REFERENCES

Arya, S., Mount, D.M., Netanyahu, N.S., Silverman, R., and Wu, A.Y., An Optimal Algorithm for Approximate Nearest Neighbor Searching in Fixed Dimensions, *Journal of the ACM*, 45(6), 891-923, Nov. 1998.

Beckmann, N., Kriegel, H.-P., Schneider, R., and Seeger, B., The R*-tree: An efficient and robust access method for points and rectangles, *Proc. of ACM SIGMOD Int'l Conf. on Management of Data*, 322-331, 1990.

Berchtold, S., Keim, D.A., Kriegel, H.-P., The X-tree: An Index Structure for High-Dimensional Data, *Proc. of the Int'l Conf. on Very Large Data Bases*, 28-39, 1996.

Cha, G.-H., Zhu, X., Petkovic, D., and Chung, C.-W., An Efficient Indexing Method for Nearest Neighbor Searches in High-Dimensional Image Databases, *IEEE Transactions on Multimedia*, Vol. 4, No. 1, March 2002.

Cha, G.-H. and Chung, C.-W., A New Indexing Scheme for Content-Based Image Retrieval, *Multimedia Tools and Applications*, 6(3), 263-288, May 1998.

Chakrabarti, K. and Mehrotra, S., Local Dimensionality Reduction: A New Approach to Indexing High Dimensional Spaces, *Proc. of the Int'l Conf. on VLDB*, 89-100, 2000.

Flickner, M., Sawhney, H., Niblack, W., Ashley, J., Huang, Q., Dom, B., Gorkani, M., Hafner, J., Lee, D., Petkovic, D., Steele, D., and Yanker, P., Query by image and video content: the QBIC system, *IEEE Computer*, 28, 23-32, 1995.

Indyk, P. and Motwani, R., Approximate Nearest Neighbors: Towards Removing the Curse of Dimensionality, Proc. of the *ACM Symp. on the Theory of Computing*, 604-613, 1998.

Kanth, K.V.R., Agrawal, D. and Singh, A., Dimensionality Reduction for Similarity Searching in Dynamic Databases, *Proc. of the ACM SIGMOD Int'l Conf. on Management of Data*, 166-176, 1998.

Katayama, N. and Satoh, S. The SR-tree: An Index Structure for High-Dimensional Nearest Neighbor Queries, *Proc. of the ACM SIGMOD Int'l Conf. on Management of Data*, 369-380, 1997.

Kushilevitz, E., Ostrovsky, R. and Y. Rabani, "Efficient Search for Approximate Nearest Neighbor in High Dimensional Spaces," *Proc. of the ACM Symposium on the Theory of Computing*, 614-623, 1998.

Lin, K.-I., Jagadish, H.V., and Faloutsos, C., The TV-tree: An Index Structure for High-Dimensional Data, *The VLDB Journal*, 3(4), 517-542, 1994.

Megiddo, N. and Shaft, U., Efficient Nearest Neighbor Indexing Based on a Collection of Space-Filling Curves, *Technical Report RJ 10093, IBM Almaden Research Center*, Nov. 1997.

Niblack, N., Barber, R., Equitz, W., Flickner, M., Glasman, E., Petkovic, D., Yanker, P., Faloutsos, C., and Taubin, G., The QBIC Project: Querying Images By Content Using Color, Texture, and Shape, *Proc. of the SPIE Conf. on Storage and Retrieval for Image and Video Databases II*, 173-187, 1993.

Shepherd, J., Zhu, X. and Megiddo, N., A Fast Indexing Method for Multidimensional Nearest Neighbor Search, *Proc. of the IS&T/SPIE Conference on Storage and Retrieval for Image and Video Databases VII*, 350 – 355, 1999.

Weber, R., Schek, H.-J., and Blott, S., A Quantitative Analysis and Performance Study for Similarity-Search Methods in High-Dimensional Spaces, *Proc. of the Int'l Conf. on VLDB*, 194-205, 1998.

BIOGRAPHY

Guang-Ho Cha received his Ph.D. degree in computer engineering from the Korea Advanced Institute of Science and Technology, Taejon, South Korea in 1997. Since 1997, he has been an Assistant Professor of Multimedia Engineering, Tongmyong Univesity of Information Technology, Busan, South Korea. From 1999 to 2000, he was a Visiting Scientist at the IBM Almaden Research Center, San Jose, CA. His research interests include content-based image/video/music indexing and retrieval, XML and semi-structured databases, and distance learning/education.

THE SEGMENTATION AND CLASSIFICATION OF STORY BOUNDARIES IN NEWS VIDEO

Lekha Chaisorn and Tat-Seng Chua
The School of Computing, National University of Singapore
Singapore 117543
{Lekhacha, chuats}@comp.nus.edu.sg

Abstract The segmentation and classification of news video into single-story semantic units is a challenging problem. This research proposes a two-level, multi-modal framework to tackle this problem. The video is analyzed at the shot and story unit (or scene) levels using a variety of features and techniques. At the shot level, we employ a Decision Tree to classify the shot into one of 13 pre-defined categories. At the scene level, we perform the HMM (Hidden Markov Models) analysis to eliminate shot classification errors and to locate story boundaries. We test the performance of our system using two days of news video obtained from the MediaCorp of Singapore. Our initial results indicate that we could achieve a high accuracy of over 95 % for shot classification. The use of HMM analysis helps to improve the accuracy of the shot classification and achieve over 89% accuracy on story segmentation.

Keywords: News Video classification; multi-modal approach; learning-based approach; Story Segmentation

1. INTRODUCTION

The effective management of the ever-increasing amount of broadcast news video is essential to support a variety of user-oriented functions, including the browsing, retrieval and personalization of news video. One effective way to organize the video is to segment the video into small, single-story units and classify these units according to their semantics. Research on segmenting an input video into shots is well established [Zhang et al 1993, Lin et al 2000]. A shot represents a contiguous sequence of visually similar frames. It is a syntactical representation and does not usually convey any coherent semantics to the users. In order to overcome this problem, recent works have been done to group related sequence of shots into scenes [Chang & Sundaram 2000, Wang et al. 2001]. The other challenge is to classify the shots and scenes created into well-defined categories.

Our research aims to develop a system to automatically segment and classify news video into semantic units. We propose a two-level, multi-modal framework to tackle this problem. We adopt the domain of news video in this study because news video is more structured and has clearly defined story units. The video is analyzed at the shot and story unit (or scene) levels using a variety of features. At the shot level, we use a set of low-level and high-level features to model the contents of each shot. We then employ a Decision Tree to classify the video shots into one of the 13 pre-defined categories. The result of shot level analysis is a set of shots tagged with one of the predefined categories. As the classification is performed independently at shot level, errors and ambiguity in shot tagging will occur. To overcome this problem, we perform HMM analysis [Rabiner & Juang 1993] at the scene level in order to eliminate the classification errors and to identify news story boundaries. Our approach is similar to that employed in natural language processing (NLP) research in performing part-of-speech tagging at the word level, and higher level analysis at the sentence level [Dale 2000].

Briefly, the content of this paper is organized as follows. *Section 2* describes related research and *Section 3* discusses the design of the multi-modal two-level classification framework. *Section 4* presents the details of shot level classification and *Section 5* discusses the details of story/scene segmentation. *Section 6* discusses the experiment results. *Section 7* contains our conclusion and discussions of future works.

2. RELATED WORKS

Video classification is a hot topic of research for many years and many interesting research has been done. Because of the difficulty and often subjective nature of video classification, most early works examined only certain aspects of video classification in a structured domain such as the sports or news.

Ide et al. [1998] tackled the problem of news video classification and used videotext, motion and face as the features. They first segmented the video into shots and used clustering techniques to classify each shot into one of the five classes of: Speech/report, Anchor, Walking, Gathering, and Computer graphics shots. Their classification technique is quite simple and seems effective for this restricted class of problems. Zhou et al. [2000] examined the classification of basketball video into the restricted categories of Left-court, Middle-court, Right-court, and Closed-up. They considered only motion, color and edges as the features and employed a rule-based approach to classify each video shot (represented using a key frame). Chen and Wong [2001] also used a rule-based approach to classify news video into the classes of: news, weather, reporting, commercials, basketball, and football. They used the feature set of motion, color, text caption, and cut rate in the analysis.

Another category of methods incorporated information within and between video segments to determine class transition boundaries using mostly the HMM approach. Eickeler et al. [1997] considered 6 features, deriving from the color histogram and motion variations across the frames, and employed HMM to classify the video sequence into the classes of Studio Speaker, Report, Weather Forecast, Begin, End, and the editing effect classes. Huang et al. [1999] employed audio, color, and motion as the features and classified the TV programs into the categories of news report, weather forecast, commercials, basketball games, and football games. Alatan et al. [2001] aimed to detect dialog and its transitions in fiction entertainment type videos. They modeled the shots using the features of audio (music/silence/speech), face and location changed, and used HMM to locate the transition boundaries between the classes of Establishing, Dialogue, Transition, and Non-dialogue.

In summary, most reported works considered only a limited set of classes and features, and provided only partial, intermediate solutions to the general video organization problem. In our work, we aim to consider all possible categories of shots and scenes to cover all types of news video. Another major difference between our approach and existing works is that we plan to perform the story segmentation analysis at two levels, similar to that employed successfully in NLP.

3. THE MULTI-MODAL TWO-LEVEL FRAMEWORK

3.1 Structure of News

Most news videos have rather similar and well-defined structures. Figure 1 illustrates the structure of a typical news video. The news video typically begins with several Intro/Highlight shots that give a brief introduction of the up coming news to be reported. The main body of news contains a series of stories organized in term of different geographical interests (such as international, regional and local) and in broad categories of social political, business, sports and entertainments. Each news story normally begins and ends with Anchor-person shots and several in between Live-reporting shots. Most news ends with reports on Sports, Finance, and Weather. In a typical half an hour news, there will be at least one period of commercials, covering both commercial product and self-advertisement by the broadcast station.

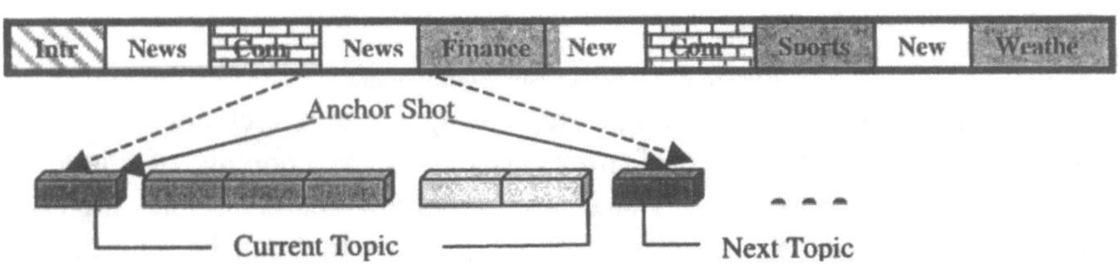

Figure 1: The structure of local news video under study

Although the ordering of news items may differ slightly from broadcast station to station, they all have similar structure and news categories. In order to project the identity of a broadcast station, the visual contents of each news category, like the anchor person shots, finance and weather reporting etc., tends to be highly similar within a station, but differs from that of other broadcast stations. Hence, it is possible to adopt a learning-based approach to train a system to recognize the contents of each category within each broadcast station.

3.2 The design of a news classification and segmentation system

Although news video is structured, it presents great challenges in classifying them and in particular identifying the story boundaries. The classification is difficult because there are many categories that are highly similar and can only be differentiated by using an appropriate combination of features. Examples of similar and ambiguous categories include: (a) the speech, interview, and meeting shots; (b) certain live reporting and sports; and (c) between different types of sports. For example, we might need a combination of face, text caption, visual background and audio features to differentiate between anchor-person, interview and meeting shots. The identification of story boundaries is even more difficult as it requires both visual and semantic information.

To tackle the problem effectively, we must address three basic issues. First, we need to identify the suitable units to perform the analysis. Next, we need to extract an appropriate set of features to model and distinguish different categories. Third, we need to adopt an appropriate technique to perform the classification and identify the boundaries between stories. To achieve this, we adopt the following strategies as shown in Figure 2:

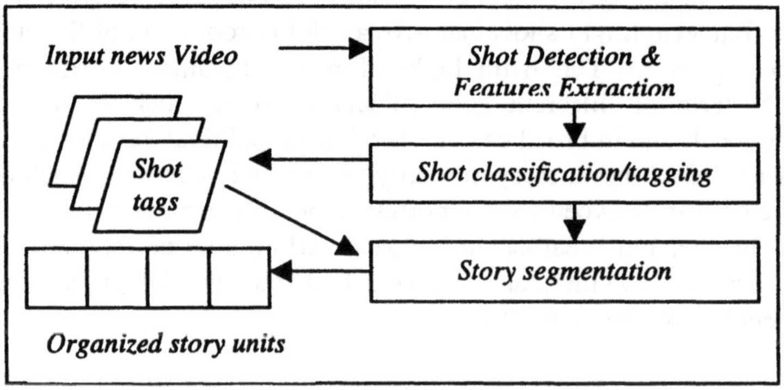

Figure 2: Overall system component

a) We first divide the input video into shots using a mature technique.
b) We extract a suitable set of features to model the contents of shots. The features include low level visual and temporal features, and high-level features like faces. We select only those features that can be automatically extracted in order to automate the entire classification process.
c) We employ a learning-based approach that uses multi-modal features to classify the shots into the set of well-defined subcategories.

d) Finally, given a sequence of shots in respective subcategories, we use a combination of shot content features, categories, and temporal features to identify story boundaries using the HMM technique.

4. THE CLASSIFICATION OF VIDEO SHOTS

This section describes the details of shot classification, including: shot segmentation; choice of appropriate shot categories and feature set; and the classification process.

4.1 Shot Segmentation and Key Frame Extraction

The first step in news video analysis is to segment the input news video into shots. We employ the multi-resolution analysis technique developed in our lab [Lin et al. 2000] that can effectively locate both abrupt and gradual transition boundaries effectively.

After the video is segmented, there are several ways in which the contents of each shot can be modeled. We can model the contents of the shot: (a) using a representative key frame; (b) as feature trajectories; or, (c) using a combination of both. In this research, we adopt the hybrid approach as a compromise to achieve both efficiency and effectiveness. Most visual content features will be extracted from the key frame while motion and audio features will be extracted from the temporal contents of the shots. This is reasonable as we expect the visual contents of shots to be relatively similar so that a key frame is a reasonable representation. We select the I-frame that is nearest to the center of the shot as the key frame.

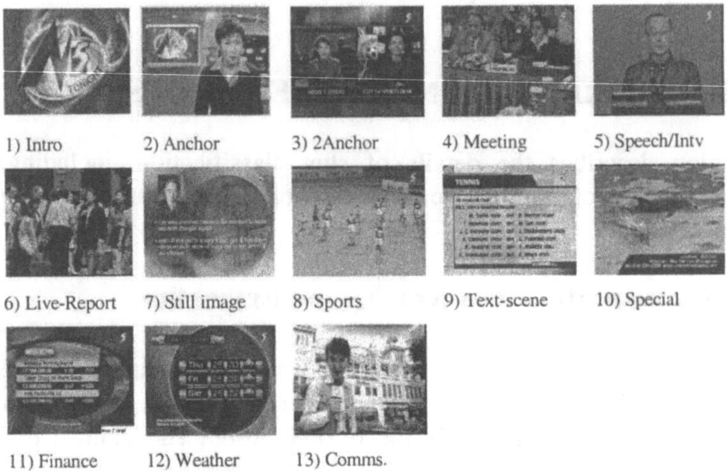

***Figure 3*: Examples of the predefined categories and example shots**

The next step is to determine an appropriate and complete set of categories to cover all shot types. The categories must be meaningful so that the category tag assigned to each shot is reflective of its content and facilitates the subsequent stage of segmenting and classifying news stories. We studied the set of categories employed in related works, and the structures of news video in general and local news in particular. We arrive at the following set of shot categories: *Intro/Highlight, Anchor, 2Anchor, Meeting/Gathering, Speech/Interview, Live-reporting, Still-image, Sports, Text-scene, Special, Finance, Weather, and Commercial*. These 13 categories cover all essential types of shots in typical news video. Some categories are quite specific such as the Anchor or Speech categories. Others are more general like the Sports, Special or Live-reporting categories. Figure 3 shows a typical example in each category.

4.3 Choice and extraction of features for shot representation

The choice of suitable features is critical to the success of most learning-based classification systems. Here, we aim to derive a comprehensive set of features that can be automatically extracted from MPEG video.

4.3(a) Low-level Visual Content Feature

Color Histogram: Color histogram models the visual composition of the shot. It is particularly useful to resolve two scenarios in shot classification. First, it can be used to identify those shot types with similar visual contents such as the weather and finance reporting. Second, the color histogram can be used to model the changes in background between successive shots, which provides important clues to determining a possible change in shot category or story. Here, we represent the content of key frame using a 256-color histogram.

4.3(b) Temporal Features

Background scene change: Following the discussions on color histogram, we include the background scene change feature to measure the difference between the color histogram of the current and previous shots. It is represented by 'c' if there is a change and 'u' otherwise.

Speaker change: Similar to background scene change feature, this feature measures whether there is a change of speaker between the current and previous shot. It takes the value of 'u' for no change, 'c' if there is a change, and 'n' if this feature is not applicable to the shots that do not contain speech.

Audio: This feature is very important especially for Sport and Intro/Highlight shots. For Sport shots, its audio track includes both commentary and background noise, and for Intro/Highlight shots, all the narrative is accompanied by background music. Here, we adopt an algorithm similar to that discussed in Lu et al. [2001] to classify audio into the broad categories of speech, music, noise, speech and noise, speech and music, or silence

Motion activity: For MPEG video, there is a direct encoding of motion vectors, which can be used to indicate the level of motion activities within the shot. We usually see high level of motion in sports and certain live reporting shots such as the rioting scenes. Thus, we classify the motion into *low* (like in an Anchor-person shot where only the head region has some movements), ***medium*** (such as those shots with people walking), *high,* or *no* motion (for still frame shots).

Shot duration: For Anchor-person or Interview type of shots, the duration tends to range from 20 to 50 seconds. For other types of shots, such as the Live-reporting or Sports, the duration tends to be much shorter, ranging from a few seconds to about 10 seconds. The duration is thus an important feature to differentiate between these types of shots. We set the shot duration to *short* (if it is less than 10 seconds), *medium* (if it is between 10 to 20 seconds), and *long* (for shot greater than 20 seconds in duration).

4.3(c) High-level Object-based features

Face: Human activities are one of most important aspects of news videos, and many such activities can be deduced from the presence of faces. Many techniques have been proposed to detect faces in an image or video. In our study, we adopt the algorithm developed in Chua et al. [2000] to detect mostly frontal faces in the key frame of each shot. We extract in each shot the number of faces detected as well as their sizes. The size of the face is used to estimate the shot types.

***Shot type*:** We use the camera focal distance to model the shot type, which include *closed-up, medium*-distance or *long*-distance shot etc. Here, we simply use the size of the face to estimate the shot type.

Videotext: Videotext is another type of object that appears frequently in news video and can be used to determine video semantics. We employ the algorithm developed in Zhang and Chua [2000] to detect videotexts. For each shot, we simply determine the number of lines of text appear in the key frame.

***Centralized Videotext*:** We often need to differentiate between two types of shots containing videotexts. The normal shot where the videotexts appear at the top or bottom of a shot to indicate its contents. The Text-scene shot where only a sequence of texts is displayed to summarize an event, such as the results of a soccer game. A text-scene shot typically contains multiple lines of centralized text, which is different from normal shots that may also contain multiple lines of text but normally un-centralized. Hence, we include this feature to identify Text-scene shots. It takes the value "true" for centralized text and "false" otherwise.

4.4 Shot representation

After all features are extracted, we represent the contents of each shot using a color histogram vector and a feature vector. The histogram vector is used to match the content of a shot with the representative shot of certain categories, while the feature vector is used by the classifier to categorize the shots into one of the remaining categories.

The feature vector of a shot is of the form:

$$S_i = (a, m, d, f, s, t, c) \tag{1}$$

where

- a the class of audio, $a \in$ {t=speech, m=music, s=silence, n =noise, tn = speech + noise, tm= speech + music, mn=music+noise}
- m the motion activity, $m \in$ {l=low, m=medium, h=high}
- d the shot duration, $d \in$ {s=short, m=medium, l=long}
- f the number of faces, $f \in \mathrm{N}$
- s the shot type, $s \in$ {c= closed-up, m=medium, l=long, u=unknown}
- t the number of lines of text in the scene, $t \in \mathrm{N}$
- c set to "true" if the videotexts present are centralized, c $\in$ {t=true, f=false}

For example, the feature vector of an Anchor-person shot may be (t, l, l, 1, c, 2, f). Note that at this stage we did not include the scene change and speaker change features in the feature set. These two features are not important for shot classification and will be included in story boundary detection using HMM.

4.5 The classification of video shots

We first remove the commercials before performing the classification of the remaining shots using a learning-based approach.

In most countries, it is mandatory to air several black frames preceding or proceeding a block of commercials. However, this is not always the case in many countries, like in Singapore. Our studies have shown that commercial boundaries can normally be characterized by the presence of black frames, still frames and/or audio silence [Koh and Chua 2000]. We thus employ a heuristic approach to identify the presence of commercials and detect the beginning and ending of the commercials blocks. Our tests on six news videos (180 minutes) obtained from the MediaCorp of Singapore demonstrate that we are able to achieve a higher detection accuracy of over 97%.

We break the classification of remaining shots into two sub-tasks. We first identify the shot types that have very similar visual features. Examples of these shot types include the Weather and Finance reports. For these shot types, we simply extract the representative histogram of the respective categories and employ the histogram-matching algorithm developed in Chua & Chu [1998] to compute the shot-category similarity that takes into consideration the perceptually similar colors. We employ a high threshold of 0.8 to determine whether a given shot belongs to the Weather or Finance category. By simply using this measure, we could achieve a very high classification accuracy of over 95% for these two categories.

For the rest of the shots, we employ a decision tree to perform the classification in a learning-based approach. Decision Tree (DT) is one of the most widely use methods in machine learning. The decision tree has the advantages that it is robust to noisy data, capable of learning disjunctive expression, and the training data may contain missing or unknown values [Quinlan 1986]. The decision tree approach has been successfully employed in many multi-class classification problems [Dietterich & Bakiri 1995, and Zhou et al. 2000]. We thus select the Decision Tree for our shot classification problem.

5. STORY/SCENE SEGMENTAION

After the shots have been classified into one of the pre-defined categories, we employ HMM to model the context of shot sequences in order to correct the shot classification errors and identify story boundaries. We use the shot sequencing information, and examine both the tagged category and appropriate features of the shots to perform the analysis. This is similar to the part-of-speech (POS) tagging problem in NLP that uses a combination of POS tags and lexical information to perform the analysis.

We model each shot by: (a) its tagged category; (b) scene/location change (c= change, u = unchanged); and, (c) speaker change (c = change, u = unchanged, and n = not applicable). We use the tag id as defined in Figure 3 to denote the category of each shot. For example, an input shot represented by **(1 c c)** means that this is an Intro/highlight shot with changes in background/location and speaker from the previous shot. Example of an input sequence passed to HMM is illustrated in Figure 4.

1cc 1uu 1cu 1uu 1uu .... 1uu | 2cc | 4cc 4uu 6uu 6uu ....

<----Intro/Highlight shots---------→ AP ←-----news reporting------→

Figure 4: Example of an input sequence (AP=Anchor-person shot)

HMM is a power statistical tool first successfully utilized in speech recognition research. HMM contains a finite set of *states*, each of which is associated with a (generally multidimensional) probability distribution. Transitions among the states are governed by a set of probabilities called *transition probabilities.* In a particular state, an outcome or *observation* can be generated according to the associated probability distribution. Video is a time sequencing data similar to that of speech, we thus employ HMM to perform the news video story segmentation.

In our priliminary experiments, we simply employ a left-to-right HMM with 4 to 9 internal states to model the news video.

6. TESTING AND RESULTS

This section discusses the experimental setups and results of the shot-level classification and scene (story boundary) detection.

6.1 Training and test data

We use two days of news video (one from May 2001, the other from June 2001) obtained from the MediaCorp of Singapore to test the performance of our system. Each day of news video is half an hour in duration. One day is used for training, and the other for testing. In this study, in order to eliminate indexing errors, we manually index all the features of the shots segmented using the multi-resolution analysis algorithm [Lin et al. 2000]. After the removal of commercials, the training data set contains 200 shots and testing data set contains 183 shots. The numbers of stories/scene boundaries are respectively 39 and 38 for the training and test data sets.

6.2 Shot level classification

6.2(a) Results of shot-level classification using Decision Tree

The results of shot-level classification using the Decision Tree are presented in Table 1. The diagonal entries in Table 1 show the number of shots correctly classified into the respective category, while the off-diagonal entries show those wrongly classified. It can be seen that the largest classification error occurs in the Anchor category where a large number of shots is misclassified as Speech. This is because their contents are quite similar, and we probably need additional features like background or speaker change, and the context of neighboring shots to differentiate them. Overall, our initial results indicate that we could achieve a classification accuracy of over 95%.

***Table 1*:** The classification results from the Decision Tree

Classified as->	a	b	c	d	e	f	g	h	i	j	k	l
a) Intro/highlight	26					1						
b) Anchor		16					4					
c) 2anchor			2									
d) Gathering				13								
e) Still image					1							
f) Live-reporting						82				1		
g) Speech		1					11					
h) Finance								*				
i) Weather									*			
j) Sport						1				8		
k) Text-scene											6	
l) Special												5

Figure 5 presents the partial Decision Tree learned from the training data. As can be seen from the tree generated, face is the most important feature for shot-level classification followed by audio and shot type.

6.2(b) Effectiveness of the features selected

In order to ascertain the effectiveness of the set of features selected, we perform separate experiments by using different number of features. As face is found to be the most important feature, we use the face as the first feature to be given to the system. With the face feature alone, the system returns an accuracy of only 59.6%. If we include the audio feature, the accuracy increases rapidly to 78.2%. However, this accuracy is still far below the accuracy that we could achieve by using all the features. When we successively add in the rest of features in the order of shot type, motion, videotext, text centralization, and shot duration, the performance of the system improves steadily and eventually reaches the accuracy of 95.10%. The results of the feature analysis are summarized in Figure 6. The analysis indicates that all the features are essential in shot classification.

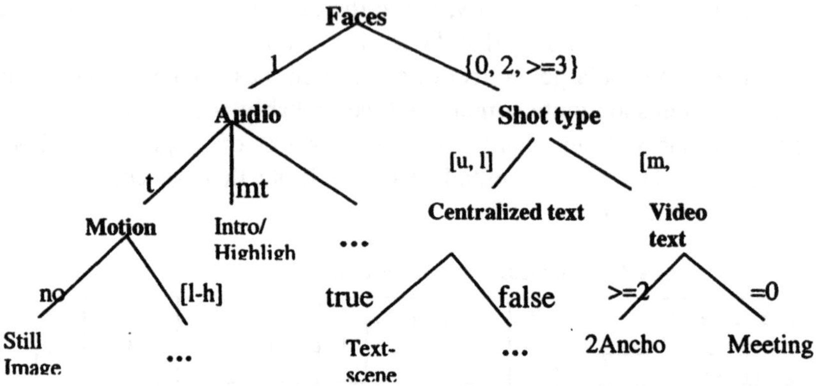

Figure 5: Part of the decision tree created from the training sample

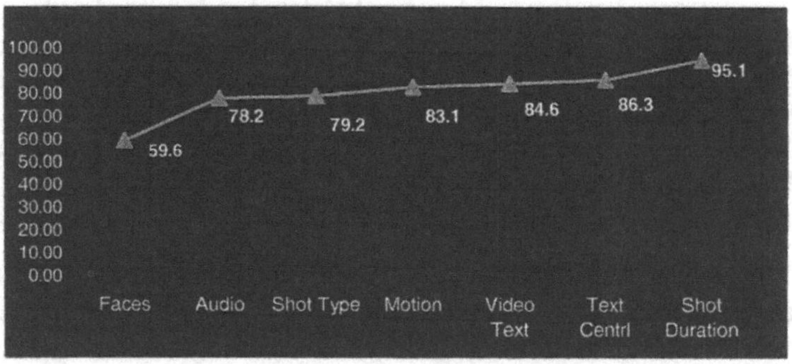

Figure 6: The results of features base-line analysis

6.3 Scene/News Story Segmentation

As stated in Section 5, we employ the left-to-right HMM to model news video sequences. We performed several experiments by setting the number of states ranging from 4 to 9. Our experiments showed that the number of states equals to 4 gives the best results.

In the first test, we assume that all the shots are correctly tagged and perform the HMM to locate story boundaries. The results indicate that out of the 38 correct story boundaries in the test set, we could achieve about 92% accuracy with two missing and one wrongly identified story boundary. This experiment demonstrates that HMM is effective in news story boundary detection.

Next, we perform HMM analysis on the set of shots tagged using the earlier shot classification stage with about 5% tagging error. The analysis aims to correct the shot tagging errors and locate story boundaries. The results demonstrate that: (a) we are able to correct 5 wrongly tagged shots to push the shot classification accuracy to over 97%; and (b) we are able to achieve over 89% accuracy on story boundary detection.

The results show conclusively that our two-level framework is effective in detecting and classifying story boundaries in news video.

7. CONCLUSIONS AND FUTURE WORKS

We have developed a multi-modal two-level framework that can automatically segment an input news video into story units. We use a set of low-level and high-level features to perform the analysis. Given an input video stream, the system performs the analysis at two levels. The first is shot classification, which classifies the video shots into one of 13 pre-defined categories using a combination of low-level, temporal and high-level features. The second level builds on the results of the first level and performs the HMM analysis to locate story (or scene) boundaries and classify news stories. Our results demonstrate that our two-level framework is effective and we could achieve an accuracy of over 89% on scene or story boundary detection,

We are now in the process of incorporating speech to text feature to enhance the system performance. Our eventual goal is to convert an input news video into a set of news stories together with their classification. This will bring us a major step towards supporting personalized news video for general users.

ACKNOWLEDGMENTS

The authors would like to acknowledge the support of the National Science & Technology Board and the Ministry of Education of Singapore for the provision of a research grant RP3960681 under which this research is carried out. The authors would also like to thank Chin-Hui Lee, Rudy Setiono and Wee-Kheng Leow for their comments and fruitful discussions on this research.

REFERENCES:

A. Aydin Alatan, Alin N. Akansu, and Wayne Wolf (2001). "Multi-modal Dialog Scene Detection using Hidden Markov Models for Content-based Multi-media Indexing". *Multimedia Tools and applications*, 14, pp 137-151.

Shiu-Fu Chang and Hari Sundaram (2000). " Structural and semantic analysis of video", IEEE International Conference on Multimedia and Expo (II): pp. 687-

Y. Chen and E. K. Wong (2001). " A knowledge-based Approach to Video Content Classification", Proceeding of SPIE Vol. 4315, pp.292-300.

Tat-Seng Chua and Chunxin Chu (1998). Color-based Pseudo-object for image retrieval with relevance feedback. International Conference on Advanced Multimedia Content Processing '98. Osaka, Japan, Nov. 148-162.

Tat-Seng Chua, Yunlong Zhao and Mohan S. Kankanhalli (2000). "An Automated Compressed-Domain Face Detection Method for Video Stratification", Proceedings of Multimedia Modeling (MMM'2000), USA, Nov, World Scientific, pp 333-347.

Robert Dale, Hermann Moisl, and Harold Somers (2000). "Handbook of natural language processing", Imprint New York: Marcel Dekker.

T. G. Dietterich, and G. Bakiri (1995). "Solving Multi-class Learning Problems via Error-Correcting Output Codes", Journal of Artificial Intelligence Research, pp 263-286

Stefan Eickeler, Andreas Kosmala, Gerhard Rigoll (1997). "A New Approach To Content-based Video Indexing Using Hidden Markov Models", IEEE workshop on Image Analysis for Multimedia Interactive Service (WIAMIS), pp 149-154.

J. Huang, Z. Liu, Y. Wang (1999). "Integration of Multimodal Features for Video Scene Classification Based on HMM", IEEE signal processing Society workshop on Multimedia Signal processing, Denmark, pp 53-58.

Ichiro Ide, Koji Yamamoto, and Hidehiko Tanaka (1998). "Automatic Video Indexing Based on Shot Classification", Conference on Advanced Multimedia Content Processing (AMCP'98), Osaka, Japan. S. Nishio, F. Kishino (eds), Lecture Notes in Computer Science Vol.1554, pp 87-102.

Michael I. Jordan (1998) (Eds). "Learning in Graphical Models", MIT Press.

Chun-Keat Koh and Tat-Seng Chua (2000). "Detection and Segmentation of Commercials in News Video", Technical report, The School of computing, National University of Singapore.

Yi Lin, Mohan S Kanhanhalli, and Tat-Seng Chua (2000). "Temporal Multi-resolution Analysis for Video Segmentationtion", Proceedings of SPIE (Storage and Retrieval for Media Databases)., San Jose, USA. Jan 2000, Vol 3972, pp 494-505.

Zhu Liu , Jingcheng Huang, and Yao Wang (1998). "Classification of TV Programs Based on Audio Information using Hidden Markov Models", IEEE Signal Processing Society, Workshop on Multimedia Signal Processing, Los Angeles, California, USA, pp 27-31.

Lie Lu, Stan Z. Li and Hong-Jiang Zhang (2001). "Content-based Audio Segmentation using Support Vector Machine", IEEE International Conference on Multimedia and Expo (ICME 2001), Japan, pp 956-959.

J. R. Quinlan (1986). "Induction of Decision Trees. Machine Learning" vol. 1, pp. 81-106.

L. Rabiner and B. Juang (1993). "Fundamentals of Speech Recognition", Prentice-Hall.

Jihua Wang, Tat-Seng Chua, and Liping Chen (2001). "Cinematic-based Model for Scene boundary detection", to appear in Proc. of Multimedia Modeling conference (MMM'01), Amsterdam, Netherlands.

Hong-Jiang Zhang, A. Kankanhalli and S.W. Smoliar (1993). "Automatic Partitioning of Full-motion Video", *Multimedia Systems*, 1(1), pp 10-28.

Yi Zhang and Tat-Seng Chua (2000). "Detection of Text Captions in Compressed domain Video". Proceedings of ACM Multimedia'2000 Workshops (Multimedia Information Retrieval), California, USA. Nov, pp 201-204.

WenSheng Zhou, Asha Vellaikal, and C–C Jay Kuo (2000). "Rule-based Classification System for basketball video indexing", Proceedings of ACM Multimedia'2000 Workshops (Multimedia Information Retrieval), California, USA. Nov, pp 213-216.

BIOGRAPHIES

Lekha Charson received her B.Sc. in Mathematics in 1982 from the Prince of Songkhla University, Thailand, and her MSc in Information and Computer Science in 1996 from the National University of Singapore. Presently, she is a PhD. candidate at the School of Computing,, National University of Singapore. She has worked as a senior lecturer at the Computer Science Department, in the Prince of Songkhla University, Thailand, since 1989. Her current research interests include news video segmentation and classification, and speech and audio classification.

Tat-Seng Chua obtained his PhD from the University of Leeds, UK. He joined the School of Computing, National University of Singapore, in 1983. He was the Acting and Founding Dean of the School of Computing from 1998-2000. He spent three years as a research staff member at the Institute of Systems Science (now KRDL) in late 1980s. Dr Chua's main research interest is in multimedia information processing, in particular, on video and text retrieval and information extraction. Dr Chua has organized and served as program committee member of numerous international conferences in the areas of computer graphics and multimedia. He is the conference co-chair of: Multi-Media Modeling (MMM) '93, '95, '97 and '03; Computer Graphics International (CGI) '90, '00 and '01; and Pacific Graphic '98. He serves in the editorial boards of: IEEE Transactions of Multimedia (IEEE); The Visual Computer (Springer-Verlag); and Multimedia Tools and Applications (Kluwer).

ARCHITECTURE AND IMPLEMENTATION OF AN INTERACTIVE TOOL FOR THE DESIGN AND VISUALIZATION OF ACTIVE CAPABILITY

Sharma Chakravarthy and Seokwon Yang

Computer Science and Engineering Department, The University of Texas at Arlington, Arlington, TX 76109-0015

Email: sharma@cse.uta.edu

Abstract: Active capability has been proposed as a paradigm to meet the demands of many database and other applications that require a timely response to situations. Event – Condition – Action (or ECA) rules are used to support active capability in a system. The design of an active DBMS for a particular application entails the design of schema for that application as well as ECA rules that correspond to business rules, constraints, invariants, and situations to be monitored in that application.

This paper concentrates on: i) architecture and development of a general-purpose lightweight proxy that enables us to support interfaces on distributed or web-based environment uniformly and ii) design and implementation of an interactive visualization tool for Active Database systems (ADBs). The tool is intended both as a debugging tool and a visualization tool based on the proposed architecture. The tool allows the designer/user to set breakpoints on event occurrences and rule execution or to enable/disable events and rules at run time. The priority and other attributes of rules can be changed interactively to study the behavior of rule interaction among themselves and with transaction/applications.

Key words: ECA rules, Event graph, Visualization

1. INTRODUCTION

Active database technology provides a means for database applications to react automatically to user-requested or system-generated events. Specification of this active capability can be tricky requiring new tools for the management of Event-Condition-Action (ECA) rule abstraction. Use of ECA rules for real-life DBMS applications has added a new dimension to the traditional validation or analysis phase. For the traditional DMBS, we used to have only schema design for the application and the main form of validation was to make sure that the design captured all of the requirements of the application and browsing the data returned as a result of user requests. In contrast, in active database systems, we have schema design as well as rule design for an application that uses active capability. The schema design for applications can be done statically with respect to the application semantics; however, the design of ECA rules requires that the rules be validated with respect to transactions and applications, as there is semantic interaction between rules and applications. Furthermore, there is a clear need for regression analysis to make sure additions and deletions of ECA rules does not change the outcome of currently used applications/transactions in an undesirable way. The tool should help the designer understand the impact of changes in rules while rules are added or removed as the business rules change over a period of time in application. For the designer of the rules, the tool will behave as a debugger and a regression analysis tool at a higher level of abstraction as compared to conventional debugging tools (such as dbx/xdbx). Designers are interested in understanding events and rules relevant to a particular transaction/application, order of rule execution, interaction among rules, and potential cycles among the set of rules. The ability to interact with the tool is critical from a designer's viewpoint. On the other hand, for an end user, the actual set of rules executed, the policies enforced for a particular application, and whether policies interact inconsistently are more important than the ability of interaction.

The tool described in this paper is a redesign that not only supports batch mode, but extends it further to on-line and interactive modes as well. In addition, we also have distributed event detection capability (GED) for which the previous tool was not useful. We wanted an architecture that will be useful for debugging distributed applications and can be used from a remote site as well. Hence, the initial portion of this paper discusses the architectural needs and our approach using which visualization as well as monitoring tools could be developed.

The rest of the paper is structured as follows. Section 2 discusses related work. Section 3 elaborates on the design consideration of the visualization tool. Section 4 discusses the web-based architecture of the visual interface components that can also support distributed applications. Section 5 describes the implementation details of the visualization tool and termination analysis. Section 6 contains conclusions.

2. RELATED WORK

DEAR [1] keeps track of both rules and events. It automatically detects inconsistencies and potential conflicting interactions among rules. But, the approach taken by DEAR works only for primitive events, such as insert, delete, update, and the rules defined over these events. Second, they do not support interactive features that we feel are necessary for a debugger of this sort. The debugging features of PEARD [2] also include detecting potential cycles in rule execution and a utility to examine different rule execution paths from the same point in the rule triggering process. This tool is similar to our visualization tool especially with respect to rule browsing, breakpoint setting, and rule enabling/disabling. But, the approach does not differentiate the external events generated by the applications and the internal events coming from the nested rule execution. SAMOS [3] has several tools, such as a rule analyzer, a rule browser and a rule explanation component. The termination analyzer assists users in checking the termination of rules. One limitation of SAMOS is that it does not differentiate the internal (or nested) event from the external event as it does not support a nested transaction model. A visualization tool was implemented earlier [4] as part of Sentinel that was mostly a post-analysis tool with limited interactive capability.

3. VISUALIZATION TOOL REQUIREMENTS

In contrast to a conventional debugging tool, which concentrates on changes to variables, the debugging context of the visualization tool is to verify or validate the correctness of business rule execution with respect to transactions and applications, based on schema and rules specified.

3.1 General design requirements

1. **Support of different user perspectives:** For the rule designer, the tool will behave as a debugger and a regression analysis tool at a higher level of abstraction as compared to conventional debugging tools (such as dbx/xdbx). Rule designers' interests go well beyond a specific application's running behavior of an application. The interactive mode of the tool is critical from the designer's viewpoint. It is also important that as part of the interaction, the designers are able to disable events and rules selectively, and to further indicate what they want to see highlighted (or removed from the display). On the other

hand, end users are more interested in the application behavior at run time, based on schema and rule design.

2. **Portability:** Users should be able to use the same tool on multiple platforms and operating systems as well as in a web-based environment (to allow visualization and debugging at locations non-local to the application) uniformly. Scalable architecture should be taken into account to make the tool available in heterogeneous environments.
3. **Multiple modes of usage:** The tool should provide multiple modes of usage so that a user can choose the mode that is most appropriate for her. The tool at the least needs to support run-time and post-analysis trace modes. In addition, an interactive mode will be helpful to debug a rule set at run time.
4. **Multiple visualization:** The tool should be able to support visualizations of participating applications in a distributed setting so that the entire distributed application can be debugged and visualized. In addition, multiple visualization of one application is equally important as groups of developers can debug the same application from different perspectives and from different locations.

3.2 Design Consideration for the Visualization tool

When we consider the debugging context of sentinel (an Object-Oriented DBMS into which active capability has been incorporated in the form of event-condition-action or ECA rules), we need to take into account the following specific design considerations.

1. **Rule and event interaction**: The visualization tool is mainly used to help the user to see the interaction among rules and events in an ADBMS. When event(s) occur, the corresponding rules are triggered. And a rule may raise an event, which in turn triggers rules that invoke other events. Without visual aid, this interaction may turn out to be too complicated to analyze and understand.
2. **Presentation of nested rule execution to users**: In Sentinel (or any active DBMS), rule execution (i.e., condition and action portions of a rule) is done in a sub-transaction. In other words, rules in turn fire other rules in a nested (as cascading) fashion. Sub-transactions can be nested to arbitrary levels and are represented by n-ary tree in the visualization tool. The transaction tree grows in a top-down way.
3. **User Interaction in application**: ADBMS application developers often realize the importance of the debugging tool that is able to provide mechanisms to change the characteristics of rules and events (enable/disable, change in priority, change in coupling mode etc.) at an abstract level. The same tool should allow the user to intervene during an application execution for this purpose.
4. **The tool in a Distributed Environment:** Allowing multiple instances of the tool to visualize and explore the same rule set simultaneously would be another interesting direction. Starting several (at least two) visualization tools, loaded with same events, but each tool having different set of rules, would be helpful for debugging. Each visualization tool would be responsible for the actual visualization of corresponding rule set, but operations such as breakpoint, disable, enable operation or generating reports, etc, would be performed as needed for each rule set at each display by users/designers. Our proposed architecture will facilitate this without any problem.

4. VISUALIZATION TOOL ON THE WEB

Figure 1 shows two different scenarios where Java user interface interacts with sentinel (or any other) applications. Figure 1-(a) illustrates the typical environment where each application and GUI creates a socket to listen to the incoming message, exchanging information in both directions. Provided that the GUI knows where each applications is executing and applications know where the GUI waits for notifications in some way, applications and GUI can either be executed on the same machine or on different machines. Figure 1-(b) demonstrates the additional requirement

Figure 1 Distributed Environment vs Distributed Web Environment

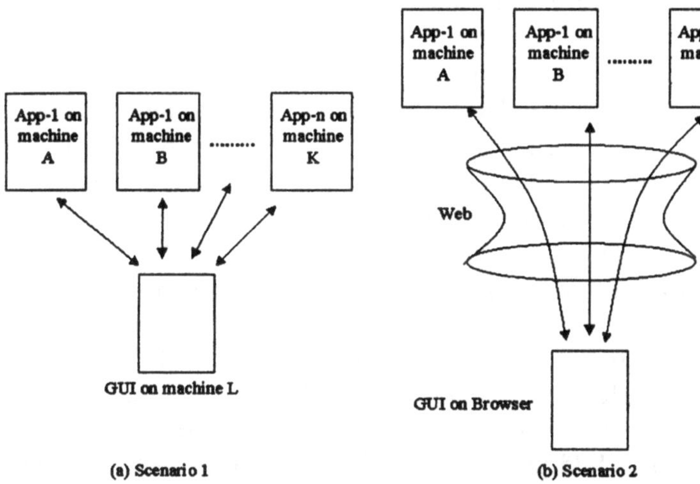

when we design the GUI components. A GUI should be able to run on top of a browser in which case the communication channel between GUI and applications goes through web. In this context, we define the "Distributed Web environment" as follows. A GUI element runs on a web browser and applications run on remote machines, while bi-directional communication is established through the web server.

The difficulty in reusing the GUI components is related to security restrictions of GUI on top of a browser. In short, the restrictions are as follows:

1. Current commercial browsers do not allow the downloaded GUI components to open a listening port for accepting connections. This restriction comes from the fact that Java applets run on a virtual machine in the browser, which insulates them from direct contact with the host system. This so-called 'sand-box' around the applet enforces restrictions that prevent it from interfering with the host.
2. Messages can only be received after initiating a connection or interaction with the host web server. GUI components on top of a browser cannot create a server

socket as it is normally done. It cannot receive information from remote applications without initiating a request. It cannot play a role as a server and wait for incoming messages.

3. GUI components are not allowed to open network connections to any computer, other than the web server machine that provided the class files [5].

We use a 3-tier architecture to overcome the above restrictions and create a lightweight proxy. The proxy maintains all connections after the GUI components initialize and register themselves. The information from remote applications to GUI can be transferred through these maintained connections. The user request from GUI to remote applications running on other than web server can be routed through the proxy.

In addition to these security restrictions, we encountered another proxy requirement in the web-based environment. We have Java applets as a front-end interface running on the web browser. One of these GUI components' tasks is to launch the Sentinel (or any general) applications either on the web server machine or a remote machine. In other words, we want to have process control mechanisms similar to that of a UNIX terminal using a browser. For this purpose, we have to add an additional capability in the proxy to receive remote execution requests through the web channel from clients and launch specific processes on the remote machine.

We consider two alternative architectures to implement the proxy. The first architecture uses the fork, semaphores, and shared memory. The other one uses threads and one linked-list for storing the open socket connection. Figure 2-(a) shows the first approach. The proxy creates a child process for each client. It has one global semaphore to coordinate the child processes and one inter-process shared memory to transfer messages received by one child process to another child process. Initially, the child process is in wait state. When any child process receives a message from the client, it first put the message in the shared memory, wakes up the other child process that serves the other client, using the semaphore operation. At the same time, the awakened child process accesses the shared memory, accesses the message and sends the message to the client it serves. Again, the state of child process is also changed into wait state after it sends the message to the destination.

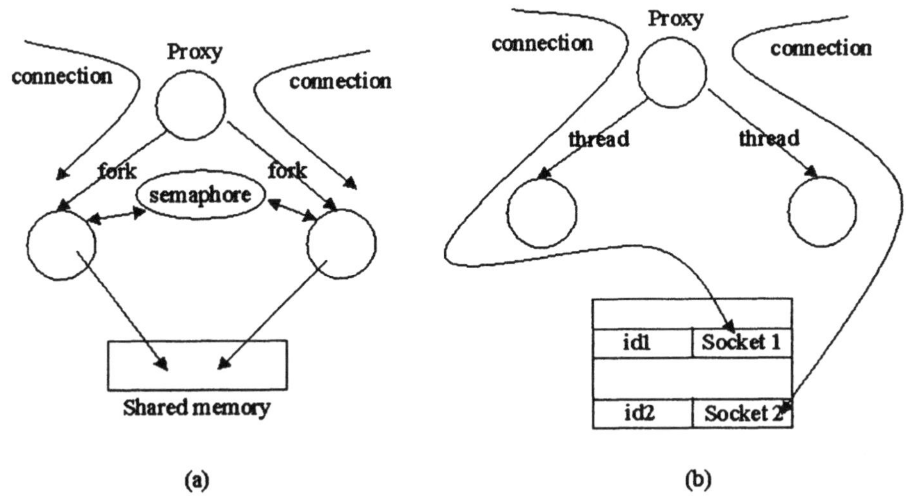

Figure 2 Two Alternatives of Proxy Architecture

The second approach is shown in Figure 2-(b). When a proxy receives the registering request for connection, it creates a daemon thread to serve each client and puts the socket connection with a unique ID into a global list. The proxy does not close the socket connection that is on the list until the client explicitly asks to close it or the client closes the other end of the socket connection. Each daemon thread is given access privilege to look up the socket connection with a given ID. When a daemon thread receives the request for transferring a message, it first looks up the list to find the destination socket connection with ID, which is contained in the message, and write the message into that socket connection. This will wake up the client and the client processes the message according to the semantics.

We chose the second approach, due to the several limitations of the first approach. One is related to shared memory. Each machine defines a minimum allocation size for shared memory. If the size of shard memory requested does not match the minimum allocation size, the shared memory would not be granted. In some cases, a machine may not have any more shared memory to grant. The other limitation is the number of semaphores required. The first approach uses a semaphore to coordinate the child processes. The number of semaphores needed is determined at run time. Therefore, we cannot make a general-purpose proxy using this architecture. Besides, the first approach cannot port directly to an NT operating system. The resources such as semaphore, shared memory and fork system calls are all specific to an operating system. Also, the size of a process is also large compared to a thread and furthermore process switching is more expensive.

5. IMPLEMENTATION OF THE INTERACTIVE VISUALIZATION TOOL

Sentinel [6] [7] is an integrated active DBMS incorporating ECA rules using Open OODB Toolkit from Tex Instruments [8]. Sentinel allows users to specify events and rules at an abstract level using Snoop [9] language, which is incorporated into the C++ language. Any method of an object class can be a potential event generator (in our case, primitive Event).

Event are classified into i) primitive event which are pre-defined in the system and ii) composite events that are formed by applying a set of operators to primitive and composite events. Primitive events correspond to database operation, such as retrieve, insert, update and delete in RDBMS or method invocation in OODB. Composite events are formed by applying a set of operators to primitive and composite events, recursively. The operators consist of OR, AND, ANY, Seq, Not, Aperiodic Operator, and Periodic Operator. Periodic and aperiodic operators were introduced to meet the requirements of process control, network management, and CIM applications.

Sentinel uses an event tree for each composite event. The trees are merged to form an event graph to detect a set of composite events. Event propagation is performed in a bottom-up fashion. Leaf nodes in event graph correspond to primitive or external events. Internal nodes correspond to event sub-expressions. Each node has a list of subscribers to whom it has to notify once the event denoted by that node is detected.

A sequence of primitive event occurrences (over a period of time) may make a composite occur which is detected in LED. Hence, the local event detector needs to record the occurrence of each event and save its parameters so that they can be used to compute the parameter set of the composite event.

Rules are specified at class definition time as a part of an application. The class-level rule specification is pre-processed into C++ statements and inserted in the application program. Sentinel also support rule activation and deactivation at run time. Rules are specified with a priority. A scheduler, based on the rule priority, controls the execution of the rule thread. If several rules have the same priority, we have concurrent execution of the rules. This may result in the conflict to access data. To deal with this problem, the nested transaction model executes a rule thread as a sub-transaction and uses the transaction synchronization scheme. The order of rule execution can be varied according to the relative priority of its sibling rules.

5.1 Visual Analysis of ECA Rules

We have extended the visualization tool developed for Sentinel to enable user interaction at run time. Interaction through a two-way communication channel, rather than passively receiving information, allows the user to make changes (enable, disable) on the rule set at run time. The user can set breakpoints during a debugging session so that the state of current rule/event execution can be inspected, and enable/disable rules or events at run time. Other debugging features include a utility for detecting potential cycles in rule execution and a utility to examine different paths from the same point in the rule triggering process [2].

The tool supports 3 modes of operation: post-analysis, real time analysis, and interactive analysis. The difference between the modes is how the rule execution information is supplied to the tool at run time and whether the mode accepts any user interaction during run time. Post-analysis does not allow any interaction while the user application runs. Instead, the LED and transaction management module writes event occurrences and rules that are fired into a log file as they happen. The visualization tool reads the log file through the proxy server, and simulates the event occurrence and rule execution. Besides, the user can select either step mode or continuous mode with post-analysis mode [10].

Real-time analysis is used to show the changes in active database application as it happens. But, Real time analysis does not allow any user interaction while the applications executes. While the tool and the user application runs, the event occurrences and rule executions, detected by LED, are sent to the tool through proxy using socket connection. When the tool receives the message, the tool parses the message and draws the corresponding action on canvas.

Interactive-analysis mode allows the user to intervene during application execution. The user, typically, selects this mode to set breakpoints during a debugging session so that the state of current rule/event can be inspected. In addition, the user has a choice to enable/disable rules or events at breakpoints.

The visualization tool reads the static information about event trees and rule definitions, which is generated by spp (sentinel pre-processor) when the application is compiled, constructs the event graph on the canvas, and stores the event and rule information in memory (Figure 3). The run time information such as event occurrence and rule execution is supplied in the form of a log file or socket connection according to the 3 different modes we have discussed. The data structure that captures the nested rule execution is an n-nary root transaction is called the top-level transaction and all others are called sub-transactions. The transaction tree grows in a top-down way: It starts from the top-level transaction and spans to descendents.

The transaction manager generates the transaction ID, which is used to infer the parent and child relationship among transactions. The naming is a general-purpose one and accommodates multiple levels and multiple sub-transaction. Figure 4 shows an execution snapshot of the visualization tool. It shows the composite AND event on stock_e1 and stock_e2 and sequence event on the AND event and stock_e_get_price defined on CLASS stock. It also present the nested rule execution in n-ary tree, comparing with the event graph. The numbers below the boxes indicate the transaction ID, from which the tool knows the nested rule level.

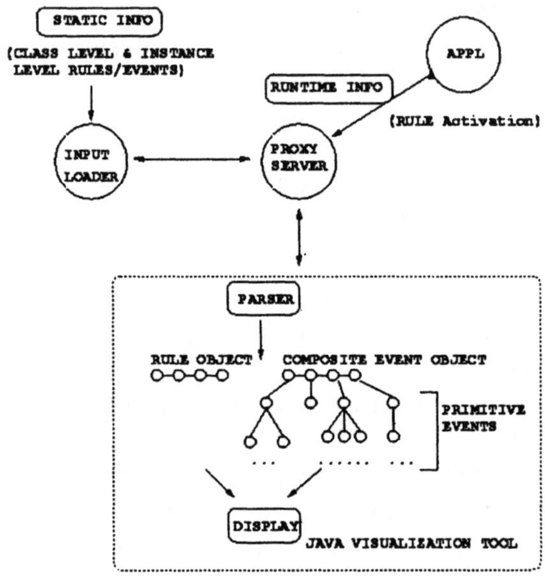

Figure 3 Input to the Visualization Tool

When an event occurs, the visualization tool only changes the color of the event node on the canvas. The user can know from this color change that the event has occurred. When a rule is actually scheduled, LED sends a message to the visualization tool with its sub-transaction ID, and the visualization tool determines the position where the sub-transaction will be drawn from the ID. LED also includes the event ID or event name in Rule execution output so that it can display the relationship between sub-transaction and the triggering event.

Coupling mode specifies the point of time after the event occurrence when condition evaluation and action execution begin. To visualize the deferred rule execution separately from the immediate rule execution, the OODB_commitT primitive event is shown as an event in the visualization. While the immediate rules are connected to the triggering event, the deferred rules are connected to the OODB_commitT primitive event when they are schedule. In this way, we can display the semantics of the deferred rule.

In order to interactively set breakpoints and enable/disable rules, the underlying system needs to support that capability. It is also necessary that events (primitive or composite) are not propagated when there are no rules associated with them. Otherwise, these events will be sent to the visualization tool which will display their detection and propagation. Also, it should be independently possible through the visualization tool to disable events (primitive or composite) even if they have rules associated with them. This is accomplished using a hash table and counters to detect the presence or absence of rules. We define the semantics of disabling a rule as follows.

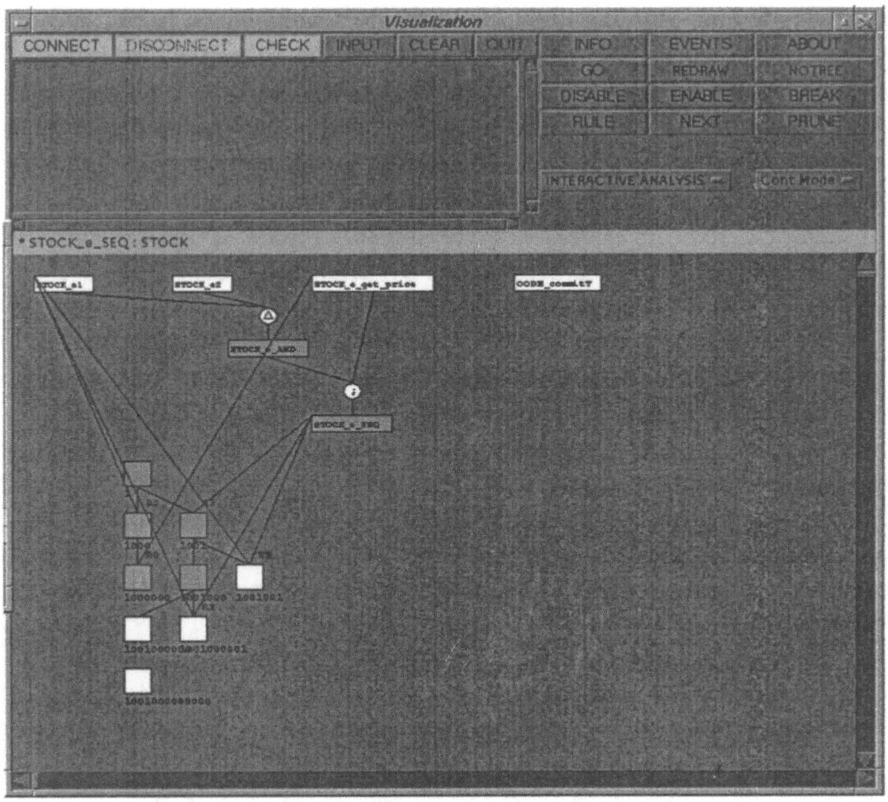

Figure 4 Execution Snapshot of the Visualization Tool

When all the rules subscribed to a particular event are disabled, then LED will stop detecting the event. This is one of the many performance optimizations that have been incorporated into the Sentinel system. This is done at run time.

5.2 Termination Analysis

The visualization tool is also extended to find potential cycles that could occur during the execution of an application and identify the rule subset potentially leading to an infinite loop. This information helps the rule designer to find the cycle within the narrow scope of rules, instead of going over all defined rules.

5.2.1 Non-deterministic behavior in rule execution

The difficulty in performing termination analysis statically is due to the dynamic behavior of rules. The condition evaluation can vary according to the Active DB state, and its execution may change the database state. This dynamic behavior becomes more complicated when we consider the priority and rule-scheduling schemes. Rules may behave differently when scheduled in different orders, yielding unexpected results. Suppose we have two rules when an event occurs. We assume that the execution of the first rule will change the database state into a state, which will make the second rule's condition true. If we execute the second rule first, both rules may not get executed. But, in the reverse order, both rules would be triggered. The same discussion applies to the priorities among rules.

In addition, the rule behavior is very closely related to the semantics of the associated event, and the behavior of event propagation. *Figure 5* shows an example of how these factors affect the termination analysis. Event tree shown in both diagrams consists of e1, e2, AND, and sequence events. Event e3 occurs by the execution of rule R2. The time when each event occurs is also shown as $\mathbf{t_i}$. Also, $\mathbf{t_k}$ is assumed to be greater than $\mathbf{t_j}$ if is greater than j. As the semantics of sequence event is to detect the event when left child event occurs before the right child event, LED will not detect the sequence event in *Figure* 5-(a). As a result, R3 will not be fired in Figure-(a). As a result, there is no cycle in the graph in the first diagram. But, in the similar event tree in *Figure* 5-(b), the sequence event occurs repeatedly and fires rule R3.

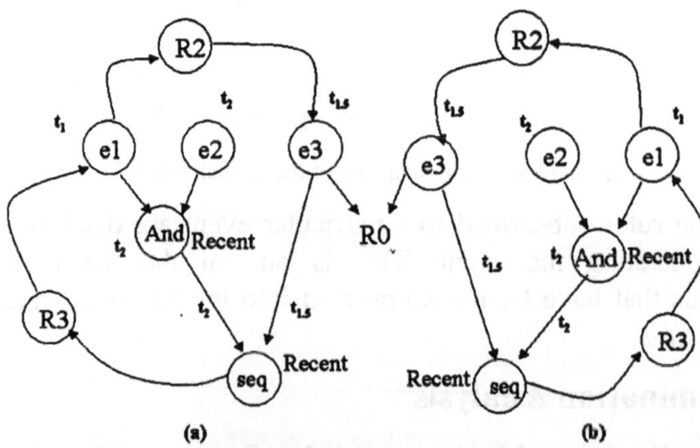

Figure 5 Cyclic Rule Set Example

If we consider the dynamic behavior according to context, the problem becomes more complicated. For instance, we may have a different result if R3 is created in a context other than RECENT.

Another difficulty is that the rule execution may change the database state in such a way that some cyclic rules may stop at some point. This can only be determined at run time.. For example, suppose we have a rule whose action is to deduct $100 from saving account only when saving account has more than $100. If this rule is part of a cycle, then the cycle eventually stops.

5.2.2 Our approach

We consider two approaches to this problem, in our case. One is a passive approach, similar to a conventional programming debugger. The debugger just displays the execution trace and lets the user infer the details of the problem. The debugger does not find the rule set that is potentially cyclic. Refer to [11] for further details of this approach. We shall describe the second approach here. The second one is an active approach, which displays the cyclic rules graphically to users at run time to help users visualize the nature of the problem.

5.2.3 Visualization of the Cyclic Rules

The tool would be user-friendly if it is able to show the cyclic behavior to users at run time, in the same way it shows the rule execution and event occurrence. Besides, the stack frame approach has a limitation. It needs an arbitrary numbers of stack frames to be grouped to detect repeating patterns. For example, *Figure 6* shows 3 simple different cyclic rules and the change of their stack frames at run time. Note that the cyclic rule path length determines the number of stack frames to identify the repeated pattern. Of course, the examples in *Figure 6* are simple cases so it is easy to identify the groups. But, in the real applications, which also have composite events and concurrent rule execution, this grouping is not easy for users.

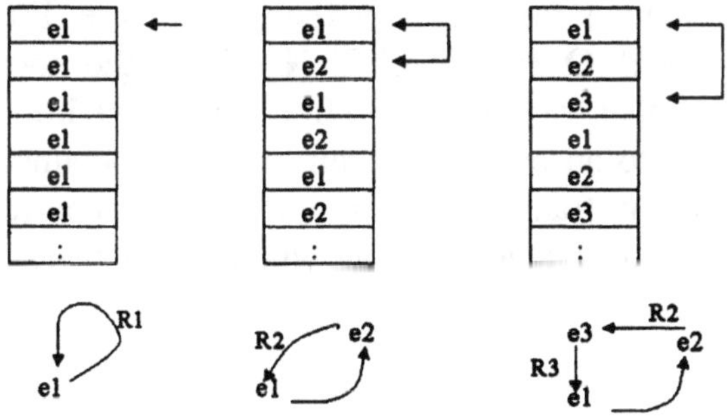

Figure 6 Grouping stacks to identify the repeated patterns

Figure 7 shows one of ways visualizing cyclic rules to users. Each event

Figure 7 Visualization of Cyclic Rules as Types

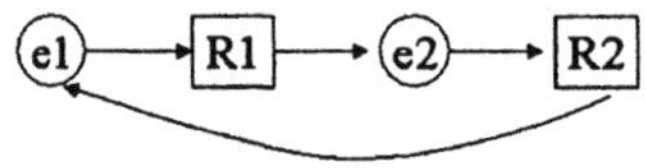

Figure 8. Visualization of cyclic rules in instance level

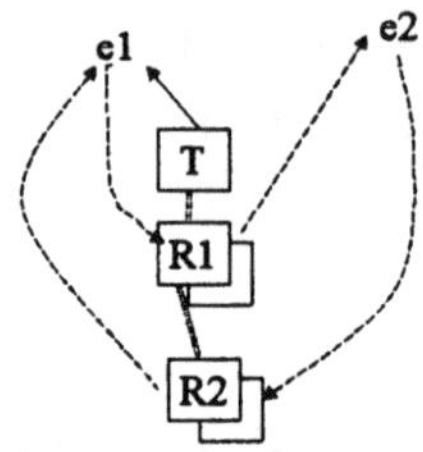

and rule is treated as a type. It does not show the instance level of event occurrence and rule firing. The graph can be generated statically, but needs to be verified at run time. The visualization tool currently generates event graph statically from event definition and displays the rule execution at the instance level to visualize the nested execution of rules. The edges between events and rules are generated at run time.

Figure 8 shows the visualization of cyclic rules at the instance level, which overcomes the disadvantages of the display scheme in Figure 7. Instead of displaying the n-ary tree, the tool positions the same rules at different transaction level side by side. In other words, when the tool detects the same rule execution at different transaction level, the tool assumes a cyclic mode, which is differentiated from display mode of rule execution as a transaction hierarchy explained earlier. To visualize cyclic rules such as the one shown in Figure 7, the tool should be able to identify the rule that generates a certain event and to identify the event that triggers certain rules. In other words, to draw the edge between R1 and e2 and edge between e2 and R2 in Figure 7, the tool should be able to identify, from the run time trace, which event is generated by the execution of a rule and which rule is triggered by an event. The tool would obtain this information from LED and draw direct edges between events and rules in the above graph at run time. Current implementation generates messages for the second case. From the message **"Rule RULE_NAME O_ID EVENT_NAME"**, the tool can find the identity of the event that triggers a rule. In addition, the information to draw an edge from a rule to an event also can be easily obtained from LED by generating the current transaction ID with event occurrence. From the transaction ID, the tool is able to know which rule generates an event and show it graphically.

6. CONCLUSION AND FUTURE WORK

This work significantly extends the previous visualization tool developed for Sentinel. The tool has been changed to incorporate the nested sub-transaction model, and extended to have user interaction at run time. The functionality includes the setting of breakpoints, disabling/enabling events and rules. The work also covers the passive cycle detection mechanism to interrupt the application execution when they show the repeated stack frame and static cycle in ETG. Besides, this paper presents a general way to extend active capability to the web-based distributed environment. The work extends the previous 3-tier architecture for designing a proxy to make web-based GUI possible. The redesigning of proxy has considered the portability and making remote process invocation possible to set up the communication among processes. For more details refer to [11].

BIBLIOGRAPHY

1. O. Diaz, A.J., and N.W. Paton. DEAR: A Debugger for Active rules in an Object Oriented Context. in 1st International Conference on Rules in Database Systems. September 1993.
2. Alexander, S.D. Urban, and S.W. Dietrich, PEARD: A Prototype Environment for Active Rule Debugging. Intelligent Information Systems : Integrating Artificial Intelligence and Database Technologies, 1996. **7**(2).
3. Anca Vaduva, s.G., and Klaus R. Dittrich. Investigating Rule Termination in Active Database Systems with Expressive Rule Languages. in 3rd International Workshop on rules in Database Systems (RIDS 97). June 1997, Sweden.
4. Chakravarthy, S., Z. Tamizuddin, and J. Zhou, SIEVE: An Interactive Visualization and Explanation Tool for active Databases, in Proc. of the 2nd International Workshop on Rules in Database Systems 1995. p. 179--191.
5. Gosling, J. and H. McGilton, The Java Language Environment: 1996.
6. Anwar, E., L. Maugis, and S. Chakravarthy, A New Perspective on Rule Support for Object-Oriented Databases, in 1993 ACM SIGMOD Conf. on Management of Data. 1993: Washington D.C. p. 99-108.
7. Chakravarthy, S., et al., Design of Sentinel: An Object-Oriented DBMS with Event-Based Rules. Information and Software Tech., 1994. **36**(9): p. 559--568.
8. David, L.W., A.B. Jose, and W.T. Craig, {Architecture of and Open Object-Oriented Database Management System}. IEEE Computer, 1992: p. 74--81.
9. Chakravarthy, S. and D. Mishra, Snoop: An Expressive Event Specification Language for Active Databases. D&KE, 1994 **14**(10): p. 1 26.
10. Han, S., Three-Tire Architecture for Sentinel Applications and Tools: Separating Presentation from Functionality. 1997, Univ. of Florida: Gainesville.
11. Yang, S., Interactive Visualization Tool for Supporting ECA Rule Design, in MS Thesis. 1999, CISE Department, Univ. of Florida: Gainesville.

INDEXING IMAGES IN HIGH-DIMENSIONAL AND DYNAMIC-WEIGHTED FEATURE SPACES

King-Shy Goh and Edward Chang
Electrical & Computer Engineering
University of California, Santa Barbara
kingshy@engineering.ucsb.edu, echang@ece.ucsb.edu

Abstract As information retrieval systems evolve to deal with multimedia content, we see the dimensions of content feature space increasing, and relevance feedback being employed to provide more accurate query results. In this paper, we propose using Tree-structured Vector Quantization (TSVQ) to index high-dimensional data for supporting efficient similarity searches and effective relevance feedback. To support efficient similarity searches, we first use TSVQ to cluster data and store each cluster in a sequential file. We then model a similarity search as a classification problem—similar objects are much more likely to be found in the clusters into which the query object is classified. When relevance feedback is considered, and thereby features are weighted differently, we show that our approach remains very effective. Our empirical study on both a 51K and a one-million-image dataset shows that tackling indexing as a classification problem and solving the problem with TSVQ is efficient, effective, and scalable with respect to both data dimensions and dataset size.

Keywords: Approximate search, high-dimensional index, similarity search, TSVQ.

1. INTRODUCTION

As information moves from text-based content towards multimedia content, existing infrastructure may be inadequate for organizing and indexing the new richer forms of data. In many applications, we are given a query object and we search for similar objects (also known as nearest neighbors) in the database. Similarity is usually measured by some distance function between feature vectors, and a good indexing structure is crucial for achieving efficient and accurate searches.

Very often, the multimedia content is characterized by very high-dimensional features (e.g., color, shape and texture features), which cause traditional indexing structures to succumb to the well-known "curse of dimensionality." The search space expands exponentially with the number of dimensions, and objects adjacent to each other in that space are not likely to occupy contiguous space on disk. In addition, many retrieval systems try to personalize search results by learning the user's query concept with relevance feedback. This interaction allows the system to map the user's high-level query to a set of low level features of varying importance. That is, features may be weighted differently from one query to another, and from one user to another. Most indexing structures are built to work with features having a fixed set of weightings, not a dynamic set.

To deal with the dimensionality-curse problem and to support dynamic feature weightings, we propose an indexing scheme using clustering and classification methods for supporting *approximate similarity searches*. In many applications it is sufficient to perform an approximate search that returns many but not all nearest neighbors [2, 12, 10, 20, 22, 24]. (A feature vector is often an approximate characterization of an object, so we are already dealing with approximations.) For instance, in content-based image retrieval [7, 14, 30] and document copy detection [6, 9, 15], it is usually acceptable to miss a small fraction of the target objects. Thus it is not necessary to incur the high cost of an exact search.

Our indexing method is a statistical approach that works in two steps. It first performs non-supervised clustering using Tree-Structured Vector Quantization (TSVQ) to group similar objects together. To maximize IO efficiency, each cluster is stored in a sequential file. A similarity search is then treated as a classification problem. Our hypothesis is that if a query object's class prediction yields C probable classes, then the probability is high that its nearest neighbors can be found in these C classes. This hypothesis is analogous to looking for books in a library. If we want to look for a calculus book and we know calculus belongs in the math category, by visiting the math section we can find many calculus books. Similarly, by searching for the most probable clusters into which the query object might be classified, we can harvest most of the similar objects.

To achieve accurate class prediction, we experiment with cluster centroids and variance. We also study the effect of cluster size and different metrics for measuring search results. Furthermore, we assess the feasibility of supporting dynamic feature weighting during a similarity search on TSVQ clusters formed without feature weightings. Our empirical study on both a 51K and a one-million-image dataset shows that tackling indexing as a classification problem and solving the problem with TSVQ clustering is efficient, effective, and scalable with respect to both data dimensions and dataset size.

The rest of this paper is organized as follows. In Section 2 we discuss related work. In Section 3 we introduce the TSVQ clustering algorithm and the classification method. We also provide an overview of how a similarity search is conducted and how feature weighting is done. We present the results of our experiments in Section 4. Finally, we offer our conclusions in Section 5.

2. RELATED WORK

In this section we discuss related work in three categories:

1. Tree-like index structures for similarity search,
2. Approximate similarity search, and
3. Indexing for dynamic feature weighting.

2.1. Tree-like Index Structures

Many tree structures have been proposed to index high-dimensional data (e.g., R*-tree [3, 17], SS-tree [32], SR-tree [21], TV-tree [25], X-tree [5], M-tree [11], and K-D-B-tree [27]). A tree structure divides the high-dimensional space into a number of subregions, each containing a subset of objects that can be stored in a small number of disk blocks. Given a vector that represents an object, a similarity query takes the following three steps in most systems [16]:

1 It performs a *where-am-I* search to find the subregion in which the given vector resides.

2 It then performs a *nearest-neighbor* search to locate the neighboring regions where similar vectors may reside. This search is often implemented using a *range* search, which locates all the regions that overlap with the search sphere, i.e., the sphere centered at the given vector with a diameter d.

3 Finally, it computes the distances (e.g., Euclidean, street-block, or L^{∞} distances) between the vectors in the nearby regions (obtained from the previous step) and the given vector. The search result includes all the vectors that are within distance d from the given vector.

The performance bottleneck of similarity queries lies in the first two steps. In the first step, if the index structure does not fit in the main memory and the search algorithm is inefficient, a large portion of the index structure must be fetched from the disk. In the second step, the number of neighboring subregions can grow exponentially with respect to the dimension of the feature vectors. If D is the number of dimensions, the number of neighboring subregions can be on the order of $O(3^D)$ [16]. Roussopoulos et al. [28] propose the *branch-and-bound* algorithm and Hjaltason and Samet [18] propose the *priority queue* scheme to reduce the search space. But, when D is very large, even the reduced number of neighboring regions can still be quite large. Berchtold et al. [4] propose the pyramid technique that partitions a high dimensional space into $2D$ pyramids and then cuts each pyramid into slices that are parallel to the base of the pyramid. This scheme may not perform satisfactorily when the data distribution is skewed or when the search hypercube touches the boundary of the data space.

In addition to being copious, the IOs can be random and hence exceedingly expensive. An example can illustrate what we call the *random-placement* syndrome faced by traditional index structures. Figure 1(a) shows a 2-dimensional Cartesian space divided into 10 equal stripes in both the vertical and the horizontal dimensions, forming a 10×10 grid structure. The integer in a cell indicates how many points (objects) are in the cell. Most index structures divide the space into

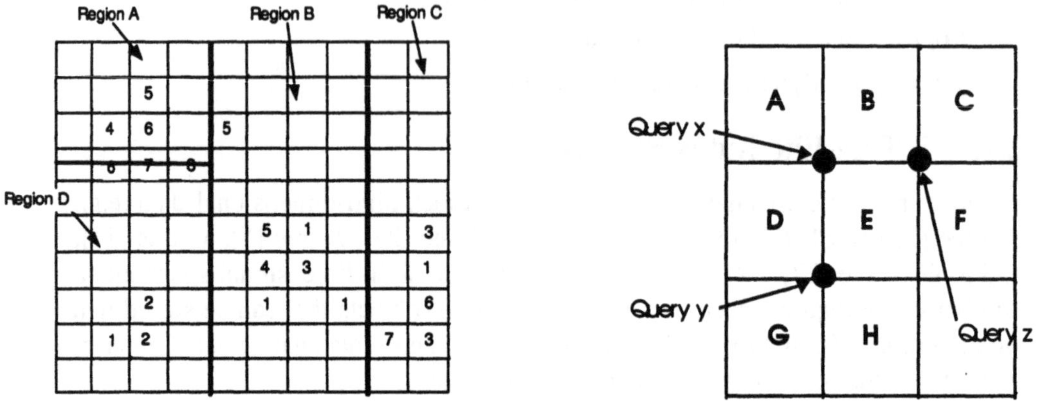

(a) Clustering (b) Random Placement

Figure 1. The shortcomings of tree structures.

subregions of equal points in a top-down manner. Suppose each disk block holds 20 objects. One way to divide the space is to first separate it into three vertical compartments (i.e., left, middle, and right), and then to divide the left compartment horizontally. We end up with four subregions – A, B, C and D – containing about the same number of points. Given a query object residing near the border of A, B and D, the similarity query has to retrieve blocks A, B and D. The number of subregions to check for the neighboring points grows exponentially with respect to the data dimension.

Furthermore, since in high-dimensional spaces the neighboring subregions cannot be arranged sequentially for all possible query objects, the IOs must be random. Figure 1(b) shows a 2-dimensional example of this random phenomenon. Each grid in the figure, such as A and B, represents a subregion corresponding to a disk block. The figure shows three possible query objects x, y and z. Suppose that the neighboring blocks of each object are its four surrounding blocks. For instance, blocks A, B, D and E are the four neighboring blocks of object x. If the neighboring blocks of objects x and z are contiguous on disk, then the order must be $CFEBAD$, or $FCBEDA$, or their reverse orders. Then it is impossible to store neighboring blocks of object y contiguously on disk, and this query will suffer random IOs. This example suggests that in high-dimensional spaces, neighboring blocks of a given object are dispersed randomly on disk by tree structures.

Many theoretical papers (e.g., [2, 20, 22]) discuss the cost of an exact search, independent of the data structure used. In particular, these papers show that if N is the size of a dataset, D is the dimension, and $D >> log\ N$, then no nearest-neighbor algorithm performs significantly faster than a linear search.

2.2. Approximate Similarity Search

Many studies propose conducting an approximate similarity search for applications where trading a small percentage of recall for a faster search speed is acceptable. For example, instead of searching in all the neighboring blocks of the query object, study [31] proposes performing only the where-am-I step of a similarity query, and returning only the objects in the disk block where the query object resides. However, this approach may miss some objects similar to the query object. Take Figure 1(a) as an example. Suppose the query object is in the circled cell in the figure, which is near the border of regions A, B and D. If we return only the objects in region D where the query object resides, we miss many nearest neighbors in A.

Arya and Mount [2] suggest doing only ε-approximate nearest-neighbor searches, for $\varepsilon > 0$. Let d denote the function computing the distance between two points. We say that $p \in P$ is an ε-approximate nearest neighbor of q if for all $p' \in P$ we have $d(p,q) \leq (1+\varepsilon)d(p',q)$. Many follow-up studies have attempted to devise better algorithms to reduce search time and storage requirements. For example, Indyk and Motwani [20] and Kushilevitz et al. [24] give algorithms with polynomial storage and query time polynomial in $logn$ and d. Indyk and Motwani [20] give another algorithm with smaller storage requirements and sublinear query time. Most of this work, however, is theoretical. The only practical scheme that has been implemented is the *locality-sensitive hashing* scheme proposed by Indyk and Motwani [20]. The key idea is to use hash functions such that the probability of collision is much higher for objects that are close to each other than for those that are far apart. Approximate search has also been applied to tree-like structures; [10] shows that if one can tolerate $\varepsilon > 0$ relative error with a δ confidence factor, one can improve the performance of M-tree by 1-2 orders of magnitude.

Although an ε-approximate nearest-neighbor search can reduce the search space significantly, its recall can be low. This is because the candidate space for sampling the nearest neighbor becomes exponentially larger than the optimal search space. To remedy this problem, a follow-up study of [20] builds multiple *locality-preserving* indexes on the same dataset [19]. This is analogous to building n indexes on the same dataset, with each index distributing the data differently. To answer a query, one retrieves one block following each of the indexes and combines the results. This approach achieves better recall than can be achieved by having only one index. But in addition to the n times pre-processing overhead, it has to replicate the data $n-1$ times to ensure that sequential IOs are possible via every index. Furthermore, a hash-based scheme like this cannot support dynamic feature weightings, a support which is critical for personalizing a query.

2.3. Indexing for Dynamic Feature Weighting

Our indexing approach can perform a similarity search on the clusters using a weighted distance function. Many researchers have shown that by assigning proper feature importance, a nearest-neighbor search can be personalized and hence improved [23]. Feature weighting has the effect of transforming the feature space. For a tree-like structure, supporting dynamic weightings may not cause too severe a problem, since the splitting conditions can also be transformed. (However, tree-like structures are ill-suited for searches in high-dimensional spaces.) For a hash-based approach, such as the locality-preserving hashing scheme [19], a new set of hash functions is needed for every set of feature weights. Most feature weightings are learned through relevance feedback by a user in a multimedia information retrieval system. This means that a new structure must be built each time the user changes the weights assignment; this is clearly not acceptable.

3. CLUSTERING AND CLASSIFICATION METHODS

Since traditional approaches suffer from a large number of random IOs, our design objectives are to reduce the number of IOs, and to make the IOs sequential as much as possible. To accomplish these objectives, we propose a statistical clustering/classification approach. The design goals of this approach are:

1 Cluster similar data on disk to minimize disk latency,

2 Use classification to select clusters that can give k nearest objects, commonly called top$-k$ Nearest Neighbors ($k-$NNs), to query objects, and

3 Support relevance feedback, which adjusts feature weights dynamically during a search.

We first use TSVQ to perform non-supervised clustering on a set of training vectors. TSVQ is based on sound statistical theory and is adaptive to data distribution. More importantly, TSVQ is fast and is scalable to large and high-dimensional datasets[1].

Once the clusters are formed, we can process a similarity search by retrieving *selected* clusters into memory, then scanning the clusters for objects that are similar to the query. To minimize the number of IOs, we rank the clusters such that a highly-ranked cluster has high probability of providing the greatest number of k nearest objects. To achieve this goal, we model cluster ranking as a classification problem. We treat the query as an object to be classified. The cluster to which the query "belongs" is likely to contain objects that are similar to it.

In the remainder of this section, we describe the TSVQ clustering algorithm, followed by a description of two cluster ranking schemes. Finally, we outline how a similarity search and feature weighting are conducted.

3.1. Tree-structured Vector Quantization (TSVQ)

A $D-$dimensional tree-structured vector quantizer (TSVQ) is a fixed-rate (R) quantizer whose encoding requires the traversal of a binary tree of depth DR. The rate R gives the average number of bits per vector or codeword. A greedy method

[1] Clustering techniques have been studied in the statistics, machine learning, and database communities. Recent works include CLARANS [26], BIRCH [33], DBSCAN [13], CLIQUE [1], and WaveClusters [29]. The speed of these algorithms lags TSVQ substantially. For example, TSVQ clusters 1-million 144-dimensional image vectors on a Pentium-III PC in less than an hour, whereas a quadratic algorithm can take more than a week.

based on the generalized Lloyd algorithm (GLA) is applied on a training set to construct the tree.

Figure 2 illustrates the case for a dimension of two. In the first step (Figure 2(a)), the Lloyd algorithm produces the root node. The centroid of the entire training set will be the 0-bit codeword for the root node. In the next step, the Lloyd algorithm will split the root node into two as shown by the open circles in Figure 2(b). These seed nodes will then produce two children nodes that are 1-bit codewords. The training set is now separated into two with the centroids as the 1-bit codeword. In Figure 2(c), the two nodes are split again to generate four 2-bit codewords. From this step onwards, the Lloyd algorithm needs only be applied to the training set associated with the codeword that is generating more children nodes.

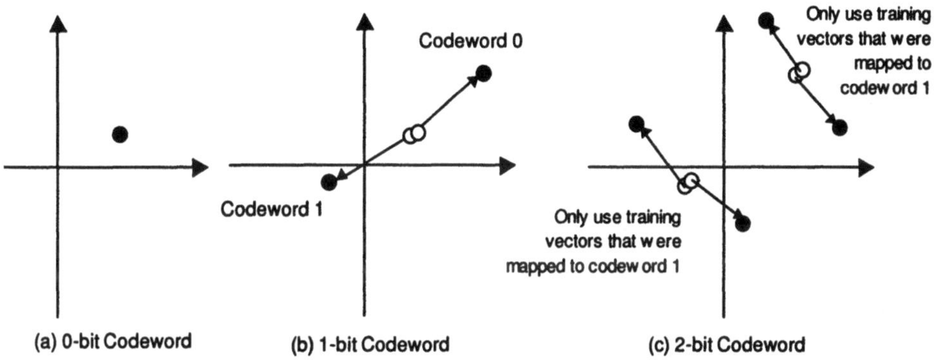

Figure 2. Example of Node Splitting in TSVQ

Two different techniques for choosing a node to split are employed in the Lloyd algorithm. The first method will find a node that has a high distortion (which is the average mean squared error of the training vectors). The split nodes are the current node and a slightly perturbed version of it. Upon failing to find a node with distortion, or when finding that one of the new children nodes has zero distortion, we use the second method. The split will be done by using the current node and the training vector that is farthest from it. The tree construction stops when a specified rate R is achieved, or when the number of training vectors associated with a node is less than the specified minimum vector parameter, or when the splitting of nodes is not possible.

There are two main advantages with using TSVQ for clustering:

1 To quantize a vector x, we begin by finding which of the two nodes originating from the root node has the closer testvector to x, then we find which of the two nodes stemming from this node has the closer testvector. We arrive at a terminal node after DR binary decisions. By increasing R, we have more levels of decisions leading to codewords with greater discriminating powers. This adaptive selection of bits allows more clusters and thus leads to better partitioning of densely populated space.

2 TSVQ is a very fast method for building clusters. It requires only $2DR$ distortion computations while constructing the quantizer, compared to 2^{DR} for an unstructured quantizer.

Each terminal node's codeword is the centroid of the training vectors associated with it. To translate the tree into clusters, only the terminal nodes are used. Each terminal node forms a cluster, the codeword gives the centroid of the cluster, and the node's training vectors are objects in the cluster. While the rate R controls the number of clusters formed by controlling the bits of the codeword, there are many instances when only one training vector is associated with a terminal node. A more effective way to control the number of objects in a cluster is to tune the minimum vector parameter, which controls the number of objects associated with a terminal node. The formal TSVQ algorithm is given in Figure 3.

```
• Inputs: stopping_rate, training_vectors;
• Output: Cluster;
• Variables:
  float  rate;
  struct node_type {
    *vect; /* Vector set associated with the node */
    codeword; /* centroid of vector set */
    distortion; /* average mean squared error of vector set */
  } *Tree, *nodelist, root, next_node;
• Algorithm:
  1: Init Tree:
    root.vect ← training_vectors;
    root.codeword ← centroid(root.vect);
    root.distortion ← avg_mean_sq_error(root.vect);
    Tree ← root;
  2: Lloyd(root); /* Split node and do GLA */
  3: nodelist ← root; /* Insert root into list of nodes to split */
  4: while (rate ≤ stopping_rate)
    • next_node ← get_next_node(); /* Choose node to split from nodelist. If the node's
  vector set is less than a specified number or no node is found, set distortion = 0 */
    • if (next_node.distortion = 0.0) break;
    • Tree ← (next_node.left, next_node.right); /* insert nodes into Tree */
    • rate ← update_rate(next_node);
    • Lloyd(next_node.left); nodelist ← next_node.left;
    • Lloyd(next_node.right); nodelist ← next_node.right;
    • remove_nodelist(next_node);
  5: for each t ∊ (terminal_nodes) /* Assign terminal nodes to clusters */
    • Cluster.id ← num++;
    • Cluster.centroid ← (t.codeword);
    • Cluster.vect ← (t.vect);
```

Figure 3. TSVQ Algorithm for Clustering.

3.2. Cluster Ranking Schemes

In this section, we describe two cluster ranking schemes. The first scheme is based on the commonly used cluster centroid; the second scheme makes use of both centroid and variance.

We store a cluster index containing the cluster ID and centroid in memory. To determine a query object q's proximity to a cluster, we measure the L_2 distance from q to the cluster centroid c as follows:

$$d_c(q,c) = (\sum_{i=1}^{D}(q_i - c_i)^2)^{\frac{1}{2}} \quad \text{where } D \text{ is the dimension of features.} \qquad (1)$$

We call this the centroid scheme. We also evaluate the effect of incorporating cluster variance into our centroid ranking. Consider a cluster of objects in a two-dimensional space. The cluster will be more densely packed if the cluster variance is low. Thus it is likely to contain more nearest neighbors. The new distance with variance d_{cv} is computed as follows:

$$d_{cv}(q,c) = \frac{d_c(q,c)}{\sigma} \quad \text{where } \sigma \text{ is the cluster variance.} \qquad (2)$$

We rank a cluster highly when its distance (d_c or d_{cv}) from the query object is comparatively small. The top-1 cluster will be one with the shortest distance.

3.3. Similarity Search and Feature Weighting

Given a query object, a similarity search proceeds in two steps:

1 We compute the distance from the query object to the clusters. The definition of distance takes different forms depending on the type of cluster ranking scheme used. A highly-ranked cluster is closer to the query object and hence more likely to contain similar objects called nearest neighbors (NNs). A cluster list contains the ranked cluster sorted in descending order.

2 We read the top-ranked cluster from disk into memory and perform a sequential scan on the cluster to find the top-k NNs. If more NNs are desired, we can read additional clusters from the cluster list.

Theoretically, having more features should allow us to distinguish between objects more distinctly and hence ease the task of similarity search. However, finding meaningful features to encode an object is difficult. Very often, we end up with a sizable number of irrelevant features that only add noise during a similarity search. One popular solution is to use a weighted distance function as follows:

$$d(q,x) = (\sum_{i=1}^{D} w_i \times (q_i - c_i)^2)^{\frac{1}{2}}, \qquad (3)$$

where w_i is the weight for each feature i and $\sum_i^D w_i = 1$, D is the dimension of features, q is the query and x is any object. The weights w_i can be changed dynamically through relevance feedback. To deal with dynamic weightings, we adjust the cluster ranking schemes slightly. When comparing distance between the query point and clusters, instead of using Equation 1, we use Equation 3, which takes into account the weights w_i for each feature.

4. EMPIRICAL STUDY

Given a query, we perform a similarity search to return the k most similar objects, or k nearest neighbors ($k-$NN). We first establish a benchmark by scanning the entire dataset to find the top-k NNs for each query; this constitutes the "golden" results set. The metric we use to measure the search result is *recall after X IOs*. In other words, we are interested in what fraction of top-k golden results are retrieved after X IOs are performed.

Our experiment consists of three parts:

1. We first evaluate the two cluster ranking schemes. Given a query, the objective is to achieve the highest recall with the minimum number of IOs.
2. We then investigate the effect of cluster size on recall and IO time.
3. We evaluate two feature weighting schemes and study their impact on recall.

We perform our experiments on two sets of images:

- **51K-image-dataset**. From Corel Image CDs, we select 51,000 images to cluster. Images from this collection are widely used by the computer vision and image processing research communities. We then randomly select an additional 1830 separate images from the CDs to be used as the query set.
- **1-million-image dataset**. The second set is generated from a base of 70,000 images that includes images from Corel CDs and the Internet. We perform 24 transformations on these images. The transformations include rotation, cropping, scaling up and down, down-sampling and GIF-to-JPEG conversion. We then select one million images to cluster, and from the remaining ones, choose 1000 images to be used as queries. Due to space limitation, we do not present the results of this dataset. An extended version of this paper can be found at *mmdb.ece.ucsb.edu/~ kingshy/vdb6-extended.pdf*.

Each image has 144 features: 108 for the 11 colors and 36 for textures [8].

4.1. Cluster Ranking Schemes

We use the 51,000−image set to evaluate each of the ranking schemes. We first apply TSVQ to the image set to obtain396 clusters with sizes ranging from 17 to 199. The clusters are then ranked by the schemes described in Section 3.2. We compute the accumulated recall, from the top−30 clusters, for 10−NN and 20−NN searches.

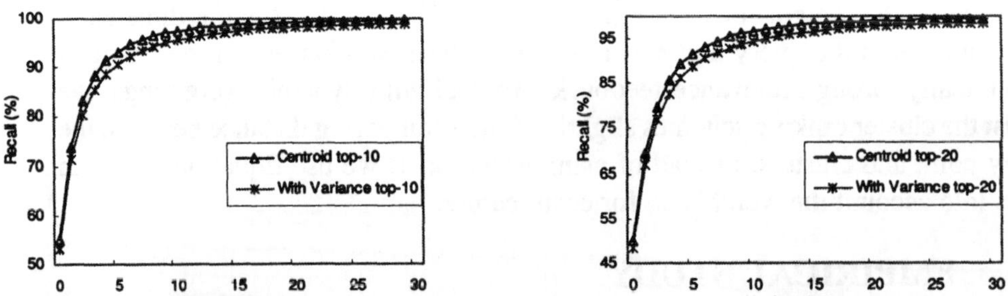

(a) 10−NN (b) 20−NN

Figure 4. Recalls of Centroid and Variance Ranking Scheme on 51K Image Set

The centroid scheme computes the L_2 distance from the query to the centroids of the clusters. The clusters are then sorted by distance in ascending order. Figure 4 compares the 10−NN and 20−NN recall of using d_c and d_{cv} to rank the clusters. The x-axis shows the number of IOs that are performed to achieve a particular recall. Given one IO, we retrieve the cluster with the smallest centroid to query distance d_c and achieve recall of 55% for 10−NN and 50% for 20−NN. After three IOs, the recall improves to 83% and 80% respectively. As more clusters are retrieved, the rate of improvement slows down.

In the same figure, we see that using variance degrades the recall results by about 2%. We believe that the variance estimate with a relatively small number of training instances in a high-dimensional space may not accurately characterize the density of objects in the cluster. (We use centroids in subsequent experiments.)

4.2. Effect of Cluster Size

In this section, we evaluate the importance of cluster size on recall using centroid and SVM schemes. We control the size of the clusters by varying the minimum vector parameter to produce cluster sizes shown in Table 1.

Minimum Vector Parameter	100	200	300	400	500
Number of Clusters	710	396	265	199	155
Average Size	69	128	191	255	327
Cluster Size (kBytes)	120	225	336	448	575

Table 1. Cluster Sizes for 51k-image Dataset

Figure 5 shows the effect of cluster size for 10−NN and 20−NN. For both the centroid and SVM schemes, we see that having a larger cluster size aids recall. By changing the cluster size from 69 to 327, the recall after one IO changes by 14% for the centroid scheme and 18% for the SVM. With larger clusters, the top−1 cluster containing the top−1 nearest neighbor is likely to enclose more of the additional nearest neighbors. The same is also true for subsequent retrieved clusters; hence the overall recall improves.

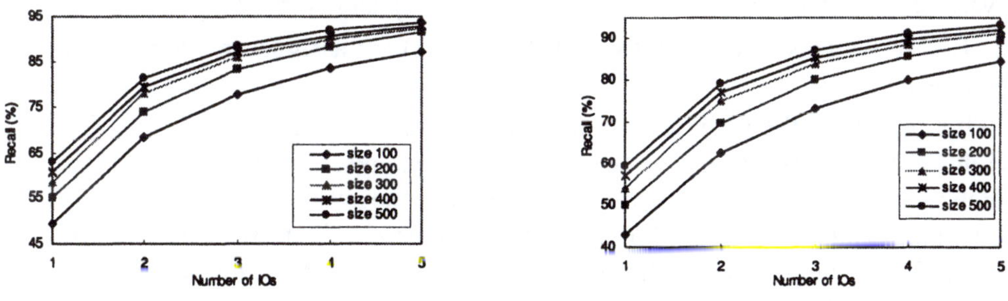

(a) Centroid 10−NN (b) Centroid 20−NN

Figure 5. Recalls for various Cluster Size

The penalty of larger cluster size is in IO time. We use a quantitative model to compute IO time. Let C be the cluster size in bytes, N be the number of IOs,

TR be the transfer rate, and T_{seek} be the average disk seek time. The IO time is estimated as

$$T = N \times T_{seek} + \frac{C \times N \times 8}{TR} \tag{4}$$

Assuming a transfer rate TR of 130Mbps, seek time T_{seek} of $14ms$, the IO times for each set of clusters are plotted in Figure 6. We observe that to achieve 60% recall, we need only to retrieve a small number of clusters, hence having a smaller cluster size translates to a faster retrieval. However, as the recall increases, we need to retrieve fewer clusters if the cluster size is large. This translates to a faster IO time. At recall of 95%, cluster sizes of 128 and 327 give the minimum IO time.

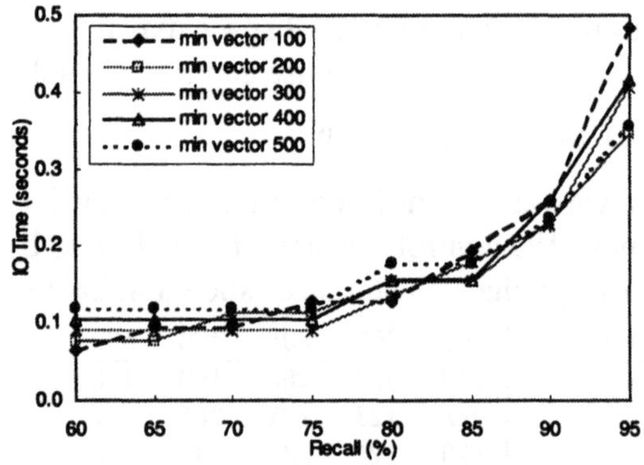

Figure 6. IO Time vs. Recall for 51K-image Dataset (10–NN)

4.3. Feature Weighting

Our goal is to evaluate the feasibility of using feature weightings for a similarity search on clusters built without weightings. Using the centroid cluster ranking with L_2 distance computed as shown in equation 3, we assign the weights in two ways:

1. Binary Weights. Two values are used as weights. We choose N features randomly and assign W to them. The remaining $(D - N)$ features are given We evaluate the recall for $W = \{0.0, 0.1, 0.2, 0.3, 0.4\}$ and $N = 44$.

2. Linear Weights. Values between 0 to $(D - 1)$ are assigned randomly to D features.

After assigning the weights, we normalize them such that $\sum_i^D w_i = 1$. The weights are then accordingly reassigned to the features. We run the similarity search for each query object 10 times, then compute the average recall. Figure 7(a) shows the recall versus IO result when using binary weights with the centroid scheme. When we plot the recall using no weights, we find that using weights only reduces the recall by 1% to 4% depending on the value of W. The reduction for using linear weights is about 4% (Figure 7(b)). We get only a slight degradation of recall when features are weighted, despite the fact that the clusters are constructed on features without weights. This means that one indexing structure will suffice to support relevance feedback.

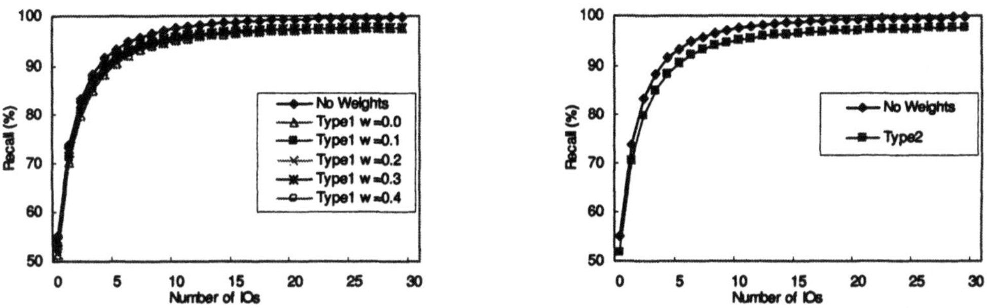

(a) Binary Weights (b) Linear Weights

Figure 7. 10−NN Recall Using Feature Weightings for 51K-image Dataset

5. CONCLUSIONS

We have presented a clustering approach using TSVQ to index data in high-dimensional spaces. We are able to support efficient similarity searches as well as relevance feedback via feature weightings. Using images as our testbed, we cluster similar images together and store them in a sequential file. A similarity search is modeled as a classification problem. We identify the cluster to which the query image belongs, and retrieve that cluster to search for similar images. We show that the use of a cluster centroid to classify the query image yields good recall. More importantly, we show that our approach is able to support relevance feedback, which is equivalent to modifying the features' weight. Using clusters constructed without feature weightings, our experiments show that the addition of weights during a similarity search lowers recall by only 1% to 4%. Lastly, we have shown that our approach is scalable to a 1−million-image dataset.

We are extending this work in several directions. First, we are evaluating additional cluster ranking schemes that use classification accuracy boosting. Next, we are extending our scheme to index data residing in a non-metric space.

REFERENCES

[1] R. Agrawal, J. Gehrke, D. Gunopulos, and P. Raghavan. Automatic subspace clustering of high dimensional data for data mining applications. *Proceedings of ACM SIGMOD*, 1998.

[2] S. Arya, D. Mount, N. Netanyahu, R. Silverman, and A. Wu. An optimal algorithm for approximate nearest neighbor searching in fixed dimensions. *Proc. of the 5th SODA*, 1994.

[3] N. Beckmann, H.-P. Kriegel, R. Schneider, and B. Seeger. The R*-tree: an efficient and robust access method for points and rectangles. *Proceedings of ACM SIGMOD*, May 1990.

[4] S. Berchtold, C. Bohm, and H.-P. Kriegel. The pyramid-technique: Towards breaking the curse of dimensionality. *ACM Sigmod*, May 1998.

[5] S. Berchtold, D. A. Keim, and H.-P. Kriegel. The X-Tree: An index structure for high-dimensional data. *Proceedings of the 22nd VLDB*, August 1996.

[6] S. Brin and H. Garcia-Molina. Copy detection mechanisms for digital documents. *Proceedings of ACM SIGMOD*, May 1995.

[7] E. Chang, B. Li, and C. Li. Toward perception-based image retrieval (extended version). *UCSB Technical Report*, February 2000.

[8] E. Chang, B. Li, and C. Li. Towards perception-based image retrieval. *IEEE Content-Based Access of Image and Video Libraries*, pages 101–105, June 2000.

[9] E. Chang, J. Wang, C. Li, and G. Wiederhold. RIME - a replicated image detector for the www. *Proc. of SPIE Symposium of Voice, Video, and Data Communications*, November 1998.

[10] P. Ciaccia and M. Patella. Pac nearest neighbor queries: Approximate and controlled search in high-dimensional and metric spaces. *Proceedings of ICDE*, pages 244–255, 2000.

[11] P. Ciaccia, M. Patella, and P. Zezula. M-Tree: An efficient access method for similarity search in metric spaces. *Proceedings of the 23rd VLDB*, August 1997.

[12] K. Clarkson. An algorithm for approximate closest-point queries. *Proceedings of the 10th SCG*, pages 160–64, 1994.

[13] M. Ester, H.-P. Kriegel, J. Sander, and X. Xu. A density-based algorithm for discovering clusters in large spatial databases with noise. *Proceedings of the 2nd International Conference on Knowledge Discovery in Databases and Data Mining*, August 1996.

[14] M. Flickner, H. Sawhney, J. Ashley, Q. Huang, B. Dom, M. Gorkani, J. Hafner, D. Lee, D. Petkovic, D. Steele, and P. Yanker. Query by image and video content: the QBIC system. *IEEE Computer*, 28(9):23–32, 1995.

[15] H. Garcia-Molina, S. Ketchpel, and N. Shivakumar. Safeguarding and charging for information on the internet. *Proceedings of ICDE*, 1998.

[16] H. Garcia-Molina, J. Ullman, and J. Widom. *Database System Implementation*. Prentice Hall, 1999.

[17] A. Guttman. R-trees: a dynamic index structure for spatial searching. *Proc. of ACM SIGMOD*, June 1984.

[18] G. R. Hjaltason and H. Samet. Ranking in spatial databases. *Proceedings of the* 4th *SSD*, pages 83–95, August 1995.

[19] P. Indyk, A. Gionis, and R. Motwani. Similarity search in high dimensions via hashing. *Proceedings of the 25th VLDB*, September 1999.

[20] P. Indyk and R. Motwani. Approximate nearest neighbors: Towards removing the curse of dimensionality. *Proceedings of the 30th STOC*, pages 604–13, 1998.

[21] N. Katayama and S. Satoh. The SR-Tree: An index structure for high-dimensional nearest neighbor queries. *Proceedings of ACM SIGMOD*, May 1997.

[22] J. M. Kleinberg. Two algorithms for nearest-neighbor search in high dimensions. *Proceedings of the 29th STOC*, 1997.

[23] R. Kohavi, P. Langley, and Y. Yun. The utility of feature weighting in nearest-neighbor algorithms. *Proc. of the European Conference on Machine Learning*, 1997.

[24] E. Kushilevitz, R. Ostrovsky, and Y. Rabani. Efficient search for approximate nearest neighbor in high dimensional spaces. *Proceedings of the 30th STOC*, pages 614–23, 1998.

[25] K.-L. Lin, H. V. Jagadish, and C. Faloutsos. The TV-tree: an index structure for high-dimensional data. *VLDB Journal*, 3(4), 1994.

[26] R. T. Ng and J. Han. Efficient and effective clustering methods for spatial data mining. *Proceedings of the 20th VLDB*, September 1994.

[27] J. T. Robinson. The K-D-B-Tree: A search structure for large multidimensional dynamic indexes. *Proceedings of ACM SIGMOD*, April 1981.

[28] N. Roussopoulos, S. Kelley, and F. Vincent. Nearest neighbor queries. *ACM Sigmod*, 1995.

[29] G. Sheikholeslami, S. Chatterjee, and A. Zhang. Wavecluster: A multi-resolution clustering approach for very large spatial databases. *Proceedings of the 34th VLDB Conference*, 1998.

[30] J. R. Smith and S.-F. Chang. Visualseek: A fully automated content-based image query system. *ACM Multimedia Conference*, 1996.

[31] D. A. White and R. Jain. Similarity indexing: Algorithms and performance. *Proc. SPIE Vol.2670, San Diego*, 1996.

[32] D. A. White and R. Jain. Similarity indexing with the SS-Tree. *Proc. of the 12th ICDE*, 1996.

[33] T. Zhang, R. Ramakrishnan, and M. Livny. Birch: An efficient data clustering method for very large databases. *Proceedings of ACM SIGMOD*, June 1996.

MODELING MULTIMEDIA DISPLAYS USING ACTION BASED TEMPORAL LOGIC

Graciela González
Sam Houston State University
Dept.of Mathematics, Computer Science, and Statistics
Huntsville, TX, U.S.A.
csc_ghg@shsu.edu

Chitta Baral
Arizona State University
Department of Computer Science and Engineering
Tempe, AZ 85287-5406, U.S.A.
chitta@asu.edu

Peter A. Cooper
Sam Houston State University
Dept.of Mathematics, Computer Science, and Statistics
Huntsville, TX, U.S.A.
csc_pac@shsu.edu

Abstract We present a metalanguage, named Alan that can be used to model dynamic multimedia displays, particularly those that display multimedia database query results. Alan is an action language that uses temporal logic to model non-Markovian systems. We show how it can be used for specifying the behavior of fairly complex dynamic multimedia display systems, modeling all graphical user interface elements on the display plus the effects of actions and of the passage of time on media such as video and audio.

Keywords: Multimedia, modeling, semantics, temporal logic, action languages, presentations, temporal presentations.

1. INTRODUCTION

The display of multimedia documents and presentations is usually built around common graphical user interface elements, such as buttons, checkboxes, lists, images, video and audio players, to name a few. The relationship among the different elements and the data that is displayed on them can be either pre-built or dynamically allocated in response to user queries or requests. Dynamically constructed *multimedia documents* that allow the user to interact with the data are the primary concern of this paper.

The semantics of a multimedia document are not obvious. There might be constraints on the behavior of elements that are dependant on not only the most recent action, but past actions as well. For example, consider a display that contains a video. By analyzing the layout, all we can say is where the video will play, but not for how long, or starting from which point in time. These two conditions might be determined by user actions that occur just before the video plays, or while it plays. A formal semantics or a formal model provides a means to unambiguously express such behavior.

We propose a way to model the behavior of multimedia displays, particularly those derived from database queries, using a new action language with temporal extensions we have called Alan. It allows enough descriptive power to express the behavior of complex, dynamic multimedia displays, modeling user-initiated actions and system actions, temporal presentations, triggers, and the behavior of data elements that span over time, like video and audio files.

The specification of the layout is not our primary concern. Any display specification language or formalism can be used to define the layout (positioning) of the elements on the display, or even natural language.

2. THE LANGUAGE ALAN

Action languages are logical formalisms used to represent dynamic environments in which actions affect the state of the environment. We refer to the language we present as Alan, short for Action LAnguage for Non-markovian domains. It is an action language that can model systems where the Markov restriction does not necessarily hold. The Markov restriction states that the future state of the world is independent of the past states given the current state (Shanmugan & Breipohl, 1988). If the Markov restriction holds, conditions placed on the executability of actions or on their effects can only be based on the current state of the world.

Formulas in Alan are used to determine whether an action is possible or not. Unlike in traditional action languages, formulas in Alan can incorporate past temporal operators such as "previously" or "lasttime" to reference points in the past. Therefore, Alan allows the definition of systems where the future state of the world depends not only on the current state, but also on past states of the world. That is, of non-Markovian systems.

Even though Alan uses the syntax of action description languages *A* and L_o presented in (Baral et al., 1997) and extended in (Watson 1999), its semantics are radically different, since *A* and L_o can only define Markovian systems. In this section we present an overview of Alan, enough to understand how it is used to model dynamic displays.

2.1 Basic notions

In Alan, we assume an alphabet for the language consisting of two disjoint, nonempty sets of symbols: a set **F** of *fluents* and a set **A** of *actions*.

As in all action languages, a *fluent* is a proposition whose truth-value might vary from one state of the world to the next. A literal is a fluent *f* or its negation $\neg f$. A *state* consists of a set of fluents that give a snapshot of the state of the world at some point in time. Consecutively indexed letters *s* denote states. *Actions* change the truth-value of fluents, determining new states. Actions can be elementary or compound. A compound action is a set of elementary actions that occur concurrently.

An alternating sequence of states and actions is called a *path*. A path that conforms to certain properties is called a *trajectory*. It is the means to represent the flow of time and the key to interpret formulas and propositions.

2.2 Formulas, Propositions, and Action Description

The simplest construct in Alan is a ***formula***, which can be an action, state, and temporal formula. We refer to them indistinctively as *formulas* when something applies to all or when the type of formula is clear by context. An ***action formula*** is of the form "occurs *a*", where *a* is a compound or elementary action from A. A ***state formula*** is an action formula or a literal, or, if p, p_1, and p_2, are state formulas, their negation, conjunction, or disjunction, written $\neg p$, $p_1 \wedge p_2$ and $p_1 \vee p_2$ are also state formulas.

A state formula can also be considered a ***temporal formula***. In addition, if p, p_1 and p_2 are formulas, then (1) **lasttime** *p*, (2) **previously** *p* (3) p_1 **before** p_2, and (3) p_1 **since** p_2 are temporal formulas. The negation, conjunction, and disjunction of temporal formulas are considered temporal formulas. The temporal operators (1) to (4) above can also be used to write the temporal connectives always and never, which we will use as well:

always *p* (*p* was true always in the past) can be written **¬previously ¬*p***

never *p* (p has never been true in the past) can be written **¬previously p**

Since we can express implication $p_1 \rightarrow p_2$ for any pair of formulas p_1 and p_2 in terms of '$\neg$' and '$\wedge$' as $\neg(p_1 \wedge \neg p_2)$, we will also use implication freely.

Formulas are used to form ***propositions***, which express the conditions upon which actions are performed, and the effects of those actions.

If a is an action, a_e is an elementary action, λ is a literal, and p is a formula, propositions take one of four forms in Alan (1) λ **if** p, called a *static proposition* (2) a_e **causes** λ **if** p, called a *causal proposition*, (3) **impossible** a **if** p, called an *impossibility proposition*, and (4) **defined** λ **if** p, called a *definition proposition*.

A collection of propositions is called an ***action description***.

The following example illustrates the use of Alan to describe a general non-Markovian system.

Example 1. *Upon receiving a check, a credit card company deposits it, and gives credit to the customer. However, if the check is returned (bounces), then they deposit it again, without giving credit twice. If it bounces a second time, then the credit is reversed.*

In Alan, these facts can be expressed as follows:

DEPOSIT **causes** CREDITED **if** $\neg$previously occurs *DEPOSIT*
$\neg$CREDITED **if** occurs *BOUNCES* $\wedge$ previously occurs *BOUNCES*

2.3 Interpreting formulas

An action description in a Markovian language defines a collection of acceptable paths or "possible trajectories" of the corresponding domain. However, given that Alan is non-Markovian, auxiliary definitions are needed, which are presented in (Gonzalez 2000) in the full semantics of the language. In a nutshell, the full semantics define when an action is executable, the effects of actions, the closure of a path with respect to an action description, and the set of possible trajectories in the non-Markovian setting.

Suffice here to say that in general, formulas have a truth-value only over a path π. Intuitively, this is because formulas might include temporal connectives such as "**previously**" that refer to properties of past states or properties that hold throughout past states. Given a path $\pi = \langle s_0, a_1, s_1, \ldots, a_n, s_n \rangle$, in Alan, by π_j, $j \leq n$, we denote $\langle s_0, a_1, s_1, \ldots, a_j, s_j \rangle$, that is, the suffix of π that ends at state s_j. Given a path π of length n, an action a, and state formulas p, q, we determine the **truth of formulas** as follows:

1. A literal λ is true in π_n if $\lambda \in s_n$.
2. **occurs** a is true in π_n if $a \in a_n$.
3. $\neg$(**occurs** a) is true in π_n if $a \notin a_n$
4. **lasttime** p is true in π_n if n>0 and p is true in π_{n-1}.
5. $\neg$(**lasttime** p) is true in π_n if n=0 or $\neg p$ is true in π_{n-1}.
6. **previously** q is true in π_n if n>0 and for some $0 \leq j < n$, q is true in π_j.
7. $\neg$(previously q) is true in π_n if n=0 or for all $0 \leq j < n$, $\neg q$ is true in π_j.

8. *p* before *q* is true in π_n if for some $0 \leq j \leq n$, *p* is true in π_j, and for every $i \leq j$, $\neg q$ is true in π_j.
9. $\neg$(*p* before *q*) is true in π_n if for every $0 \leq j \leq n$ *such that* $\neg p$ is not true in π_j (i.e., p could be true in an extension of π_j) there is $i \leq j$ *such that* *q* is true in π_i.
10. ***p* since *q*** is true in π_n if for some $0 \leq j \leq n$, *q* is true in π_j, and for every $j \leq i \leq n$, *p is true in* π_i.
11. $\neg$ (***p* since *q***) is true in π_n if for every $0 \leq j \leq n$, such that $\neg q$ is not true in π_j, there is $j \leq i \leq n$ *such that* $\neg p$ *is true in* π_i.
12. $p \wedge q$ is true in π_n if both *p* and *q* are true in π_n.
13. $\neg(p \wedge q)$ is true in π_n if either $\neg p$ or $\neg q$ is true in π_n.
14. $p \vee q$ is true in π_n if either *p* or *q* is true in π_n.
15. $\neg(p \vee q)$ is true in π_n if both $\neg p$ and $\neg q$ are true in π_n.

We can say that a formula F is false in a path if $\neg$F is true in the path, and F is unknown if neither F nor $\neg$F is true in the path.

2.4 Observations

In addition to describing the laws that rule a dynamic system, which we do with an action description, we also need a way to express observations about the domain: what is true and what actions are occurring. The expressions used to record such observations are called *observations* or ***axioms***, and are statements of the form: (1) **initially** λ, (2) a_e **occurs_at** t, or (3) λ **observed_at** t, where λ is a literal, a_e is an elementary or compound action, and t is a non-negative integer from [0...n]. Axioms of type (1) declare what is true in the initial state, axioms of type (2) state that "the elementary action a_e occurred at situation t", and axioms of type (3) state that "the literal λ was observed to be true at situation t". The set of axioms that reflects the observations in a domain is referred to as the *recorded history* of the domain.

A particular instance of the system being described is given by a tuple formed by an *action description* and its *recorded history*, and is called a ***domain description***.

2.5 Queries

One of the main purposes of a representation such as the one given in a domain description is to be able to extract answers to queries about a particular domain. A query in Alan is an expression of one of three types (1)*p* holds at t, (2) *p* holds in [t_1, t_k], or (3) *p* after A at t, where *p* is a formula, A is a sequence of actions, and t, t_1, and t_k are either time points or t_c, denoting the current or most recent time point in history.

Queries of type 1 ask if the given formula holds at the given time point. Queries of type 2 ask if the given formula holds over a period between time points t_1 and t_k. Queries of type 3 can be read as "if the sequence A of user actions were executed at situation t, would p hold afterward?".

By being able to model multimedia displays and answer such queries for a display specification, we can verify whether a resulting display indeed is the display intended by the user.

3. MODELING MULTIMEDIA DISPLAYS

Features of multimedia displays that can be modeled in Alan include:

- Navigation buttons that allow the user to go through different records in the database query answer.
- Displays with static data elements such as text and images.
- Displays with lists and triggers.
- Displays with multi-page documents (like e-books or PDFs).
- Displays with video and audio elements.

In general, to model a multimedia display system, its description is written as an action description in Alan. Objects that reflect particularities of the display are used as parameters for actions and fluents in predicates, and also in axioms when an actual multimedia document is modeled. The action description with particular recorded histories form a *domain description* that can then be used to formally verify the behavior of the display. The verification is done by queries that test the desired aspects of the behavior.

It is not our intention to reconstruct in a single framework the display features of all multimedia formats or displays. Rather we provide a metalanguage that can be used and adapted to suit the modeling of particular multimedia environments. Particularities of different environments are reflected through the use of objects. For example, if in the display being described one is using an xy-coordinate system to indicate the position of an element on the screen, then the object that represents that type of elements should include parameters for the x and y coordinates.

If the display being modeled is specified using a formal specification language, like SQL+D (Baral et al., 1998) then an automatic translation algorithm from the specification language into an action description in *Alan* can be written. In this paper we do not assume a formal specification of the display, nor a particular layout paradigm, but assume a general description in English of the expected functionality of the multimedia display and a description of the schema of the database in question. This demonstrates the flexibility of our proposed method in modeling any multimedia display.

For each feature that needs to be modeled, we present the objects, actions, and fluents needed, as well as a set of predicates that reflect the behavior being modeled.

3.1 Modeling a multimedia tutorial

As a typical example of the uses of multimedia database applications, we will model the multimedia training materials developed for the U.S. Corps of Engineers Research Laboratory land management (Cooper & Smith, 2001). We will refer to it simply as the Peace Corps tutorial. It was developed independently from the modeling language presented here.

Elements in a database that include data and references to multimedia files (audio, video, images, animation) are used in the tutorial to compose *pages*. Pages result from a query and are built dynamically. A group of pages forms a *unit*, of which there are several in a training manual.

The interface has a two-level navigation system. Tabs displayed on top provide access to units. Within each unit, the user can navigate through pages using the buttons on the top left, as shown in Figure 1. The interface allows navigation to related material through hyperlinks in the Related Topics area, or to Keywords. Navigation through any of the methods provided changes the answer set shown in the display area.

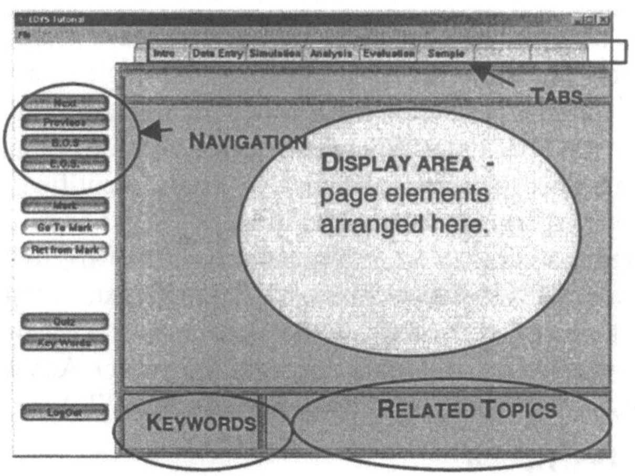

Figure 1. Display Environment of the US Corps of Engineers training manual.

3.2 Modeling navigation buttons

Almost all multimedia displays generated from database query answer include navigation buttons to go from record to record. Here we will model their behavior.

3.2.1 Objects, fluents, and actions

Table 1 shows the basic set of constructs needed. Objects are introduced to the domain as an axiom using the fluent DECLARED.

Table 1. Basic constructs to model any display specification

CONSTRUCT	TYPE	DESCRIPTION
Panel(u, w, x, y, V)	Object	Panel u is located within panel w at x, y and has content V. Parameter w is 'null' if u is the main panel. V is a set of panels and/or display elements.
Ctrl_Button(x, y)	Object	There is button x on panel y.
Answer_Set(R, x, Y, n)	Object	R is the relation or answer set currently being displayed on area x, its attributes are the set Y, and it contains n records.
ACTIVE_RECORD(x, y)	Fluent	Record y is the currently selected record from answer set x.
DECLARED(x)	Fluent	x is an object in the domain.
CLICK(x, y, z)	Action	The user "clicked" on x. Parameters y and z if used, indicate particular occurrence of x, and a particular record clicked.

As a general organizational element for the Peace Corps tutorial, we chose the object "Panel" to group of a display into logical units. The whole display area is referred to as the "main panel", and is also introduced via an object, Panel(main, NULL, 0,0 V), where V is a set of ids of all other panels in it, including one for each of the five areas identified in Figure 1: navigation, tabs, display, keywords, and links.

In the navigation panel, there is an instance of the Ctrl_Button object for each of the navigation buttons, like Ctrl_Button(Next, navigation). These objects are included in all displays. If the answer set is a relation R obtained from an SQL Query that returns n records, the object Answer_Set would look as follows: Answer_Set(UnitPages, navigation, {PID}, *n*).

3.2.2 Action Description

We model the behavior of navigation buttons with rules such as (P1).

(P1) *CLICK*(Ctrl_Button(Next, navigation)) **causes** ACTIVE_RECORD(R, i+1) ,
¬ACTIVE_RECORD(R, z) **if** ¬EQ(z, i+1), ACTIVE_RECORD(R, i),
DECLARED(Answer_set(R, navigation, _, n)), LT(i,n)

(P1) can be read as follows: the action of clicking on the "Next" button *causes* the active record to become *i+1* and not any other if the current active record is *i* for the answer set to which the button is related, and *i* is less than the total number of records in the answer set.

To "disable" a button when its action is not applicable, like for the "Next" button when we reach the last record, we use propositions like (P2).

(P2) **impossible** *CLICK*(Ctrl_Button(Next, navigation)) **if** ACTIVE_RECORD(R, n),
DECLARED(Answer_Set(R, navigation,_,n))

3.3 Displays with static elements

Consider the display shown in Figure 2. Aside from the navigation buttons, we see an image and some text above it displayed in the display panel. These two elements are what we call "static": there is no time-dependency associated to them, and actually not too much of a "behavior", aside from being "visible". We will use these elements to build our action description a little bit further.

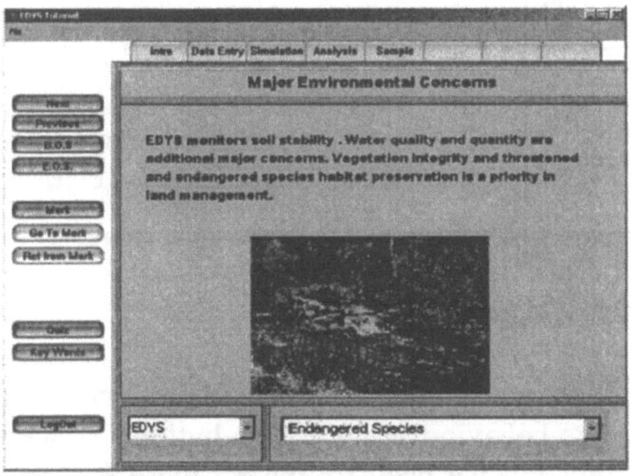

Figure 2. Multimedia display with static elements.

3.3.1 Objects, fluents, and actions

Table 2 shows the basic set of constructs needed to model the GUI elements of a display that are not time-dependant (static).

3.3.2 Action Description

The propositions in the action description to model these features deal mainly with determining what should be shown where. In multimedia documents we do not deal with the "when", since all elements are shown at the same time when the record becomes active. The timing at which each element becomes visible becomes important in multimedia presentations, which are outside the scope of this paper, presented in (Gonzalez 2000).

Each element included in a page is modeled by its corresponding instance of the "Disp_Element" object. For example, say an element of type "image" at position (300, 400) on the main screen, containing the file indicated in the attribute "Content" from the answer set R, is identified as Img1. Its corresponding object would be:

Disp_Element(Img1, image, Main, 300, 400, R.Content)

We now introduce some propositions to tell us which elements are visible. Consider Propostion (P3).

(P3) **define** VISIBLE(R, i, j) **if** ACTIVE_RECORD(R, j), DECLARED(Disp_element(y,t,p,_,_,C)), BT(R.i, C), ¬EQ(t, "list").

The above rule can be read "the value of record j, attribute i of relation R is visible if record *j* is active, and there is a display element that includes it in its contents. Otherwise, the attribute is not visible". We exclude elements of type "list" from this rule.

Table 2. Constructs to model static components of a display.

CONSTRUCT	TYPE	DESCRIPTION
Disp_Element(u, v, w, x, y, z)	Object	Display element u of type v is located in w at position x, y, and its contents are z.
ISELEM(x, y)	Fluent	x is a display element of type y
INCLUDES(y, x)	Fluent	y includes display element x, directly or indirectly (that is, x might be inside a frame or panel).
VISIBLE(R, y, z)	Fluent	The value of attribute y of record z in answer set R is visible.

3.4 Modeling triggers and lists

Triggers and lists are a very common feature in multimedia displays. This is similar to the behavior of navigation buttons, which trigger a change of the active record, but we need to expand the effects of such actions to model the launching of separate applications, or of derived displays (nested queries). For example, a button might link to a video file, and an application such as Real Player might be launched.

3.4.1 Objects, fluents, and actions

Table 3 shows the basic set of constructs needed to model displays with triggers and lists.

Table 3. Constructs needed to model triggers and lists.

CONSTRUCT	TYPE	DESCRIPTION
Trigger(x, y, z)	Object	Display element x has a trigger which launches the query or application y passing z as parameters, where z can be a fixed value or an attribute of the database associated with the display element.
LAUNCHED(x,y)	Fluent	External application y launched and is running as a separate window from display element x.
PARAM(x,y)	Fluent	y is a parameter list associated with display element x when a trigger is launched.
DOUBLE_CLICK(x)	Action	Like *CLICK*.

3.4.2 Action Description

Proposition (P4) states that a double click on an element that has a trigger associated to it will cause the related query or application to be launched.

(P4) *DOUBLE_CLICK*(x) **causes** LAUNCHED(x,y) **if** DECLARED(Trigger(x, y, z))

We can also model the parameters passed by using rules (P5) and (P6).

(P5) PARAM(y, R_j[A]) **if** DECLARED(Trigger(x, y, z), BT(R.A, z), ACTIVE_RECORD(R, j), LAUNCHED(x, y)

(P6) PARAM(y, s) **if** DECLARED(Trigger(x, y, z), BT(s, z), ISA_STRING(s), LAUNCHED(x, y)

Proposition (P3) determined which attribute values are visible for display elements other than lists. Proposition (P7) accounts for the fact that a list shows the associated attribute of all records at the same time.

(P7) **define** VISIBLE(R, A, j) **if** DECLARED(Disp_element(y, t, z, _,_ ,V)), INCLUDES(p, z), EQ(t, "list"), BT(R.A, V), DECLARED(Answer_Set(R,p, _, n)), GTE(j, 1), LTE(j,n)

In the Peace Corps tutorial, double clicking on an element of the list, like the Keywords or Related Topics lists, causes a new query to be triggered, displaying a new page. This is handled through a rule similar to (P4).

3.5 Modeling a document display element

A document display element is any that displays multi-page documents. Documents are similar to video and audio data elements in that they are composed of discrete elements ordered in a sequence that forms the whole. We call each of these constituent elements a "sample". Unlike the samples for video and audio files, a page in a document does not have a specified duration in time. It only changes when the user performs an action.

3.5.1 Objects, fluents, and actions

We introduce the notion of "occurrence" as a parameter in the fluents Current_Sample and Slider, allowing for multiple occurrences of the same display element. This additional parameter can easily be retrofitted into the rules previously presented. Table 4 shows the constructs needed.

Table 4. Constructs needed to model documents.

CONSTRUCT	TYPE	DESCRIPTION
Ctrl_Slider(t, x)	Object	Object x has a slider of type t.
SAMPLE_SIZE(x, y)	Fluent	The size, in samples, of the attribute in x is y.
CURRENT_SAMPLE(x, c, y, z)	Fluent	z is the sample of the file displayed on occurrence c of display element x for record y.
SLIDE(x, c, v)	Action	Occurrence *c* of Ctrl_Slider object x was dragged to value v, interpreted by the type of Slide control.

3.5.2 Action description

Proposition (P8) shows a rule that can be read "clicking on the Previous page button *causes* the current sample to become *s-1* if the current sample is *s* and *s* is not 1", in which case the action would be declared impossible (the button is disabled). Similar rules would be added for the Next button and simpler ones for the First and Last buttons of the document display element.

(P8) *CLICK*(Ctrl_Button(PrevPage, x), c) **causes** CURRENT_SAMPLE(x, c, j, s-1), ¬CURRENT_SAMPLE(x, c, j, z) **if** ¬EQ(z, s-1), CURRENT_SAMPLE(x, c, j, s), GT(s, 1), ACTIVE_RECORD(R, j)

Proposition (P9) states that by default, the first page of the document is the current sample when the record becomes active for the first time. Otherwise, the sample it was at in the previous visit is the current sample.

(P9) CURRENT_SAMPLE(x, c, j, 1), ¬CURRENT_SAMPLE(x, c, j, z) **if** ¬EQ(z, 1), ACTIVE_RECORD(R, j), ¬**previously** ACTIVE_RECORD(R, j), ISELEM(x,y), EQ(y, "document") ∨ EQ(y, "video") ∨ EQ(y, "audio")

The same rule applies to video and audio display elements. This proposition is the first one to use a temporal operator, "previously", and is the introduction of the non-Markovian aspects of the model.

The initial axiom set for such a display would include all the DECLARED fluents for the different Disp_element objects in the different panels. Consider adding the following observations to the initial axiom set :

SAMPLE_SIZE(B, 105) **observed_at** 0
CLICK(Ctrl_Button(NextPage, doc)) **occurs_at** 1
CLICK(Ctrl_Button(Next, navigation)) **occurs_at** 2
SAMPLE_SIZE(B, 30) **observed_at** 3
CLICK(Ctrl_Button(Previous, navigation)) **occurs_at** 3
SAMPLE_SIZE(B, 105) **observed_at** 4

These axioms are observations that reflect what is happening on the screen: on the first record, the user looked at page 2, then went to the next record, and then back to the first. The axioms, in combination with the action description, form a *domain description*, and allow us to ask queries about the behavior of the above display. We can verify with a simple query that when returning to the first record, page 2 will be displayed:

CURRENT_SAMPLE(Doc1, 1, 1, 2) holds_at 4

The proof is outside the scope of this paper, appears in (Gonzalez, 2000).

3.6 Video and audio files

We want to model the general contents and behavior of the display at particular points in time. In displays that include audio, video, and temporal presentations, display elements change constantly. We want to define "points in time" in this continuum that will reasonably represent the display contents. If the frame rate of a video were six frames per second, we should be able to represent every time a new frame is shown, that is, every $^1/_6$ of a second. A smaller granularity would serve no practical purpose, since the display does not change within that interval. For audio files it is not practical to try to refer to each sampling, since sampling rates are very small. Usually, sound samplings are given in seconds and fractions of a second.

3.6.1 Objects, fluents, and actions

Table 5 shows the set of constructs needed to model video and audio.

Table 5. Constructs needed to model triggers and lists.

CONSTRUCT	TYPE	DESCRIPTION
STOPPED(x, c), PLAYING(x, c), PAUSED(x, c)	Fluent	The occurrence c of display element x is Stopped, Playing, or Paused
CLOCK(x, c, i, y)	Fluent	The occurrence c of display element x for record j has clock value y.
SAMPLING_RATE (x, r)	Fluent	The sampling rate for a video or audio object displayed in x is r frames per second, in the case of videos, or r kHz, in the case of audio files.
RUNNING_TIME (x, t)	Fluent	The time t in seconds is the running time for a video or audio object displayed in display element x.
CLOCK_TIC(t)	Action	An action that occurs every time the system time advances t milliseconds.

3.6.2 Action description

Consider the screen from the Peace Corps application where only a video is shown with some control buttons for allowing user interaction while it is playing: Play, Stop, and Pause. We use instances of the Ctrl_Button object. For example, Ctrl_Button("Play", x) will associate a "Play" button to display element x. PAUSED, STOPPED, and PLAYING give the status of the video or audio display elements, and are mutually exclusive. Propositions such as (P10) model the effect of clicking on the buttons, in this case, "Play".

(P10) *CLICK*(Ctrl_Button("Play", x), c) **causes** PLAYING(x, c), ¬STOPPED(x, c), ¬PAUSED(x, c)

The fluent CLOCK is a timer set for a particular occurrence of a display element. It takes the id of the display element in question, plus an identifier of the particular occurrence of the display element, the record number, and a value as parameters. The behavior of the clock of a particular display element in response to different events, like passing time or the user sliding forward to a later point in the video, is modeled using propositions such as (P11), which shows that the value of the clock is set to zero when the "Stop" button is pressed, and proposition (P12), which shows how the system action

CLOCK_TIC causes an increment in the value of the CLOCK fluent for all display element that are PLAYING. For clarity, we are not including in the rules the fact that the clock value is unique, but it is assumed.

(P11) *CLICK*(Ctrl_Button("Stop", x), c) **causes** CLOCK(x, C, j, 0) **if** ACTIVE_RECORD(R, j), DECLARED(Answer_Set(R, navigation,_,n))

(P12) *CLOCK_TIC*(t) **causes** CLOCK(x, c, j, y+ t) **if** CLOCK(x, c, j, y), PLAYING(x, c), ACTIVE_RECORD(R, j), DECLARED(Answer_Set(R, navigation,_,n))

There is also a rule that reflects the effects of the action *SLIDE*, which changes the value of the fourth parameter of Clock directly, setting it to the point in time where the Slide is released. The fluents SAMPLING_RATE, RUNNING_TIME, and SAMPLE_SIZE characterize the particular video or audio file. Based on any two of them and the CLOCK fluent, propositions determine the current sample. Proposition (P13) shows that the CLOCK value of a particular element is greater than or equal to its running time, the status of the element becomes "Stopped".

(P13) STOPPED(x, c), ¬PLAYING(x, c), ¬PAUSED(x, c) **if** ISELEM(x, y), EQ(y, "video") ∨ EQ(y, "audio"), PLAYING(x, c), ACTIVE_RECORD(R, j), DECLARED(Answer_Set(R, navigation,_,n)), CLOCK(x, c, j, t), RUNNING_TIME(x, T), GEQ(t, T)

The current sample is calculated by multiplying the corresponding CLOCK value by the sampling rate of the attribute being shown.

Other propositions specify that the status of a video or audio elements is "Stopped" by default when the record becomes active for the first time. Similarly, and illustrating the use of the non-Markovian features of the modeling language, (P14) specifies that the status of a video or audio element is "Paused" when the record that contains it has been active before and just became active again. Just as we did for the document display element, the first sample showed would be the one last seen when the user left the record. The current sample would be calculated to be the same since the Clock does not change while the record is not active.

(P14) PAUSED(x, c), ¬PLAYING(x, c), ¬ STOPPED(x, c) **if** ISELEM(x, y), EQ(y, "video") ∨ EQ(y, "audio"), ACTIVE_RECORD(R, j), DECLARED(Answer_Set(R, navigation,_,n)) **lasttime** ¬ACTIVE_RECORD(R, j), **previously** ACTIVE_RECORD(R, j)

4. RELATED WORK

To our knowledge, the only other direct attempt at constructing formal semantics of dynamic displays is that by (Scherl et al., 1998), which presents a Situation Calculus model of Hypertext. However, the features are limited to modeling the dynamic aspects of link traversal and the functionality of buttons. As for the non-Markovian action language, this approach is also unique to the best of our knowledge. (Gabaldon, 2000) presents a non-Markovian extension to Situation Calculus, which is more limited than action languages. A more extensive analysis of related work is presented in the full version of this paper and in (Gonzalez, 2000).

REFERENCES

Gonzalez, Graciela (2000), *An SQL extension for specification of multimedia displays: its syntax, architecture, and semantics based on a non-Markovian action language.* Dissertation. University of Texas at El Paso.

Baral, C., Gelfond, M., and Provetti, A. (1997), "Representing Actions: Laws, Observations and Hypotheses", *The Journal of Logic Programming*, 31(1-3):201-244.

Watson, Richard (1999), *Action Languages and Domain Modeling*, Doctoral Dissertation, University of Texas at El Paso.

Baral, C., Gonzalez, G., and Nandigam, A. (1998) "SQL+D: Extended Display Capabilities for Multimedia Database Queries" Proceedings of ACM's Multimedia 98, ACM, September, 1998.

Scherl R., Bieber M., and Vitali F. (1998) "A Situation Calculus Model of Hypertext" *Proceedings of the 31st Hawaii International Conference on System Sciences*, IEEE Press

Cooper, P.A., and Smith G.W. (2000) A Development of a Hydrology Data Repository and Models Tutorial, Project funded through U.S. Corps of Engineers Research Laboratory and the Texas Research Institute for Environmental Science.

Gabaldon, Alfredo (2000) "Non-Markovian Control in the Situation Calculus", The Second International Workshop on Cognitive Robotics (held in conjunction with ECAI2000).

Shanmugan, S. and Breipohl, A.M.(1988) "Markov Sequences and Processes", Random Signals: Detection, Estimation, and Data Analysis, John Wiley & Sons.

BIOGRAPHIES

Graciela Gonzalez is an Assistant Professor of Computer Science at Sam Houston State University. She received his M.S. (1994) and PhD (2000) in Computer Science from the University of Texas at El Paso. During the course of her studies, she was the main author to published papers in conferences such as ACM Multimedia '98, IEEE's ICDE '98 and ICMCS '99, among others, and worked as a Software Engineer and Multimedia Development Manager. Her main research interests include multimedia databases, human-computer interaction, theories of actions and logic programming.

Chitta Baral is an associate professor at the Arizona State University. He obtained his B.Tech(Hons) degree from the Indian Institute of Technology, Kharagpur and his M.S and Ph.D degrees from the University of Maryland at College Park. He has been working in the field of knowledge representation and logic programming since 1988, and his research has been supported over the years by National Science Foundation, NASA, and United Space Alliance. He received the NSF CAREER award in 1995 and led successful teams to AAAI 96 and 97 robot contests. He has published more than 65 articles in Logic Programming, Knowledge Representation, and Artificial Intelligence conferences and Journals.

Peter Cooper is an Associate professor of Computer Science at Sam Houston State University. He received his M.A.(1990) and Ph.D.(1993) from the University of Missouri-Columbia. His main research interests include two and three dimensional imaging and human computer interaction.

AN ENTROPY-BASED APPROACH TO VISUALIZING DATABASE STRUCTURE

Dennis P. Groth*
Indiana University
Computer Science
dgroth@indiana.edu

Edward L. Robertson*
Indiana University
Computer Science
edrbtsn@cs.indiana.edu

Abstract This paper explores the use of entropy for visualizing database structure. In particular, we show how visualizing the entropy of a relation provides a global perspective on the distribution of values and helps to identify areas within the relation where interesting relationships may be discovered. The type of structure we are interested in discovering is related to functional dependencies. Our approach is not dependent on the underlying domain of the data, providing a view of the dependency landscape within a relation. Using these techniques, we describe comparative results for a wide variety of synthetic and real data.

Keywords: Database visualization, entropy, information dependency, functional dependency

1. Introduction

Developing visualizations of database content is of extreme interest to the research community. There are numerous examples of applications developed around a graphical display of database content, including relationship discovery, outlier detection, and trend analysis.

Our approach to visualizing the structural, information content (which is distinct from the data content) of databases is motivated by the disci-

*Both authors were supported by NSF Grant IIS-0082407

pline of information theory. In particular, we utilize entropy as the basis for our visualizations. Within the field of information theory, entropy is the central concept, related to the encoding of messages. As such, entropy is a statistic that provides a global description of the information content of data. This research utilizes entropy to visualize the structure of a database relation, independent of the underlying domain datatype. We defer to Section 2 for the definition of entropy, as well as other formal notions.

When developing effective visualizations of database content there are three significant challenges that must be addressed. First, we are often faced with high-dimensional data. Second, databases are awash with categorical data, which often lack any meaningful order or scale. Thirdly, the sheer mass of data in even a moderately sized database may overwhelm the user when trying to simply display a two-dimensional scatter plot.

There has, of course, been a great deal of research effort aimed at addressing these challenges. For example, a number of techniques have been applied to high dimensional data, such as parallel coordinate displays, worlds within worlds, dimensional stacking, and grand tour methods.(Inselberg and Dimsdale, 1987; Inselberg and Dimsdale, 1990; LeBlanc et al., 1990; Feiner, 1992) Likewise, the field of information visualization has many techniques for dealing with abstract, categorical data.(Card et al., 1999) For techniques dealing with visualizing the contents of large databases see (Keim et al., 1994; Keim, 1996a; Keim, 1996b).

Whereas the goal of almost all other visualization techniques is to facilitate understanding of particular values, our approach specifically remains aloof from those values in two distinct ways. First, we are interested in large-scale properties of instances – properties that are related to attributes rather than values. For example, a relation with 10 attributes requires 45 different 2D scatter plots to provide the same amount of information our technique provides in a *single* 2D scatter plot. Indeed, the axes for many of the visualizations we present are the collection of attributes in the relation, or characteristics of those attributes, rather than the values in a particular attribute. Second, even within a particular attribute, it is the distribution of values rather than the actual presented values that matter. Indeed, we typically code values as integers to simplify processing.

This second distinction is a consequence of the notion that the structure of data is independent of data values. Formally, structure is *generic*, in that it is invariant under 1-1 substitution of data values (hence the encoding with integers). For example, functional dependencies describe a particular type of structure - independent of the actual values. The definition of the functional dependency $X \rightarrow Y$, namely "$\forall t_1 \in r, \forall t_2 \in r(t_1[X] = t_2[X] \Rightarrow t_1[Y] = t_2[Y])$", exhibits this formal genericity. Information theory, which uses only probabilities associated with values and not the values themselves, therefore provides techniques that allow us to view value-independent structure. Because entropy-based visualizations show global properties, they are more in tune with natural uses of visualization, where global structure and detail through drill-down are most effective.

Naive attempts at global visualization often fail when our perceptual mechanisms confront the above challenges. For example, Figure 1 illustrates how our natural perception is sometimes misleading - a glance suggests that the left pane is more "function-like", while in fact the right pane exhibits the functional dependency $A \rightarrow B$ while the left does not. While the presence or absence of these functional dependencies is easy to evaluate in Figure 1, with only eight data points, this task becomes increasingly difficult as the number of data points increases. In addition, determining when the data contains an approximate dependency (Kivinen and Mannila, 1992), in which a functional dependency holds except for a small number of violations, is equally difficult.

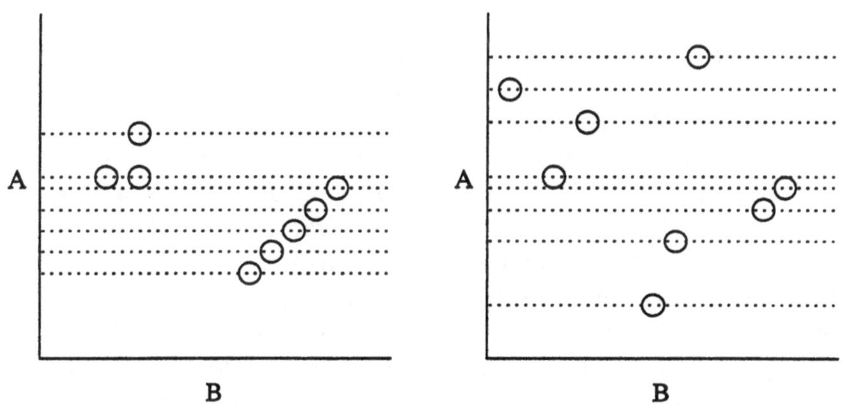

Figure 1. On the left, a scatter plot of data where the functional dependency $A \rightarrow B$ does not hold. On the right, a scatter plot where the functional dependency does hold. The dashed lines have been added to show the alignment of the points along the vertical dimension.

This paper is structured as follows. Section 2 provides the formal notation and definitions used throughout the paper. Section 3 explores the use of entropy to visualize frequency distributions of attribute values in database relations. Section 4 demonstrates the use of entropy for visualizing dependencies, or relationships between attributes. Section 5 provides examples of these these techniques for making broad comparisons of different datasets. Lastly, Section 6 provides future directions and concluding remarks.

1.1. User Interaction

In order to visualize database structure we have developed a system to support interactive displays of database visualizations. Based on an architecture we proposed in (Groth and Robertson, 1998), the system supports the specification of database queries and the mapping of the query results to a graphical representation. These mappings are entirely under the control of the user.

The system is implemented in Java, using JDBC for query processing. The visualizations are implemented using Java 3D, allowing the user to manipulate the display for standard actions such as rotating, scaling and translating. In addition, the user is able to drill down at any data point to see the raw data values, as well as identifying datapoints that are particularly interesting to them. These selected points can be utilized in subsequent visualizations for comparative purposes.

2. Definitions

This section provides the formal notation and definitions used in this paper. Our focus is on visualizing database information, so we begin with the basics of the relational model. Let $R = \{A, B, C, \dots\}$ be a relation schema for instance $\mathbf{r}$. For attribute $A \in R$, A denotes $\{A\}$. Sets of attributes are denoted by $X, Y, Z \subseteq R$. For X and $Y \subseteq R$, XY denotes $X \cup Y$. The notation we use for tuples is $t \in \mathbf{r}$, with $t.A$ representing the value for attribute A in tuple t.

With its genesis in message theory, entropy is defined over a set of messages $M = \{m_1, \dots, m_n\}$, with associated probabilities $P_M = \{p_1, \dots, p_n\}$. The entropy of M is $\mathcal{H}_M = \sum_{i=1}^{n} p_i \log \frac{1}{p_i}$. Entropy provides us with an average cost (in bits) for each message. The upper bound on the entropy of M is $\log n$, which occurs when each message has equal probability. Additional details on entropy, as well as other information theory topics, are covered in (Cover and Thomas, 1991).

For databases, the message set we are interested in is taken from the relation instance $\mathbf{r}$. When projecting attributes from R, we do not eliminate duplicate values, which allows us to compute the probabilities using the counts of each value in the active domain. For example, the probability $P(A = a) = \frac{count(\sigma_{A=a}(\mathbf{r}))}{count(\mathbf{r})}$.

For any set of attributes $X \subseteq R$, we can compute $\mathcal{H}_X$ using an SQL aggregate query. The query is shown in Figure 2 for the case of $A \in R$.

For the purposes of the visualizations generated for this research, we pre-compute $\mathcal{H}_A$ for each $A \in R$, as well as $\mathcal{H}_{AB}$ for each $A, B \in R$. Note that $\mathcal{H}_A \leq \log |\mathrm{Adom}(A)|$, where Adom($A$) is the active domain of A. When $\mathcal{H}_A = \log |\mathbf{r}|$, A is a key.

```
Select   SUM((R1.frequency/R2.rowcount) *
              LOG(2,1/(R1.frequency/R2.rowcount)))
From     (Select    A, COUNT(*) as frequency
          From      R
          Group By  A) as R1,
         (Select    COUNT(*) as rowcount
          From      R) as R2
```

Figure 2. SQL query to calculate the entropy of A

2.1. Information Dependencies

Within the database research field, the concept of functional dependencies is well understood. The functional dependency $A \rightarrow B$ holds in instance $\mathbf{r}$, when for any two tuples $t_1, t_2 \in \mathbf{r}, t_1.A = t_2.A \implies t_1.B = t_2.B$. While functional dependencies always hold for an instance, a particular functional dependency may be specified as a constraint over instances of a relation and commercial database management systems have mechanisms for entering such constraints.

As is often the case, however, large, complex data rarely exhibits many functional dependencies beyond those specified as constraints. As shown in (Dalkilic and Robertson, 2000), an *Information Dependency Measure* is defined using entropy. The information dependency measure $\mathcal{H}_{X \rightarrow Y}$ provides a measure indicating the average number of bits we need to use to determine Y if we know a value for X. Another way to look at this measure is in terms of surprise. In other words, how surprising is a particular value for Y when we know X.

The information dependency $\mathcal{H}_{X \rightarrow Y}$ defined as $\mathcal{H}_{XY} - \mathcal{H}_X$. For more details on information dependencies, as well as an equivalent definition, see (Dalkilic, 2000). When $\mathcal{H}_{X \rightarrow Y} = 0$, the functional dependency $X \rightarrow Y$ holds. The upper bound on $\mathcal{H}_{X \rightarrow Y}$ is $\mathcal{H}_X + \mathcal{H}_Y$, which is the case of independence of X and Y.

Another weakness of using a traditional approach for identifying dependencies is shown in the right pane of Figure 1. We can verify by checking across the display that there are no violations of the dependency $A \rightarrow B$. However, as the number of datapoints increase the task becomes increasingly difficult. In addition, determining when the data contains an approximate dependency (Kivinen and Mannila, 1992), in which a functional dependency holds except for a small number of violations, is equally difficult. Figure 1 may be used to illustrate the applicability if the information dependency measure: $\mathcal{H}_{A \to B}$ is 0.25 in the left pane and 0 in the right. Whereas a visual estimation of approximate functional dependencies does not scale, estimation via $\mathcal{H}_{A \to B}$ does.

3. Visualizing Distributions

Using the measures defined in Section 2, we turn to the visualization problem addressed in this research. The data we use in our visualization is drawn from a variety of sources, including the U.S. Census (cen, 2000), the U.C.I. Machine Learning Repository (Blake and Merz, 1998), and the Wisconsin Benchmark (DeWitt, 1993). The specific dataset we used for the Census was the 1990 Indiana Public Use Microdata Sample (PUMS), which has 125 attributes.

Our first application is the visualization of frequency distributions. An obvious technique for visualizing frequency distributions is to use histograms, with the height of each bar representing the frequency. Figure 3 shows the log of the size of the active domain for each attribute in the U.S. Census (Left) compared to the calculated entropy value for each attribute value (Right). The leftmost bar in each display corresponds to a key in the relation; otherwise, the attributes are arbitrarily ordered.

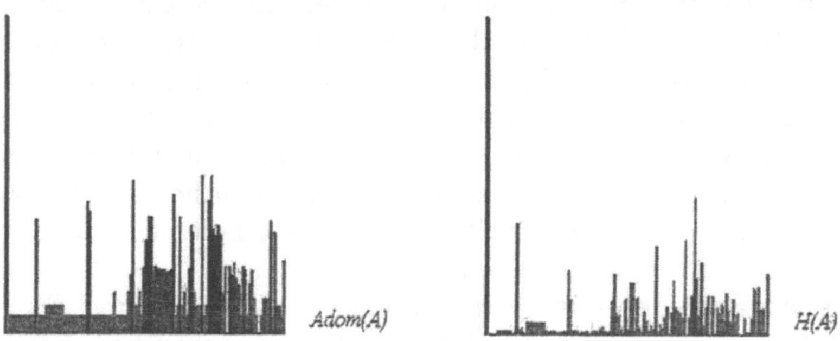

Figure 3. **Comparing the size of the active domain for each attribute (Left) to the entropy of each attribute (Right) in the U.S. Census dataset.**

Note that the height of the bars varies according to the probabilities associated with each value in the active domain, resulting in differences in the heights for the same attribute in each display. To highlight these differences, consider Figure 4, which shows the same information for a subset of the attribute space. The attributes displayed include: Hours Worked Per Week, Immigration Year, Income, Non-farm Income, Farm Income, Interest and Dividend Income, Social Security Income, Public Assistance Income, and Retirement Income. In this case, we can see that certain attributes that have dominant values have their corresponding entropy values reflect this dominance.

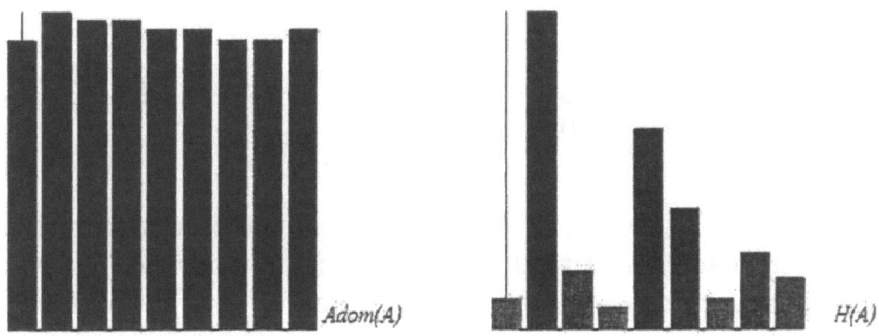

Figure 4. **A view of the differences between the size of the active domain for (Left) compared to the entropy values for the same attributes (Right).**

In order to gain an overall view of the attribute space, we can compare $\mathcal{H}_A$ to log |adom(A)| using a two-dimensional scatterplot. This visualization is shown in Figure 5, in which the attribute that is a key has been omitted. In the visualization, points that lie on the diagonal have an (approximately) uniform distribution. The further a point is from the diagonal, the less uniform is the associated distribution.

4. Visualizing Relationships

While the previous section demonstrated the use of entropy to gain insight into frequency distributions within database relations, this section extends the technique in order to explore relationships between attributes. In particular we utilize the information dependency measure described earlier to visualize these relationships.

While we have formally described the concept of an information dependency, we have not yet discussed visualizing them. The left pane of Figure 6 characterizes the space of $\mathcal{H}_{A \rightarrow B} \times \mathcal{H}_B$, which is encountered when visualizing the values in a 2D scatter plot. This type of visual-

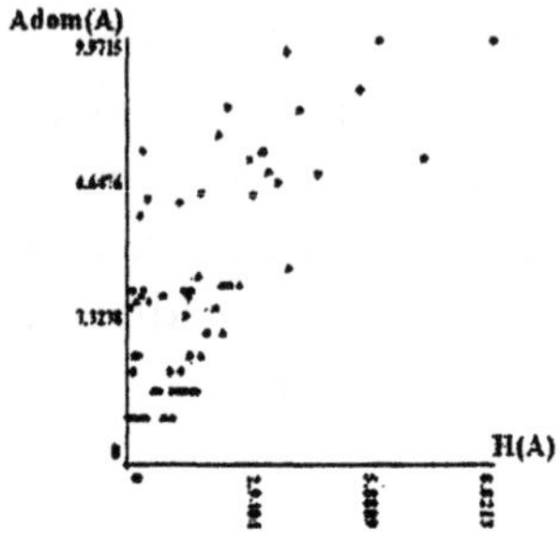

Figure 5. Comparing the entropy of each attribute in the census data to the log of the size of the corresponding active domain.

ization allows us to get an overall view of all possible attribute pairs in a compact space. A critical advantage of this approach is that the visualizations do not depend on the actual values or types of data.

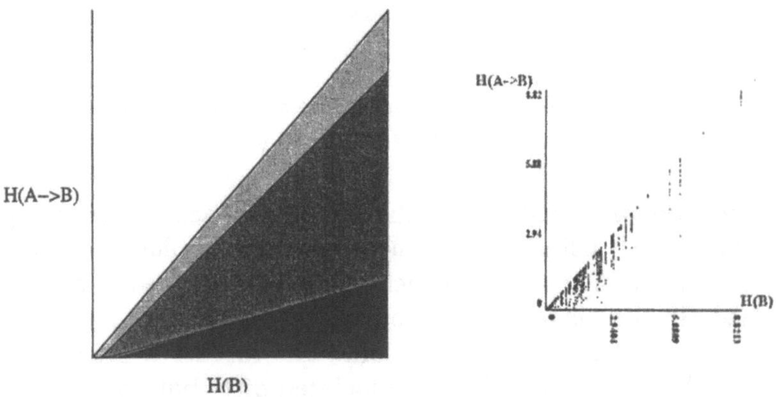

Figure 6. On the left, characterizing the space $\mathcal{H}_{A \to B} \times \mathcal{H}_A$. On the right, a visualization of this space for the census data.

The dark area in the figure represents functional dependencies in the relation. Above the diagonal the space is empty, since the upper bound of $\mathcal{H}_{A \to B}$ is $\mathcal{H}_B$. As you move away and below the diagonal, the structure becomes more like a functional dependency. There is an area of potential interest close to the horizontal axis, in which the space represents approximate functional dependencies that are *almost* a pure functional dependency. The space closest to the diagonal contains attribute pairs where B does not significantly depend on A (we cannot say that A and B are independent since $B \rightarrow A$ is not ruled out).

The right pane of Figure 6 shows a scatter plot comparing $\mathcal{H}_{A \rightarrow B}$ to $\mathcal{H}_B$ for the census data. We can easily see individual attributes, which correspond to the vertical bands (since of course $\mathcal{H}_B$ is determined only by B. Unfortunately, a black-and-white rendition of this image does not indicate points that lie exactly on the horizontal axis - points that correspond to true functional dependencies. Certain points close to that axis are of obvious interest. In addition, one isolated point about 1/3 up and 2/3 right begs investigation in detail. However, we cannot tell whether points on the upper right merely correspond to A's with small entropy.

This suggests a more detailed examination using three dimensions, comparing $\mathcal{H}_{A \rightarrow B}$, $\mathcal{H}_A$ and $\mathcal{H}_B$. Figure 7 shows two perspectives on this visualization - the left image looks out along the $\mathcal{H}_A$ axis with $\mathcal{H}_B$ vertical and $\mathcal{H}_{A \rightarrow B}$ going off to the right and the right image rotates the left around the vertical axis. Both images are zoomed somewhat, as is evident by the axis labels. The origin is zero for each axis. The fact that $\mathcal{H}_{A \rightarrow B} \leq \mathcal{H}_B$ is clearly shown by the empty space in the lower right of the image.

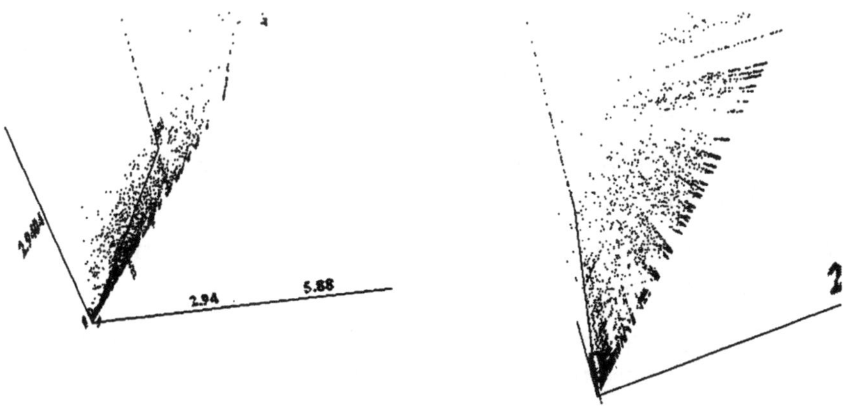

Figure 7. 3D plot comparing $\mathcal{H}_{A \rightarrow B}$, $\mathcal{H}_A$ and $\mathcal{H}_B$.

We can observe several properties of the space. The vertical line of data points at the far end of the $\mathcal{H}_A$ axis (Z dimension) arises when A corresponds to the key of the relation, which of course functionally determines every attribute. The rotation from the left to right image also shows that most points lie near the $\mathcal{H}_{A \rightarrow B} = \mathcal{H}_B$ plane, althought this is less evident with still images than when image manipulation is possible.

Two bands along the edge of the $\mathcal{H}_B = \mathcal{H}_{A\rightarrow B}$ plane, corresponding roughly to $\mathcal{H}A \leq 0.5$ or $\mathcal{H}_B \leq 0.5$, line very close to the plane. This indicates the surprising fact that each low entropy attribute is independent of other attributes except each other

In addition to identifying potentially interesting relationships between attributes, the visualizations also highlight additional information. For example, when $\mathcal{H}_A$ is low and $\mathcal{H}_{AB} - \mathcal{H}_A = 0$, it is possible to decompose the original relation into smaller sub-relations, taking advantage of space savings. When the difference is very near to zero, you may decide to ignore the noise entirely and clean the data by removing the noisy data.

4.1. Drilling Down

The discussion thus far has involved global characterizations of attributes, but information-based visualization can also drill-down to reveal local structures. This makes use of the fact that the functional dependency $A \rightarrow B$ holds iff $\mathcal{H}_{A\rightarrow B} = 0$ and thus the quantity $\mathcal{H}_{A\rightarrow B}$ is a measure of how close $A \rightarrow B$ is to holding in an instance. The characterization of $\mathcal{H}_{A\rightarrow B}$ as $\sum_{a\in A} p(a) \times \mathcal{H}_B(\sigma_{A=a}(r))$ suggests that the "landscape" of $p(a)$ and $\mathcal{H}_B(\sigma_{A=a}(r))$ might reveal something about local structure related to $A \rightarrow B$. Indeed this is the case, as we see in examples from the census data.

The first example examines AGE $\rightarrow$ DEPART (with AGE as A and DEPART as B). The plot of $p(a)$ versus $\mathcal{H}_B(\sigma_{A=a}(r))$, shown in the first panel of Figure 8, has several interesting features:

1 AGE values with low probability have low diversity of associated DEPART, and this holds uniformly

2 the relationship of $\mathcal{H}_B(\sigma_{A=a}(r))$ versus $p(a)$ is essentially a smooth function for low $p(a)$ values

3 when $p(a)$ exceeds a certain value, the corresponding $\mathcal{H}_B(\sigma_{A=a}(r))$ is typically close to the maximum; this cutoff is surprisingly sharp

4 there are a few higher probability AGEs which differ from the typical by having $\mathcal{H}_B(\sigma_{A=a}(r))$ values that are lower or 0; these AGEs are interesting in themselves. Indeed, further investigation of these values seems to indicate anomalies in the way the census data was collected.

5. Visual Comparisons Of Datasets

In previous sections we have demonstrated the use of entropy to visualize the information content of database relations. In this section we

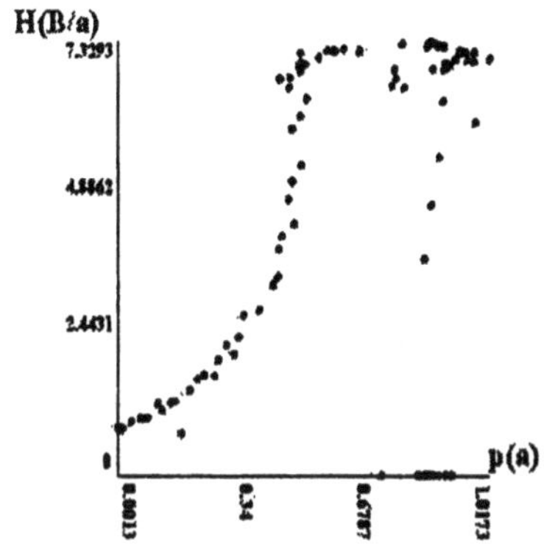

Figure 8. Comparing $p(a)$ to $\mathcal{H}_B(\sigma_{A=a}(r))$ for census data. In this example, A is AGE and B is DEPART.

show how multiple, diverse datasets can be compared within the same display in order to understand the degree to which the datasets might be similar in terms of their structure.

We have used this particular technique to compare various benchmark datasets in order to evaluate their structure. Although benchmark datasets are used for a variety of applications, a primary use is the performance evaluation of new algorithms. For example, the Wisconsin benchmark (DeWitt, 1993) has been used to test various join algorithms. Within the machine learning community a large number of benchmark datasets are available.(Blake and Merz, 1998) Many of these datasets have been used for evaluating various data mining techniques.

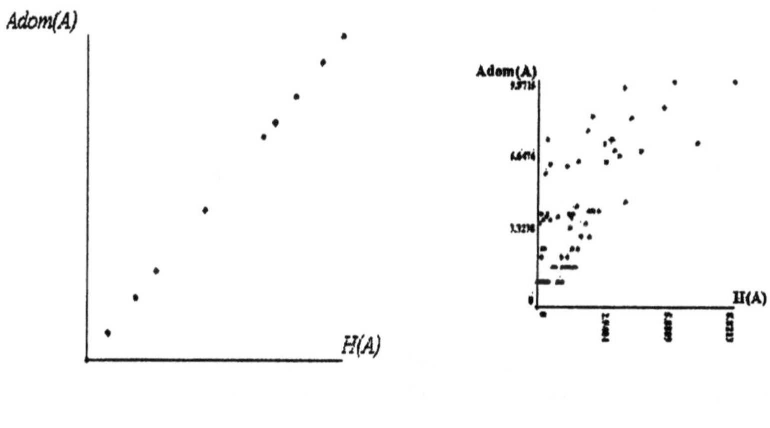

Figure 9. $\mathcal{H}_A$ compared to log $|\text{adom}(A)|$ for the Wisconsin benchmark data (Left). The same comparison from the census data (Right).

Figure 9 (Left) shows $\mathcal{H}_A$ compared to log |adom(A)| for the Wisconsin benchmark data. The Wisconsin data can be seen to have a nearly perfect uniform distribution within each attribute. When compared on the census data, seen in Figure 9 (Right), it is clear that this synthetically generated data demonstrates significant differences from real data, which has much more complexity to its structure.

As another example, Figure 10 shows a number of datasets from the machine learning repository displayed for comparison. We can see in this visualization that these datasets have different structure as well, although the sparseness of the data does have an effect. In addition, these datasets tend to have a large number of boolean valued attributes.

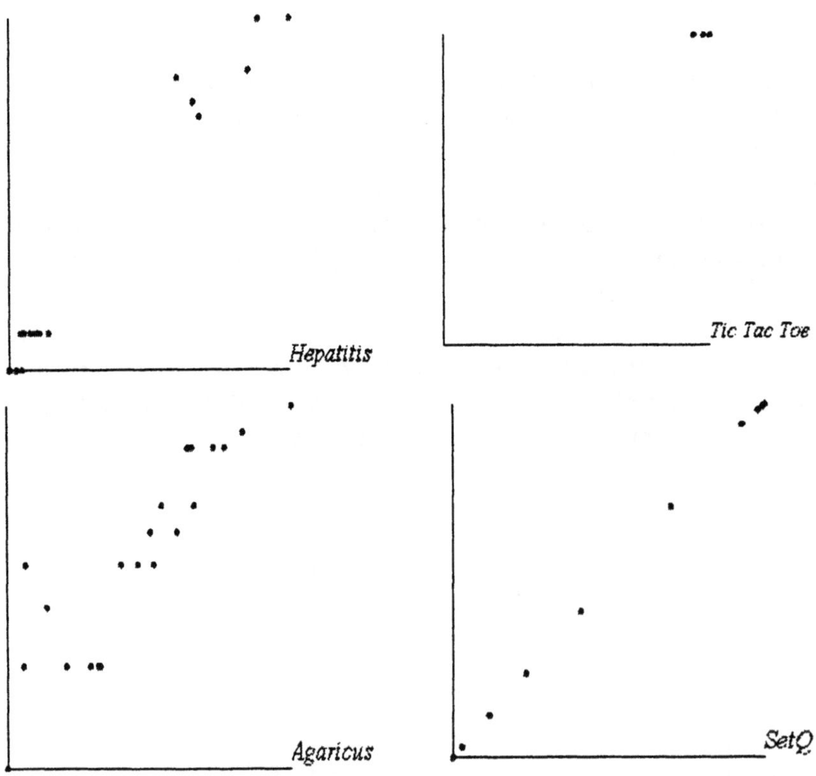

Figure 10. $\mathcal{H}_A$ compared to log |adom(A)| for datasets taken from the machine learning repository. Clockwise from top left - Hepatitis, Tic Tac Toe, Agaricus, SetQ.

6. Conclusion

In this paper we have shown how entropy, a central concept in information theory, can be used for visualizing the structure of information within database relations. The technique simplifies the display of complex relationships, allowing for dependencies to be spotted. Our use of entropy is independent of the underlying datatypes, handling all in a consistent fashion. Furthermore, we have demonstrated the technique on a wide variety of data, some of which are quite large. The census dataset, for instance, contains 125 attributes and approximately 300,000 rows of data.

While this particular research is reported in terms of database visualization problems, the techniques we have employed are applicable to several areas. Within data mining we envision that these techniques can be used to assist an expert in exploring their particular problem space. In addition, database designers can use the visualization to assist in the construction of decompositions, either for OLTP systems, or for OLAP data warehouses.

Acknowledgments

The authors wish to thank Mehmet Dalkilic, Philip Berg, Chris Giannella and Dirk Van Gucht for their support.

References

www.census.gov. On The Web.

Blake, C. and Merz, C. (1998). UCI repository of machine learning databases. http://www.ics.uci.edu/~mlearn/MLRepository.html.

Card, S. K., Mackinlay, J. D., and Shneiderman, B., editors (1999). *Readings in Information Visualization: Using Vision to Think*. Morgan Kaufmann Publishers, Inc.

Cover, T. M. and Thomas, J. A. (1991). *Elements of Information Theory*. John Wiley & Sons, New York, NY, USA.

Dalkilic, M. M. (2000). *Foundations of Data Mining*. PhD thesis, Indiana University, Computer Science.

Dalkilic, M. M. and Robertson, E. L. (2000). Information dependencies. In *Proceedings of the Nineteenth ACM SIGMOD-SIGACT-SIGART Symposium on Principles of Database Systems, May 15-17, 2000, Dallas, Texas, USA*, pages 245–253. ACM.

DeWitt, D. J. (1993). The wisconsin benchmark: Past, present, and future. In Gray, J., editor, *The Benchmark Handbook for Database and Transaction Systems (2nd Edition)*. Morgan Kaufmann.

Feiner, S. (1992). Virtual worlds for visualizing information. In *Advanced Visual Interfaces*, pages 3–11.

Groth, D. P. and Robertson, E. L. (1998). Architectural support for database visualization. In *Proceedings of the Workshop on New Paradigms in Information Visualization and Manipulation*.

Inselberg, A. and Dimsdale, B. (1987). Parallel coordinates for visualizing multi-dimensional geometry. In *Proceedings of Computer Graphics International '87*, Tokyo. Springer-Verlag.

Inselberg, A. and Dimsdale, B. (1990). Parallel coordinates: A tool for visualizing multi-dimensional geometry. In *Proceedings of IEEE Visualization '90*, pages 361–375, Los Alamitos, CA. IEEE Computer Society Press.

Keim, D. A. (1996a). Databases and visualization. In Jagadish, H. V. and Mumick, I. S., editors, *Proceedings of the 1996 ACM SIGMOD International Conference on Management of Data, Montreal, Quebec, Canada, June 4-6, 1996*, page 543. ACM Press.

Keim, D. A. (1996b). Pixel-oriented database visualizations. *SIGMOD Record*, 25(4):35–39.

Keim, D. A., Kriegel, H.-P., and Seidl, T. (1994). Supporting data mining of large databases by visual feedback queries. In *Proceedings of the Tenth International Conference on Data Engineering, February 14-18, 1994, Houston, Texas, USA*, pages 302–313. IEEE Computer Society.

Kivinen, J. and Mannila, H. (1992). Approximate dependency inference from relations. In Biskup, J. and Hull, R., editors, *Database Theory - ICDT'92, 4th International Conference, Berlin, Germany, October 14-16, 1992, Proceedings*, volume 646 of *Lecture Notes in Computer Science*, pages 86–98. Springer.

LeBlanc, J., Ward, M. O., and Wittels, N. (1990). Exploring n-dimensional databases. In *Proceedings of IEEE Visualization '90*, pages 230–237, Los Alamitos, CA. IEEE Computer Society Press.

Dennis Groth received the BS in computer science from Loyola University of Chicago in 1983 and the PhD in computer science from Indiana University (expected) in 2002. He is currently a Lecturer in the School of Informatics at Indiana University, Bloomington. His research interests include database visualization, data mining, and human computer interaction. He is a member of the Association for Computing Machinery.

Edward Robertson received the BS in mathematics from Cal Tech in 1966 and the MS and PhD in computer science from the University of Wisconsin in 1968 and 1970, respectively. He is currently Professor of Computer Science and Associate Dean of the School of Informatics at Indiana University, Bloomington. He has served on the faculty of the University of Waterloo, Ontario, and the Pennsylvania State University. In 1987 and 1988 he was Fulbright Scholar and Visiting Professor at the University of Nairobi, Kenya. His research interests include database systems, datamining, and computer systems design and implementation, especially software engineering. He is a member of the Association for Computing Machinery (having served as Vice Chair of the ACM Education Board), the Computer Society of the Institute of Electrical and Electronics Engineers, and Computer Professionals for Social Responsibility.

VISUAL QUERY PROCESSING FOR GIS WITH WEB CONTENTS

Ryong Lee
Department of Social Informatics, Kyoto University
ryong@db.soc.i.kyoto-u.ac.jp

Hiroki Takakura
Data Processing Center, Kyoto University
takakura@rd.kudpc.kyoto-u.ac.jp

Yahiko Kambayashi
Department of Social Informatics, Kyoto University
yahiko@db.soc.i.kyoto-u.ac.jp

Abstract

In many geographic objects such as a travel planning, the use of web information is significantly increasing. For an efficient support of such work, it is very important to combine web information with map semantics. Current web systems usually do not support map semantics. Conversely, conventional Geographic Information Systems (GIS) do not utilize the web resources. The purpose of the research is as follows: (1) to get semantics from the web contents to realize advanced GIS functions on geographic web searches, and (2) to develop a user interface which can utilize web contents and map semantics in an effective integrating way. For such a purpose, we construct two map semantics about geographic characteristics and relationships available on the web. Utilizing semantics, we have developed a prototype system, KyotoSEARCH; its main function is to support users' information navigations among the web, the map and web-based geographic knowledge, in an integrated way.

Keywords: Map-based Web Search, Map Semantics, Geographic Web Search

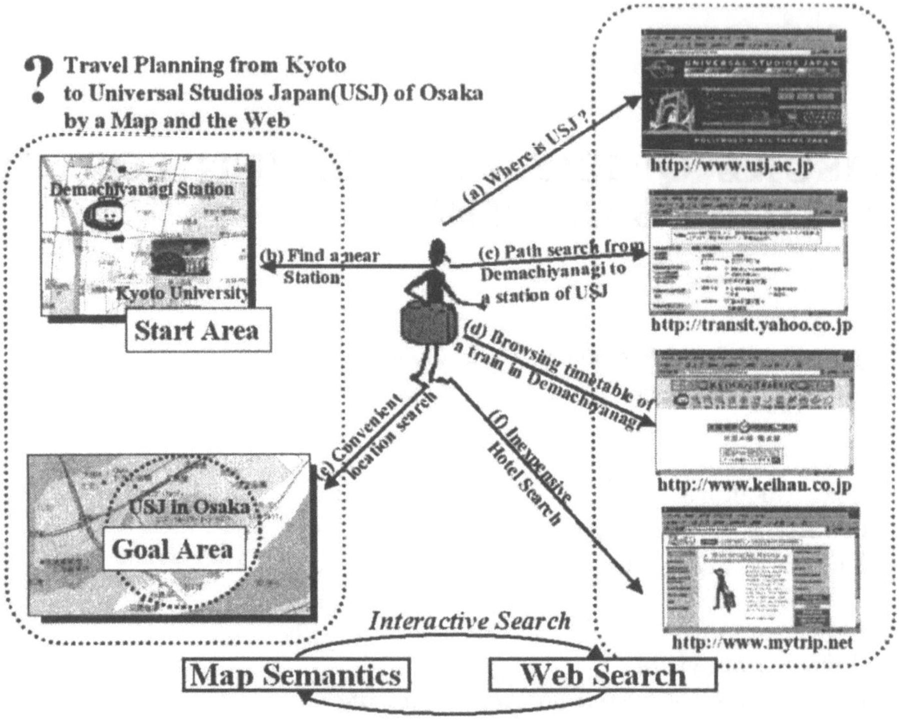

Figure 1. Geographical Information Search by a map and the web

1. INTRODUCTION

In the context of Geographical Information Systems(GIS), the current web resources should be another important database of human geographical information. In recent years, there are various kinds of significant efforts to integrate the web and geographical resources such as place names. Most of the efforts and possible extensions can be categorized as follows:

Indexing the Web by Relevant Locations

[Ding00; McCurley00; Arikawa00; Buyukkokten99]

By extracting place names from a page, a set of relevant geographic locations can be calculated. These locations represent the page's geographical coverage and relevancy. This will introduce new web classifying and indexing ways. We can use it for improving most the current web search engines that have been less focused on geography of the web.

Use of the Map as a User-Friendly Web Interface

[Lee00; Yates00; Hiramatsu01; McCurley00; Kumar99; BIGwhat; Mapion]
Instead of specifying locations by place names or latitude/longitude pairs, a user can select a location on the map precisely. In this case, other keywords should be specified separately, but it is possible to use geographical operations such as range and distance constraints.

Integrating of the Web Information with Map Semantics

If we can aggregate web resources highly related to a specific geographical location, it will be possible to perform spatial knowledge discovery on the web. That is, the web as a human geographical database will reveal unknown spatial knowledge. Then, it will be also used to improve web searches in geographic query processing.

The major objectives of this paper are as follows.

- *To realize an integrated system to advance GIS functions with the web*
- *To utilize the web as geographical knowledge base*

In order to describe problems of geographical web searches on the current web, let us consider a following scenario when we make a travel plan using the web.

A Motivated Scenario:
A foreign person who will participate in a Symposium at Kyoto University also would like go to Universal Studios Japan(USJ), that is a theme park in Osaka in Japan. We assume that she has only a map and a mobile computer connected to the web. First she will browse the USJ's web page as shown in Fig.1(a). Then, she can know the precise location of USJ. However, she wants more to know how to go there by train. To search for a route, the next query she posed is to browse a page about the train route search at a Yahoo! service page like Fig.1(b). This search, now, needs to be inputted 'starting station' and 'targeting station'. The latter one can be known by the USJ's page. For the determination of the 'starting station', she opens the map, and finds the nearest station 'Demachiyanagi' from 'Kyoto University'. Returned to the route search, she can now find a path which will be the best solution in conditions of charge, time, the number of transferring. In the next search, to find the timetable about a train of 'Demachiyanagi' station, she searches a page in the step of Fig.1(d). Furthermore, to reserve a hotel at a convenient place near the USJ, she will look for places around USJ on the map, and

found some hotels drawn by an image(Fig.1(e)). In order to compare price, facilities, etc. and to reserve one of them, she accesses to a hotel guide page.

As the above scenario shows, the web must be a useful resource for decisions of the planning which requires much of geographical knowledge with a map. Through her investigations with a map and the web, she could finish her preparations with much efforts and long time to this step. In the result, it is a very hard work, because the web and the map information are not integrated.

In order to utilize the web as a geographical knowledge base for advanced GIS, we focus on two kinds of important factors, geoword(place names, G) and non-geoword(N) founded in web pages(P). On the basis of the two kinds of word domains, we examine co-existence and association rules such as $G \rightarrow G$ *and* $G \rightarrow N$ by applying data mining methods. Here, for example, $G \rightarrow G$ shows an association rule for two geographical words(when W_1 exists there in many cases, W_2 exists in the same page). These relationships will derive a new semantic model for GIS such as **geographical characteristics and geographical relationships**. Moreover, we can benefit from utilizing these relationships in performing advanced geographic web search and web knowledge discovery.

The remainder of the paper is organized as follows. In Section 2, problems of conventional GIS's are discussed by the stand point described above. Section 3 describes how to compute associations and constraints of three domains(G, N, and P). Section 4 introduces a user-friendly comprehensive visual interface. It can extend GIS functionalities to Map-based Keyword Retrieval and Keyword-based Map Retrieval. In order to describe how to solve spatial queries efficiently on the domains, we discuss a web-based spatial query processing strategy in Section 5.

2. PROBLEMS OF CONVENTIONAL GEOGRAPHIC INFORMATION RETRIEVAL ON THE WEB

In solving spatial queries as the above example, searching for well-arranged tour guide web sites may be one solution today. However, as a generalized solution to these spatial queries with various purposes, web search engines should be integrated to GIS functions and resources.

All of these searches must be solved in two very fundamental domains; *spatial and non-spatial information domains.* Moreover, we need to refine each search results by applying *spatial constraints* such as region or distance, and *non-spatial constraints* such as term hierarchy. However,

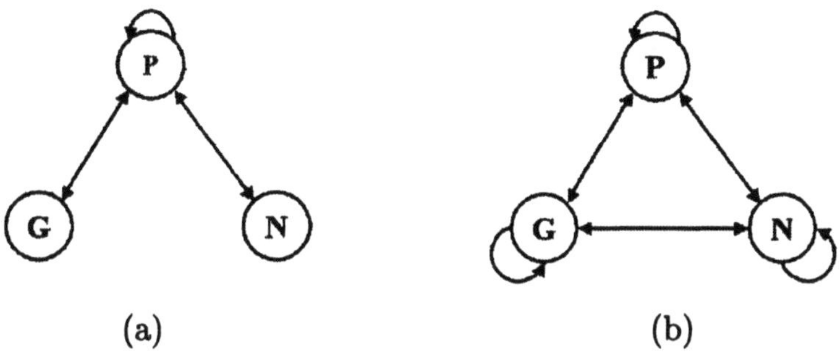

Figure 2. Relationships among P, G, and N, for conventional and advanced systems: (a) Conventional Web Information Systems, and (b) Relationships for Advanced GIS

most of current web search engines support only information navigations on domains of pages and related keywords. For complete navigations including geographical knowledge, the two domains, spatial and non-spatial information spaces should be strongly connected as shown in Figure 2. In the current Web, concepts in G(geoword) and N(nongeoword) are not directly connected with each other and itself as shown in Fig.2(a). We can say that they have some relationships (if they appear in the same web page). By analyzing web pages users can generate relationships between G and G' (other location names), between N and N' (other keywords), and between G and N. In the pairs, a geoword and a non-geoword can be related even if they do no appear in one particular page the user is interested in. However, it will give users an opportunity to know other interesting knowledge.

Generally, these kinds of relations can be a new semantics for GIS and Geographic Web Searches.

- *G-domain* has map semantics such as range or distance relationships in real worlds. In order to specify a geographical query and to display query result, map interface can be integrated to conventional web browsers.

- *N-domain* represents conceptual networks of terms which have been studied for a long time in textual processing study. It already has been constructed many terminology relationships such as similarity and term hierarchy. Languages have dynamic nature, there are also relationships among non-geoword(Ns) not contained in conventional dictionary such relationships can be found from the contents of web pages.

- *P-domain* has been constructed well-developed web search technologies in web search fields based on links and contents of the web.

By combining of these semantics, more powerful spatial knowledge supports are possible. This paper will construct the knowledge based on the association and constraints of the three domains. Comparable studies in information navigation is DualNAVI[Takano00]; it supports an information navigation on association of document and word space. Users can move from one document to another associative document by their link, and from one document to its most associative keyword. At the same way, movement from one keyword to another keyword or to the document space is possible. Our purpose is more general form to realize geographical information search by integrating web document space with map semantics.

3. CONSTRUCTION OF WEB-BASED MAP SEMANTICS

The term *Web Mining* has been used to refer to three kinds of data mining to Content, Usage, and Structure of the Web. The first one, on which we mainly focus in this paper, involves the discovery of meaningful knowledge from a large collection of primarily unstructured web data. This type of analysis is generally performed by means of interpreting statistical attributes of the discovered rules or patterns. In this paper, we exploit such discovery of the web in order to reveal the following geographical knowledge produced and shared by web users, where $G+$(or $N+$) shows a set consisting of elements in G(or N) respectively excluding empty sets.

Geographical Relationships : $G \rightarrow G+$

Geographical Characteristics : $G \rightarrow N+$

For example, results of most web search services about a location name 'Seoul in Korea'(G) in the end of May, 2002, will be shown many web pages extensively including related-location names ($G+=\{$'Niigata in Japan','Ulsan in Korea',...$\}$) and characteristic words($N+=\{$'FIFA', 'World-Cup','Match Schedule','Team','Ticketing',...$\}$), since the two cities take place '2002 FIFA World-Cup' together. Such relationships are very important at that moment and later its important will be decreased.

These kinds of knowledge extracted from the web are very different from those of conventional GIS based on the relational/object databases. Since the web space is constantly updating its contents in a large amount, well-refined geographical knowledge of the Web can be a valuable source in geographical object applications. In the following subsection, we describe how to compute associations between geoword and non-geoword from web pages, and constraints in each domain for more efficient query processing.

Association Construction from Web Pages

The most straightforward and effect way in mining associations is to find the patterns which are relatively strong, i.e., which occur frequently together in most cases. In the data mining field, an association rule is a general form of dependency rule on transaction-based database; the rule has the form of "$W \rightarrow B$" (c%), explained as "if a pattern W appears in a transaction, there is c% possibility(confidence) that the pattern B holds in the same transaction", where W and B are a set of attribute values. In order to ensure that frequently encountered patterns is covered enough, the concept of the support of the rule was introduced, which is defined as the ratio that the pattern of W and B occurring together in the transactions vs. the total number of transactions in the database [Agrawal94].

Table 1. Fundamental Matrix

	nid_0	nid_1	nid_2	$\cdots$	$\cdots$	nid_m
pid_0	0	0	1	$\cdots$	$\cdots$	0
pid_1	0	0	1	$\cdots$	$\cdots$	0
pid_2	0	1	0	$\cdots$	$\cdots$	1
$\vdots$	$\vdots$	$\vdots$	$\vdots$	$\ddots$	$\ddots$	$\vdots$
pid_n	1	1	0	$\cdots$	$\cdots$	0

(a) Matrix $M : P \times Noun$

	nid_0	nid_1	nid_2	$\cdots$	$\cdots$	nid_m
nid_0	20	2	3	$\cdots$	$\cdots$	9
nid_1	2	34	7	$\cdots$	$\cdots$	2
nid_2	3	7	16	$\cdots$	$\cdots$	3
$\vdots$	$\vdots$	$\vdots$	$\vdots$	$\ddots$	$\ddots$	$\vdots$
nid_m	9	2	3	$\cdots$	$\cdots$	75

(b) $M^T M$

Table 2. Geo-Matrix

	gw_0	$\cdots$	gw_k	ngw_0	$\cdots$	ngw_l
pid_0	0	$\cdots$	0	0	$\cdots$	0
pid_1	1	$\cdots$	0	1	$\cdots$	0
pid_2	0	$\cdots$	0	0	$\cdots$	1
$\vdots$	$\vdots$	$\ddots$	$\vdots$	$\vdots$	$\ddots$	$\vdots$
pid_n	0	$\cdots$	0	1	$\cdots$	0

(c) Matrix $G : P \times \{G, N\}$

	gw_0	$\cdots$	gw_k	ngw_0	$\cdots$	ngw_l
gw_0	10	$\cdots$	3	32	$\cdots$	5
$\vdots$	$\vdots$	$\ddots$	$\vdots$	$\vdots$	$\ddots$	$\vdots$
gw_k	3	$\cdots$	7	8	$\cdots$	13
ngw_0	32	$\cdots$	8	93	$\vdots$	12
$\vdots$	$\vdots$	$\ddots$	$\vdots$	$\vdots$	$\ddots$	$\vdots$
ngw_l	5	$\cdots$	13	27	$\cdots$	75

(d) $G^T G$

We mine the web by constructing a matrix M illustrated in Table 1., which defines the relationship between Page and Nouns. A row in (a) the matrix M represents noun-list appearing in a page pid_j. As the conventional mining work, the $page_{id}$ is corresponding with each shopping transaction, while the words of $page_{id}$ is a set of items included in each transaction. The co-citation matrix M^TM also can show the frequently associated noun-pairs. Here we consider a constraint that the occurrence of a noun in a page is counted just onetime for a brief description. Then, to find most relevant terms, the matrix M^TM has integer values, while M has binary values.

A mining rule that we are targeting is a rule of the form "$X \rightarrow Y$", where X and Y can be a set of $G+$ and $N+$; here, $G+$ is a set of geo-referential text(place names or geographical names), while $N+$ is a set of generic nouns excluding $G+$. For this, we introduce a matrix G in Table 2., which is made by distinguishing G from N. The co-citation matrix G^TG represents the three important relationships described in Figure 2, (i) $P \rightarrow \{P+, G+, N+\}$, (ii) $G \rightarrow \{P+, G+, N+\}$, (iii) $N \rightarrow \{P+, G+, N+\}$. Here, the relationship $P \rightarrow P+$ can be constructed from link structure among pages, i.e., $P+$ is a set of pages linked from page P.

In making above matrix, there are two way to process it from the web. One is for starting from aggregation of unknown data set of the web. In such case, we need to perform analysis work as following steps:

step 1. Extraction of *Page-Links, G, N* from contents of web pages
$P \rightarrow \{P+, G+, N+\}$

step 2. Indexing for G, N search: Using G and N, we can construct index for web pages
1) $G+ \rightarrow P+$, 2) $N+ \rightarrow P+$

step 3. Association Construction: The following relationships are derived by the occurrence relationships of identical web pages.
1) $G+ \rightarrow G+$, 2) $G+ \rightarrow N+$, 3) $N+ \rightarrow G+$, 4) $N+ \rightarrow N+$

For information retrieval, words in $G+$ and $N+$ are determined, using index defined in step 2, and corresponding pages are obtained.

4. A WEB-BASED SPATIAL INFORMATION RETRIEVAL SYSTEM

In this section, we introduce a prototype system, KyotoSEARCH, to support information navigation among *G, N, and P.* The system has two main functions necessary to resolve the query about $G \rightarrow N$ and

$N \rightarrow G$. For that, new retrieval ways as Map-based Keyword Retrieval and Keyword-based Map Retrieval are introduced.

Our system has the following components as shown in Figure 3:

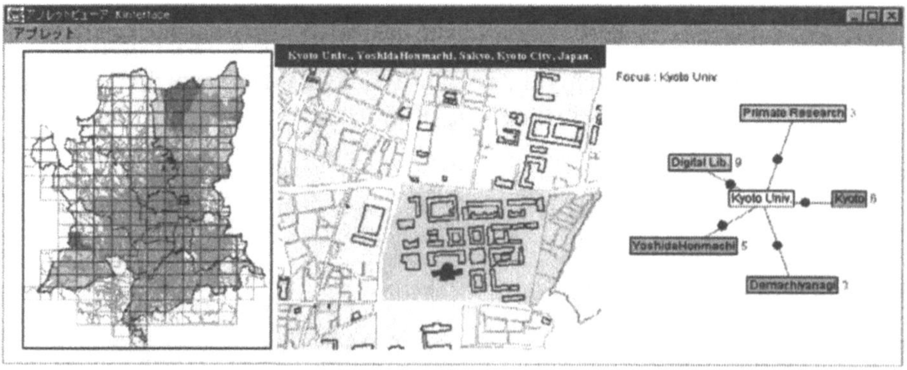

Figure 3. A user interface for KyotoSEARCH

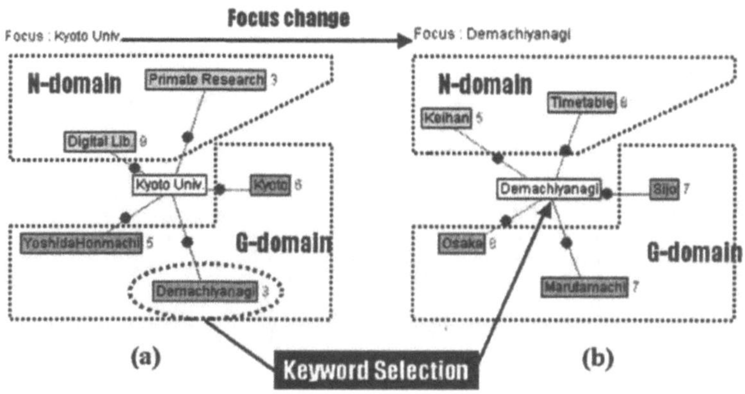

Figure 4. Knowledge Navigation on the Keyword Interface

- **Map Interface** is a great user interface to specify a location. The result of a query can be also shown on a map, which is easy to understand. Here we develop two maps: The left one is for show the number of web pages in each town. The right one is a detailed map at a specified location.

- **Keyword Interface** is used for exploiting the relationships of G and N introduced in the previous sections. In the center of this interface, a focused keyword(G or N) is positioned. Its related $G+$ and $N+$ are placed around the focused keyword together with lines showing the semantic relationships(each relationship can be expressed by a label or a kind of line). If users click one of the related words, it becomes to a new focus, moves to center position, and re-shows its relatives as shown in Figure 4. In Fig.4(a), if a user selects "Demachiyanagi" as a new focused word, the graph will become the other shown in Fig.4(b).

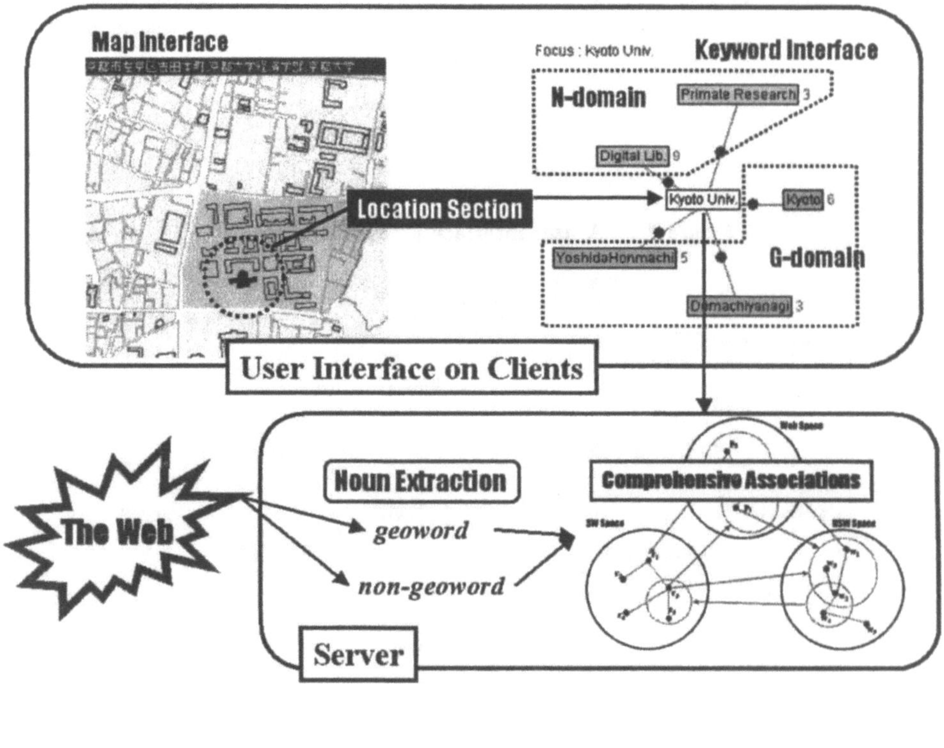

Figure 5. Map-based Keyword Retrieval

In addition, we made a URL-List Interface for displaying a list of web pages relative to focused one in above Keyword Interface. Users can browser most relative web sites by choosing one of them. In this paper, we do not describe specifically since our focus is on the above two interfaces. With above components, users can perform the following two retrieval operations alternatively.

Map-based Keyword Retrieval

By clicking a location to search on Map Interface, other interfaces are activated for receiving location key as shown in Figure 5. In Keyword Interface, the focused keyword changes into the received location keyword from the map, and shows a set of new relatives around it. URL-List Interface will show a list of web pages retrieved by the received location name. Users are then able to know relative information on them. This retrieval actually gives solutions to spatial queries starting from G, i.e. $G \rightarrow \{G+, N+, P+\}$.

Keyword-based Map Retrieval

A selection of one keyword from the relatives changes contents of Keyword Interface as shown in the above description. It also interacts with other interfaces; map interface shows the detailed map if the selected keyword is included in G. On the other hand, URL-List Interface shows a revised list related to the newly selected keyword.

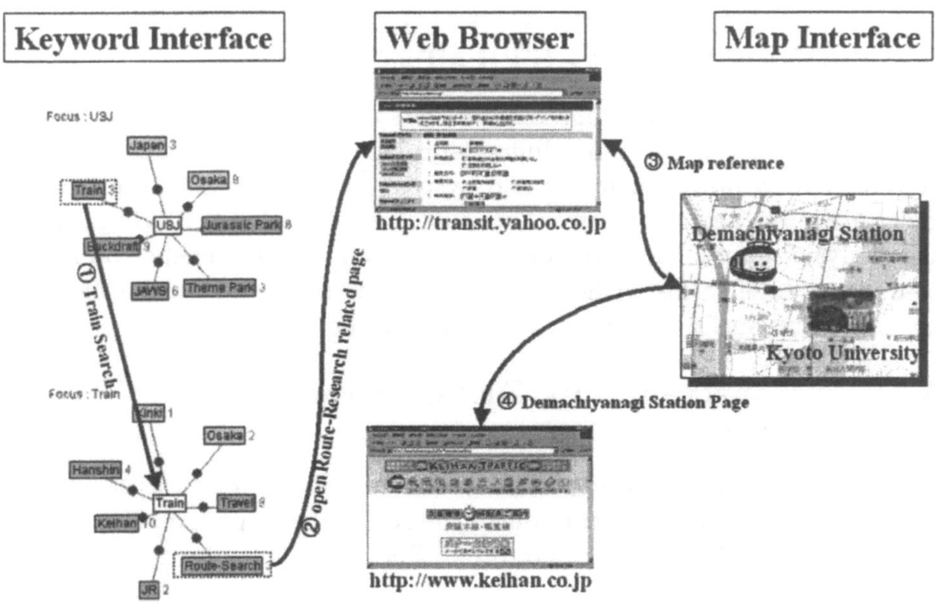

Figure 6. Protype system-based geographical knowledge navigation

We can now easily process the first scenario described in the introduction for travel planning as shown in Figure 6. The new travel plan process is as follows:

step 1. By specifying 'USJ' as the focused keyword, the corresponding map will be shown. (G='USJ' → K+={'Jurassic Park', 'JAWS', 'Train', ... }, G+={'Japan','Osaka'})

step 2. As one of the related words to the 'USJ' shown in Figure 6, we specify the 'train' as a new focused word. Then, as the result, new list of related words will be shown such as 'Route-Search', 'JR', 'Keihan', etc. (G='USJ' → K='Train' → P="http://transit.yahoo.co.jp')

step 3. By specifying Kyoto University as the focused keyword to view a map near the university, the most near station "Demachiyanagi" is found on the map. If it is selected, a web page related to "Demachiyanagi" will be retrieved. From this page, we get the information about the location of the station, timetable, etc.

step 4. By performing route search with "Demachiyanagi" as another web browser, we will get a list of most low-cost courses to 'USJ'.

5. DISCUSSIONS: EFFICIENT QUERY PROCESSING STRATEGIES

In the developing works and experiments using a large number of web resources, we faced to many difficult problems. First, the goal of our system was to make an integrated system to support multi-purposed geographic web search system. This made us suffer about how to reason the analysis results. Since the prototype system simply depends on high co-occurrence of terms without a consideration of any constraint or any pre-classification, it is very hard to evaluate the efficiency.

5.1. Constraints by Distance and Term Hierarchy

In order to improve the current search result, we discuss two constraints. One is spatial restriction to the results by applying actual distance constraint for filtering geowords. The other is for term hierarchy for filtering non-geoword.

For show what aspects will be improved with these constraints, we first consider the following example which has different characteristics from the previous examples.

Example) Simple Restaurant Search
One wish to find a good restaurant for dinner in a town the person does not know. This query now goes through the following steps:

step 1. Inquire into a location list that each location has many restaurants in the town

step 2. Choose a location from above location list

step 3. Request a restaurant type list in a selected location

step 4. Select one restaurant in above type list

step 5. Access to a web site of the selected one for more specific information

The result of above step 1 is desirable to show many related geographical regions on the map, so that one of the resulting regions need to be selected by users or automatically recommended ways. In step 3, she now need to know more specific information about what kinds of restaurant exist in the selected region. This question must be answered by using term hierarchy for 'restaurant'; it will have Chinese-, Italian-, France-, Japanese-, Korean restaurant, etc. as child terms. In step 4, one of the restaurants is selected by her favorites. She choose a 'Korean restaurant'. Finally, she access to a web page of the selected 'Korean restaurant' for looking at food menu and making reservation.

In resolving the above query, we first consider the following steps to solve the user query without constraints.

Formalized Simple "Restaurant" Search :

step 1. $LocationSearch('restaurant') : N \rightarrow G+$

step 2. $RestaurantList(G_{selected}) : G \rightarrow N+$

step 3. $PageSearch(restaurant_{selected}) : N \rightarrow P+$

In above search, the user needs to traverse on the whole information domains; First query is that what locations are related to "restaurant". It needs an association from N to $G+$ described in Section 2. Secondly the user asks what restaurants exist there. This involves $G \rightarrow N+$ search with selected G. By the result of this search, the user is given a restaurant list filtered by G and N conditions. With a final restaurant selection by the user, for the more specific information such opening/closing time, food menu, cost, etc., by use of $N \rightarrow P+$ association, the restaurant page is opened by web browser. Associations described in previous sections perform these transition from one domain to another. Through the traversal, users will get a comprehend spatial knowledge with non-spatial one based on the web resources. However, the simplified search will be resulted in large amount of low-quality answers to each query, since any constraints is yet considered. Therefore, we need to refine above query in the constraints about two domain G and N as follows:

Constraint-based "Restaurant" Search:

step 1. $LocationSearch('restaurant') : N \rightarrow G$

step 2. $Inside(1km, G_{list}) : G \rightarrow G$ as **Distance Restriction**

step 3. $RestaurantList(G_{selected}) : G \rightarrow N$

step 4. $ResturantType(N)$: $N \rightarrow N$ as **Categorization Restriction**

step 5. $PageSearch(restaurant_{selected}) : N \rightarrow P$

This search is now will show a list of the restaurants, restricted regions and categorized into Italian-, France-, Chinese restaurants, etc. These added constraints involves self-traverse in each domain of G and N which are possible at the strong connection we described in Section 2.

6. CONCLUSION

The association on the Keyword Interface is built on analysis of aggregated web pages from many web searches. The number of the aggregated web pages, we stored in local disks, is 2 millions as about 30GB data size. For extracting geowords and non-geowords from each page, we perform the morphological analysis, resulting in about 20GB output data size. As a future work, we will develop an efficient knowledge discovery method to handle such a large volume of web data.

The developed system, we described in Section 4, is implemented with Java Applet for using on the web after our further experimental work. This comprehensive interface realizes information navigation which we discussed at the strong connection in Section 2. We believe that many of difficult spatial queries in conventional GIS will be resolved by our proposed system by the following facts.

- Map interface is an intuitive interface for representing geographical regions of web resources and formulating user query in spatial domain.

- Keyword Interface utilizes a result from web contents mining in respect to G and N. It gives background and unknown knowledge to users by relations such geographical characteristics($G \rightarrow N$) and relationships($G \rightarrow G$).

Our another future work will focus on object-based knowledge discovery on the G-N-P graph, constructed by actual analysis work to millions of aggregated web pages.

ACKNOWLEDGEMENT

This work has been supported by 'Universal Design in Digital City' Project in CREST of JST (Japan Science and Technoloy Corporation).

REFERENCES

R. Agrawal and R. Srikant. *Fast algorithms for mining associations*, VLDB1994, pp. 487-499, 1994.

M. Arikawa, K. Okamura. *Spatial Media Fusion Project*, Proc. of Kyoto International Conference on Digital Libraries: Research and Practice, pp.75-82, Nov. 2000.

O. Buyukkokten, J. Cho, H. Garcia-Molina, L. Gravano, and N. Shivakumar. *Exploiting geographical location information of web pages*, In Proc. of the ACM SIGMOD Workshop on the Web and Databases, WebDB, 1999.

J. Ding, L. Gravano,and N. Shivakumar. *Computing Geographical Scopes of Web Resources*, VLDB2000, pp.545-556, 2000.

K. Hiramatsu and T. Ishida. *An Augmented Web Space for Digital Cities*, IEEE/IPSJ Symposium on Applications and the Internet (SAINT-01), pp.105-112, 2001.

V. Kumar, A. Bugacov, M. Coutinho, and R. Neches. *Integrating Geographic Information Systems*, Spatial Digital Libraries and Information Spaces for conducting Humanitarian Assistance and Disaster Relief Operations in Urban Environments", ACMGIS, 1999.

F. Lee, S. Bressan, and B. C. Ooi. *Global Atlas: Calibrating and Indexing Document from Internet in the Cartographic Paradigm*, Internation Conference on Web Information Systems Engineering. Vol 1, pp. 117-124, 2000.

K.S. McCurley. *Geospatial Mapping and Navigation of the Web*, WWW10, 2000.

A. Takano, Y. Niwa, S. Nishioka, M. Iwayama, T. Hisamitsu, O. Imaichi, and H. Sakurai. *Associative Information Access Using DualNAVI*, Proc. of Kyoto International Conference on Digital Libraries: Research and Practice, pp.285-289, Nov. 2000.

J.D. Yates and X. Zhou. *Searching the Web Using a Map*, Proc. of the 1st International Conference on Web Information Systems Engineering, pp. 222-229, Jun., 2000.

BIGwhat. *http://www.bigwhat.com*

Mapion. *http://www.mapion.co.jp*

SPATIO-TEMPORAL MODELLING AND QUERYING VIDEO DATABASES USING HIGH-LEVEL CONCEPTS

Surya Nepal and Uma Srinivasan
CSIRO Mathematical and Information Sciences,
Locked Bag 17, North Ryde NSW 1670, Australia
{Surya.Nepal,Uma.Srinivasan}@cmis.csiro.au

Abstract: Modelling and querying video content involves understanding the spatio-temporal relationships of objects[1] represented in a video sequence. In this paper, we present a binary representation-based framework for modelling and querying video object relationships at a semantic level. The framework supports spatio-temporal queries using high-level concepts. We propose a set of semantic (qualitative) terms to describe the spatio-temporal relations between objects and then show how such qualitative terms can be calculated within the proposed framework using a fuzzy-logic-based approach. We also report the experimental results performed on a video clip from the MPEG-7 video content archive.

Key words: content-based retrieval, spatio-temporal relations, multimedia databases.

1. INTRODUCTION

The growing number of video databases has placed content-based modelling and search tools in high demand. A number of commercial products as well as academic prototype systems have been developed to facilitate content-based search. Prominent examples are QBIC (Flickner 1995), and Virage (Hampapur et al. 1997). These systems generally extract features from raw images/videos and use them for retrieval. Features such as

[1] When using to the terms *objects or video objects,* we are referring to objects or region(s) of features that are identified in a video sequence.

colour, texture, shape, motion trajectories, and edges are commonly used. Many modelling and querying techniques have been developed and used for emerging features (Baral, Gonzalez and Son 1998). Initially, most of these modelling and querying techniques were developed for image databases. More recently, multimedia applications have started paying attention to spatio-temporal modelling and querying video content (Bolle et al 1997, Sistla et al. 1997, Hjelsvold and Midstraum 1994). There have been a few techniques for modelling and querying multimedia databases based on spatio-temporal relations (Li et al 1997, Kuo and Chen 2000). These approaches are motivated from the low-level feature-based techniques. In this paper, our aim is to present a framework that enables users to query video content using high-level concepts. These high-level concepts are described using spatio-temporal relations.

Most feature-based systems index content using extracted features, where users need to be familiar with the underlying feature representation schemes to express their queries. We call this a "bottom up approach", as users need to know how to express their queries in terms of low-level features. Our framework is based on "top-down" approach, where users express their queries using high-level concepts that are more natural. The "concepts" we defined are based on spatio-temporal relations at the frame and shot levels.

In section 2, we review various spatio-temporal relations used in geographical information systems and provide a set of semantic terms to describe spatio-temporal relations in video databases. In section 3, we use binary representation-based modelling techniques to model spatio-temporal relations at different levels. Using an object detection algorithm, we illustrate some fundamental relationships and provide experimental results. These are reported in Section 4.

2. BACKGROUND

We present background work in the areas of spatial and temporal relations and provide a set of semantic terms that are useful for expressing spatio-temporal queries in video databases

2.1 Topological relations

Topological relations are spatial relations that are invariant under bijective and continuous transformations that also have inverses. Topological equivalence does not necessarily preserve distances and directions. Instead, topological notions include continuity, interior, and boundary, which are defined in terms of neighbourhood relations. Egenhofer and Franzosa (1991) have specified eight fundamental topological relations that can be applied between two planar regions. These relations are used in geographical information systems and spatial databases (Papadias and Delis 1997, Delis, Christos and Spiros 1999). The eight topological relations are *Disjoint, Meet, Equal, Inside, Contains, Covered_By, Covers,* and *Overlap*.

2.2 Directional relations

Directional relations are used to define the order of objects in the space. Frank (1996) has defined the eight directional relations based on a qualitative approach. These relations are studied under two different groups: strict directional relations such as N, S, W and E, and mixed directional relations such as NE, SE, SW and NW. Qualitative approaches are highly desirable in similarity-based retrieval systems (such as image and video databases), because precision is not always desirable nor available. The eight directional relations are North, NorthEast, East, SouthEast, South, SouthWest, West, and NorthWest.

2.3 Temporal relations

As a video is a continuous medium, temporal interval relations provide important cues for video data retrieval. Allen (1983) has defined 13 temporal interval relations. These are *Before, Meets, Overlaps, Finishes, Starts, Contains, Equals, During, Started by, Finished by, Overlapped by, Met by,* and *After*. Many variations of Allen's temporal interval relations have been proposed and used in temporal and multimedia databases. These relations are used to define the temporal relationships of events within a multimedia document. For example, weather news *after* the sports news in a daily TV news broadcast.

A partial taxonomy of spatio-temporal relations for video databases is shown in Figure 1. The list of conceptual terms and relationships are not limited to the ones provided in the figure. We have shown spatio-temporal relations and concepts that are of interest in this paper. We categorize spatio-temporal relations into two categories based on the number of objects involved: unary and binary relations. For a single object, unary spatio-temporal relations describe location of the object, motion of the object, etc. In binary relations, our focus is on the relative positions and movements of related objects. We next describe the framework and show how it is used in mapping semantic terms to spatio-temporal positions.

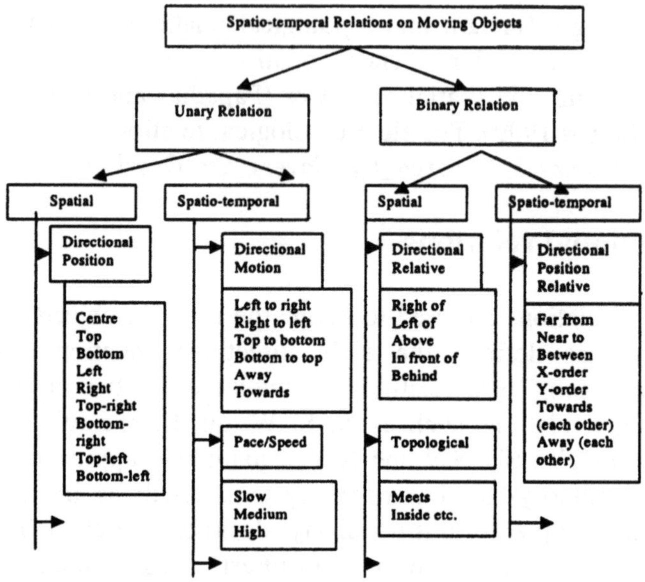

Figure 1: A few semantics describing spatio-temporal relations in video databases.

3. PROPOSED FRAMEWORK

3.1 Binary representation scheme

In this section, we describe a binary representation scheme for positions as defined in (Delis, Christos and Spiros 1999) for spatial reasoning (they are also called relations in literature). We first describe how spatial positions are represented using 1D binary string. The positions are defined using reference points. The reference points partition the given interval into a number of smaller intervals. Each partitioned interval is represented by a single bit. Thus, the number of bits required to represent positions depends on the reference points. A single reference point within a given interval yields two positions: "*left*" and "*right*". We could have infinite number of reference points that yield infinite number of positions. The question is how do we determine the number of reference points. There are no standard rules. We have considered two factors: high-level concepts and fuzzy concepts. The first approximation is that we should be able to describe each region (or partition) using semantic terms. In our case, we have considered nine semantic terms to describe positional relations. So based on the first approximation, we map nine terms (to be described later) to nine partitions shown in Figure 3. There does not exist distinct boundary between two concepts. In order to represent this fuzziness we introduce buffer (fuzzy) regions in between two adjacent semantic regions. The number of buffer regions depends on the level of preciseness (or the granularity of fuzzy membership values). In our case, we introduce one fuzzy region in between two adjacent semantic regions.

Let n be the number of reference points within a given interval. Then we need n+1 bits to represent positions. Let AB = $<X_1, X_2 .. ,X_n>$ be partitions of given interval (a,b) . Given an interval X, let X.l and X.r represent its left and right end points. X.l and X.r determine the boundaries for calculating the binary string.

Definition (Positional Binary String): *Assume a reference interval X. A resolution scheme AB (X) = $<X_1, X_2, ..., X_n>$ is a partition of X by (n-1) reference points where a position of an interval (x1,x2) over AB is a binary string $t_1,t_2,...,t_n$ such that t_i belongs to {0,1}, t_i="1" iff $X_i \cap [x_1, x_2] \neq$ Null and t_i = "0" otherwise, i=1,...,n, complying with the following constraints (i) it has exactly one substring of consecutive "1"'s and (ii) there is at least one t_i = "1" in a position "i" such that X_i is a non-zero length interval.*

The positional binary string is defined for a single object. That is, the positional binary string is calculated for each object rather than each image/frame. Thus, a calculated binary string provides a spatial position of an object in a particular dimension.

Definition (Spatio-temporal Positions) *The spatio-temporal relation of an object O consists of spatial and temporal positions $O<P_x, P_y, P_t>$, where $<P_x, P_y>$ gives the spatial positions and P_t the temporal position. $Pos(O<t>)$ = $<P_x, P_y>$ represents the spatial position of an object O at time t.*

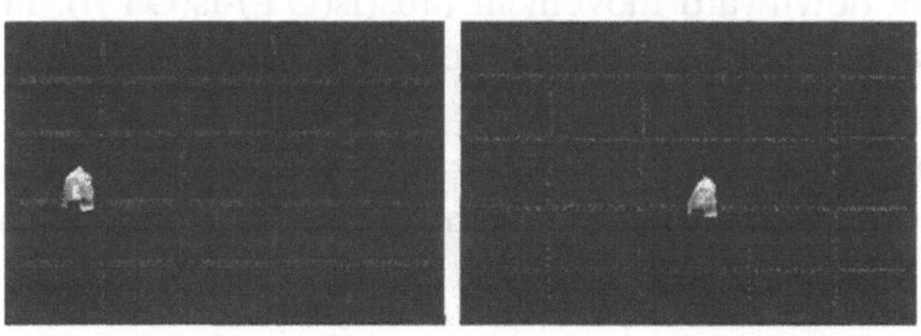

Figure 2: **The figure shows objects identified in the frames at time t_1 and t_2.**

Figure 2 shows objects identified in a video at time t_1 and t_2, respectively. The frame is partitioned into 25 different parts where each part represents a spatial position significant to human perception. We will elaborate about these partitions. The spatio-temporal relations of an object shown in the figure are represented as follows.

Pos(O<t_1>) = <10000, 11100>, Pos(O<t_2>) = <00100, 11100>

Being raw data these binary strings neither help users to express their queries nor are meaningful perceptually. In the later section, we describe techniques that map high-level concepts that are used to express spatio-temporal relations to these binary strings.

3.2 Similarity measurement

Video/image retrieval systems use similarity-based search which is usually often based on perceptual features. The similarity is measured using distance functions over feature values. In our scheme, spatio-temporal relations are expressed using binary strings as defined above. The question is how do we measure the similarity of binary strings. Our similarity measure is based on fuzzy logic. We first define some functions that are needed to define similarity measures.

rs(X) : this is a right shift function which returns the position of the rightmost "1" in a binary string X.

ls(X) : this is a left shift function which returns the position of the leftmost "1" in a binary string X.

Let *QX* and *QY* be the query binary strings representing positions in *X* and *Y* directions, respectively. Let *OX* and *OY* be the binary strings of an object in the database. The distance between these two are then defined as follows.

Dist(Q,O)=abs(rs(QX)–rs(OX)) + abs(rs(QY)-rs(OY)) + abs(ls(QX)-ls(OX)) + abs(ls(QY)-ls(OY))

The distance function is a combination of four different movements: distance in right movement (abs(rs(QX)–rs(OX))), distance in left movement (abs(ls(QX)-ls(OX))) , distance in upward movement (abs(rs(QY)-rs(OY))), and distance in downward movement (abs(ls(QY)-ls(OY))). In most of the circumstances, the right and upward movement would be equal and opposite to left and downward movement.

The similarity value of the query binary string Q with any database binary string O in fuzzy logic is given by (Nepal, Ramakrishna and Thom 1998)

$$\mu_Q(O) = \frac{(Max - Dist(O,R))}{Max}$$

where Max is the maximum possible distance between the two binary strings representing spatio-temporal positions, and $\mu_Q(O)$ is the similarity of a database binary string O with the query string Q or the membership value of the binary string O in a fuzzy set Q.

3.3 Spatio-temporal queries

In this section we describe how we can map the spatio-temporal relations defined in Section 2 to the positional strings given in binary representation.

3.3.1 Unary relations: spatial: directional Positions

The directional relations such as *North* and *South* discussed in Section 2 are used for spatial reasoning in large-scale spaces, i.e., spaces that cannot be seen or understood from a single point of view. Such relations are useful in application areas such as Geographical Information Systems. In case of still images and video frames, we mainly deal with small-scale spaces, i.e., spaces that can be seen or understood from a single point of view. Nextwe describe our qualitative (concept-based) spatial reasoning approach that can be used in multimedia databases.

In order to support such spatial reasoning, we provide a set of positional relations. We classify positional relations into two groups: (1) absolute and (2) relative. In unary directional positions, we only consider absolute positional relations. We define nine absolute positional spatial relations and their corresponding representations in binary strings are shown in Table 1 and Figure 3.

Relations	Symbol	QX	QY
Top	T	00100	00001
TopRight	TR	00001	00001
Right	R	00001	00100
BottomRight	BR	00001	10000
Bottom	B	00100	10000
BottomLeft	BL	10000	10000
Left	L	10000	00100
TopLeft	TL	10000	00001
Centre	C	00100	00100

Figure 1: Nine basic positional relations and their corresponding symbols, and X and Y binary strings of relations.

Figure 3 shows the partition of spatial space into semantic and fuzzy terms. The white regions correspond to specific regions labelled with appropriate semantic terms. Since the boundary between two semantic regions is not clear, we introduce a fuzzy region. We represent fuzzy regions by shaded areas in the figure. The number of fuzzy regions increases the possible membership values for an object to be at certain semantic position (i.e., the granularity of fuzzy values increases). The possible membership values with the partition shown in figure are 1, 0.75, 0.5, 0.25 and 0. If we introduce two fuzzy regions between adjacent semantic regions, then the possible membership values would be 1, 0.85, 0.68, 0.51, 0.34, 0.17 and 0.

Computation: If a query contains directional position relations such as Top and Bottom, the query string is generated as shown in Table 1. The database strings are then compared with the query string using the similarity measure defined above. For example, the similarity value for a query "Center" is 1 if an object appears at the region specified by "C" in the Figure 7. If the object appears in the shaded region between "C" and "B", then the similarity value would be 0.5. The qualitative semantic terms and their corresponding binary representation scheme are shown in Table 6.

Consider a query Q = Bottom-left (logo), where Bottom-left is a positional spatial qualitative term and logo is a visual feature (or object). This query is then converted to a binary form as Q = <QX, QY> = <00001, 10000>. Consider a database position string where the logo appears at the center is represented as O = <OX, OY> = <00100, 00100>. The similarity of O with Q is then calculated as follows.

rs(QX) = 1, ls(QX) = 5, rs(QY) = 5, ls(QY) = 1
rs(OX) = 3, ls(OX) = 3, rs(OY) = 3, ls(OY) = 3
Dist(O, R) = 2 + 2 + 2 + 2 = 8
Max = 4 + 4 + 4 + 4 = 16
The similarity of Q with X is then given by $\mu_Q(R)$ = (16-8)/16 = 0.5.

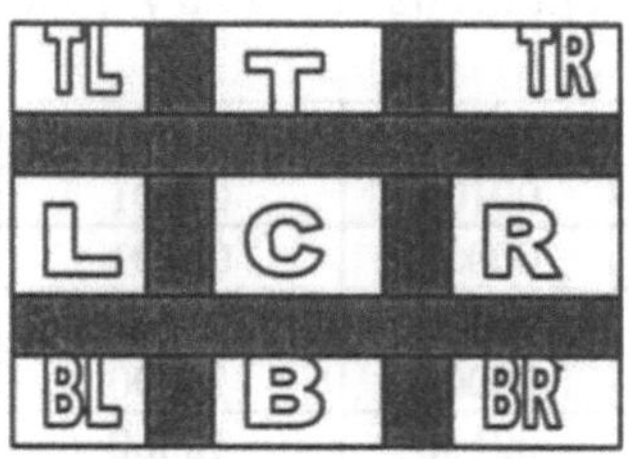

Figure 3: Nine positional relations in a two dimensional space

3.3.2 Unary relations: spatio-temporal: directional

Moving object is an important cue for video analysis and retrieval (Li, Ozsu and Szafron 1997, Sistla et al. 1997). Many applications such as video surveillance have used techniques that deal with moving object detection (Cedras and Shah 1995). The movement of a object can be described in terms of direction of movements. Next we develop a set of semantic query terms to describe the movement of objects and evaluate them under our binary representation scheme. The semantic terms defined here are applicable at the shot level.

Definition (spatial-factor): *this is the factor by which an object changes its spatial position over the duration of that shot. This change could either be induced by camera motion or by the object's intrinsic motion.*

We use this spatial-factor to compute various concepts and terms. We first compute the horizontal and vertical movements: left to right, right to left, top to bottom and bottom to top. Let OX_1 and OX_n be the X binary positional strings of the object O in the first and last frames of the shot. Let OY_1 and OY_n be the Y binary positional strings of the object in the first and last frames of the shot. Then the distances of right, left, top and bottom movements are calculated as follows.

Let the Right movement $D_1 = rs(OX_1)- rs(OX_n)$, Left Movement $D_2 = ls(OX_1) - ls(OX_n)$, Upward Movement $D_3 = rs(OY_1)-rs(OY_n)$, Downward Movement $D_4 = ls(OY_1)-ls(OY_n)$, Sim = the similarity value for the query, w_1 = weight assigned to the horizontal movement, w_2 = weight assigned to the vertical movement, D_1Max = maximum right movement, D_2Max = maximum left movement, D_3Max = maximum upward vertical movement, D_4Max = maximum downward vertical movement.

Consider a query Q = "left-to-right" that requests for objects moving from left to right. D_1 plays an important role in the right movement. Here, we consider that if an object does not have right movement ($D_1 < 1$), then its fuzzy membership value to the result set is 0. If it has a right movement (if $D_1 >= 1$), then the membership value is given by $\mu_Q(R)$.

$$\mu_Q(R) = \frac{abs(w_1.D_1 - w_2 \frac{(abs(D_3) + abs(D_4))}{2})}{(w_1.D_1Max + w_2 \frac{D_3Max + D_4Max}{2})}$$

There are various types of left to right movements. An object moving from left to right in a straight line (that is, without having any vertical motion) should have greater membership value than one that has vertical motion. We take this fact into account by considering D_3 and D_4 while evaluating the above membership function. The total effect of horizontal and vertical movements is controlled by their corresponding weights. That is, if w_2 is 0, then the membership function depends only on the total horizontal movement. Similarly, we calculate other directional unary relations such as "Right-to-left", "Bottom-to-top" and "Top-to-bottom" (Nepal and Srinivasan 2001). Next we demonstrate the capability of the proposed framework in representing and querying moving objects.

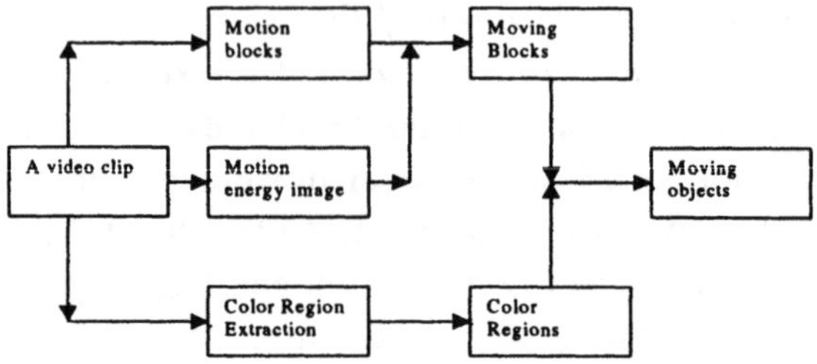

Figure 4: A diagram showing our approach of detecting/capturing moving objects.

4. EXPERIMENTAL RESULTS

4.1 Data set

We used MPEG-7 video content (etri_od_b.mpg) to evaluate the effectiveness of our approach. We identified 17 shots within the video. This can be done using one of the many shot detection algorithms. The first, middle and last frames of the shots are given in the appendix.

4.2 Moving Object detection algorithm

The block diagram of our approach for moving object detection is shown in Figure 4. While moving object detection is not the focus of this paper, this section is introduced to demonstrate how moving objects are modelled in this framework. The pre-processing stage uses a combination of visual features (such as colour and motion vectors) to generate regions for colours and motions and then combine them to obtain the moving objects present in a video clip. The algorithm detects moving object in a stationary background.

The colour regions extracted using 13 perceptually meaningful colours (Carson and Ogle 1996). We use the notion of uniform regions in images and treat each region as an object present in the image. Motion information in a MPEG video is based on 16 x 16 blocks (Gall 1995). We use such motion information to extract motion regions. Let C_{reg} and the M_{reg} be the sets colour and motion regions (or blocks), respectively. The object regions O_{reg} are then given by,

$$O_{reg} = | M_{reg} \cup C_{reg} |$$

where, $C_{reg} = \{C_1, C_2, \ldots, C_m\}$ where m is the number of color regions, $M_{reg} = \{M_1, M_2, \ldots, M_n\}$ where n is the number of motion regions. The moving object is then given by

$$MO_{reg} = \{C_i \mid th > 0.7 \wedge th = \frac{|M_j \cap C_i|}{|C_i|} > 0.7 : i = 1,..,m : j = 1,..n\}$$

where *th* is a threshold value. In our experiments, we calculate the threshold value in such a way that 70% of the colour region has motion, for it to be considered it as a region belonging to a moving object.

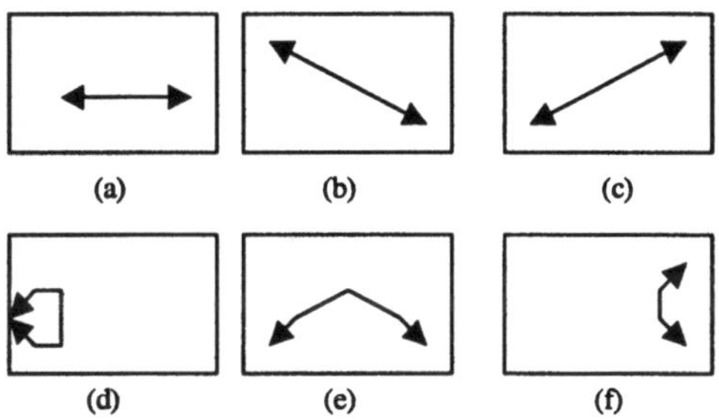

Figure 5: A set of example directions of object movements.

4.3 Results

We used Figure 3 as the basis for binary representation for each moving object. The shot number, frame number and their binary representation in both *X* and *Y* dimensions are stored in the database. A set of sample shots with first, middle and last frames are shown in Appendix A. In order to keep it simple, we discarded shots such as shot 3 having more than one object.

We posed a set of directional queries on our experimental data set. A summary of the query results is shown in Table 2. We explain the results in terms of a set of example directional object movements shown in Figure 5. Shots 1, 2, 5, 6, 7, 9, 10, 11, 12 15, 16 and 17 have movements of type Figure 9(a), either the object is moving from left to right or right to left. Shot 3 has multiple objects that we have not considered in this experiment. Shots 4 and 13 have movements of types Figures 9(c) and 9(e), respectively. As can be seen moving objects have both right to left and top to bottom motions. Shot 8 has a motion of type Figure 9(d) with no vertical movements. That is, our current modelling and querying framework does not recognize this kind of movements. This is a limitation of our framework. We plan to improve our query processing techniques in order to recognize such object movements. Our object recognition algorithm could not identify the motion of objects on shot 14. This is due to the fast movement of the object that gives false motion to background objects as well. This is a limitation of our object recognition algorithm rather than the modelling and querying framework presented in this paper. In our experiment, we discarded the effects of vertical movements on horizontal movements and vice versa by setting the weights to 0. We are further investigating the effects of weights and how to optimise such weights to get better similarity values.

Shot No	Left to Right $W_1=1$ $w_2=0$	Right to Left $w_1=1$ $w_2=0$	Top to Bottom $w_2=1$ $w_1=0$	Bottom to Top $w_2=1$ $w_1=0$
1	0.8	0.0	0.0	0.0
2	0.0	0.6	0.0	0.0
3	NA	NA	NA	NA
4	0.0	0.8	0.6	0.0
5	0.0	0.8	0.0	0.0
6	0.8	0.0	0.0	0.0
7	0.6	0.0	0.0	0.0
8	0.0	0.0	0.0	0.0
9	0.6	0.0	0.0	0.0
10	0.0	0.8	0.0	0.0
11	0.0	0.8	0.0	0.0
12	0.8	0.0	0.0	0.0
13	0.0	0.4	0.6	0.0
14	0.0	0.0	0.0	0.0
15	0.8	0.0	0.0	0.0
16	0.8	0.0	0.0	0.0
17	0.8	0.0	0.0	0.0

Table 2: A summary of shot level directional queries on the experimental data set.

We also posed a set of directional positional queries for all shots. We explain a set of query results here. We posed three directional position queries "left", "right" and "centre" into the database. We recorded the similarity values of each frame from all shots for all three different queries. We choose three shots to explain the results as shown in Figure 6. Figure 6(a) shows the similarity values of each frame in shot 1, where the object is moving from left to right. When an object is having smooth left to right movement, the ideal result would be the one shown in Figure 6(b). Similarly, Figures 6(c) shows the result for the shot 5, where the object is moving from right to left.

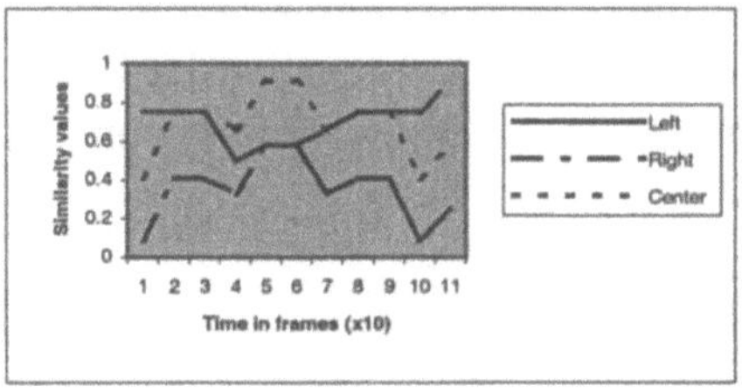

(a)

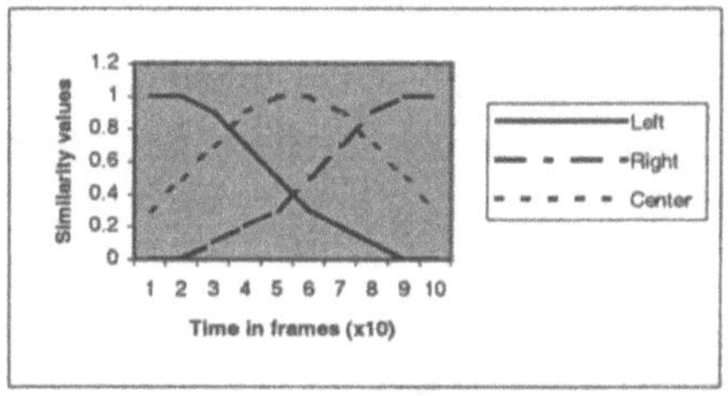

(b)

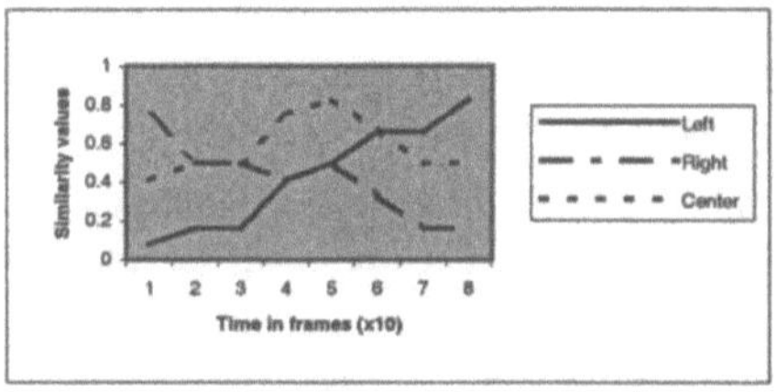

(c)

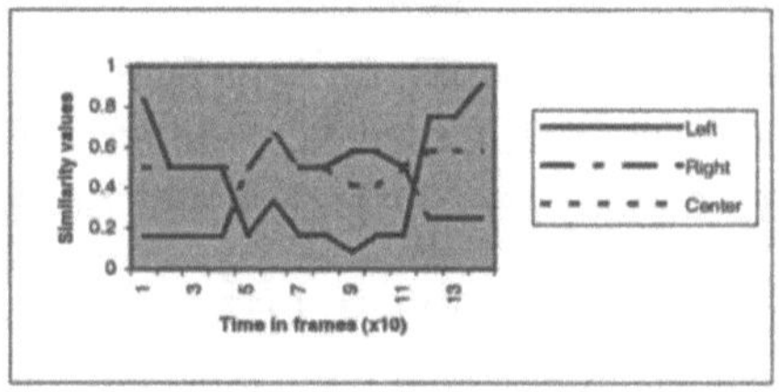

(d)

Figure 11: A set of results for the positional semantic terms left, right and center.

Figure 6 (d) shows the results of three positional queries for each frame in shot 8. We have seen in Figure 10 that shot 8 has similarity values 0.0 for all movement queries like left to right. As we can see in the figure, the similarity values for left and right queries for the first and last frames are almost the same. That means the position of the object in the first and last frame is the same though the position of the object is changed within the shot. This and other similar questions related with movements need to be answered; for example are they important to users? What kinds of terms do people use to express such movements in real life? And how do we evaluate such queries? We leave these queries for our future research.

5. CONCLUSIONS

In this paper we have presented a framework for modelling and querying video databases using spatio-temporal relations. We provided a set of semantic terms that can be used to describe unary and binary spatio-temporal relations. However, our focus in this paper was on a set of unary relations. We proposed a binary string based representation scheme for positions, which offers an efficient technique for mapping high-level semantic terms to low-level feature. We presented a fuzzy logic based approach for computing similarity of spatial positional and spatio-temporal directional semantic terms. We reported the results of our experiment on a sample video from the MPEG-7 data set. Our future work involves mapping other high-level semantics to binary spatio-temporal relations in order to support concept-based querying.

REFERENCES

ALLEN, J.F (1983) Maintaining Knowledge about Temporal Intervals. *Communication of the ACM*. 1983. pp 832-843.

BARAL, C., GONZALEZ, G., AND SON, T (1998). Conceptual Modeling and Querying in Multimedia Databases. *Multimedia Tools and Applications, Vol 7*, pp 37-66, 1998.

BOLLE, R.M., YEO, B.L., AND YEUNG M. (1997) Video Query and Retrieval, in SATTAR, A. (Ed.) *Advanced Topics in Artificial Intelligence,* Lecture Notes in Artificial Intelligence 1342, pp 13-24, 1997.

CARSON, C. AND OGLE, V.E. (1996). Storage and retrieval of feature data for a very large online image collection. *Bulletin of the IEEE Computer Society Technical Committee on Data Engineering, Volume 19, Number 4, Pages 19-27*, December 1996.

CEDRAS, C. AND SHAH, M. (1995) Motion-Based Recognition: A Survey. *Image and Vision Computing,* Volume 13 Number 2 March 1995 pages 129-155.

DELIS, V., CHRISTOS, M. AND SPIROS, S. (1999) A Provably Efficient Computational Model for Approximate Spatiotemporal Retrieval. *ACM GIS* 1999. pp. 40-46.

EGENHOFER, M. and FRANZOSA, R. (1991). Point-set topological spatial relations. International Journal of Geographic Information Systems, 5(2):161—174, 1991

FLICKNER, M. , SAWHNEV, S., NIBLACK, W., ASHLEY, J., HUANG, O., DOM, B., GORKANI, M., HAFNER, J., LEE, D., PETKOVIC, D., and STEELE, D. (1995) Query by Image and Video Content: The QBIC System. Computer. Vol 28, No. 9, 1995, pages 23-32.

FRANK, A.U. (1996) Qualitative Spatial Reasoning: Cardinal Directions as an Example. *International Journal of Geographic Information Systems,* Vol. 10 (3), 269-290

GALL L. (1995) MPEG: A Video Compression Standard for Multimedia Applications. *Communications of the ACM* Volume 34 Number 2 April 1995 pages 47-58, 1996.

HAMPAPUR, A. et al. (1997) Virage Video Engine. *SPIE Vol. 3022*. pp 188-198, 1997.

HJELSVOLD, R. AND MIDTSTRAUM, R. (1994) Modelling and Querying Video Data. *Proceedings of the 20th VLDB Conference*, Santiago, Chile, 1994.

KUO, T.C.T. AND CHEN A.L.P. (2000) Content-Based Query Processing for Video Databases. *IEEE Transaction on Multimedia Vol 2* No 1, March 2000.

LI, J.Z., OZSU, M. T., AND SZAFRON, D. (1997) Modeling of Moving Objects in a Video Database. ICMCS, 1997, pages 336-343.

NEPAL, S., RAMAKRISHNA, M.V., and THOM, J.A.(1998) A Fuzzy System for Content Based Image Retrieval. 2nd *IEEE International Conference on Intelligent Processing Systems* (IEEE ICISP98), Gold Coast, Australia, August 4-7, 1998. Pages 335-339

NEPAL, S., AND SRINIVSAN, U. (2001). Spatio-temporal modelling and querying video databases using high-level concepts, CSIRO Mathematical and Information Sciences, Technical Report Number 2001/66, 2001.

PAPADIAS, D. AND DELIS, V. (1997) "Relation-Based Similarity", In *Proceedings of the 5th ACM Workshop on GIS*, Las Vegas, ACM Press, 1997.

SISTLA, A. P., WOLFSON, O., CHAMBERLAIN, S., AND DAO, S. (1997) Modeling and Querying Moving Objects, ICDE 1997, pages 422-432.

Appendix a

Shot 1

Shot 3

Shot 4

Shot 8

Shot 13

PERFECT LINE SIMPLIFICATION FOR VISUALIZATION IN DIGITAL CARTOGRAPHY

Sham Prasher
School of Information Technology and Electrical Engineering
University of Queensland
sham@itee.uq.edu.au

Abstract Spatial data is often voluminous and, as a result, difficult to process or manipulate efficiently. In digital cartography spatial data is presented to provide accurate information regarding real-world geography. However because available data may often exceed that which is needed, techniques for the reduction of the data load have long been a focus of study. Cartographic generalization looks at reducing the amount of map data while preserving the quality of visually conveyed information. We look at current techniques of cartographic generalization, simplification algorithms in particular, and show their dependence on unreliable geometric properties can cause imperfect results. We introduce an algorithm that produces visually perfect simplifications of spatial objects in linear time where previous algorithms have failed to do so. We show how the algorithm can be used with standard co-ordinate data and as well as z-value data.

Keywords: simplification, cartographic generalization, spatial data

1. INTRODUCTION

Generalization is the process of reproducing images in reduced versions whilst maintaining as much visual quality and convey as much meaning as the original. Similarly cartographic generalization is the process of reproducing maps at smaller scales (i.e. different levels of detail) while retaining as much information as the resulting image will allow. Where cartographers traditionally performed this task manually, the advent of modern computing power and geographic information systems has brought promise to automating the process.

Automatic cartographic generalization techniques have been the focus of study for the past 30 years especially with the recent growth of geographic information systems. The aim of cartographic generalization is to derive small scale, less detailed, maps from larger scale maps. Automated generalization of spatial information should simulate the work of the human cartographer [9]. This condition poses the greatest challenge in all attempts of automation. The reason is that processes that allow human vision to distinguish relationships between buildings, rivers, roads and other topographic elements are difficult to identify and classify, let alone computerize. With spatial data becoming more widespread there is a growing need for efficient data manipulation (generalization) to satisfy various commercial uses. This need is particularly high in online systems where the processing and retrieval time of data are correlated with quality of service.

Typically spatial data are stored as images in either raster or vector format. The raster format stores the content of each pixel of an image individually. Storage is higher but the image is complete and ready for display. Spatial databases are commonly used to store and manage vector data. Vector data includes only information on objects within the image that are put together to form a complete picture. Storage requirements are lower but some computation is needed to assemble the picture. Vector data (points) are usually stored in some co-ordinate system format such as (x,y) grid values, longitude-latitude or Lambert Azimuthal coding for geographic data. Alternatively z-values [12], which are generated from the regular decomposition of space, can also be used to describe spatial data. The development of efficient ways to encode, index and manipulate z-values has proven them useful in many spatial database applications. Although we look at the possible use of z-values, a full explanation of them goes beyond the scope of this paper.

In our work the vector format is preferred because it allows for easier image manipulation and can be cached more readily for future use, such as zooming and panning by using cached data.

Generalising maps has thus far proven non-trivial. Like many other tasks it requires complex human reasoning regarding the visual and topological relationships between multiple elements. Cartographic generalization deals with making sense of spatial data at the macro level. As a result numerous processes are employed to make an image that may be overloaded with detail, visually legible during generalization. Examples include amalgamation and smoothing. Non-spatial operators like SQL *'selection'* statements on spatial layers can also be used to remove unwanted clutter such as *'all minor roads'*. An important factor in automated generalization is deciding which techniques, if any, to use or are necessary. The choice usually depends on context and exactly what kind of result is desired. Different kinds of manipulation can mean different information is presented in the final image. The scope of this paper takes the approach of geometric generalization [7]. The focus is solely on simplification of elements within a map at the micro level. The issue here is reducing the amount of data required to represent objects in an already legible image.

Our goal is to produce simplifications of cartographic objects, stored as spatial data, that look as close as possible to their originals. For this purpose we introduce the concepts of *perfect generalization* and *minimal perfect* generalization (PG/MPG). In the section 2 we provide an overview of research to date in this area. Section 3 introduces the concepts of PG and MPG. Section 4 outlines a methodology for PG. The paper is concluded, and notes on future work are given in section 5.

2. BACKGROUND

Generalized images are usually produced with a certain level of accuracy. With current techniques not being perfect, this level may vary between situations and is what warrants the utilisation of several different correctional and supporting techniques. Among several different approaches to the problem, line simplification algorithms are one of the most fundamental. A number of such algorithms have been developed and refined over the past few decades. One of the most widely used, the Douglas Peucker algorithm [3] works by initially building a baseline connecting the first and last points. The distance of a constructed line joining each point to the baseline perpendicularly is measured as the selection factor. The point with the longest distance is kept and included in a new baseline. The process iterates until a set number of points are selected or points fail to exceed some pre-defined threshold distance from the baseline.

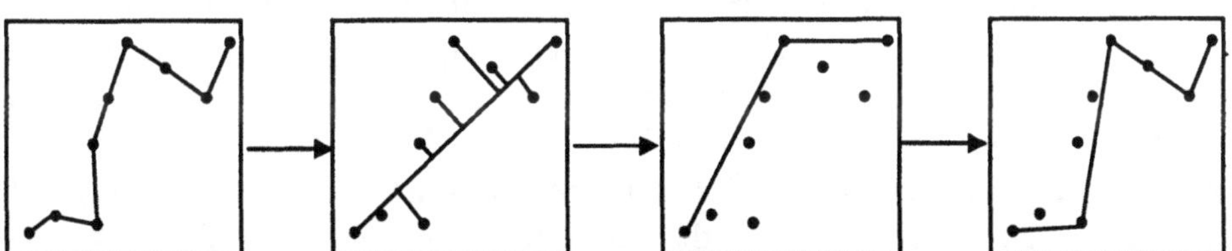

(a) Original line. (b) Calculated distances from baseline. (c) Baseline after 1 point is added. (d) Baseline after 3 points are added.

Figure 1 Douglas Peucker Line Simplification

A similar approach is taken by the line-length [1] and angular-change [9] algorithms. The first eliminated points iteratively based on how little difference their absence makes. This difference is measured as the distance between a point's two (previous and next) neighbouring points. The point whose neighbours form the shortest line is eliminated. Similarly the angular-change algorithm eliminates points based on what change of angle neighbouring points will produce. The notable issue with these is that their criteria alone cannot determine the actual shape of the line or guarantee the accuracy of the result. Taking it one step further, the Visvalingam Whyatt [13] algorithm calculates area changes before and after point elimination. Again this single criterion is not very useful, as distance and line shape cannot be derived from a single area measure. Like the line-length and angular-change approaches this algorithm makes an assumption that the minimal measure of its metric (i.e. area displacement) correlates to a minimal change in the polyline's shape.

Individually these algorithms are easily tested based on how well their results resemble the original image. However testing between algorithms, and determining which is the best, is difficult because each is usually evaluated using different metrics [14]. As with the Douglas Peucker algorithm these techniques do not always preserve the original shape of objects. The main reason the shape is often compromised is the algorithms only consider the vector properties of line elements meaning that no consideration is given to how the simplification will affect the look of the data once mapped to a digital display. This also contributes to the reason why conversions between vector and raster formats are error-prone. Although there are a number of refining and smoothing techniques [10] that are designed to handle such after-effects, they are themselves imperfect and still cannot completely prevent the chance for error.

Another algorithm designed by Li and Openshaw [8] considers the equivalent raster representation of given vector data during the simplification process. The algorithm uses the concept of the Smallest Visible Object (SVO) as the finest cartographic detail visible by a human user. In raster format this equates to a single pixel. A list of points is first given as the polyline to be simplified. Then a layer of pixels is placed over the vector data. The pixels are defined at the resolution of the digital environment onto which the resulting simplified data is to be displayed. Wherever a pixel contains a point from the given list, the centre of that pixel is returned as a new point in the simplified line, which is then used to represent all points within that pixel. Another difference is that new points are returned, not one from the original list.

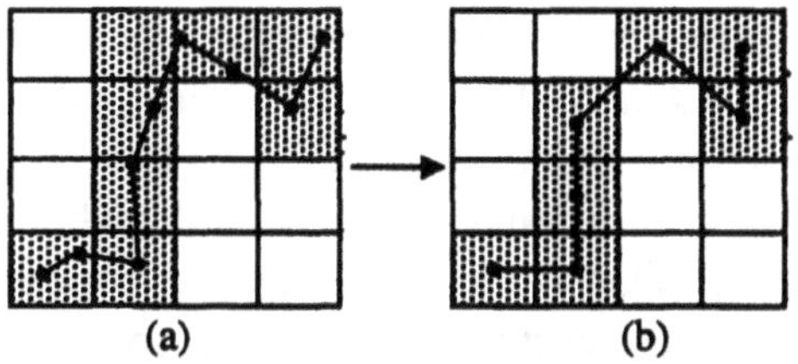

Figure 2 (a) The original image rendered to pixels (represented as shaded blocks) and (b) the Li Openshaw simplification of the same data rendered at the same resolution.

There is no guarantee the original shape is preserved because newly created points govern the simplified line's shape (3b), not original ones. Revisiting the Douglas Peucker algorithm we can see how inaccuracies can occur. Given vector displacement as a point discriminator there is no particular vector distance (from the baseline) that is suitable for all points at that resolution. If this distance, or tolerance, was set to lower than a resolution's pixel width then the simplified line could be identical to the original. It also does not consider cases where points within this tolerance are located in different pixels because the baseline itself passes close to a pixel border. The other geometry-based algorithms suffer the same drawback.

Other trends in digital cartography include scale-indexing techniques [5] that take a paradigmatically opposite approach by using pre-processing to construct indexes. This allows easy scale-based access to data instead of employing on-the-fly generalization algorithms. The issue with using such methods is that pre-computation cannot easily anticipate, therefore accommodate all possible uses of the data by users, which themselves may change. To accommodate large changes often recomputation of the entire index is required.

An important goal of generalization is to preserve topology that often can convey most of an image's meaning. If these relationships cannot be shown given a purely geometric transformation using polyline simplification, other techniques mentioned earlier can be used. Smoothing, amalgamation, exaggeration, collapse and displacement are common ways of modifying the resulting image to convey important or relevant information. Works presented in [6][15] discuss criteria that must be satisfied in order to guarantee some level of quality from the generalization. The involvement of these techniques also usually calls for manual intervention and so has led to the conceptualisation of large complex frameworks [10, 2, 11] for generalising. This can complicate things more than is desirable, involving additional processes, time and resources to what may be intended as an efficient procedure. One evaluation method [6] in particular uses a similar concept to the Li Openshaw algorithm for correctness checking. It works by overlaying a gird on the result and measuring whether the generalization process was done consistently throughout the original map by comparing levels of 'clutter' within each grid cell. In this paper we focus on simplification and avoid additional 'correctional' techniques that may add unnecessary complexity. Our work builds on the concept of overlaying a raster grid of pixels over vector spatial data to serve as a guide for simplification.

3. DEFINITION OF PG AND MPG

The aim of PG/MPG is to generate a set of spatial data, which is visually indistinguishable, in a digital environment, to the larger original dataset on which it was based. Therefore it can provide exactly the same visual experience at a fraction of the storage requirement and, hence, transmission time or processing cost.

First we must clarify the use of scale and resolution. Scale is the term used by cartographers to state how far reduced elements on a map are from their real life counterparts. Since maps are reduced images of real life areas the scale factor can reach well into the millions. A small scale corresponds to a highly detailed map whereas a large scale denotes lower detail. The term resolution is often used interchangeably with scale, sometimes to the point of confusion. In this paper resolution is used to the detail at which some display hardware (i.e. CRT/LCD) renders spatial data. A high or low resolution corresponds to high or low display detail respectively.

When data, stored at a particular scale, is rendered to some physical display there is no guarantee that the scale and screen resolution are exactly match. That is if the screen resolution is low then only some of the data is made physically visible (figure 4). Conversely at high resolutions a larger amount of data can be handled and viewed. Ideally some automated decision-making would be used to determine the best amount of data to use and display at a particular resolution. This leads to the concept of *perfect generalization.*

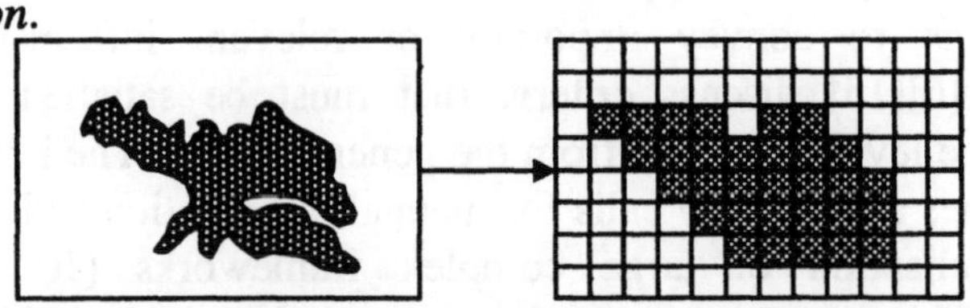

Figure 3 Original data mapped to a low resolution.

If a simplification algorithm modifies a dataset and that modified data set renders to the computer screen an identical picture to that which is rendered by the original dataset, then that simplification algorithm is said to be *perfect*. More precisely, given a set of data d that is rendered to a screen at a particular resolution r an image i is produced. We note this as $ren(d, r)=i$. If d is initially generalised by some simplification method to a reduced data set d' then rendered to r another image, i' is produced; $ren(d', r)=i'$. If i' looks exactly the same as i, $(i'=i)$, using the same display and resolution, then the generalization is said to be perfect. More formally, if $d' \subseteq d \wedge i = i'$. In some situations it may be necessary to replicate the same visual effect of an image, as much as possible, at a lower resolution. The change equates to a transition from a high to a low-resolution image requested by a user or forced by some hardware restrictions such as a low resolution WAP screen. *Perfect* simplification occurs when every pixel rendered in the original image is represented by some 'equivalent' lower resolution pixel on the output device. Also no pixels at the lower resolution are rendered that are not represented by some pixel in the original image. This follows the definition $d' \subseteq d \wedge i = i'$ as closely as the output resolution is able. Section 5.2 covers this point in more detail.

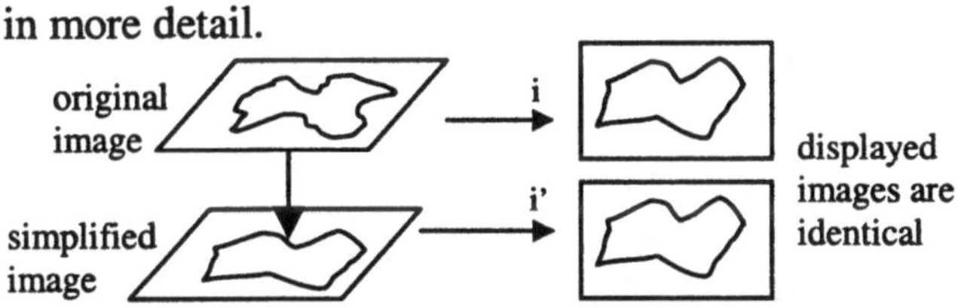

Figure 4 Perfect generalization.

The problem with *perfect generalization* is that an algorithm that takes a vector object and returns the same vector object is considered ideal or perfect. The concept of *minimal perfect generalization* is introduced to express the fact that an algorithm is preferable if it greatly reduces the size of data needed to represent an object. *Minimal perfect generalization* refers to a generalization that uses the minimal number of points of d to construct a *perfect generalization* d'.

So if $(d' \subseteq d \wedge i = i') \wedge (\neg\exists p, p\in d' \bullet (d' - p) = d'' \wedge ren(d'', r) = i'' = i)$ then d' is minimal.

4. PERFECT GENERALIZATION ALGORITHM

4.1 Assumptions and notations

For data storage we use a single relational table containing one field for object IDs and another for the object's geometry. We specify the geometry of a single object as a sequence of spatial (x,y) coordinates using Oracle's

SDO_GEOMETRY spatial data type. Alternatively points could be stored as z-values using quadtree coding [12]. The object may be closed (polygon) or open (polyline). An index is placed on the table to allow spatial querying[1].

We must make note that the data structures and algorithms provided in this paper serve only to provide an example of the PG and MPG methods as applied to data points. Since such structures are usually defined based on what queries are expected of the database [4] they are subject to change with context.

Given a spatial object O that is comprised of a set of points in 2D space; i.e. $O = \{t_1...t_k\}$. O may represent either a closed polygon or an open polyline. In either case points can be retrieved in a linear sequence. A function F applied to O will generate an object O' comprised of a set of points such that $F(O) = O' = \{q_1...q_m\}$ where $O' \subseteq O$. In other words $F(O)$ is a simplification of O.

The purpose of the MPG is to render the original object to a display at a given resolution using only a fraction of its data. Therefore we must consider the display of objects in terms of resolution. A small resolution is limited to low detail whereas high resolution allows for high detail. A resolution r is required for the original object O to be rendered with no visual loss of detail. To render O to some display with a resolution r', such that $r' < r$, with no visual loss of detail, O can be generalised to object O' to reduce the amount of needed data. First r must be mapped to r':

Using r we can define a resolution $r = [r_x \times r_y]$; eg 640×480. The range of r must cover the spatial extent of some digital display (such as an LCD screen), which can be given as $[ext_x \times ext_y]$ and is specified in some metric measurement. The points in O cover a spatial range sr = [sr-x_{max}, sr-y_{max}, sr-x_{min}, sr-y_{min}] such that $0 \leq$ [sr-x_{max}, sr-x_{min}] $\leq ext_x$ and $0 \leq$ [sr-y_{max}, sr-y_{min}] $\leq ext_y$. Each point in O has spatial coordinates (x, y) such that $0 \leq x \leq ext_x$ and $0 \leq y \leq ext_y$.

The resolution r is made up of a grid of pixels. Each pixel p in r has its own spatial extent. That is $\forall p \in r \Rightarrow p_{ext} = [x_{max}, y_{max}, x_{min}, y_{min}]$ such that $0 \leq [x_{max}, x_{min}] \leq ext_x$ and $0 \leq [y_{max}, y_{min}] \leq ext_y$. Each pixel essentially covers a square area having four edges and four vertices[2]. The latter is drawn from the pixel's spatial extent and is given as [p-x_{max}, p-y_{max}], [p-x_{min}, p-y_{min}], [p-x_{min}, p-y_{max}], [p-x_{max}, p-y_{min}]. Vertices and edges may belong to multiple neighbouring pixels.

The width length of a pixel s is given by (ext_x/r_x). The ext_y does not need to be included because it is assumed that pixels cover square areas and that a given resolution is always properly scaled to fit the display area. Therefore

[1] The exact index technique is not vital to the paper's focus; for instance we assume an R-Tree is used.

[2] While a pixel is a dot we represent its extent as the square area covered by its dimensions.

$(r_x \times s) = ext_x$ and $(r_y \times s) = ext_y$. For example if $ext_x = 1000$ and $ext_y = 500$, and $r_x = 500$ then r_y must be 250.

Next r must be converted to the desired resolution r'. To do this we define $[r'_x, r'_y]$ on r' such that $r'_x < r_x$ and $r'_y < r_y$, and $(r'_x \times s) = ext_x$ and $(r'_y \times s) = ext_y$. The desired resolution spans the extent of the display because the number of pixels is reduced hence they are a different size. In r' a pixel's width is given by (ext_x/r'_x).

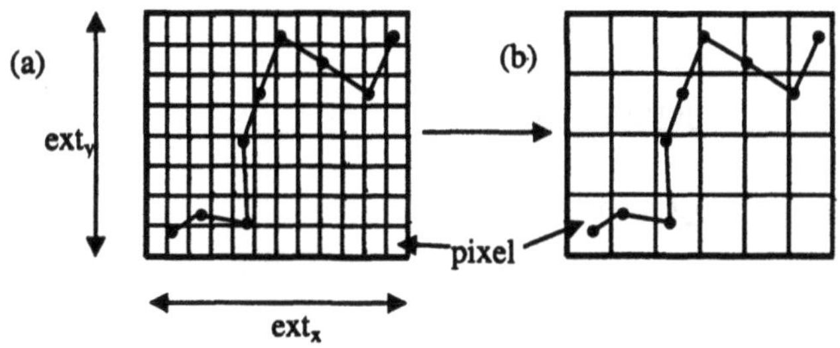

Figure 5 Grid over object O at resolution r (a) and r' (b).[3]

Pixels in r' have the same properties as those in r except they cover different spatial extents.

4.2 Method

The preliminary step gives us a foundation similar to that used by the Li Openshaw algorithm. Knowing how the spatial data would appear on display serves as the guide to simplifying O into O'. In the following algorithm we use a *transform* function on spatial (x,y) co-ordinates to transform the resolution of data points to that of the overlaid grid. We define another function *truncate* that performs the same transformation except on z-values. The function can be used for both simplification at the same resolution or simplification to a lower resolution as mentioned in section 3. Like the Li Openshaw method, the PG algorithm requires a single pass through the point sequence thus operating in $O(n)$ time.

<u>Algorithm Parameters:</u>
Q: A single object of the data table in the form ObjectID, geometry($x1,y1$, ... , xn,yn).
ObjectID(x): The xth point in the object's geometry.
R: An empty object of the form ObjectID, geometry($x1,y1$, ... , xn,yn).

---

[3] We show the grid of resolution r at a slightly coarser level than it actually is for legibility. Realistically r would be set at a finer level in order to describe the polyline in the illustration.

transform(*a*): Function that changes a point *a*, specified at the original resolution *r*, to its equivalent value *b*, which is specified at a lower resolution *r'*. For example given *r*=[1000 × 500], *r'* = [500 × 250] and *a*=(500, 250) then *b*=(250,125).
truncate(*a*, *x*): Function that removes the *x* rightmost digits of a z-value *a* thus changing *a* to a z-value of a larger scale. This function can be used interchangeably with *transform(a)* if z-values are used instead of (x,y) co-ordinates.

<u>Algorithm: Perfect Generalization</u>

```
begin
 //put the first point of Q into R
   R = ObjectID(1);
   For each subsequent point i:
     //check if the point is in the same pixel as the previous point
     if transform(i) = transform(i-1) then
       //if the next point is not in the same pixel keep this point
       if transform(i+1) ≠ transform(i-1)
         R=R+(ObjectID(i))
       else
         R=R+(ObjectID(i))
       end if
    go to next point i=i+1
loop
Check if first point can be removed, joining its predecessor and successor.
end
```

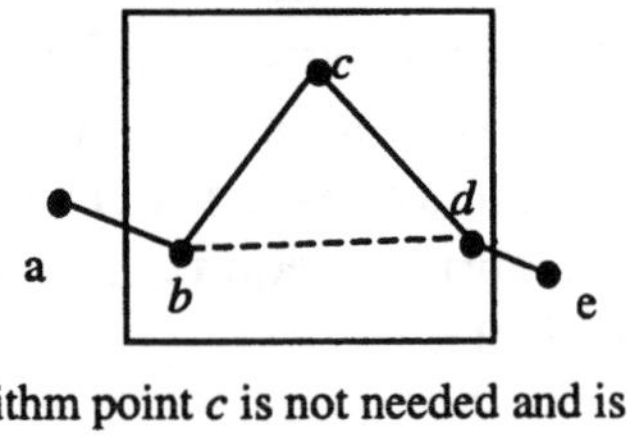

Figure 6 From the algorithm point *c* is not needed and is removed, linking *b* to *d*.

Using z-values allows quick conversion from one resolution to another. The drawback of z-values is they can only be truncated to a discrete number of specific resolutions. Each digit truncated sets the value to a different resolution. If the display resolution *r'* does not match one of these resolutions then the result may have to be stretched or condensed slightly to fit the output display.

To begin with the first point is kept as a starting point. The algorithm eliminates points that form lines within a pixel since their inter-connections become insignificant when the whole pixel is rendered. Lines that enter or exit different pixels, i.e. the endpoints occur in two different pixels after transformation, are kept. The reason is that these lines' directions contribute to preserving the image's overall appearance by determining which pixels are covered or crossed by the object, as follows:

1. The direction of lines entering and exiting two different pixels is determined by the position of their endpoints within those pixels.
2. Given 3 points *A*, *B* and *C* the lines *AB* and *BC* are formed. The elimination of the exiting point *B*, forming a new line *AC*, produces no change if *AC* does not cross different pixels than those crossed by *AB* and *BC*. Otherwise the visualization of *AC* is different to *ABC*.
3. We denote the set of pixels crossed by a line *l* as P(*l*). Therefore elimination of point B is where P(*AC*) = P(*AB*) ⊕ P(*BC*).
4. A line *l* crosses a pixel edge or vertex at a specific point called an intersection point or IP.[4]
5. An intersection point, being on a border can touch multiple pixels. For a given IP these pixels are denoted P(IP).
6. Given any pixel and some point IP*x* occurring on its border there can be up to eight different instances of P(IP*x*), four for the sides and four for each vertex of the pixel. If we move an IP *x* along a pixel border we can see that encountering any vertex will cause a change in the set P(*x*).
7. For any 2 intersection points IP1 and IP2 where P(IP1)=P(IP2) they must lie on either the same pixel side or vertex.
8. Conversely for any IP1, IP2 where P(IP1)≠P(IP2) then one of the following must hold:
    - IP1 is on a pixel edge *e1*, IP2 is on a pixel edge *e2* and *e1*≠*e2*.
    - IP1 is on any pixel edge, IP2 is on any pixel vertex.
    - IP2 is on any pixel edge, IP1 is on any pixel vertex.
9. Using the lines *AB*, *BC*, *AC* the instance of a pixel vertex occurring on the edge of or within the triangle *ABC* denotes that P(*AC*) ≠ P(*AB*) ⊕ P(*BC*).
10. If a pixel vertex is not found in the triangle *ABC* then *AC* touches on or passes through the same pixels as the polyline *ABC*.

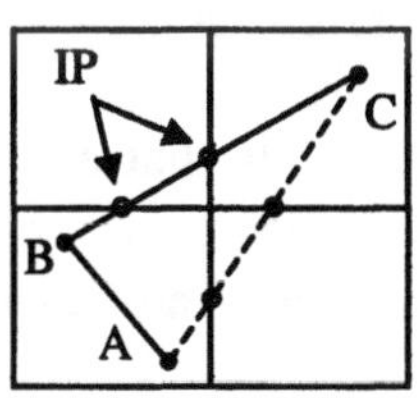

[4] Crosses means travelling from one pixel into another, touching on a pixel side or vertex does not count as crossing.

Figure 7 B is not removed as AC will render different pixels to AB and BC together.

To ensure that the shape of the polyline is not compromised the PG method automatically retains all entering and exiting lines for each pixel. Another benefit to this is that is creates the base of a hierarchical data structure. The data can thus be used for future image manipulation that is commonly used in digital cartography; i.e. zooming in and out, and panning.

4.3 Minimal Perfect Generalization

Given R from the PG algorithm we wish to further reduce it by eliminating points that are not crucial to preserve the visual quality of the image. The MPG simplification follows the definition given in Section 3 that the simplified line must only occupy or cross pixels at r' containing pixels that are originally rendered at r.

The point sequence is processed from head to tail. Given a point p_i and another point p_n where $n > i+1$ all intermediate points p_m, where $i<m<n$, are checked for possible elimination. To do so we must ensure that the set of pixels crossed by p_i-p_n is equal to the cumulative set of pixels crossed by all line segments that occur between p_i and p_n. Or $P(p_i - p_n) = P(p_i - p_{(i+1)}) \oplus \ldots \oplus P(p_{(n-1)} - p_n)$. To obtain the best simplification p_i must be checked with each subsequent point to the end of the point sequence. The last pair p_i-p_n that satisfies the above equality condition is taken as the simplified line segment. This reduction is maximised because there exists no point p_q where $q>n$ such that $P(p_i - p_q) = P(p_i - p_{(i+1)}) \oplus \ldots \oplus P(p_{(q-1)} - p_q)$. The process is then repeated beginning with p_n. The process ends when p_n is the last point in the sequence. The result is a simplified polyline S. If the polyline is originally open then the MPG is complete. However if the object is a closed polygon then the first point p_i has not been checked and may not be needed. Starting with the endpoint p_n a final pass is performed on the now simplified point sequence S using the same equality condition mentioned earlier. One problem that arises from this approach is that MPG simplification S is resultant from using P_i as the starting point. Given any other starting point in the original sequence it is possible that a different simplification S' is produced that has fewer points than S.

This naive approach demands that every possible permutation of S must be computed, and the smallest one chosen. However the added computation makes such an approach inefficient and leaves the door open for better solutions to MPG.

4.4 Perfect Visualization

Once the simplified object *O'* is obtained it can be rendered to the screen. However, rendering points that are specified at the end resolution *r'* will not produce the desired effect of PG (figure 11b). Points from different simplifications may be located in different parts of a pixel, but when rendering the only information that can be passed to the rendering device is which pixels to render. This is because a pixel is the smallest definable graphical feature on the device, or a SVO. This defeats the purpose of PG retaining original points since it is the exact location of points within those pixels, and their connection to other such points, that determine the perfect generalization.

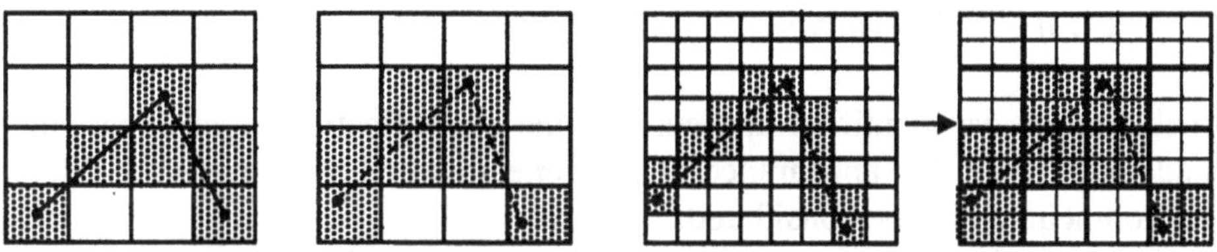

(a) A line simplified by the Li-Openshaw method.

(b) The same line in (a) simplified by PG.

(c) Rendering of the PG line in (b) at *r*.

(d) Scaling of (c) from *r* (thin grid) to *r'*(thick grid).

Figure 8 The direct rendering to *r'* of a Li Openshaw simplification (a), and of an MPG simplification (b).

An extra processing step is needed in order for *O'* to be rendered accurately. The image must first be rendered at the original resolution, then be scaled to *r'* using some image scaling operation. Figure 11c illustrates a simple example of the MPG line displayed at a resolution double that of r'[5]. When scaled back to *r* in 11d those pixels in which *r'* resolution pixels are contained are rendered. This results in the same pixels being rendered as those in figure 9b.

As a result of PG the shapes of individual objects are preserved as well as the final resolution r' will permit. That is objects occupy the same area they did originally except are represented by pixels of a coarser resolution covering this area. At r' these pixels are equivalent to a Li Openshaw SVO. It does not matter where in each SVO the original data was located, since anything inside a SVO is visually indistinguishable. The important thing is that all of the SVOs the object originally occupied are

[5] This resolution is used instead of the line's actual resolution only for display purposes, the latter being too fine to demonstrate with.

retained. This is where the PG method differs to the Li Openshaw algorithm; the result will not omit areas originally covered (figure 3b) or cover new areas that did not contain the original data.

Topological relationships that exist in the same SVO, are technically not preserved since they are too small to display. Similarly relationships such as the disjointedness of two objects that occur in adjacent SVOs cannot be shown because the gap between them is too small (i.e. it at least needs 1 SVO between the object SVOs to be represented). In this sense topological relationships will only be kept if they are large enough to be visually significant on the display resolution. The full effect of PG on topological relationships required further study.

5. CONCLUSIONS

In this paper we identified that current line simplification algorithms were inadequate when the appearance of the generalization, rendered in a digital environments, must be considered.

We introduced the concepts of *perfect generalization* and *minimal perfect generalization*, designed with the specific goal of generalising spatial data to a compact solution without compromising visual quality. A way to achieve perfect generalization in linear time using standard spatial data is provided. These methods are targeted for use particularly in online (GIS) applications where hardware restrictions for efficient data reduction and accuracy. Simplification algorithms work on whole datasets, which are first fetched from some database. An alternate approach to improving efficiency is the possible use of spatial database structures (eg. indexes, z-values) and operations to reduce the data before it is sent for processing by generalization algorithms. The development of support mechanisms for this approach is a topic of further study.

When discussing generalization of an image at a particular scale to suit a certain resolution the density of data has a direct effect on the application of PG. In a worst case scenario very sparse data that cannot be reduced will be returned as it is by the algorithm, wasting both CPU and I/O resources. Conversely extremely dense data, where say an individual pixel has dozens of points, guarantees great reduction in storage requirements for an image. The question of effectiveness calls for testing of PG against other simplification techniques under differently distributed data.

ACKNOWLEDGMENTS

This paper continues the work of Jackson Carroll's honours research on spatial object simplification in *Spatial Data Simplification: The World is Just Too Much,* (2000).

REFERENCES

[1] Barber C., Cromley R. & Adrle R. (1995) Evaluating Alternative Line Simplification Strategies for Multiple Representations of Cartographic Lines, *Cartographic and Geographic Information Systems, vol 22, no. 4, pp 276-290.*

[2] Brassel K.E. & Weibel R. (1988) A Review and Conceptual Framework of Automated Map Generalization, *International Journal of Geographic Information Systems, 2(3), pp229-244.*

[3] Douglas D.H. & Peucker T.K. (1973) Algorithms for the Reduction of the Number of points Required to Represent a Digitized Line or its Caricature, *The Canadian Cartographer, vol 10, no. 2, pp112-122.*

[4] Hoel E. & Samet H. (1991) Efficient Processing of Spatial Queries in Line Segment Databases, *Symposium on Large Spatial Databases, pp237-255.*

[5] Horhammer M. & Freeston M. (1999) *Spatial Indexing With A Scale Dimension,* Symposium on Large Spatial Databases, pp 52-71.

[6] Jansen, M. & M. van Kreveld (1998) Evaluating the consistency of cartographic generalization, *In T.K. Poiker and editors N. Chrisman, M., editors, Proceedings 8th International Symposium on Spatial Data Handling, pp. 668-678.*

[7] Jones C.B (2001):
http://www.geog.utoronto.ca/gozdyra/teach/Lectures_GGR272/16_MapGeneralization.htm.

[8] Li Z. & Openshaw S. (1992) Algorithms for Automated Line Generalization Based on a Natural Principle of Objective Generalization, *International Journal of Geographical Information Systems, vol 6, no. 5, pp 373-389.*

[9] McMaster R.B. (1983) A Mathematical Evaluation of Simplification Algorithms, *Auto Carto 6 Proceedings, vol 2. pp 267-276.*

[10] Peter & Weibel (1999) Using Vector and Raster-Based Techniques in Cartographical Map Generalization, *Third ICA Workshop on Progress in Automated Map Generalization, Ottawa.*

[11] Ruas A. & Plaznet C. (1996) Strategies for Automated Generalization, *Proceedings of the 7th International Symposium on Spatial Data Handling, vol 1, pp9A.1-9A.14.*

[12] H. Samet. (1984) The Quadtree and Related Hierarchical Data Structures, *ACM Computing Surveys, 16(2):187—260.*

[13] Visvalingam & Whyatt (1993) Line Generalization by Repeated Elimination of Points, *The Cartographic Journal, vol 30, no.1, pp46-51.*

[14] Weibel. R (1995) Map Generalization in the context of Digital Systems, *Cartographic and Geographic Information Systems, Vol 22. pp259-263.*

[15] Weibel R. (1996) A Typology of Constraints to Line Simplification, *In Proceedings of the 7th International Symposium on Spatial Data Handling, pp9A.1-9A.14.*

BIOGRAPHY

Sham Prasher is a PhD student in the department of Information Technology and Electrical Engineering at the University of Queensland. His research interests include spatial databases and geographic information systems.

BALANCING FIDELITY AND PERFORMANCE IN VIRTUAL WALKTHROUGH

Yixin Ruan, Jason Chionh, Zhiyong Huang, Lidan Shou, Kian-Lee Tan
Department of Computer Science, National University of Singapore, Singapore 117543
[ruanyixi, jchionh, huangzy, shoulida, tankl]@comp.nus.edu.sg

Abstract In a virtual reality (VR) system, users expect both high visual quality as well as a high constant frame rate when they interact with the system (walkthrough). However, realizing these two requirements for very large virtual environments (VE) that cannot fit in the main memory has not been adequately addressed in the literature. In this paper, we present a novel access method, called ViSA (Visibility and Spatial data Access method) that, given a region of the current view point, returns the set of 3D objects of VEs that are visible from, as well as those that are in, the region. Ideally, these 3D objects will be loaded into memory and rendered during walkthrough. However, to balance the visual fidelity (showing all visible objects) and constant high frame rate, we dynamically determine the number and set of objects that are to be loaded based on the current memory size and frame rate. In order to minimize I/O cost, we propose an optimized search technique. We have implemented the ViSA structure in a prototype walkthrough system and our experiments show that it can provide quality visual fidelity with an acceptable constant real time frame rate.

Keywords: Visual Fidelity, Visibility and Spatial Data, Virtual Environment, Secondary Storage Indexing

1. INTRODUCTION

Traditionally, in walkthrough applications, the Virtual Environment (VE) is stored in its entirety in the main memory. However, this assumption is no longer reasonable. For a realistic VE, secondary storage must be used. However, relying on the OS's virtual memory management for walkthrough gives unacceptable results because the OS is application independent.

One promising strategy that has been adopted in the literature is to exploit spatial index structures, e.g., R-trees (Guttman, 1984), for VE data (Pajarola et al., 1998; Shou et al., 2001). While these works can achieve high frame rates for real-time walkthrough, they have not adequately addressed the issue of visual fidelity. This is because spatial index structures are designed to cluster objects that are spatially close together. As such, a window query may miss "distant" objects that are visible from the viewpoint (i.e., those that do not intersect the query box) resulting in unsatisfactory visual quality. Clearly, using a sufficiently large window size that bounds the region for the maximum viewing distance of human eye sight is certainly not a practical solution.

In this paper, we capture two categories of information from the VE data. First, the VE space is split into regions, and for each region, we keep track of its *visibility set* (i.e., objects that are visible from at least one point within the region). (We assume a static environment so that visibility information can be pre-computed.) Second, the VE objects are organized into clusters so that those that are spatially close are in the same cluster. The first set of information is used to enhance the visual quality of the scene, while the second category is used to facilitate high frame rates. We present a novel access method, called ViSA (*Vi*sibility and *S*patial data *A*ccess method), to facilitate speedy retrieval of these two types of information. It is essentially an extended R-tree where nodes contain information on the spatial and visibility information of their entries. Given a window query, ViSA can therefore restrict the search space to regions that are close to the query region. The additional information along the paths of the nodes traversed provide the (pre-computed) visibility set that should be accessed for these candidate regions.

While the set of objects obtained from ViSA can guarantee visual fidelity (showing all visible objects), the system may not be able to sustain a constant and high frame rate. We propose a novel scheme to balance these two potentially conflicting user requirements. For each region, we pre-compute the contribution of each visible object to the scene. These objects can then be sorted using the contribution values in a non-ascending order. During walkthrough, visible objects are loaded according to this sorted order (i.e., objects with higher contribution values are loaded first) until some thresholds are violated. Two important thresholds can be used – available memory and the frame rate, i.e., if the available memory or frame rate drops below a predetermined value, then no further loading is performed. In order to minimize I/O cost, we propose an optimized search technique.

We have implemented a prototype walkthrough system that employs the proposed mechanisms. Our experiments on a large dataset show that the proposed mechanisms can facilitate high and constant rendering frame rates and excellent visual fidelity.

The rest of this paper is organized as follows. In the next section, we review some related work. In Section 3, we present the ViSA framework in detail. In Section 4, we describe an optimized search technique. Section 5 presents our experimental study and report our findings, and finally, Section 6 concludes the paper.

2. RELATED WORK

Existing works have addressed the problem from two different perspectives – either from the visibility (Cohen-Or et al., 1998; Panne and Stewart, 1999; Yagel and Ray, 1995) or from the spatial proximity (Kofler et al., 2000; Pajarola et al., 1998; Shou et al., 2001) point of views. Detecting objects that are visible from at least one point in a 3D view cell is a non-linear 4D problem (Teller, 1992). Most of these works assume that the entirety of the VE can fit in the main memory.

A straightforward approach to indexing visibility information for large VEs is to decompose the VE space into regular grid cells, and maintain cell-to-cell visibility information. However, this method is shown to be inefficient (Shou et al., 2001). Works on spatial proximity have largely employed the R-tree to organize the data space to facilitate searching. In Figure 1, we illustrate a sample dataset with 8 objects (Minimum Bounding Rectangles (MBRs) are shown in Figure 1(a)), and the corresponding R-tree structure (Figure 1(b)). The works in (Pajarola et al., 1998; Shou et al., 2001) consider only the spatial proximity of objects, while (Kofler et al., 2000) adapted the R-tree structure to also store multiple level of details of an object. R-tree, however, is not adequate in addressing the issue of visual fidelity.

3. THE VISA STRUCTURE

In this section, we shall present the ViSA structure. After giving an overview of the structure, we shall present the basic search algorithm. Next, we shall examine how ViSA can be used to balance visual fidelity and constant high frame rate. We shall end this section by looking at how ViSA can be created.

3.1. The Big Picture

ViSA is a *Vi*sibility and *S*patial data *A*ccess method to facilitate speedy retrieval of visibility as well as spatial proximity information. For pedagogical reasons, we shall use the example in Figure 1(a) in our discussion. Figure 2(a) shows the cell-to-object visibility information of the MBRs of the objects. For example, objects 2, 3, 4 and 5 are visible from MBR 1. This means that if the viewpoint is in MBR 1, then (ideally) objects 2-5 should also be loaded to ensure high visual fidelity walkthrough. Figure 2(c) shows the ViSA structure for our example dataset and visibility information.

As can be seen from Figure 2(c), the core of ViSA is an R-tree structure that provides the spatial proximity information (compare the structure given by the box with the R-tree in Figure 1(b)). However, ViSA extends the R-tree in several ways. First, each leaf node contains entries of the form (MBR, OP, VP) where MBR is the minimum bounding rectangle of the object, OP is the pointer to the object, and VP (which is newly added) is a pointer to the list of objects visible from at least one position in MBR. As shown in Figure 2(c), MBR 1 points to objects 2-5.

Each internal node contains entries of the form (MBR, NP, VP) where MBR is the minimum bounding rectangle that bounds all regions in its child node pointed by NP, and VP is a pointer (newly added) to the visibility information of MBR. Clearly, the visibility information of MBR is a superset of the visibility information of its children regions. To enhance performance, the visibility information of MBR is determined by excluding those of its children regions. However, since the region bounded by MBR can be very large, the visibility information can be very large. For example, consider MBR 14 in Figure 1(a), even if we have excluded MBRs 5, 6, 7 and 8, the region covered by MBR 14 is still large, and the visibility set of this space can be very large. Thus, if a query window, Q (see Figure 1(a)), intersects MBR 14, the entire visibility set corresponding to MBR 14 may have to be retrieved. We resolve this problem by splitting the region into smaller subregions. As an example, in Figure 2(b), the regions of MBRs 12 and 14 have been further decomposed into 4 and 7 subregions respectively. This decomposition is done such that each subregion contains approximately the same number of visible objects. Thus, VP points to a list of regions, each of which provides the visibility information for the region. Using the same query example where query window Q intersects MBR 14, we now only need to access visibility set corresponding to MBR 14.6 which is much smaller than MBR 14! The root node structure is similar to the internal node.

3.2. The Basic ViSA Search Algorithm

Figure 3 shows the algorithmic description of the basic ViSA search algorithm. The algorithm is very similar to the R-tree search algorithm, except for lines 5-7 and 12-13. Given a query window, the search begins from the root node, and traverses down the tree. For each internal node of ViSA examined (lines 1-7), the Bounding Boxes (BB) of the entries within the node are first checked against the query window (line 2). If the BB of an entry E overlaps the query window, it means that objects covered by the BB may be spatially close to or within the query window. As such, the search will continue with the child node associated with E (line 4). Next comes the differences from R-tree. Since ViSA internal nodes also keep track of visibility information of the space covered by the BB of E, the VP pointer is used to retrieve the list of regions not covered by E's children nodes. For those regions that intersect the query window, we return the pointer to the list of the visible objects (lines 5-7). In this way, all potentially visible objects along the path can be accessed.

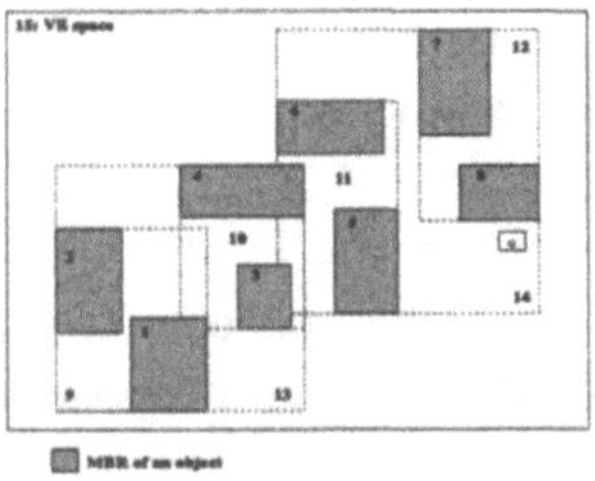

(a) A sample dataset.

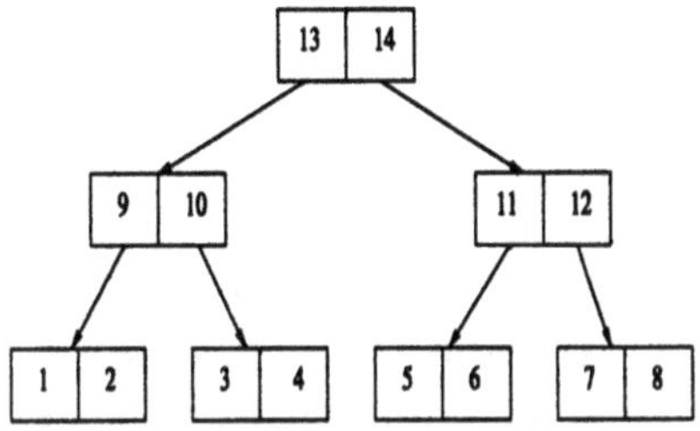

(b) The corresponding R-tree.

Figure 1. An R-tree example.

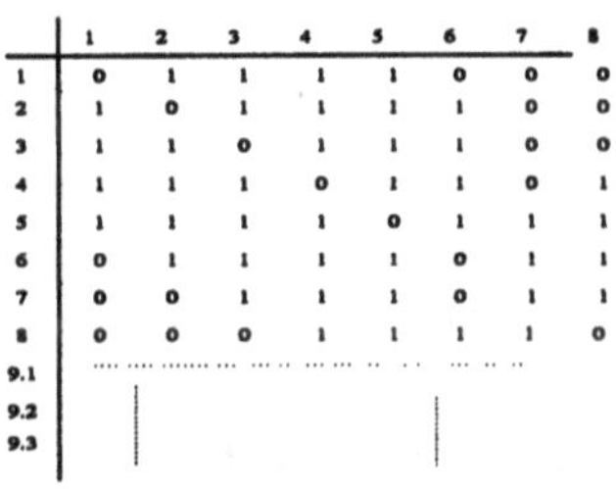

(a) Visibility information.

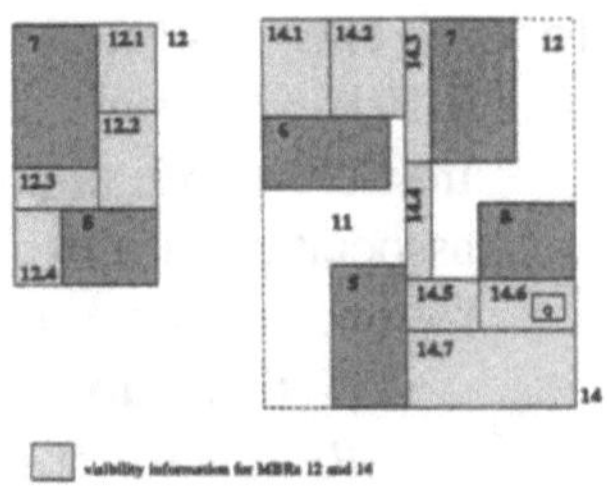

(b) Partitioning of MBR.

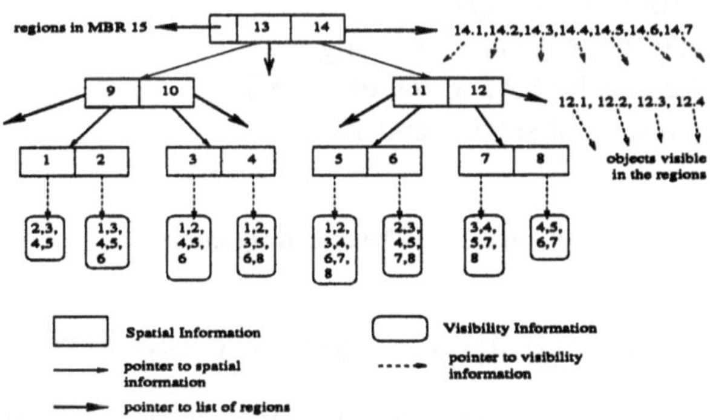

(c) The ViSA structure.

Figure 2. A ViSA example.

Now, for a leaf node, similar process is performed (lines 9-12). If the BB of an entry E of the leaf node overlaps the query window, then we know that E is a qualifying record. So, both the pointer to the object corresponding to E and the pointer to the list of objects visible from E are returned. Finally, we need to merge the query results of steps 7 and 12. The reason is that the same object can be queried more than once, e.g., one object can be visible from two different regions.

As in the R-tree search algorithm, those entries that do not intersect with the query window can be pruned away. Thus, ViSA facilitates speedy retrieval of spatial and visibility data. In order to minimize I/O cost, we propose an optimized search algorithm that will be described in Section 4.

Algorithm Search (T, C)
Input: T: pointer to node, C: Query window

```
1.   if T is not a leaf node /* search subtrees */
2.       for each entry E of node T do
3.          if (BB(E) Overlaps C)
4.             Invoke Search on the sub-tree whose root is the node
               associated with E
5.             for each region V obtained via pointer VP associated with E
6.                if (V Overlaps C)
7.                   Return VP of node T, the pointer to list of visible objects
8.   else /* search leaf node */
9.       for each entry E of node T do
10.         if (BB(E) Overlaps C)
11.            E of node T is a qualifying record
12.            Return the SP and VP of node T
13.  Merge the results of steps 7 and 12
```

Figure 3. The search algorithm.

3.3. Visual Fidelity vs High Frame Rate

Given a query window Q, we can obtain the set of objects that are in Q as well as objects that are visible from any point in Q. However, depending on the memory size and the computational power of the system, it may not always be possible to sustain high frame rates as well as visual fidelity. Under such a situation, our approach is to provide as much visible data as possible as long as the frame rate does not degrade beyond a certain predetermined threshold, i.e., when the frame rate falls below a certain prescribed threshold, we will sacrifice the visual quality by dropping some visible objects.

Essentially, given a region, we associate with each object in its visibility set a contribution value. An object's contribution value reflects its importance to the rendered image. In other words, it is more valuable to load an object with a larger contribution value than one with a lower contribution value. Thus, all we need is to sort the objects in non-ascending order of their contribution values. During a walkthrough session, visible objects with higher contribution values are loaded first, followed by those with smaller values. In this way, whenever the frame rate drops below the threshold value, we stop loading the visibility objects.

3.4. Creation of the ViSA Structure

To create a ViSA structure from a VE is a fairly complex and time consuming task. Fortunately, this process is done offline, and only need to be done once for a static VE. As described in the previous subsections, the major data structures of ViSA are (1) the hierarchical cells that represent the spatial adjacency of 3D objects (referred by SP) and (2) the visible set of each node and regions (referred by VP).

The creation is split into three steps. First, we construct the R-tree component of ViSA. This process is straightforward by using the R-tree construction scheme proposed in (Guttman, 1984). However, we need to allocate space for all the additional visibility pointers that are needed in ViSA. The process is essentially an iterative inserting process: for each object and its MBR in the scene, we traverse a single path down the tree from the root to the leaf and insert the entry into the leaf node. At each level of the traversal, we choose the child node whose MBR needs the least enlargement to contain the MBR of the object. In our implementation, we adapted the linear node split algorithm of (Ang and Tan, 1997). This algorithm minimizes both the coverage and the overlap of the cells of SP. It is very efficient with linear time complexity for the number of 3D objects in a VE.

Second, we determine the regions in which visibility set should be computed. We traverse the R-tree component bottom up, i.e., from the leaf levels first, followed by the level above the leaves and so on. At each leaf node, for each data object, its MBR corresponds to the region. For each internal node, the space that is not captured by the children nodes are split into regions. In our current work, we have adopted a simple strategy: we split the space into regions whose size must be smaller than the largest MBR of the children nodes.

Third, we compute the visible set for the region defined by each node in the hierarchy. The resulting objects of the visible set will be recorded in the visible table (referred by VP). To pre-compute the visibility information, we change the model set to the k-D tree structure. For each node region R, some nearby large convex objects will be selected as the occluders. The k-D tree hierarchy of bounding boxes is then tested against the z-buffer to find which nodes are hidden by the occluder. The hidden sets for eight vertices are intersected, generating the hidden set of the occluder. And finally, all the hidden sets of all occluders are unioned to make up the global hidden set occluded by the occluder set. In such a way, we can get the visibility set for each region.

4. THE OPTIMIZED SEARCH ALGORITHM

In a large VE walkthrough system, in order to minimize I/O cost, the user's viewpoint is typically associated with a *disk cell* that contains the view frustum (Shou et al., 2001). For simplicity, in our experiments, we used a box-shaped cell (i.e., typical Window query) as a disk cell. The disk cell serves two purposes. First, if the frustums of subsequent frames are totally bounded in the disk cell, there is no need to access data from secondary storage. This can lead to higher frame rate. Second, whenever a user moves such that its view frustum is no longer bounded by the disk cell, new data has to be accessed from the secondary storage. The disk cell (corresponds to a query window) serves to define the region of space in the VE that contains objects that should be accessed from the secondary storage and brought into main memory for rendering.

However, in a walkthrough environment, consecutive disk cells, say $C_1, C_2, \ldots, C_i$, issued to the retrieval engine to access data from secondary storage may contain significant overlap. Consider a user's frustum cell is initially within cell C_1. When the user's frustum cell moves out of C_1, data of cell C_2 has to be loaded. Intuitively, we should only load objects that are in C_2 but not in C_1. Similarly, if C_3 becomes the current cell, then only objects in C_3 that are not in C_2 and C_1 should be accessed. This is also true for the visible sets V_1, V_2, and V_3. Unfortunately, the non-overlapped areas of cells are usually concave geometries, so it is difficult to describe such a region in each retrieval operation. It is also difficult to search for objects overlapping such a concave area in ViSA as the original search algorithm employs only box-shaped regions.

In (Shou et al., 2001), a novel complement overlap concept was introduced to reuse overlap information to retrieve only objects in the non-overlapped regions. ComplementOverlap between two regions are defined as follows: given a cell A, the space not contained in A is the complement of A, which is denoted as $\bar{A}$. If a bounding box BB (of a virtual object or a group of objects) overlaps (or intersects) $\bar{A}$, then we say that BB complement overlaps A. ComplementOverlap can be exploited in our context as follows:

- Given that we want to load objects of a new cell C, we can use a history of cells HS = $\{C_1, C_2, \ldots, C_i\}$ to filter away (spatial) objects that are already loaded in memory by the cells in HS. Thus, the problem becomes one of retrieving objects whose bounding boxes overlap C but do not overlap any of the cells in HS.

- Similarly, given that we want to load objects that are visible from a new cell C, we can use a history of regions whose visibility objects are already loaded in memory, HV = $\{V_1, V_2, \ldots, V_i\}$, and use them to filter away visible objects that are already loaded in memory.

Referring to our example again, if C_3 is the current cell whose objects we want to retrieve, then (1) objects that overlap C_3 but not C_1 and C_2 and (2) visible objects of C_3 but not visible from C_1 and C_2 are the ones that we are interested in.

We incorporated this idea to the basic ViSA search algorithm. As it works on the spatial and visible information of a disk cell, we refer to it as the SVC-search (*S*patial-*V*isual *C*omplement search). Figure 4 gives the algorithmic description for the SVCsearch. In the figure, we use T to denote an ViSA node, use E to denote an entry of the ViSA node, and use SP and VP to denote the references (pointers) to objects inside and visible objects of the ViSA node region as described in Section 3. As shown, the main difference between this algorithm and the basic search algorithm in Figure 3 is the additional ComplementOverlaps statements that appear in lines 4 and 8.

If we denote the cells that a user accesses as $C_1, C_2, C_3, \ldots$, based on the SVCsearch algorithm, the retrieval engine will issue the following queries to the database (ViSA): C_1, $C_2 - C_1$, $C_3 - (C_1 \cup C_2)$, $C_4 - (C_3 \cup C_2 \cup C_1)$, …, $C_{i+1} - (C_i \cup \ldots \cup C_2 \cup C_1)$ and so on. As a comparison, a traditional method would issue queries C_1, C_2, C_3, …, to the database. For a SVC search like $C_{i+1} - (C_i \cup \ldots \cup C_2 \cup C_1)$, we can remove any cells from $\{C_1, C_2, \ldots, C_i\}$, if the bounding boxes of all their objects do not overlap C_{i+1}. Such cells have no effect on the query result because objects overlapping them cannot overlap C_{i+1}. Thus, before sending the query to the database, a filtering operation can be conducted on the cell list, so those cells not intersecting the current cell do not need to be considered in the SVCsearch algorithm. In our prototype walkthrough system, the number of cells in the history to be maintained is fewer than twenty in most cases. With such short cell lists, the CPU cost on the extra ComplementOverlap and Overlap testing is negligible. The above argument also applies to the ComplementOverlap operation on visibility data.

Besides exploiting the concept of complement overlap, we also keep track of the list of objects that are in memory. In this way, by comparing the IDs of the objects, we can avoid loading a memory-resident object. Since the number of objects to be compared is small, the computation cost is negligible compared to the I/O savings in loading the actual objects.

As a user "steps" out of a cell boundary, a SVCsearch returns a new result set. The algorithm guarantees that the result sets will have no overlap. However, as the object buffer in the main memory gets filled up, old objects should be freed to make space for new cells. Our solution is to delete from the buffer

Algorithm SVCsearch (T, C, HS, HV)
Input: T: pointer to node, C: Query window, HS: History of spatial search cells, HV: History of visible regions

```
1.   if T is not a leaf node /* search subtrees */
2.       for each entry E of node T do
3.           if (BB(E) Overlaps C)
4.               if BB(E) ComplementOverlaps all of C_1, C_2, ..., C_i in HS
5.                   Invoke SVCsearch on the sub-tree whose root is the node
                     associated with E
6.                   for each region V obtained via pointer VP associated with E
7.                       if (V Overlaps C)
8.                           if V ComplementOverlaps all of V_1, V_2, ..., V_i in HV
9.                               Return VP of node T, the pointer to list of visible
                                 objects
10.  else /* search leaf node */
11.      for each entry E of node T do
12.          if (BB(E) Overlaps C)
13.              if BB(E) Overlaps none of C_1, C_2, ..., C_i in HS
14.                  E of node T is a qualifying record
15.                  Return the SP and VP of node T
16.  Merge the query results of steps 9 and 15
```

Figure 4. The SVCsearch algorithm.

the objects of the cells that do not overlap the latest cell, while maintaining the objects whose cells overlap it.

5. EXPERIMENTAL STUDY

We implemented the ViSA system that employs all the proposed techniques. The system was built upon a PC with Pentium III and 128 megabytes of memory, running Windows NT4. We generated a synthetic dataset to simulate a large cityscape. There are about 100,000 virtual buildings requiring about 100 MB of harddisk space (inclusive of ViSA index), and more than 500 MB of memory space if fully loaded into main memory (in scene graph format).

We compare the ViSA system against the REVIEW system (Shou et al., 2001). REVIEW is the predecessor of ViSA designed to facilitate walkthrough in large VEs. REVIEW employs R-tree to index the VE data. However, it does not handle visibility data beyond those within a query region, i.e., given a query region, nothing outside of the region can be viewed. Currently, both systems support the same replacement and prefetching policies that are designed in REVIEW based on walkthrough semantics. The distance-priority-based replacement policy keeps those nodes that are close to the current viewpoint in memory, while replacing those nodes whose bounding boxes are distant from the current viewpoint. The prefetching scheme computes the position of the view cell that the user will be in based on the velocity in which the user is moving. Both schemes have been shown to perform better than other non-semantic-based schemes.

The metrics of measuring the quality of a walkthrough are the frame time and the smoothness of the walkthrough. Frame time is defined as the cycle time between two consecutive rendering operations. The time for database query, memory data manipulation, rendering and other overheads are all included in frame time. The smoothness of the walkthrough can be represented by how much each frame time varies from the average frame time. A walkthrough with a small average frame time and a small variance is considered to be of good quality.

Both the average frame time and the frame time variance of the ViSA and REVIEW system are listed in table 1. We can see the frame time and time variation of ViSA is close to those of REVIEW. With increasing query cell size ratio (defined as the ratio of the disk cell size over the view frustum cell size), the frame time and its variance become worse. This is because when the size of the querying box increases, more objects are loaded into memory. The average frame time of ViSA is about 3.5ms more than that of REVIEW and its average variance is about 17.3ms more than that of REVIEW. Thus, ViSA's performance is acceptable especially since it can provide much better visual fidelity than REVIEW (as we shall see shortly).

Cell size ratio	ViSA ft (ms)	ViSA vt (ms)	REVIEW ft (ms)	REVIEW vt (ms)
1.0	25.89	28.53	22.52	10.24
1.1	29.76	30.57	26.51	12.94
1.2	34.20	32.30	30.92	14.04
1.3	39.18	32.78	35.67	15.92
1.4	44.32	35.84	40.68	18.24
1.5	49.37	35.26	45.88	18.51
1.6	54.35	35.37	50.57	19.15

Table 1. Comparisons of ViSA and REVIEW on the average and variance of frame time (ft and vt) for different query cell size.

Figures 5(a) and 5(b) show the results on the rendering time for each frame when a user path is applied to ViSA system and REVIEW system. The results show that the ViSA has longer rendering time and less smooth frame rate because the visible objects were loaded and rendered. However, the performance is only marginally lower. At some frames (20 of total 500 frames), the frame time is very large for both systems because of the queries to the secondary storage.

Another straightforward approach to indexing visibility information for large VEs is to decompose the VE space into regular grid cells (REGULAR in short). We now compare the rendering time of REGULAR (Figure 5(c)) and ViSA (Figure 5(a)). REGULAR's average frame time (70.9ms) is longer than ViSA's (25.9ms). The variance of frame time of REGULAR is 343.6ms, longer than that of ViSA(28.5ms) as shown in table 1. It is due to REGULAR's longer average disk access time.

As expected, the fidelity of ViSA is significantly higher than REVIEW in walkthrough. The missing visible objects in REVIEW can be 0% (all the visible objects are occluded by the objects in the region) to ∞ (no objects in the region, e.g., a football ground, but many visible objects around, "blind spots"). To visually compare, Figure 6 displays three pairs of snapshots of display of ViSA and REVIEW using the same viewpoint for a same VE. It is clear from the figure that some visible buildings are only shown in the results of ViSA.

In the next experiment, we study the effect of trading off visual fidelity for performance. We use the cell size ratio 1.0 for this experiment. Figure 7 shows how the percentage of visible objects loaded affect the average frame time of the walkthrough. In other words, a point (x, y) in the figure means that (100-x)% of the objects were dropped, while $x\%$ were loaded into memory.

We can see that in Figure 7, as we decrease the percentage of visible objects information, the ViSA's frame time decreases. The frame time of REVIEW remains constant as REVIEW does not consider visibility information, but rather, only the spatial information. The curve of ViSA will not reach the horizontal line of REVIEW. The reason is that there is a constant additional overhead for ViSA to do the computation for the visibility part even if there is no visible object to be loaded.

The fidelity for different dropping rates also can be visually compared. One set of three snapshots is shown in Figure 8. The visual fidelity decreases as the dropping of more visible objects in the visible set. In Figure 8(a), all distant cylinder towers and lower blocks are shown. In Figure 8(b), two most distant cylinder towers and some lower blocks are not shown. In Figure 8(c), only one most close cylinder tower and lower blocks are shown.

6. CONCLUSION

In this paper, we have presented a novel access method to organize large virtual environments that cannot fit into the main memory. The proposed structure, ViSA, stores both visibility and spatial proximity information, and facilitates optimized search and speedy retrieval of objects that are visible from and

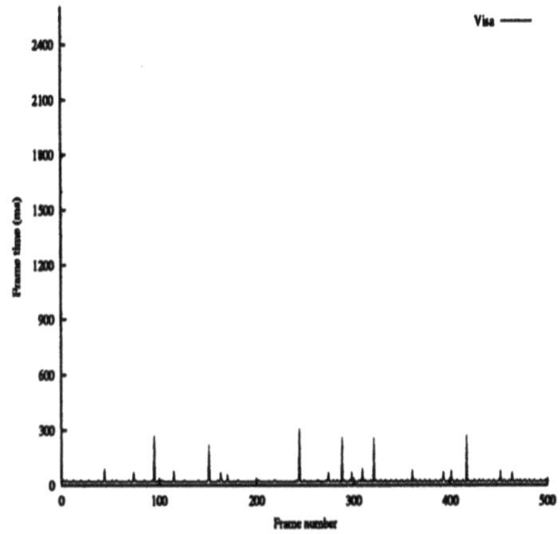

(a) ViSA

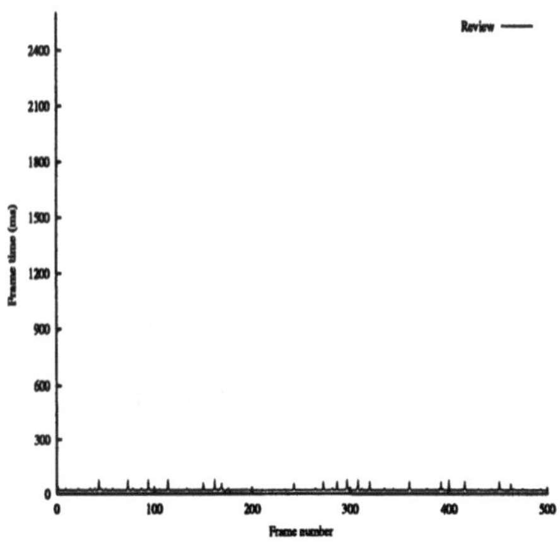

(b) REVIEW

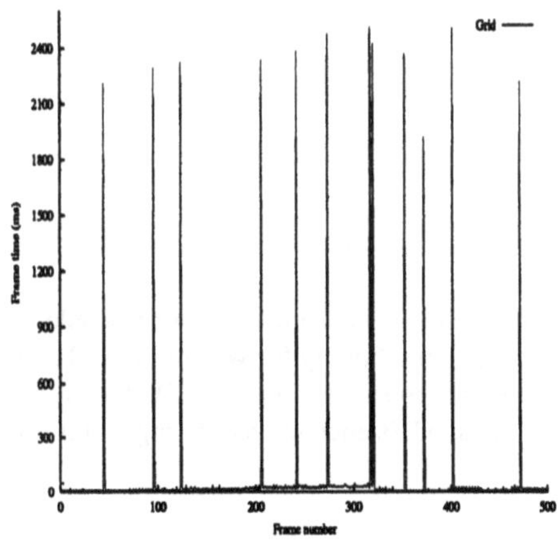

(c) REGULAR

Figure 5. Experiment results of rendering time for each frame: the spikes indicate time and frame number for disk accesses.

spatially close to the viewpoint. This approach can successfully balance the fidelity and performance for walkthrough. We plan to extend this work in several directions. First, we would like to further study data structures that can organize the visibility data (instead of using a visibility table which can become a bottleneck for large number of objects). Second, we will take Level of Detail (LOD) into consideration in our future work. We plan to integrate this into the successor of ViSA.

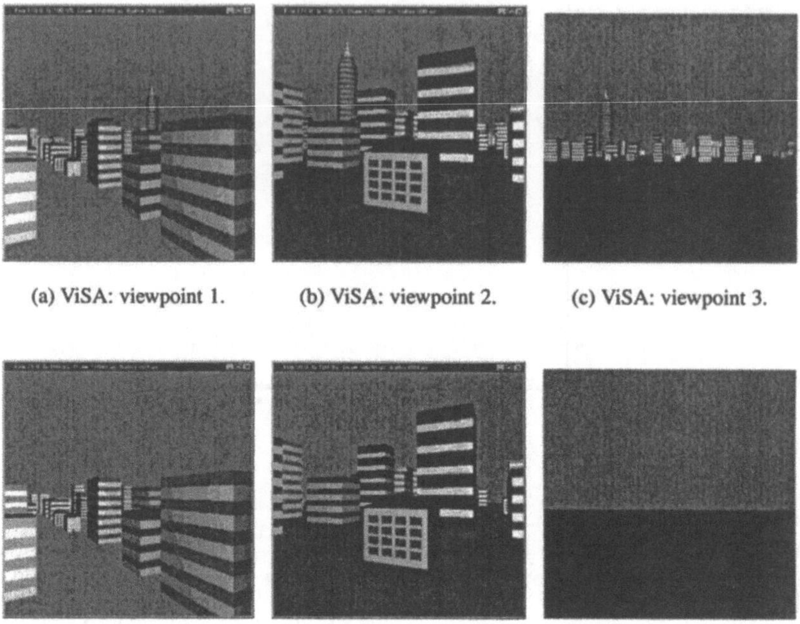

(a) ViSA: viewpoint 1. (b) ViSA: viewpoint 2. (c) ViSA: viewpoint 3.

(d) REVIEW: viewpoint 1. (e) REVIEW: viewpoint 2. (f) REVIEW: viewpoint 3.

Figure 6. Visual comparisons of fidelity for ViSA and REVIEW. It shows that ViSA has higher visual fidelity for walkthrough. For viewpoints 1 and 2, some buildings, e.g., a cylinder tower, are missing from the REVIEW system. For viewpoint 3, all objects are missing, i.e., a "blind spot" is encountered during walkthrough.

ACKNOWLEDGMENTS

Yixin Ruan and Lidan Shou are supported by the University Research Scholarship. Initial discussion with Beng Chin Ooi prompted us to look into the issue of visibility data.

REFERENCES

Ang, C. H. and Tan, T. C. (1997). New linear node splitting algorithm for r-trees. In *Advances in Spatial Databases, SSD'97*, pages 339–349, Berlin, Germany.

Cohen-Or, D., Fibich, G., Halperin, D., and Zadicario, E. (1998). Conservative visibility and strong occusion for viewspace partitioning of densely occluded scenes. *Computer Graphics Forum*, 17(3):243–254.

Guttman, A. (1984). R-trees: A dynamic index structure for spatial searching. In *Proc. 1984 ACM SIGMOD International Conference on Management of Data*, pages 47–57.

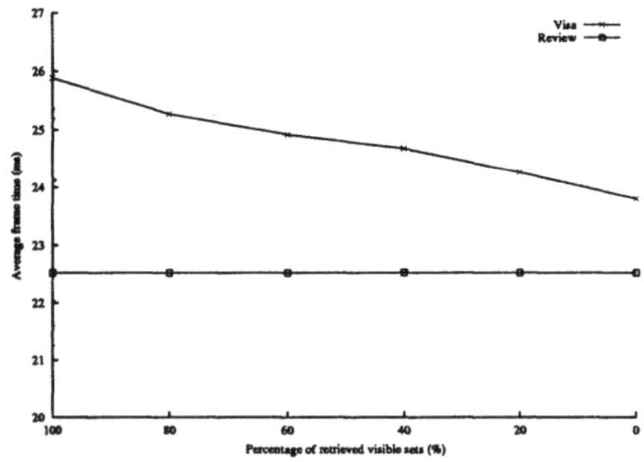

Figure 7. The average frame time of the walkthrough in ViSA, dropping the visible objects, against the REVIEW.

(a) No dropping of the visible objects.

(b) Dropping 20% of the visible objects.

(c) Dropping 40% of the visible objects.

Figure 8. Visual illustration of fidelity for ViSA when dropping the visible objects with small contribution values in order to maintain the frame time.

Kofler, M., Gervautz, M., and Gruber, M. (2000). R-trees for organizing and visualizing 3d gis databases. *Journal of Visualization and Computer Animation*, 11:129–143.

Pajarola, R., Ohler, T., Stucki, P., Szabo, K., and Widmayer, P. (1998). The alps at your fingertips: Virtual reality and geoinformation systems. In *Proceedings of the ICDE'98 Conference*, pages 550–557.

Panne, M. and Stewart, A. (1999). Effective compression techniques for precomputed visibility. In *Proceedings of Eurographics Workshop on Rendering*, pages 305–316.

Shou, L., Chionh, C., Huang, Z., Ruan, Y., and Tan, K. L. (2001). Walking through a very large virtual environment in real-time. In *Proc. VLDB 2001*, pages 401–410.

Teller, S. (1992). Computing the antipenumbra of an area light source. In *Proceedings of SIGGRAPH'92*, pages 139–148.

Yagel, R. and Ray, W. (1995). Visibility computation for efficient walkthrough of complex environments. *Presence*, 5(1):45–60.

AURAL INTERFACES TO DATABASES BASED ON VOICEXML

Beat Signer, Moira C. Norrie, Peter Geissbuehler, Daniel Heiniger
Institute for Information Systems
Swiss Federal Institute of Technology (ETH)
CH-8092 Zurich, Switzerland
signer@inf.ethz.ch, norrie@inf.ethz.ch

Abstract As part of a general framework for the development of global information systems, we include support for the development of aural interfaces. The framework uses an object-oriented database for the management of application, document content and presentation data. The access layer is based around an XML server and XSLT for document generation from default and customised templates. Specifically, aural interfaces are supported through a VoiceXML server that provides the speech recognition and synthesis mechanisms, together with XSLT templates for the generation of VoiceXML. In this paper, we describe the implementation of a generic voice browser for application databases as well as the development of a customised aural interface for a community diary managing appointments and events.

Keywords: web databases, aural interfaces, voice browser, VoiceXML

1. INTRODUCTION

We are rapidly moving towards an information society in which communities of users demand access to all forms of both personal and shared information from their work places, homes and on the move. The resulting application systems can be classified as *global information systems* that enable ubiquitous access to shared information.

To support the development of such global information systems, we require modern data management frameworks with a general and flexible interaction layer that allows access from various forms of client devices including not only desktop workstations, but also mobile phones, Tablet PCs and PDAs. We have therefore extended our OMS Java data management framework [Kobler and Norrie, 1999] with a generic database access layer to support universal client access. The resulting eXtensible

Information Management Architecture (XIMA) framework [Signer et al., 2001; Kobler et al., 2001] uses XML as an intermediate representation format and the Extensible Stylesheet Language Transformation (XSLT) for document generation from default and customised templates. The XIMA framework is very flexible and it is easy to support new forms of client devices since only the final rendering step to the client's desired output format, based on the XSLT, has to be adapted.

Recent innovations, such as the Voice Extensible Markup Language (VoiceXML), encouraged us to extend the XIMA framework with a user interface based on speech recognition and synthesised voice output [VXML, 2002]. Using voice as a potential input and output medium opens up many new possibilities in terms of, not only mobile access to information, but also access for the disabled. Aural interfaces just require the use of a regular telephone to access information stored in our databases. Today one can find telephones almost everywhere and mobile phones are far more portable and accessible than computers. Therefore the support of voice browsers was just a logical step towards realising our vision of *ubiquitous information — information for everyone, everywhere.*

Even in the case of WAP-enabled mobile phones, the use of a voice interface may be a much more convenient means of accessing information. Navigation by voice is by far more pleasant and faster than the use of touch-tone input or entering information using the small keypads of mobile WAP phones. Also, in some situations, voice output may be preferred over visual output. For example, a person may perform a manual task, while simultaneously receiving information via a voice interface. Just think of an employee driving to his office by car: He can listen to the news on the company's web portal site while his eyes are concentrating on the traffic.

With respect to the disabled, voice-enabled applications are valuable to users who can either not use their hands for keyboard input or their eyes to process visual output. Further, voice interfaces require no special instruction or experience. They also allow new forms of human-computer interaction based on a combination of visual and voice interfaces. We can build applications which are either fully based on voice or use speech technology to augment existing graphical user interfaces.

In this paper, we present an overview of the XIMA framework and describe how it has been extended with an aural interface based on VoiceXML. The enhanced framework strongly supports the database driven development of voice-enabled applications, which finally can be deployed using one of the numerously available voice server platforms [BeVocal, 2002; VoiceGenie, 2002]. We begin in section 2 by presenting our overall vision and the main advantages of aural user interfaces. After discussing existing applications which already make use of aural input and output, we outline how VoiceXML can be used to simplify the development process of voice based applications. We describe the eXtensible Information Management Architecture (XIMA), which already supports different types of client formats (HTML for regular web browsers, WML for mobile WAP phones, and CHTML for PDAs and NTT DoCoMo's imode devices) in section 3. In section 4, we then point out how the XIMA framework has been enhanced with a generic voice browser interface that allows voice access to all our OMS Java databases. Section 5 explains how a customised voice interface can be developed by adapting the generic voice browser for a specific application and we describe how this was done for a community diary. Concluding remarks are given in section 6.

2. AURAL INTERFACES

There are several good reasons for investigating aural interfaces as a new access form for database management systems. As discussed in the introduction, such interfaces may provide benefits in terms of mobility and universality, extending potential user communities to those without access to computers or special devices and also to the physically handicapped, unable to use conventional input or output devices.

Aural interfaces are most frequently used for retrieving information from a database or invoking operations on the database. However, there are also applications and circumstances where voice input may be appropriate for the entry of new data or the editing of existing data. For example, entering a new person in an electronic address book could be done by spelling out the name and the phone number. This enables entry to be done quickly and conveniently "on the spot" rather than having to later enter the data when a computer plus keyboard or business card scanner are available. Also an aural interface enables a "hands-free" and "eyes-free" mode of interaction which may be useful in many practical work situations or for the augmentation of other visual applications.

For various technical reasons, it is only in recent years that it has become possible to create useful human-computer voice interaction. Due to advances in digital speech processing technologies, it is now possible to support the application and deployment of a variety of speech technologies for aural interfaces. Figure 2 shows how voice input is processed and an aural response is generated by a computer using a speech recognition component, a language analyser, an application server connected to a database and a speech synthesiser (text-to-speech or TTS).

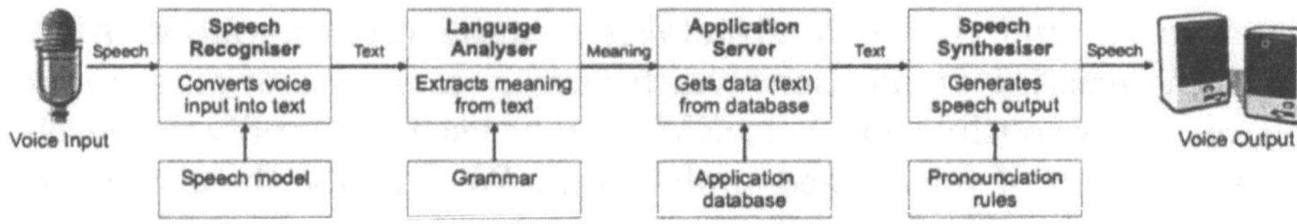

Figure 1. Voice Processing Components

The speech recognition is performed by a speech recogniser engine that processes incoming audio signals and tries to determine the most likely combination of basic spoken sound patterns (phonemes) that represent the audio input (word recognition). The language analyser then compares the resulting output to the active grammar containing all potential words and phrases which can be detected. Based on the extracted meaning, information can be fetched from an application database and a reply is built in textual form. Finally, based on prosody analysis and text-to-phoneme conversion, the output speech waveform is generated by the speech synthesiser. Today's synthesised voice output still sounds artificial, but it should continue to improve in the near future with the use of new voice modelling techniques and computing performance improvements.

The task of the application developer was further simplified when major vendors of speech technologies and tools (e.g. IBM Speech ML and Motorola VoxML) formed the VoiceXML Forum in 1999 and agreed to develop a common standard. This resulted in the specification of the VoiceXML standard which was published in March 2000.

The task of designing an aural interface to an application is not a trivial undertaking. Good speech user interfaces are significantly different from their visual counterparts. A lot of tasks that are visually possible — such as scrolling through a long list of elements — cannot be directly mapped to an aural user interface. Several projects try to adapt existing graphical user interfaces and make them accessible using voice browsers [Anderson et al., 2001; Freire et al., 2001]. The problem of such an approach is that the navigational concepts used by graphical applications are not suitable for access by voice recognition. Another problem is the audible output of large amounts of information. Since speech is transient (you hear it once and then it is gone), users tend to forget important information provided at the beginning of long dialogues. Books are available giving general guidelines for the design of aural interfaces [Balentine and Morgan, 1999].

The advantage of using the XIMA framework for the development of speech-enabled applications is that we adopt an "information-based" approach. This means that we start by developing a general information model for the application in question using OM, an object-oriented data model [Norrie et al., 1996]. The OM model supports object and association constructs and encourages the application information to be represented in terms of fine-grained "information units" which are linked together by associations. Representing information objects as small, externally linked objects allows for a greater flexibility when it comes to generating document content and access patterns for a specific interface. Through the clear separation of content and visualisation, it is possible to use completely different navigational patterns for voice and visual user interfaces. In addition, the representation of application information in terms of small units of information provides a good basis for the development of aural interfaces.

3. EXTENSIBLE INFORMATION MANAGEMENT ARCHITECTURE

XIMA uses the OMS Java system for the management of application, document content and presentation data. OMS Java is an application framework for the Java programming environment that implements the abstractions and operations defined in the OM object-oriented data model. For the purposes of this paper, it is not necessary to describe OM or OMS Java in detail. However, it is important to appreciate the main constructs of the OM model and we therefore begin this section with a description of these.

Each OM object is an *instance* of one or more *types*. A type is a set of attribute and method properties. If a type t_2 is declared to be a subtype of type t_1, then the set of properties of t_2 is composed from the set of properties defined for t_2 and those inherited from t_1. The composition is in line with usual inheritance mechanisms in object-oriented languages. We refer to the set of properties defined for t_2, and not inherited, as the *type unit* of t_2.

If an object is an instance of type t_1, then it will have a corresponding *information unit* that gives the values of all attribute properties defined in the type unit of t_1. Access to an object is always associated with a *type context* that specifies one of its types. The corresponding type instance for that object will be constructed dynamically from the appropriate information units, i.e. from the information unit for the context type together with those inherited from supertypes.

A *collection* is an object that represents a semantic grouping of objects. It has a name, a member type and an extent which is the set of ids of all member objects. Only those objects which are instances of the collection's member type can belong to the collection. The member type also specifies the type context for objects accessed through that collection.

For a given collection C, we can define one or more *subcollections* C_1, C_2,... This specifies a containment relation between the collections — every object that is a member of C_1 must also be a member of C.

An association is a *binary collection* together with constraints that specify a *source collection*, a *target collection* and cardinality constraints over the source and target. A binary collection B is a special form of collection in which the members are pairs of object ids, e.g. (O_1, O_2). Correspondingly, the member type of B must be a binary type of the form (t_1, t_2). Assume that collections C_1 and C_2 are specified as the source and target collections, respectively, of B. Then for every pair (O_1, O_2) that belongs to B, O_1 must be a member of C_1 and O_2 a member of C_2.

Although association constructs are present in a number of descriptive models such as Entity-Relationship models [Batini et al., 1992] and UML [Booch et al., 1998], they are rarely supported as a separate abstraction construct in models of operational systems. Our experience in working with object-oriented databases has shown the benefits of having a dedicated construct in order to be able to associate objects directly instead of via attributes and to perform operations over these associations.

The OMS Java framework was designed and developed to support application development through the provision of a high-level application programming interface based on the abstractions of the OM model. Further it was defined with openness and extensibility in mind which allowed us to extend and re-engineer the framework to provide universal client access and web content management facilities based on XML technologies.

In Figure 2, we present the architecture of the resulting eXtensible Information Management Architecture (XIMA). For a specific application, all client access is via a single Java servlet — the Entry Servlet. This means that all requests can be sent to the same URL, rather than having different URLs for different types of client devices. The Entry Servlet detects the user agent type from the HTTP request header and delegates the handling of the request to the appropriate servlet. For example, in Figure 2, we show servlets to handle requests from HTML browsers, WML browsers running on WAP-enabled mobile phones and voice browsers based on VoiceXML.

The request handling servlets then access the database by connecting to an OMS Java workspace via the OMS Java API. The connection may either be direct or via the OMS Java XML server. Direct connections

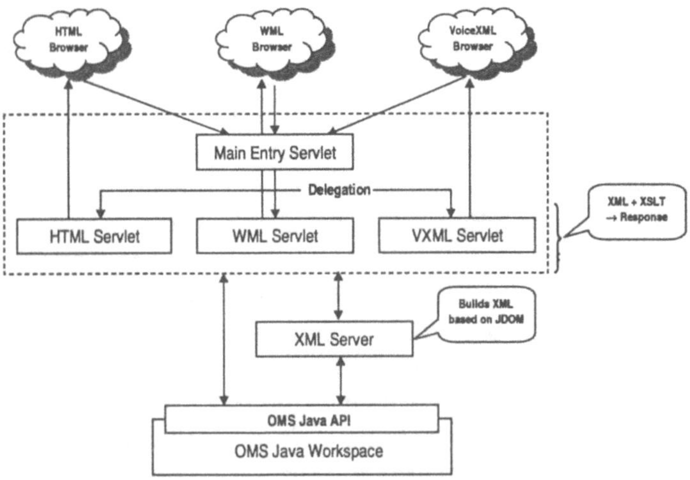

Figure 2. **eXtensible Information Management Architecture**

deal with requests that do not involve data retrieval such as checking the membership of an object in a collection or performing updates. Any requests that involve the retrieval of data go through the XML server. The XML server forwards requests to the OMS Java workspace and generates XML representations for any data objects. For all database constructs such as objects, instances, attributes, etc. there exist JDOM wrapper components, which generate a document object model (DOM) for the corresponding database object. Every wrapper object itself may use other wrapper components during its transformation process. For example, the JDOM wrapper of an *instance* database entry uses the *type*, *attribute*, *method* and *link* wrappers to add types, attributes, methods and links to the instance's document object model. The resulting DOM tree is returned to the requesting servlets (in Figure 4 of section 4 we present an XML instance representation). Finally, the servlets use the appropriate XSLT templates to transform the XML results to the desired client format.

There are a few points to note in this general architecture. First, we are not storing any XML documents, but rather generating them dynamically from the application data which is stored according to the information model. Since the information model is a loosely-coupled graph model based on object collections and associations, this gives much more flexibility than the rather restrictive hierarchical-based models imposed by XML structures. At access time, a particular hierarchical view on data is derived and the appropriate XML content generated. Second, since what we are interested in is the XML structure rather than the document per se, what we generate as an intermediate form for the XSLT processor is actually the associated DOM (document object model) structure rather than the XML document.

The generated DOM tree conforms to an OMS/XML document type definition (DTD) which defines a representation of all database objects at a fairly high level, so that the resulting XML documents provide a good basis for the succeeding XSLT transformations. There exists a second "low level" OMS/XML DTD which is only used to transfer database content from one OMS database to another OMS database. Nevertheless, it is sufficient to implement only a wrapping mechanism for the "high level" document object model representation. The resulting DOM structure can easily be transformed to an XML document conforming to the "low level" DTD by applying a simple XSLT transformation.

Using generic XSLT templates for the various client devices, we are able to provide generic browsers and editors for the current set of client types. Adding a new client type involves implementing the corresponding servlet and writing the appropriate XSLT templates.

Specific application interfaces are supported through the customisation of XSLT templates. As an example, we have developed an application for a *community diary* that manages appointments and address book entries for a user community.

Many existing tools for web site engineering either rely on a specific form of client such as an HTML browser, or they require that different forms of clients be handled separately meaning that it requires significant development time to port an application to another form of client device. The goal of XIMA was to develop a universal client framework that requires minimal development effort to access an application via another form of client device. The effort required to support a particular client device goes into optionally customising the presentation to suit the device in question. Such general frameworks are particularly important when one considers how dynamic the world of mobile devices currently is. There are many questions as to whether technologies such as WAP will really become established or whether they will be replaced by either new technologies or new devices better capable of handling existing technologies.

4. GENERIC VOICEXML USER INTERFACE

The Voice Extensible Markup Language (VoiceXML) is an application of the Extensible Markup Language (XML) which enables interactive access to the web through standalone voice browsers or regular phones. Its major goal is to bring the advantages of well established web-based content delivery techniques to Interactive Voice Response (IVR) applications. Application navigation works by voice recognition or the use of Dual Tone Multi Frequency (DTMF) keypad input. The resulting aural responses feature digitised audio or synthesised speech output.

During the design phase of the aural user interface, we used the IBM Voice Server Development Kit [IBM Voice Server, 2002] which fully supports the VoiceXML standard. It further allowed us to test the application on a personal computer using a standard microphone prior to installing it on a commercial voice server platform.

In this section, we focus on the design of the generic voice browser which enables any OMS Java application database to be accessed using speech input and output [Geissbuehler and Heiniger, 2001]. We therefore had to design general interactive sequences for navigating through a database and accessing the constructs of the OM model i.e. objects, collections and associations.

Most of the general voice interface's output is generated dynamically based on XIMA's XML server results. To avoid a discordant mixture of digitised audio and synthesised speech, we decided to use synthesised speech for all outputs. For a specific application, as described in the next section, it still makes sense to use digitised audio output for the representation of static content (e.g. help information) to improve the user experience.

To define valid navigation commands, we use rather simple grammars consisting of only basic words and phrases. In our generic voice browser, almost all grammars are built dynamically based on the returned XML content and therefore do not contain complex sentences. The main advantage of a simple grammar is better voice recognition performance. On the other hand, we had to spend additional effort in designing the system prompts so that they guide the user to only choose one of the valid responses specified by the corresponding grammar. Keeping an end-user within "bounds" is an important aspect of overcoming fragility in the interface and may have strong effects on user satisfaction [Roe and Wilpon, 1994]. Since speech is slow, only essential data should be spoken. The prompts in our general aural interface are rather terse and normally not longer than a few seconds. This leads to compact dialogue structures, which is relevant if simple grammars are used as is the case here.

A problem of the generic voice browser is that collections of objects can become quite large and therefore an aural representation of such a collection's content may take some time. As stated in [Schmandt, 1994], voice response systems must strive to minimise the amount of time required to retrieve information: They must be brief, selective about content, and they should almost always be interruptible. For this reason, we decided to use a full-duplex (barge-in) implementation which lets a user interrupt the voice output if he hears the desired object or if he already knows his next step before the aural output is finished.

We further improved the navigational component by introducing special commands which are always active and therefore accessible in any situation. The user can get information about these always-active command by using the *commands* keyword. Nevertheless we did not use any of the built-in commands of the IBM Voice Server Development Kit to remain independent of a specific voice server framework.

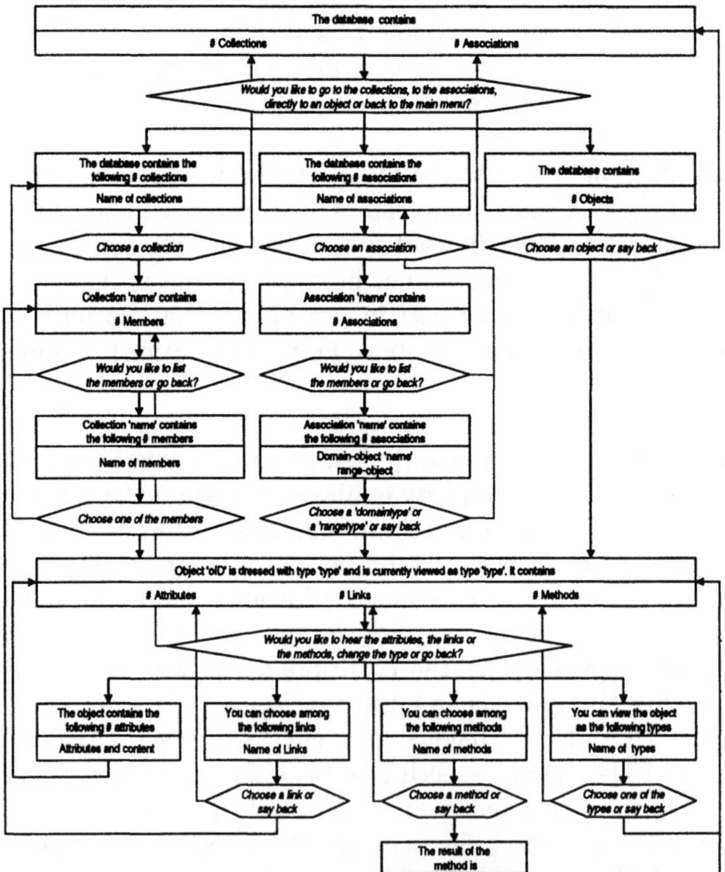

Figure 3. Generic Information Flow

An information flow chart of the generic voice interface is shown in Figure 3. The introductory prompt reads the number of collections and associations that the OMS Java database contains. A user can choose

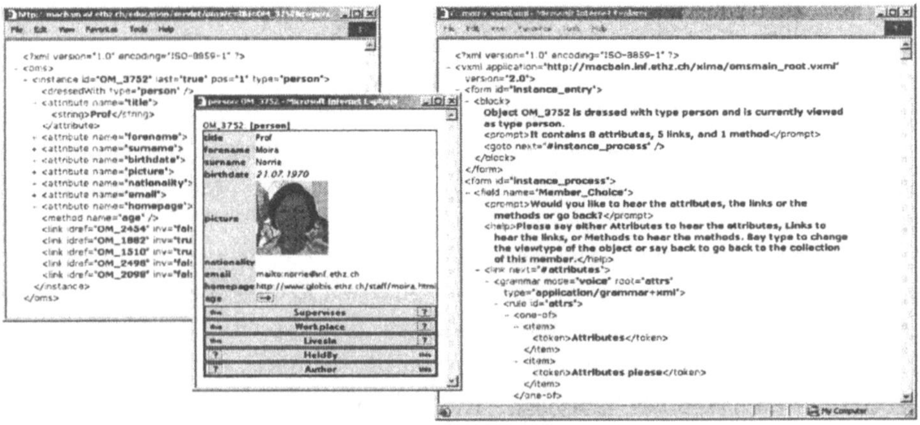

Figure 4. XML, HTML and VoiceXML Instance Representation

to go to the collections, the associations or directly to an object if he already knows the object of interest. One problem is to decide how individual objects can be referenced since it is not reasonable to expect the user to know the object ids. We have handled this by specifying an attribute within the OMS Java database, which acts as a *label* for each object type. For example, one might choose the *name* attribute of a type *person* to be the label attribute. Then a person instance could be accessed directly by giving the name of the person as the input.

An object instance contains attributes, methods and links to other objects. The links are generated dynamically based on the association information and allow easy browsing between related objects. An example of an object instance is shown in Figure 4. On the left hand side we show the XML representation of a database instance. The HTML transformation of this XML document is presented in the centre. A VoiceXML representation of the same XML content, which can be interpreted by a voice browser, is shown on the right hand side.

A first prototype of the general voice browser has been tested by several users. The test persons were given error recovery sheets on which they could mark errors or ambiguities in the application control flow. A first problem detected during this initial test phase was that the voice recognition did not always work correctly. The most common reason for voice recognition errors was the occurrence of multiple similar sounding words in our grammar. By refining the static part of the grammar and using synonyms for the "problematic" words, we could significantly improve the voice recognition performance. It was not possible to solve this problem for dynamically generated grammars. To support users in the case of voice recognition errors, we provide the always-active *back* command allowing them to browse back step by step.

Another common problem was that some users were not understood because they added additional filler words such as *please* to their commands. By extending our grammar with optional parts handling such filling constructs, we could further improve the voice recognition reliability.

In our first prototype, the *help* command always led to an aural presentation of the always-active commands. For most of the inexperienced test persons, this was not sufficient because they expected context dependent help for any potential input they had to provide. In the redesigned version, the application therefore does not switch into a separate help dialogue (help mode) when the user demands help, but uses self-revealing help. This means that suitable help information is integrated within each application dialogue and provides a specific output for the current situation. With this approach, no mode management and no audio formatting is necessary. The provided help is more specific and is closer to the dialogue style than in a help mode.

Users were often unsure as to whether the application had understood a command or if they had to repeat it. We therefore introduced an aural feedback after most of the user inputs. The application confirms every input with an *OK* prompt.

The current generic voice browser functions quite well and after a short amount of time, users are able to locate desired information within a database. However, the interaction can have a tendency to rapidly become tedious and, if little is known about the database content in advance, it is difficult for a user to keep track of their navigation within the database. In any case, it is important to remember that this generic voice browser is mainly intended as a first step in the rapid development of application specific interfaces as described in the next section.

5. APPLICATION SPECIFIC INTERFACES

To build a new application, the developer first prototypes the information model using OMS Pro [Würgler, 2000], a prototyping system for the OM model. During this early development stage, the model can already be tested by entering concrete data. In the next step, the prototype is ported to the OMS Java database management system which requires the implementation of a simple Java class for each type defined in the information model. The model and data can be exported from OMS Pro and imported in OMS Java using the Data Definition Language (DDL) and the Data Manipulation Language (DML), respectively. The OMS

Java application database is then already accessible by XIMA's generic voice browser. A final step is to customise the dialogues to improve the user experience as described in the following paragraphs.

The generic voice browser has been customised for a specific *community diary* which manages appointments and events for a user community and further offers some basic email functionality. The initial development phases of this application involved the steps described above and it was then the task of the developer to customise the XSLT stylesheets to refine the voice user interface. Note that this involved no changes to the results returned from XIMA's XML server component.

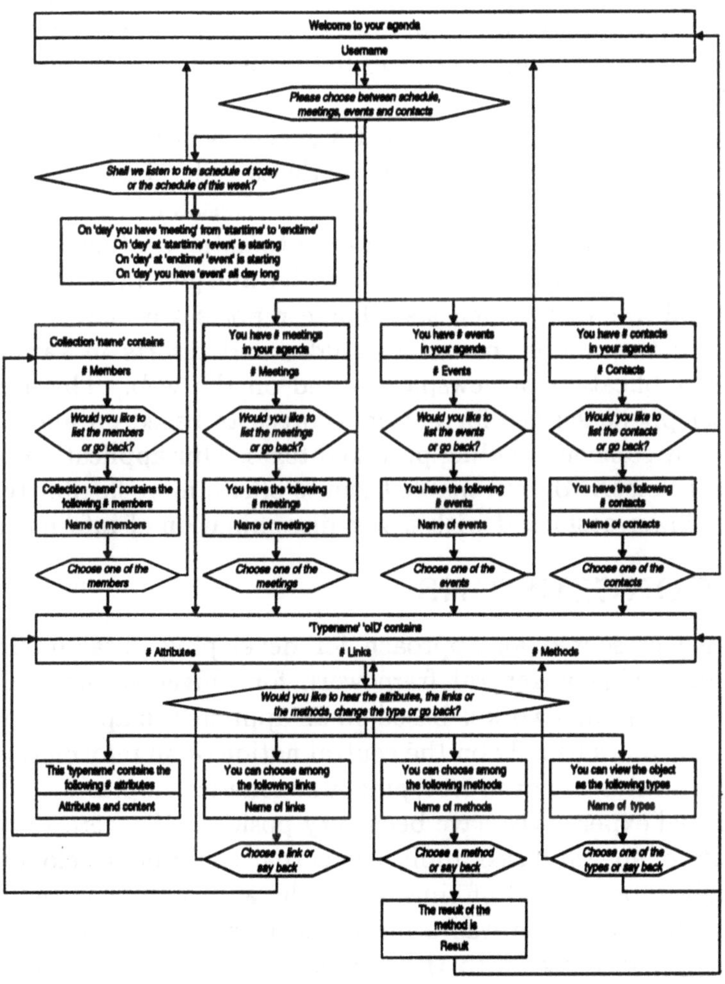

Figure 5. Diary Information Flow

By importing the generic XSLT stylesheets, we could inherit the base functionality from the existing stylesheets and only had to override specific parts. The final diary application allows a user to receive contacts information and to get a schedule of a day or the whole week. An information flow of the diary application with the customised dialogues is shown in Figure 5.

It is no longer possible to get access to all collections and associations defined in the diary's information model as explained in the description of the generic voice browser. Rather a few collections such as *meetings* or *contacts* can be accessed. We further had to add a component which allows access to the schedule of a day or a week as generated by operations defined within the database. While some parts of the generic voice browser interface have been refined, one can see that the lower part of the information flow diagram is exactly the same as the one shown before and therefore could be inherited from the generic voice browser interface.

In another project, we developed a special voice application service based on the XIMA framework for the Swiss Federal Institute for Snow and Avalanche Research (SLF) in Davos [Geissbuehler and Heiniger, 2002]. SLF gathers information from automatic weather stations and manual observers throughout the Swiss Alps and generates both national and regional avalanche forecasts. These reports are made available to members of the public, mountain guides and resorts in various ways including publication in newspapers and on the web. There is also a limited telephone service for national forecasts based on audio reports generated by someone reading prepared texts. Our application based on XIMA and VoiceXML will enable them to offer a more flexible telephone service at lower costs and with faster dissemination of information.

6. CONCLUSIONS

We have presented an approach for developing aural interfaces to applications using a general framework for universal client access to databases. The framework is based on an approach to application development that relies heavily on the central notion of an information model and the extensive use of prototyping and generic templates.

Our initial experiences have been very positive. We were surprised at the quality of speech-based applications that could be developed within a relatively short period of time given the approach that we followed. Not only that, but this was achieved as part of a general framework that also provides access to the applications from a range of desktop and mobile devices. At the same time, these experiments highlighted many challenges in terms of the best ways of designing speech dialogues — especially in the case of generic database browsers — and we intend addressing these in future projects.

REFERENCES

Anderson, C. R., Domingos, P., and Weld, D. S. (2001). Personalizing Web Sites for Mobile Users. In *Proceedings of the 10th International World Wide Web Conference*, Hong Kong.

Balentine, B. and Morgan, D. P. (1999). *How to Build a Speech Recognition Application: A Style Guide for Telephony Dialogues.* Enterprise Integration Group.

Batini, C., Ceri, S., and Navathe, S. B. (1992). *Conceptual Database Design: An Entity-Relationship Approach.* Benjamin/Cummings.

BeVocal (2002). BeVocal, Inc., http://www.bevocal.com.

Booch, G., Rumbaugh, J., and Jacobson, I. (1998). *Unified Modelling Language User Guide.* Addison-Wesley.

Freire, J., Kumar, B., and Lieuwen, D. (2001). WebViews: Accessing Personalized Web Content and Services. In *Proceedings of the 10th International World Wide Web Conference*, Hong Kong.

Geissbuehler, P. and Heiniger, D. (2001). Voice-Based User Interface for the eXtensible Information Management Architecture (XIMA). Semester work, Institute for Information Systems, ETH Zurich.

Geissbuehler, P. and Heiniger, D. (2002). Providing A Telephone Avalanche Warning Service Using XIMA, VoiceXML and WML. Diploma thesis, Institute for Information Systems, ETH Zurich.

IBM Voice Server (2002). Voice Server SDK, http://www-4.ibm.com/software/speech.

Kobler, A. and Norrie, M. C. (1999). OMS Java: Lessons Learned from Building a Multi-Tier Object Management Framework. In *Proceedings of the Workshop on Java and Databases: Persistence Options*, Denver, USA.

Kobler, A., Norrie, M. C., Signer, B., and Grossniklaus, M. (2001). OMS Java: Providing Information, Storage and Access Abstractions in an Object-Oriented Framework. In *Proceedings of the 7th International Conference on Object-Oriented Information Systems (OOIS'01)*, Calgary, Canada.

Norrie, M. C., Steiner, A., Würgler, A., and Wunderli, M. (1996). A Model for Classification Structures with Evolution Control. In *Proceedings of 15th International Conference on Conceptual Modelling (ER'96)*, Cottbus, Germany.

Roe, D. B. and Wilpon, J. G. (1994). *Voice communications between humans and machines.* National Academy Press.

Schmandt, C. (1994). *Voice Communication with Computers, Conversational Systems.* Van Nostrand Reinhold Verlag.

Signer, B., Grossniklaus, M., and Norrie, M. C. (2001). Java Framework for Database-Centric Web Engineering. In *Proceedings of the 4th Workshop on Web Engineering (in conjunction with 10th International World Wide Web Conference)*, Hong Kong.

VoiceGenie (2002). VoiceGenie Technologies, http://www.voicegenie.com.

VXML (2002). VoiceXML Forum, http://www.voicexml.org.

Würgler, A. (2000). *OMS Development Framework : Rapid Prototyping for Object-Oriented Databases.* PhD thesis, ETH Zurich.

VISUAL QUERYING IN GEOGRAPHIC INFORMATION SYSTEMS

Valéria Gonçalves Soares
Federal University of Pernambuco
Agriculture and Livestock Research Company of Rio Grande do Norte State
vgs@cin.ufpe.br,valeria@dmrh.emparn.br

Ana Carolina Salgado
Federal University of Pernambuco
acs@cin.ufpe.br

Abstract This article presents a framework that defines a visual query language for Geographical Information Systems (GIS). The main objective of the proposed framework is to improve the friendliness of a GIS interface, which is achieved by using pictorial information to build query clauses and by reducing the differences among GIS internal structures. The queries use visual elements and visual spatial operators, which are represented according to a Geographic Visual Query Language, the GeoVisualQL.

Keywords: Geographic Information Systems (GIS), Visual Query Language.

1. INTRODUCTION

A Geographic Information System – GIS is "a powerful set of tools for collecting, storing, retrieving at will, transforming and displaying spatial data from a particular set of purposes" (Burrough and McDonnell. 1998). Geographical data represent phenomena from the real world in terms of their position in coordinate systems, their attributes and their spatial interrelations with each other.

User interfaces for GIS require considerable research and technology development efforts for usability enhancement (Oliveira, 1997) (Wessel and Haarslev, 1999). An important aspect of usability in this context is the need for a visual query language to enable users to think graphically, while building queries. Most current GIS are able to generate graphical representations of query results, but only a few systems support graphical queries (Danko, 2000). It is difficult for the typical GIS users to formulate queries using complex spatial operators and related entities in a textual form. This difficulty can be reduced by the use of Visual Query Languages (VQL) (Calcinelli and Mainguenaud, 1994) and it is the motivation behind using visual queries in GIS.

Generally GIS interfaces have several differences from each other and they may offer too complex mechanisms to define queries. The proposed framework uses a Geospatial Metadata Standard (FGDC Standards, 1999) and Spatial Query Language (Open GIS Consortium, SQL, 1999) concepts to define a Geographic Data Visual Standard (*GeoVisual Standard*). The motivation behind using this GeoVisual Standard is designing user interfaces that are rather easier to use by improving data visualization and integration. This new standard is defined based on visual elements and spatial operators and is used to define the Geographic Visual Query Language (*GeoVisualQL*). The proposed GeoVisualQL is, in turn, syntactically and semantically defined to support the main Spatial Query Language structures.

Users will not need to learn the internal structures and the query language for each GIS being used. Instead, they will use the same visual language, based on metadata standard, to query several GIS. The proposed framework supports not only visual queries by the direct manipulation of visual elements, but also enables users to navigate through the metadata information at the interface, before building the queries.

The remainder of this paper is structured as follows. The next section presents some information about Visual Query Systems. Section 3 presents a discussion on Spatial Metadata Standards. Section 4 discusses on how spatial metadata can be useful in visual querying. Section 5 presents the proposed GeoVisual Query Language. Section 6 presents some related work. Finally, in section 7, the current status of our work is presented.

2. VISUAL QUERY SYSTEMS

Visual Query Systems (VQS) are database query systems that use a visual representation to depict the domain of interest and to express related requests (Catarci, et al. 1997). In addition to providing the capability to express queries in a visual form, these systems also provide different functionality to enhance human-computer interaction. The use of visual tools can help users in accessing databases without requiring previous learning on a specific query language.

The goal of a typical VQS user is to retrieve the desired data by developing two main activities: understanding the target domain and formulating the query. The query formulation can be done by four strategies that identify the VQS type: by schema navigation; by sub-queries, by matching and by range selection (Catarci, et al. 1997).

2.1 Visual Formalisms

The term visual language is used to describe several types of languages: languages for manipulating visual information; languages for supporting visual interaction and languages for programming with visual expressions (Golin and Reiss, 1990).

When we talk about visual languages we mean that they are completely different from textual languages in terms of their formalization. For example, consider a weather map: sometimes it is not clear how its syntax or semantics can be specified, or even if it has sharp and well-defined boundaries (Marriot and Meyer, 1998).

There are different approaches for specifying visual languages: the grammatical approach, that is based on grammatical formalisms used for the specification of textual languages; the first-order mathematical approach that uses forms of mathematical logic which often stem from artificial intelligence; and the algebraic approach that consists of composition functions which construct complex pictures from simpler pictorial elements.

After having analyzed different grammar approaches that can be used to specify visual languages (Gooday and Cohn, 1996) (Haarslev, 1995)(Marriot and Meyer, 1998) (Wang and Zeevat 1998) we have finally decided to use the Picture Layout Grammar – PLG (Golin, 1991) (Golin and Reiss, 1990), because it better satisfies our goals.

3. SPATIAL METADATA STANDARDS

Metadata describes the content, quality, condition and other relevant data characteristics (Hart and Phillips, 1999). The concept of metadata is familiar to most people who deal with spatial issues. A map legend, for example, is pure metadata (The Value of Metadata, 1999). Nowadays, most digital geospatial files have some associated metadata.

The Federal Geographic Data Committee (FGDC Standards, 1999) adopted a content standard for metadata, the Content Standard for Digital Geospatial Metadata (CSDGM), that is a spatial metadata standard developed to support the National Spatial Data Infrastructure (NSDI) (Tosta, 1998). The NSDI was created in order to coordinate data acquisition and provide access to geospatial data in USA. The Content Standard provides a consistent approach and format for the description of data characteristics.

In Europe, some initiatives that trend to gather research efforts shall be mentioned. A lot of different metadata formats and information systems are emerging all over Europe (Balfanz and Göbel, 1999) for example, CEN ENV 12657 and UDK 4.0. But both of them do not have neither levels of compliance or any methodology to extent the original metadata model. These are the main reasons for having used the Content Standard of FGDC in this work.

4. VISUAL QUERIES USING SPATIAL METADATA STANDARDS

We present a solution to the problem of querying GIS, especially in terms of their user interface. As mentioned above, Geographical Information Systems often do not provide friendly interfaces (Oliveira and Medeiros, 1996) (Oliveira, 1997). Generally the Query Language is specific and dependent on the Geographic Database internal structure. It is known that query formulation in traditional Spatial Query Languages (Egenhofer, 1992) is difficult because their structures are too complex. Typical users do not have the necessary knowledge of the language to express their real needs in a consistent manner (Oliveira and Medeiros, 1996) (Oliveira, 1997). Textual query clauses having several spatial entities and spatial operators related to each other are usually extremely confusing because spatial information is essentially visual.

The main objective of the proposed framework is to be as general as possible, so that the same interface can be used in several different GIS. For this purpose, users should be allowed to use exactly the same query format in any GIS.

4.1 Why Use Spatial Metadata?

The use of spatial metadata is important because we want to present geographic information from various GIS by always using the same format. In addition, the main objective of Spatial Metadata Standards, such as FGDC (FGDC Standards Reference Model, 1999), is to make spatial data clear and sharable.

The idea is to use a Standard for Digital Geospatial Metadata such as CSDGM (FGDC Standards Reference Model, 1999), because it allows users to describe several types of geographic entities by using its formalisms. Then, we aim to define a Geographic Visual Standard, the GeoVisual Standard, for several types of geodata by applying some of these spatial metadata definitions and based on the conceptual model of the OpenGIS Consortium (OGC) (OpenGIS Consortium, 1999).

We will represent spatial entities that are manipulated in GIS by visual elements in the GeoVisual Standard. In general, these visual spatial elements are represented by the following geometric entities: point, line and region.

This new visual standard describes many kinds of geographic elements, and, for each of these elements, their spatial operators allowed. The GeoVisual Standard defines how to describe geographic data visually. All the spatial entities that are manipulated in GIS are also represented by visual elements at the interface.

The Geographic Visual Query Language (GeoVisualQL) is defined using visual elements and spatial operators with syntactic rules based on the SQL Specification of the Open GIS Consortium (Open GIS Consortium, SQL, 1999). Spatial operators are also graphically represented in our system to allow users to compose queries in a completely visual form.

The syntax of GeoVisualQL was defined based on the SQL specification of the Open GIS Consortium (Open GIS Consortium, SQL, 1999). This allows all possible SQL structures to be constructed in the visual language as well. Before choosing the Spatial Query Language to be used in this definition we have done a comparative study about some of these languages (Egenhofer, 1994) (Sambura, 1998).

5. THE GEOVISUAL FRAMEWORK

The GeoVisual Framework is composed basically of four modules: GIS Components, Metadata Model, Query Manager, and Graphic Interface, as shown in Figure 1. All these modules are described in (Soares and Salgado, 2000) (Soares, 2002). In this paper we will discuss only the Query Manager Module.

The Query Manager Module is composed by the Geographic Visual Query Language – GeoVisualQL, and the Query Translator that converts the visual query to a textual query based on the SQL specification of the Open GIS (Open GIS Consortium, SQL, 1999). We will, now, present the GeoVisualQL. The Query Translator is under specification and will not be presented in this paper.

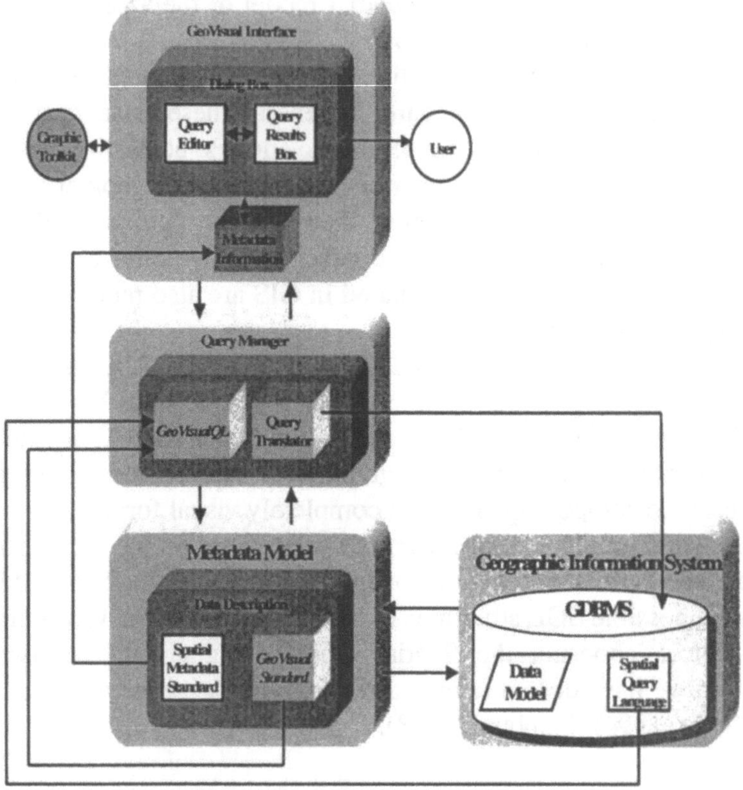

Figure 1 GeoVisual Framework

5.1 The GeoVisualQL

As stated before, the Geographic Data Visual Query Language – GeoVisualQL, is based on the SQL specification of the Open GIS Consortium (Open GIS Consortium, SQL, 1999). In order to formalize this language, some definitions have had to be specified:

Definition 5.1: The GeoVisualQL is a triple GQL = (O,R,Σ), where O is a set of graphic primitives that represent geographic objects, R is the set of spatial relationships allowed and Σ is the set of restrictions.

Pictorial Objects are geographic pictoric entities identified and with attributes. They can participate of spatial relationships that define relationships between objects and sub-objects.

Definition 5.2: A pictorial Object in GQL is a triple gql=(id,o,l) where id ε ID is the object identity derived from the set of identifiers ID, o ε O is its type and l (eventually null) is the values list of its attributes.

Definition 5.3: A pictorial relationship in GQL is a 6-tuple rp = (r,po1,po2,s1,s2,s3), where $r \varepsilon R$ is the spatial relationship type, po1 and po2 are both object identifiers or variable names and each sj (eventually null) is a set of object identifiers or variable names.

Based on the above definitions, we will define the components that are necessary to the GeoVisualQL specification.

5.1.1 Pictorial Objects

The pictorial objects of the GeoVisualQL and the Geographic Data Visual Standard, GeoVisual Standard are intrinsically related to the chosen spatial data model (Open GIS Consortium, 1999). The primitive graphic elements (i.e. the pictorial objects of GeoVisualQL) are based on the SQL Specification of the Open GIS Consortium Geometry Model (Open GIS Consortium, SQL, SQL, 1999): point, curve, line-string, line, line-ring, polygon, multicurve, multipolygon, multiline-string and multipoint.

5.1.2 Spatial Relationships

The Spatial Relationships and Spatial Operators used in GeoVisualQL with their respective restrictions are presented as follows. Consider the term any to represent any pictorial object defined above.

Definition 5.4: The following spatial relationships, and the type returned from each function compose the GeoVisualQL Language:

Equals *(any, any) : integer*

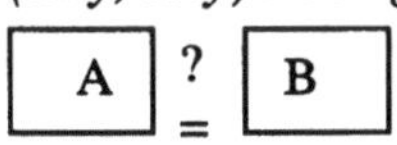

Disjoint *(any, any) : integer*

Touches *(any, any) : integer*

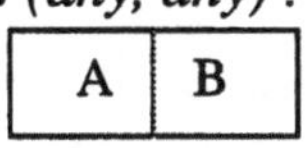

Within *(any, any) : integer*

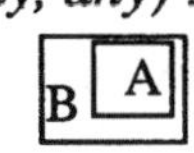

***Overlaps** (any, any) : integer*

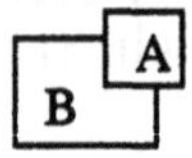

***Crosses** (any, any) : integer*

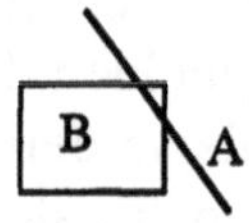

***Intersects** (any, any) : integer*

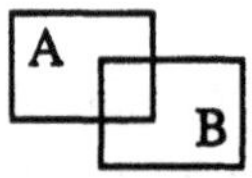

***Contains** (any, any) : integer*

***Relates** (any, any, string) : integer*

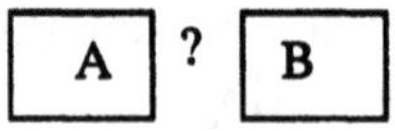

Definition 5.5: The following spatial operators also compose the GeoVisualQL Language. The resulting type is a pictorial object.

***Intersection** (any, any) : any*

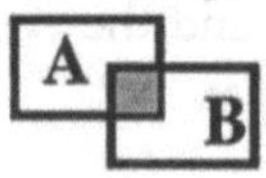

***Difference** (any, any) : any*

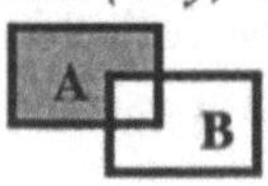

***Union** (any, any) : any*

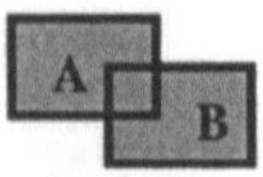

There are some others SQL functions defined in (Open GIS Consortium, SQL, 1999) but we will not represent them pictorially.

Auxiliary operators must be defined in GeoVisualQL to enhance the visual queries edition. The approach used in these editions, always consists of assigning pictorial objects to a given a spatial operator. To allow complex queries having more than one spatial operator and n pictorial objects to be executed we include logic operators to be used in these queries.

Operator AND: $\wedge$
Operator OR: $\vee$
Operator NOT: $\neg$

To group elements in the query construction we defined an auxiliary edition operator to be used if necessary. That is the Grouped edition operator. It is used to select which geometry entities are related with each chosen visual operator.

Figure 2 Operator Grouped

5.1.3 Formal Definition of Spatial Relationships in GeoVisualQL

The following definitions are some of the pictorial representations of the valid query clauses available in GeoVisualQL. After each of these clauses has been identified by the system as a valid clause, they will be translated to textual clauses based on the SQL specification of the Open GIS Consortium (Open GIS Consortium, SQL, 1999). It is important to note that all queries in GeoVisualQL are composed by visual elements that represent the geographic objects and by spatial visual operators that represent the spatial relationships among these entities. At this moment, we are not concerned about topologic analysis on the visual elements composing the query. We just check if there are two visual elements for each selected spatial operator. Then, the translation will be done and we will finally access the geographic database.

a)**Equals**

Definition: *The spatial relation* ***equals*** *is visually represented in Figure 3, and will be valid if and only if:*

EQUALS-CLAUSE →grouped (GEOMETRY1, Equals, GEOMETRY2)

Where

GEOMETRY1.feature == GEOMETRY2.feature

The **where** *restriction is a condition to accept and translate the visual query to the SQL clause.*

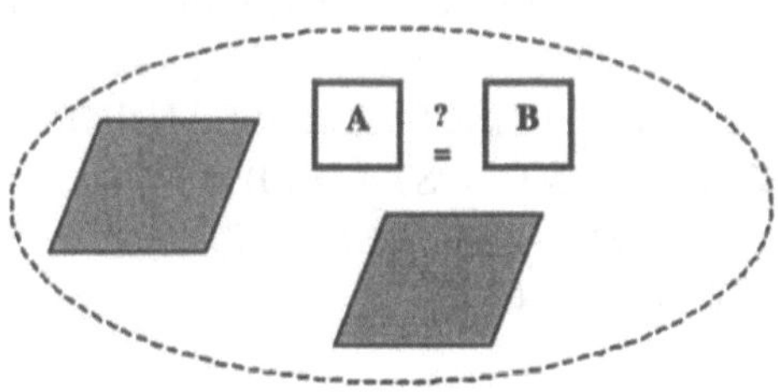

Figure 3 Representation of a visual query using the operator equals

b) **Disjoint**

Definition: *The* ***disjoint*** *operator is represented in Figure 4, and is valid if:*

DISJOINT–CLAUSE →grouped (GEOMETRY1, Disjoint, GEOMETRY2)

In this case, the DISJOINT operator can be applied to two of any known geometric objects; thus, there is no need for including any restriction.

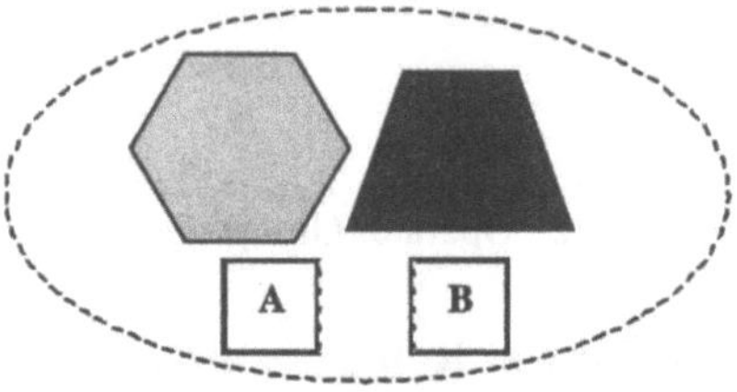

Figure 4 Symbolic representation of the visual query construction using the operator disjoint

The others operator clauses are constructed in a similar manner to these presented here and the complete definitions of these are defined in (Soares, 2002).

5.2 GeoVisualQL Grammar Definition

The start symbol of the language is the term STATEMENT. These are the production part of the language. These grammar definitions were defined based on (Golin, 1991).

GEOMETRY => point | curve| line-string| line| line-ring| polygon| multicurve| multipolygon| multiline-string| multipoint

STATEMENT => STATEMENT1 | AND-CLAUSE| OR-CLAUSE | NOT-CLAUSE

STATEMENT1 => EQUALS-CLAUSE | DISJOINT-CLAUSE | TOUCHES-CLAUSE | WITHIN-CLAUSE | OVERLAPS-CLAUSE | CROSSES-CLAUSE | INTERSECTS-CLAUSE | CONTAINS-CLAUSE | RELATE- CLAUSE | INTERSECTION-CLAUSE | DIFFERENCE-CLAUSE | UNION-CLAUSE

AND-CLAUSE => (STATEMENT $\wedge$ STATEMENT)

OR-CLAUSE => (STATEMENT $\vee$ STATEMENT)

NOT-CLAUSE => $\neg$ STATEMENT

LABEL => string

EQUALS-CLAUSE →grouped (GEOMETRY1, Equals, GEOMETRY2)

Where

GEOMETRY1.feature == GEOMETRY2.feature

DISJOINT–CLAUSE→grouped (GEOMETRY1, Disjoint, GEOMETRY2)
TOUCHES-CLAUSE→grouped (GEOMETRY1, Touches, GEOMETRY2)
WITHIN-CLAUSE → grouped (GEOMETRY1, Within, GEOMETRY2)
OVERLAPS-CLAUSE →grouped (GEOMETRY1, Overlaps, GEOMETRY2)
CROSSES-CLAUSE→grouped (GEOMETRY1, Crosses, GEOMETRY2)
Where
GEOMETRY1.type == line
INTERSECTS-CLAUSE→ grouped (GEOMETRY1, Intersects,GEOMETRY2)
CONTAINS-CLAUSE→ grouped (GEOMETRY1, Contains,GEOMETRY2)
RELATE-CLAUSE→ grouped (GEOMETRY1, Label, Relate, GEOMETRY2)
INTERSECTION-CLAUSE→grouped (GEOMETRY1, Intersection, GEOMETRY2)
DIFFERENCE-CLAUSE→grouped (GEOMETRY1, Difference, GEOMETRY2)
UNION-CLAUSE →grouped (GEOMETRY1, Union, GEOMETRY2)

The translation module will use these grammar definitions to produce valid textual clauses. We define in the next section an example of a query using the GeoVisualQL.

5.3 Example of a Query in GeoVisualQL

We shall now consider the following query where a user wants to know "*Does the Capibaribe River cross the city of Recife*?" The following steps will be needed to formulate the query:

1. Selection of the pictorial objects that best represent the query geographic entities.
   a. After selecting a polygon element, the feature associated with it must be selected (e.g. the feature ***City***). The *city* representation may either be part of the GeoVisual Standard at the interface, or it can be created and incorporated into the system for further queries. For the feature City, a specific instance must be selected and named *Recife*.
   b. A line must be selected to represent the feature ***River***. Following this, the instance must be identified and named *Capibaribe*.
2. Then the visual representation of the spatial operator *Crosses* must be selected and grouped together with the following two instantiated features: *Recife* and *Capibaribe*.
3. The query submission is executed. This query is illustrated in Figure 5.

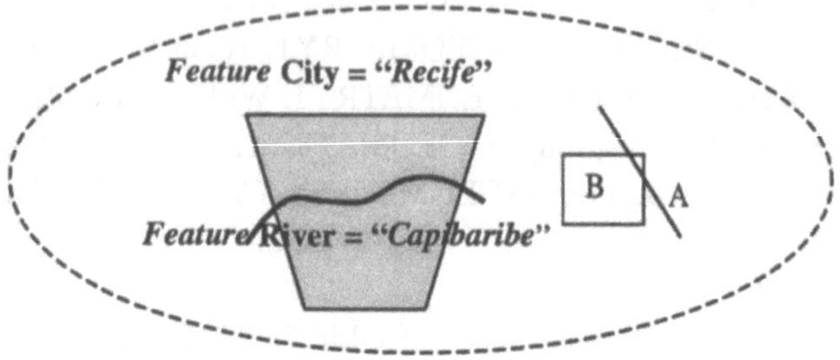

Figure 5 A Valid Query Example

After the query submission, the translation will be done by creating a textual clause in SQL, based on the specification of the OGC (Open GIS Consortium, SQL, 1999). This should be carried out by the system translation module that is now under specification.

In another example, a user could ask if the River mentioned above, *Intersects* **any** Road. This second query requires that two spatial operators are combined together by the logic operator AND, as we have specified at subsection 5.1.2. The feature *Road* does not need to be instantiated, and it need to be associated with the feature *River* named *Capibaribe* and with the spatial operator *Intersects*. So, the complete query "*Does the Capibaribe River cross the City of Recife and intersect any road?*" is shown in Figure 6.

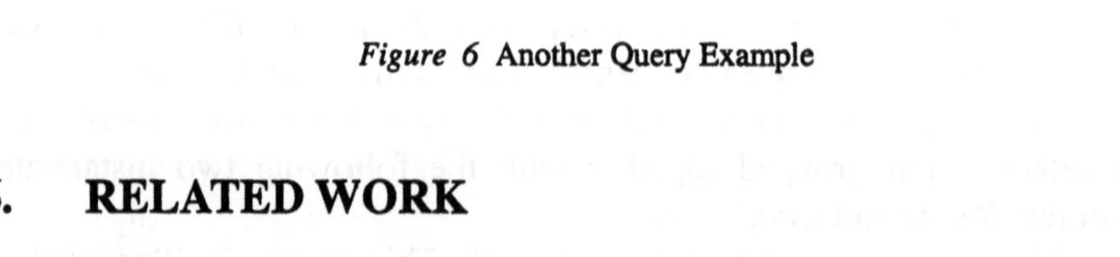

Figure 6 Another Query Example

6. RELATED WORK

There have been implementations of GIS research prototype that incorporate visual query languages (Blaser and Egenhofer , 2000) (Calcinelli and Mainguenaud, 1994). However, the shortcomings of these languages are two-fold. First, they do not use a standard to create the visual elements and spatial operators provided by their interface. Second, they are not based on metadata standards. Some of these proposals are briefly described bellow.

CIGALES (Cartographical Interface Generating an Adapted Language for Extensible Systems) is a visual and declarative query language for GIS based on a Query-By-Example approach (Calcinelli and Mainguenaud, 1994). This language is visual because a query is defined by a sketch of the spatial relationships involved in the query and is declarative because it only defines the properties to be verified by the query results. It is a graphical language, which provides users with an easy and natural means of manipulating geographical data. Cigales is designed to be an upper layer of a spatial Database Management System.

VISCO (Wessel and Haarslev, 1999) is a visual spatial query system designed for extracting information from spatial information systems, specially Geographical Information Systems. VISCO supports the retrieval of interesting sets of spatial objects based on their structural, topological, metric and geometric attributes and relationships between them. The language is based on a strong naive physics metaphor for query objects and assumes a topologically-structured vector representation of the data of interest.

At a first glance, Sketch! (Meyer, 1992) may seem to be very similar to the approach taken by the CIGALES project. However, Sketch! (Meyer, 1992) aim is to explore language concepts that are best suited for non-expert users, who are not familiar with computer language concepts, but are well informed about the structure of the data they are working with. In the Sketch! user interface, context-sensitive menus guides the user through a session so that only a little knowledge of the system is required.

Spatial-Query-by-Sketch (Blaser and Egenhofer, 2000) is a sketch-based user interface to query spatial information within a GIS environment. It associates sketching with freehand drawing, rather than with the construction of geometric figures or with the composition of icons or symbols. It also allows users to sketch what they are looking for, by using a set of interpretation algorithms, needed for pen-based querying of geographical information systems. Spatial-Query-By-Sketch focuses on the graphical interaction of drawing a spatial query.

7. FINAL CONSIDERATIONS

In this paper we have presented an approach for visual queries in GIS, which uses a spatial metadata standard, and proposes a solution to query different spatial data in several GIS. Based on the FGDC (FGDC Standards Reference Model, 1999) description of metadata, we propose a Geographic Data Visual Standard, GeoVisual Standard and a new Geographic Visual Query Language, GeoVisualQL, to be used by GIS users.

Users can build queries in a GIS with the information about the geographic database structures from the metadata information in interface and with the visual elements and spatial operators defined for the GeoVisualQL. The proposed framework also translates queries from the Visual Query Clause to the Textual Query Clause.

We presented in this paper GeoVisualQL grammar definitions and a query example, using some elements of the GeoVisual Standard. Currently we are specifying the Query Translation Process that will translate the visual query clause to a textual query clause based on the SQL specification of OGC (Open GIS Consortium, SQL, 1999). More information about this work can be found in (Soares, 2002).

REFERENCES

Balfanz, D. and Göbel, S. (1999). Bridging Geospatial Metadata Standards towards Distributed Metadata information Systems. *The Third IEEE Meta-Data Conference.* http://computer.org/conferen/proceed/meta/1999/papers/40/dbalfanz.html´

Blaser, A. D. and Egenhofer, M. J. (2000). A Visual Tool for Querying Geographic Databases. *Advanced Visual Interfaces* – AVI 2000, Palermo, Italy. http://www.spatial.maine.edu/~max/RC40.html

Burrough, P. and McDonnell, R. (1998). Principles of Geographical Information Systems. *Oxford University Press.* 1998.

Calcinelli, D. and Mainguenaud, M. (1994). Cigales: A Visual Query Language for Geographical Information System: The User Interface. *International Journal of Visual Languages and Computing, Academic Press,* Vol 5, pp 113-132. http://www-inf.int-evry.fr/~adm_bd/Cigales/Publications/cig_publi.eng.html

Câmara, G.; Casanova M. et. al. (1996). Geographic Information Systems Anatomy. *Tenth Brazilian Computer School.*

Catarci, T., et.al. (1997). Visual Query Systems for Databases: Analysis and Comparison. *Journal of Visual Languages and Computing,* Vol. 8, N. 2, pp. 215-260. ftp://ftp.dis.uniroma1.it/pub/catarci/VQSJVLC.ps.gz

Danko, D. M. (2000). Perspectives in the Development of ISO Metadata Standards. http://www.fgdc.gov/publications/documents/metadata/nimapaper.html

Egenhofer, M. J. (1992). Why not SQL! *Int. Journal Geographical Information Systems,* Vol. 6, No. 2, pp 71-85.

Egenhofer, M. J. (1994). Spatial SQL: A Query and Presentation Language. *IEEE Transactions on Knowledge and Data Engineering,* Vol. 6, No. 1.

FGDC Standards Reference Model. (1999). *Federal Geographic Data Committee.* http://www.fgdc.gov/

Golin, E. J. (1991). A Method for the Specification and Parsing of Visual Languages. PhD Dissertation, *Brown University,* Technical Report No. CS-90-19.

Golin, E. J. and Reiss, S. P. (1990). The Specification of Visual Language Syntax. *Journal of Visual Languages and Computing,* Vol. 1, No.2, pp. 141-157.

Gooday, J. M. and Cohn, A. G. (1996). Visual Language Syntax and Semantics: A Spatial Logic Approach. *Division of Artificial Language.* University of Leeds, England.

Guting, R. H. (1994) An Introduction to Database Systems. *Special Issue on Spatial Database Systems of the VLDB Journal*, Vol. 3, No. 4.
Haarslev, V. (1995). Formal Semantics of Visual Languages Using Spatial Reasoning. *IEEE.*
Hart, D. and Phillips, H. (1999). Metadata Primer – A "How To" Guide on Metadata Implementation. *National States Geographic Information Council.* http://rat.lic.wisc.edu/metadata/metaprim.htm
Marriot, K. and Meyer, B. (1998). (Editors). Visual Language Theory. *Springer Verlag.*
Meyer, B. (1992). Beyond Icons. Towards New Metaphors for Visual Query Languages for Spatial Information Systems. Interfaces to Database Systems, R. Cooper (Ed.), *Springer.* http://www.pst.informatik.uni-muenchen.de/~bmeyer/Papers/Publications.html
Oliveira, J. L. (1997). Interface Design and Implementation for Geographic Information Systems. *Phd Thesis. Unicamp*, Brazil.
Open GIS Consortium Abstract Specification (1999). Version 4. http://www.opengis.org/
Open GIS Consortium, Simple Features Specification for SQL. (1999). Revision 1.1. http://www.opengis.org/
Sambura, A. (1998). Spatial Extensions to SQL. *Proc. Of 16th Australian Conference on Urban and Regional Planning Information Systems* (URPIS 16), pp. 359-366. Australia, Sydney.
Soares, V. G. and Salgado A. C. (2000). A Metadata-based Approach to Define a Standard to Visual Queries in GIS. . In Proceedings of the International Workshop on Interacting with Databases in conjunction with the 11th International Conference on Database and Expert Systems Applications - *DEXA 2000*. London, UK.
Soares, V. G. (2002) GeoVisual – A Visual Query Framework for Geographic Information Systems. PhD thesis to be concluded. Informatics Center. Federal University of Pernambuco. Brazil..
The Value of Metadata (A NSDI Report). (1999). http://www.fgdc.gov/publications/documents/metadata/metabroc.html
Tosta, N. (1998). Continuing Evolution of the National Spatial Data Infrastructure. http://www.fgdc.gov/publications/publications.html
Wang, D. and Zeevat, H. (1998). A Syntax-Directed Approach to Picture Semantics. K. Marriot and B. Meyer (Editors). Visual Language Theory. *Springer Verlag.*
Wessel, M. and Haarslev, V. (1999). VISCO: Bringing Visual Spatial Querying to Reality. http://kogs-www.informatik.uni-hamburg.de/~mwessel/visco-engl.html

BIOGRAPHIES

Valéria Gonçalves Soares, MSc 92, UNICAMP, is a PhD Student at Informatics Center of the Federal University of Pernambuco. She works as a researcher at the Agriculture and Livestock Research Company of Rio Grande do Norte State. Her main interests are geographic databases and visual query languages.

Ana Carolina Salgado is an Associate Professor at the Universidade Federal de Pernambuco, Brazil (Center of Informatics). She obtained her Doctorate from the University of Nice (France) in 1988. Her main research interests are in the area of non-conventional databases, specially multimedia and geographical databases, data integration on the Web and cooperative systems. Dr. Salgado has published over sixty technical articles in conference proceedings and journals. She is a member of the Brazilian Computer Society. She is the head of the Center of Informatics and also held office as head of undergraduate studies.

AUTOMATIC ANNOTATION AND RETRIEVAL OF IMAGES

Yuqing Song
Department of Computer Science and Engineering
State University of New York at Buffalo
Buffalo, NY 14260 USA
ys2@cse.buffalo.edu

Wei Wang
Department of Computer Science and Engineering
State University of New York at Buffalo
Buffalo, NY 14260 USA
wwang3@cse.buffalo.edu

Aidong Zhang
Department of Computer Science and Engineering
State University of New York at Buffalo
Buffalo, NY 14260 USA
azhang@cse.buffalo.edu

Abstract We propose a novel approach for semantics-based image annotation and retrieval. Our approach is based on monotonic tree, a derivation of contour tree for discrete data. Monotonic tree provides a way to bridge the gap between the high-level semantics and low-level features. Each branch (subtree) of the monotonic tree is termed as a *structural element* if its area is within a given scale. The structural elements are classified and clustered based on their low level features such as color, spatial location, harshness, and shape. Each cluster corresponds to some semantic feature. The category keywords indicating the semantic features are automatically annotated to the images. Based on the semantic features extracted from images, high-level (semantics-based) querying and browsing of images can be achieved. The experimental results demonstrate the effectiveness of our approach.

Keywords: Content-based image retrieval, semantics, monotonic tree

1. INTRODUCTION

Although tremendous work has been done on content-based image retrieval, efficient and effective image retrieval still remains an open problem. Content-based image retrieval using low-level features such as color [Swain and Ballard, 1991; Smith and Chang, 1996b; Pass et al., 1996], texture [Manjunath and Ma, 1996; Smith and Chang, 1994; Sheikholeslami and Zhang, 1997], shape [Syeda-Mahmood, 1996; Mehrotra and Gary, 1995; Hirata and Kato, 1993] and others [Picard, 1996; Smith and Chang, 1996a; Ahuja and Rosenfeld, 1981] has been well studied.

However, retrieving images based on low-level features has been proven unsatisfactory. With the enormous growth of image databases, it is an urgent need to build image retrieval systems which support high-level (semantics-based) querying and browsing of images. Keyword indexing is a common scheme used by many picture libraries. For example, Getty Images [Bjarnestam, 1998] used over 10,000 keywords to index their collection of contemporary stock photographs. Current image indexing by keywords can only be done manually. According to [Eakins and Graham, 1999], the process of manual indexing suffers from two significant drawbacks. Firstly, it is inherently very labour-intensive. Secondly, manual indexing does not appear to be particularly reliable as a means of subject retrieval of images.

In recognizing the existing problems in the CBIR field, we believe that research efforts are needed to bridge the gap between the high-level semantics users are interested in and the low-level features that can be extracted. We propose a novel approach to extracting high-level semantics from low-level features. Our approach is based on monotonic tree [Song and Zhang, 2002]. Branches (subtrees) of the monotonic tree are termed as a *structural elements* if their areas are within a given scale. The structural elements are classified and clustered based on their low level features such as color, spatial location, harshness, and shape. Each cluster corresponds to some semantic feature. The category keywords indicating the semantic features are automatically annotated to the images. Based on the semantic features extracted from images, high-level (semantics-based) querying and browsing of images can be achieved.

We focus our attention on scenery images, which provide a popular testbed for semantics extraction. Technically, scenery images are relatively easier to analyze than other images. The reasons are following. Firstly, types of objects are limited in scenery images. Main scenery object types include sky, tree, building, mountain, lawn, water, and snow. Secondly, as compared with color, texture, or the spatial location of image elements, shape features are less important in analyzing scenery images than in other images. Thus we can avoid our weakness in shape matching when extracting semantic features.

The remainder of this paper is organized as follows. Section 2 introduces the idea of the monotonic tree. In Section 3, techniques for extracting semantic features are described. Section 4 presents case study of scenery features, while Section 5 describes our system design. Section 6 offers a performance evaluation of the proposed approach. A summary and concluding remarks appear in Section 7.

2. INTRODUCTION TO MONOTONIC TREE

Monotonic tree [Song and Zhang, 2002] is a derivation of contour tree for discrete data. Monotonic tree is used as a hierarchical representation of image structures. Contour trees [Morse, 1969; van Kreveld et al., 1997] have been used in geographic information systems (GIS) and medical imaging to display scalar data. Contours are only defined for continuous functions. For an image represented by discrete data, a continuous function is first defined as an interpolation of the data. Then the contour tree is defined on this continuous function.

We introduce a new concept termed monotonic line, which is directly defined on discrete data. An *outward-falling/climbing monotonic line* of an gray image is a boundary where the image assumes higher/lower values in the pixels adjacent to the boundary from inside than those from outside. All monotonic lines in an image form a rooted tree, called *monotonic tree*. A maximal sequence of uniquely enclosing monotonic lines is called a *monotonic slope*. All monotonic slopes in an image form the *topological monotonic tree*. A monotonic slope is called *outward-falling/climbing* if all monotonic lines in it are outward-falling/climbing. See Figure 1. For a color image, the monotonic tree and topological monotonic tree are constructed on its gray copy.

3. EXTRACTING SEMANTIC FEATURES

Our feature extraction scheme is based on the topological monotonic tree. We use the branches of the topological monotonic tree to model the basic structures in an image, which are termed as *structural elements*. Structural elements have low-level features such as color, shape, harshness, and spatial location. They are clustered to form high-level features.

Feature extraction consists of three consecutive steps: (a) classifying structural elements; (b) clustering structural elements; and (c) rendering semantic regions. See Figure 2.

3.1. Classifying Structural Elements

Each branch (a subtree) of the topological monotonic tree is called a *structural element* if it's covered area is no more than a threshold, which gives the scale in which we are interested. A structural element is called *posi-*

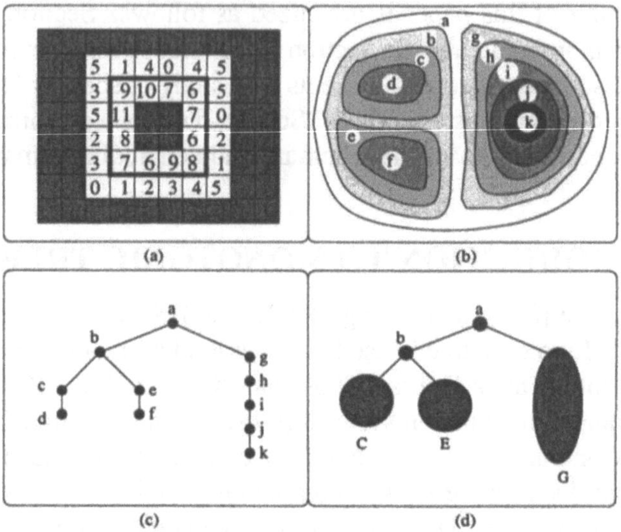

Figure 1. (a) An outward-falling monotonic line (the solid line in the figure), (b) a set of monotonic lines, (c) the monotonic tree, (d) the topological monotonic tree.

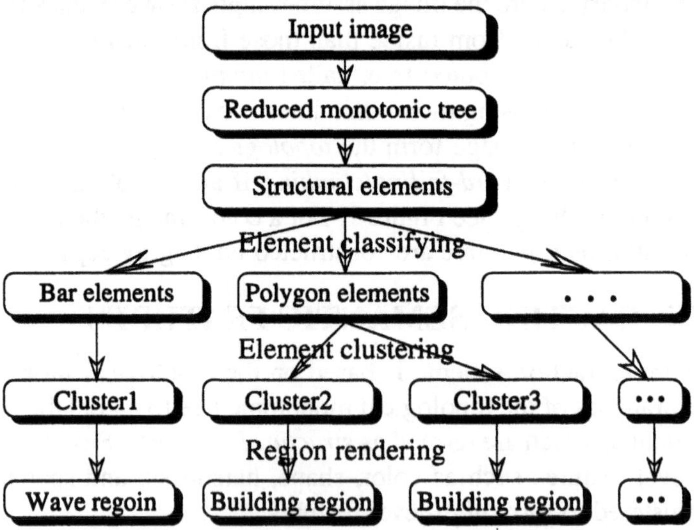

Figure 2. System design for feature extraction.

tive/negative if its root (root of the subtree) is outward-falling/climbing. See Figure 3(a). Positive/negative elements are like peaks/valleys. For a positive/negative element, we define its *altitude* to be the absolute value of the average altitude of all its pixels above/blow the highest/lowest pixels adjacent to the structural element. See Figure 3(b). The *harshness* of a structural ele-

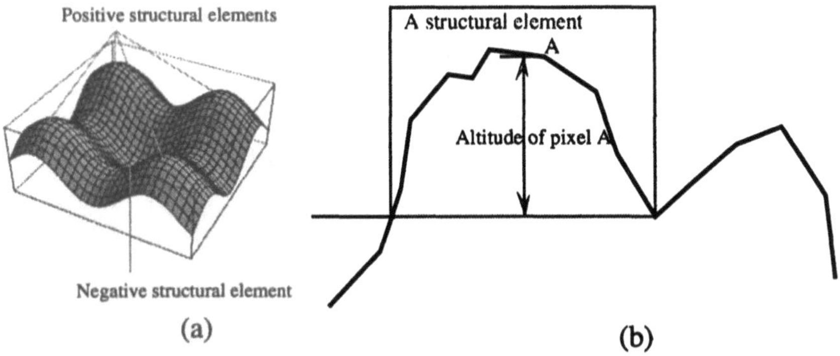

Figure 3. (a) Positive/negative structural elements; (b)the altitude of a pixel in a structural element.

ment is determined by the number, area and altitude of its sub-elements. [1] We define the harshness of an element t by

$$Harshness(t) = \frac{\Sigma_{b \in SubElementSet(t)} Altitude(b) * Area(b)}{Area(t)},$$

where $SubElementSet(t)$ is the set of sub-elements of t, $Altitude(b)$ is the altitude of b and $Area(b)$ is the area of the region covered by b.

A structural element can be classified by its (1) color (the average color of all pixels in this element), (2) altitude, (3) harshness, and (4) shape (the shape of its covered region). By shape, we can classify elements as: (a) bars, (b) polygons, (c) irregular elements, (d) boundary-smooth elements, and (e) others. For a bar element, the ratio of its length to its width is high. A polygon element is a structural element whose boundary mainly consists of line segments. For a smooth-boundary element, its boundary is a smooth curve. The irregular elements are those whose boundaries are irregular. Figure 4 shows different cases of elements.

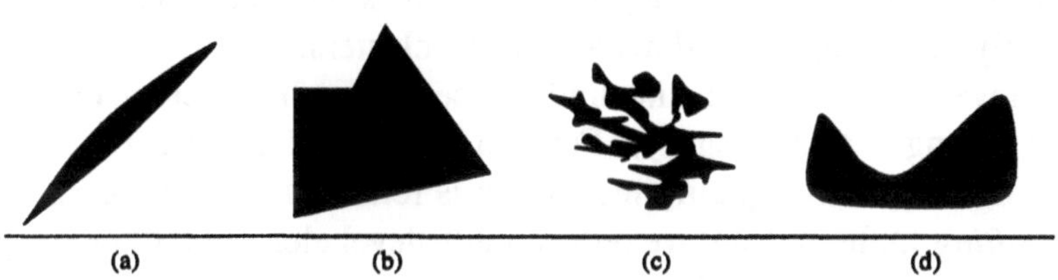

Figure 4. (a) A bar element, (b) a polygon element, (c) an irregular element, and (d) a smooth-boundary element.

The semantic features of scenery images are characterized by the categories of structural elements. Three examples of the categories are polygon elements (for building), horizontal bar elements (for wave), and green harsh irregular elements (for tree). See Figures 5 and 6.

Figure 5. An image of building (in the left) and the polygon elements (in the right) in it. The polygon elements are shown in black and white.

Figure 6. A image of river (in the left); and (a) green harsh irregular elements (shown in green or dark green), (b) horizontal bar elements (shown in black and white).

3.2. Clustering Structural Elements

Given an image, for each category of structural elements we are interested in, we apply clustering algorithms to find the clusters.

For a given category, we first find the set of qualified elements (i.e., the elements belong to this category). For two qualified elements, if they overlap, then the one with lower qualifying score [2] is removed. This process is called *element sifting*. After sifting, we reduce multi-level elements of the image into one level elements, which all belong to the given category. The elements after sifting form some element pattern in the 2D plane.

For the element pattern, we construct its Delaunay graph, which is the neighboring graph of the element pattern. We then apply clustering algorithms on the neighboring graph to find the clusters in the element pattern. In our implementation, the clustering algorithm is based on the minimal spanning tree of the neighboring graph. Reference on pattern processing by neighboring graph can be found in [Ahuja, 1982; Ahuja and Tuceryan, 1989]. Reference on clustering by minimal spanning tree can be found in [Zahn, 1971; Dugad and Ahuja, 1998].

3.3. Rendering Semantic Regions

Given a cluster of structural elements, the region rendering process consists of three steps: (1) element connecting; (2) hole filling; and (3) boundary smoothing. At the first step, we connect all elements in the cluster by line segments whose lengths are within a threshold. At the second step, we fill the holes whose areas are less than an area threshold. At the last step, we smooth the boundary of the region by removing those irregular angles and branches. Figure 7 shows an example of these steps.

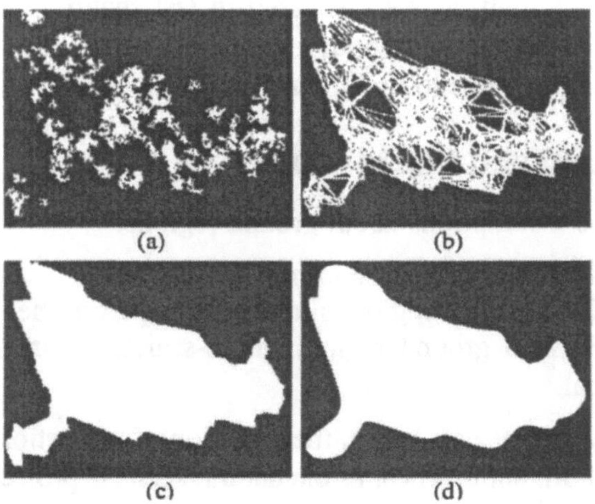

Figure 7. (a) A cluster of structural elements, (b) element connecting (c)hole filling, and (d)boundary smoothing.

4. CASE STUDY OF SEMANTIC FEATURES

In this section, we discuss the identification of high level scenery features: sky, building, tree, water wave, placid water, and ground. Water wave and placid water have different structures in images, thus they are treated with different schemes. The ground feature in images can be further split into snow, lawn and other kinds of ground.

4.1. Sky

Without clouds, a sky region is a homogeneous region consisting of blue pixels. In natural images, clouds tend to change smoothly at pixel level, due to their physical properties. In location, there is usually no other object above a sky region. To retrieve sky regions, We make three simple assumptions:

- (sky.a1) A sky region is smooth;
- (sky.a2) A sky region occupies an upper part of the image; and
- (sky.a3) The color of sky regions is either blue or the color of clouds.

For our current implementation, we assume that the color of clouds is black-white.[3]

To find the sky regions, we first find the smooth regions in the image. The smooth regions are the complement of the harsh regions, which is characterized by intensity peaks and valleys. Under monotonic tree, the intensity peaks and valleys are modeled as small structural elements whose altitudes are high. Thus we detect the harsh regions of the image by clustering the small elements whose altitudes are high, as we discussed in last section. When we get the harsh regions, we also get the smooth regions. Then we check the location and color of the smooth regions to find the sky regions.

4.2. Ground and Placid Water

We make three assumptions about ground regions.

- (ground.a1) A ground region is smooth;
- (ground.a2) A ground region is in the lower part of the image; and
- (ground.a3) In a ground region, micro-structures are more horizontal than vertical.

When scenery pictures are taken, the direction of projection is usually horizontal or nearly horizontal. Thus, as the natural scene is projected to the image plane, the structures on the ground appear more horizontal than vertical, which is the reason why we make the third assumption.

Similar to detecting background regions, we first find the smooth regions in the image. Then for each smooth region, we check if the last two assumptions hold or not. For the last assumption, we count the horizontal and vertical elements in the smooth region. The last assumption holds if the horizontal elements are more than the vertical elements in the region.

A ground region found this way could be lawn, snow, or other kinds of ground. We distinguish these kinds of regions by their colors. We assume that lawn regions are green, snow regions white.

For placid water, we make four assumptions. The first three are the same as the three assumptions of ground. Besides, we assume that the color of placid water is blue.

4.3. Wave

Small water waves have very regular patterns. When the small waves projected to a picture, they appear to be horizontal bars if the projecting direction is nearly horizontal. See the image in Figure 6. Wild waves have complicated structures. In the images with wild waves, we usually can detect a piece of surface consisting of parallel bar structures. See the image in Figure 8. We assume that a wave region is a region consisting of horizontal bar elements. We detect wave regions by clustering horizontal bar elements in the image.

Figure 8. An example of image with big wave.

4.4. Green Tree

If we look at the tree region in the Figure 6 carefully, we can find that the micro structures in the region are very irregular. Based on this observation, we assume that a tree region is a region consisting of green[4] harsh, irregular elements. The tree regions in an image are found by clustering the green, harsh irregular elements in the image.

4.5. Building

The shapes of most buildings are characterized by the line segments inside them. We assume that a building region in an image is a region consisting of polygon elements. To check whether a structural element is a polygon element, we first partition its boundary into line segments and other kinds of segments. A structural element is a polygon element if its boundary mainly consists of line segments. Reference on curve partitioning can be found in [Robl and Farber, 1998; Rosin and West, 1989; Rosin and West, 1992].

All of the above cases can be viewed in our demo system located at http://monet.cse.buffalo.edu:8888/.

5. IMAGE QUERYING

Our demo system, named SceneryAnalyzer, has three main components: (1) image database, (2) feature extraction, and (3) image querying. The feature extraction is done off-line. During feature extraction, each image is processed to generate semantic features, which are stored in a feature vector. The semantic features are automatically annotated in the gray copy of the original image. All feature vectors are stored in a vector base. To retrieve images, users can select any combination of the listed features. After the query is submitted, the icons of images with the selected features are output in pages. If users click an icon, a window is pop up with the original and annotated images.

6. EXPERIMENTS

We conducted experiments to compare the performance between our approach and traditional CBIR techniques including keyblock model [L. Zhu, A. Rao and A. Zhang, 2000], traditional color histogram [Swain and Ballard, 1991], color coherent vector [Pass et al., 1996], and wavelet (Haar and Daubechies) texture techniques [Smith and Chang, 1994; Strang and Nguyen, 1996]. The comparison is made by the precisions and recalls of each method on six scenery features: sky, building, tree, wave, ground, and placid water.

We used 6776 COREL images in the experiments. They are selected from CD7 and CD8 of COREL Gallery 1,300,000. The COREL images can be split into two parts: scenery and nonscenery parts. There are 4125 scenery images, which are pictures taken at countries all around the world. The nonscenery part has 2651 images, which cover a large variety, including different kinds of textures, marine fishes, molecules, space scenes, and insects. Table 1 shows the statistics of the scenery features in the COREL images (each entry shows the number of images with some feature).

Table 1. The statistics of scenery features in 6776 COREL images.

feature	sky	building	tree	wave	placid water	ground		
						lawn	snow	other
images	2369	1920	1479	161	882	298	68	659

For each scenery feature, to show the performance of SceneryAnalyzer, we calculate the precisions and recalls of first $\frac{n}{30}$, $\frac{2n}{30}$, $\frac{3n}{30}$, ... , and n images retrieved by SceneryAnalyzer with this feature, where n is the total number of images retrieved by SceneryAnalyzer.

Traditional CBIR techniques accept only queries by examples. Let's take an example to show how we choose query sets and calculate the precision-recall for these methods. The example is about keyblock on sky feature. There are 2369 COREL images with sky regions. For each sky image, we use it as a query on the COREL database to select top 100 images by the keyblock approach, and count the number of sky images in this retrieved set. Then we sort the 2369 sky images descendingly by the numbers of sky images in their corresponding retrieved sets. Let the sorted list be $SKYLIST$. Then we select the first 5%, i.e., 118 images of $SKYLIST$ as the query set, which is denoted as $QUERYSET$. Then for each COREL image I, we calculate its distance to $QUERYSET - \{I\}$ by the keyblock approach. The COREL images are sorted ascendantly by this distance. Top 2369 [5] COREL images are retrieved. Based on the retrieved images by keyblock, we calculate and plot the precision-recall of keyblock on sky, as we did for SceneryAnalyzer.

The result is in Figure 9. By comparing the graphs in Figure 9, we can see that our method outperforms all the others on each feature. To see the comparison clearly, we calculate the average precision-recall on the six scenery features, which is shown in Figure 10. From these comparisons, we can see that our method is much better than the traditional techniques on scenery features.

7. CONCLUSION

In this paper, we used a model termed monotonic tree to model high-level scenery features. Based on the monotonic tree representation, primitive elements of low-level features such as color, shape, harshness, and spatial location can be easily identified, clustered and combined to form semantically meaning regions (or features) for images. Thus, images can be automatically annotated with category keywords, including sky, building, tree, wave, lawn, water, snow, and ground. With this annotation, high-level (semantics-based) querying and browsing of images can be supported.

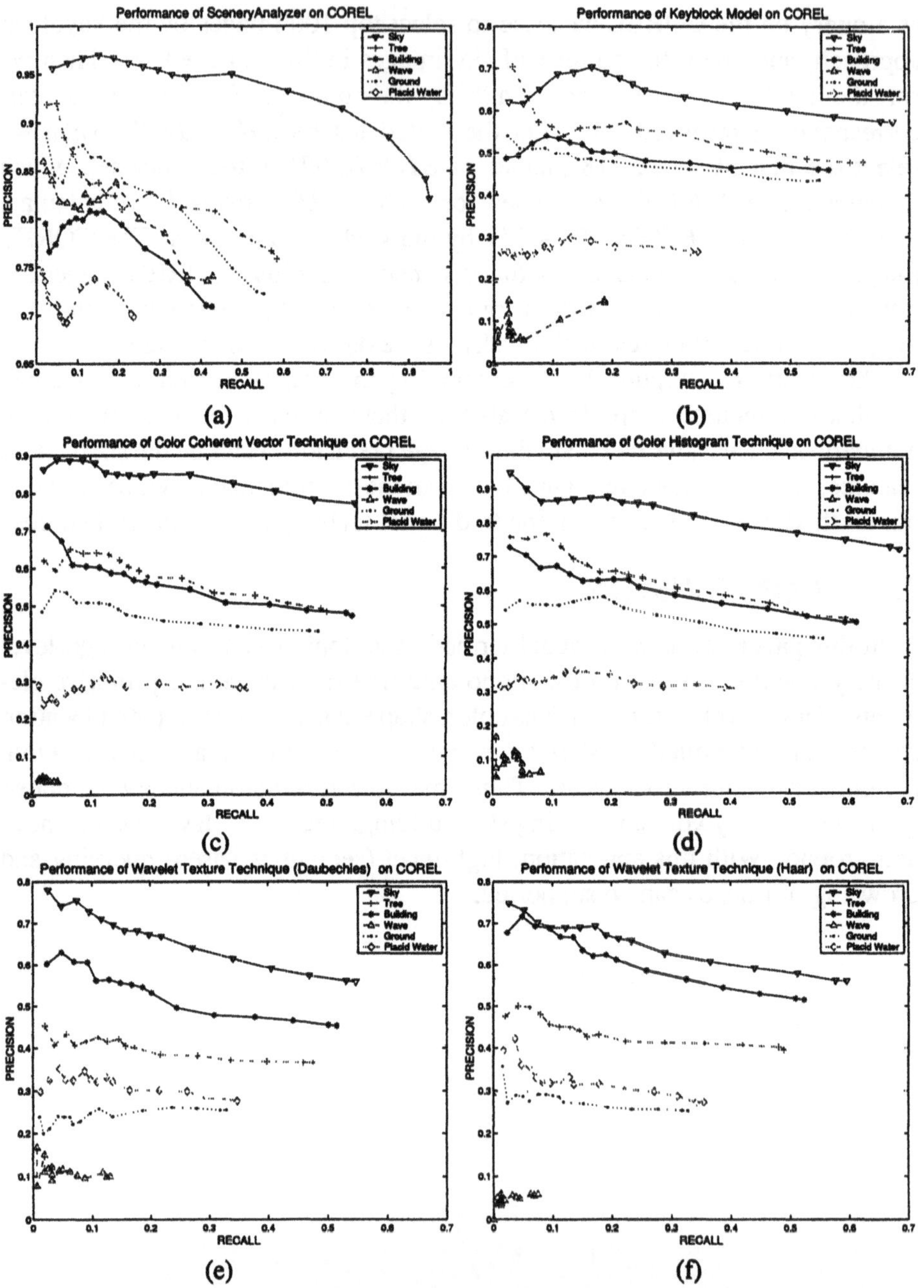

Figure 9. Performance of (a) SceneryAnalyzer, (b) keyblock model, (c) color coherent vector, (d) color histogram, (e) Daubechies wavelet, and (f) Haar wavelet on COREL images

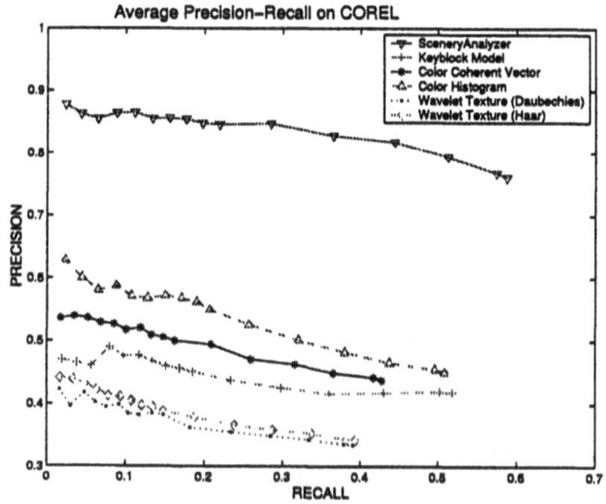

Figure 10. Average precision-recall on six features: sky, building, tree, wave, ground and placid water.

Notes

1. An element is a branch of the topological monotonic tree. All sub-branches of this branch are sub-elements.
2. For a given category, the qualifying score of an element indicates how qualified the element is to belong to this category.
3. Clouds can have more colors. In the following discussion, we also make some simple assumptions about the colors of trees, water and snow. More comprehensive color patterns of sky, trees, water, and snow can be integrated into our system, which is not the focus of this paper.
4. Again, we make a simple assumption about the color of trees.
5. This is the number of COREL images with sky.

REFERENCES

Ahuja, N. (1982). Dot pattern processing using voronoi neighborhoods. *IEEE Trans. on Pattern Analysis and Machine Intelligence*, 4(3):336–343.

Ahuja, N. and Rosenfeld, A. (1981). Mosaic models for texture. *IEEE Transactions on Pattern Analysis and Machine Intelligence*, 3(1):1–11.

Ahuja, N. and Tuceryan, M. (1989). Extraction of early perceptual structure in dot patterns: integrating region, boundary, and component gestalt. *Computer Vision, Graphics, and Image Processing*, 48(3):304–356.

Bjarnestam, A. (Feb.5, 1998). Description of an image retrieval system. In *The Challenge of Image Retrieval research workshop, Newcastle upon Tyne*.

Dugad, R. and Ahuja, N. (1998). Unsupervised multidimensional hierarchical clustering. In *IEEE International Conference on Acoustics Speech and Signal Processing, Seattle*.

Eakins, J. and Graham, M. (Jan. 10, 1999). Content-based image retrieval. In *Reports of JISC Technology Applications Programme*.

Hirata, K. and Kato, T. (1993). Rough sketch-based image information retrieval. *NEC Research & Development*, 34(2):263–273.

L. Zhu, A. Rao and A. Zhang (2000). Theory of keyblock-based image retrieval. *ACM Transactions on Information Systems.*

Manjunath, B. and Ma, W. (1996). Texture Features for Browsing and Retrieval of Image Data. *IEEE Transactions on Pattern Analysis and Machine Intelligence*, 18(8):837–842.

Mehrotra, R. and Gary, J. E. (1995). Similar-shape retrieval in shape data management. *IEEE Computer*, 28(9):57–62.

Morse, S. (1969). Concepts of use in computer map processing. *Communications of the ACM*, 12(3):147–152.

Pass, G., Zabih, R., and Miller, J. (1996). Comparing images using color coherence vectors. In *Proceedings of ACM Multimedia 96*, pages 65–73, Boston MA USA.

Picard, R. (1996). A society of models for video and image libraries. Technical Report 360, MIT Media Laboratory Perceptual Computing.

Robl, C. and Farber, G. (1998). Contour tracer for a fast and precise edge-line extraction. In *IAPR Workshop On Machine Vision Applications (MVA98).*

Rosin, P. and West, G. (1989). Segmentation of edges into lines and arcs. *Image and Vision Computing*, 7(2):109–114.

Rosin, P. and West, G. (1992). Multi-stage combined ellipse and line detection. In *British Machine Vision Conference (BMVC92)*, pages 197–206.

Sheikholeslami, G. and Zhang, A. (1997). An Approach to Clustering Large Visual Databases Using Wavelet Transform. In *Proceedings of the SPIE Conference on Visual Data Exploration and Analysis IV*, pages 322–333, San Jose.

Smith, J. and Chang, S. (1996a). Visualseek: A fully automated content-based image query system. In *ACM Multimedia 96.*

Smith, J. R. and Chang, S. (1994). Transform Features For Texture Classification and Discrimination in Large Image Databases. In *Proceedings of the IEEE International Conference on Image Processing*, pages 407–411.

Smith, J. R. and Chang, S.-F. (1996b). VisualSeek: a fully automated content-based image query system. In *Proceedings of ACM Multimedia 96*, pages 87–98, Boston MA USA.

Song, Y. and Zhang, A. (April 3-5, 2002). Monotonic tree. In *The 10th International Conference on Discrete Geometry for Computer Imagery, Bordeaux, France.*

Strang, G. and Nguyen, T. (1996). *Wavelets and Filter Banks*. Wellesley-Cambridge Press, Wellesley, MA.

Swain, M. and Ballard, D. (1991). Color Indexing. *Int Journal of Computer Vision*, 7(1):11–32.

Syeda-Mahmood, T. (1996). Finding shape similarity using a constrained non-rigid transform. In *International Conference on Pattern Recognition.*

van Kreveld, M., van Oostrum, R., Bajaj, C., Pascucci, V., and Schikore, D. (1997). Contour trees and small seed sets for iso-surface traversal. In *Proc. 13th Ann. Sympos. Comput. Geom.*, pages 212–220.

Zahn, C. (1971). Graph-theoretical methods for detecting and describing gestalt clusters. *IEEE Trans. on Computers*, C-20:68–86.

VISUALIZATION OF WEB-BASED AUSTRALIAN EXPORT TRADING

Lisa Soon and Phoebe Chen
School of Information Systems
Queensland University of Technology, Brisbane, Australia
{l.soon, p.chen}@qut.edu.au

Abstract: E-commerce applications tend to be used by a non-homogenous user population, requiring special attention to the modelling of underlying business processes, in order to make the execution of an activity as conspicuous as possible. Current modelling languages do not provide for concepts and symbols to represent all communicative aspects of a business transaction. Speech act theory offers categories that may be used to supplement the concepts and notations of current modelling languages. We are developing a Visual Business Modelling Language (VBML), for which we propose various speech acts in addition to the common symbols in a modelling language. To explore and demonstrate the expressiveness and logic of VBML, we apply it to the web-based Australian export trade. In particular, we show how an export trader can make a cargo declaration through the web to facilitate a document exchange with the Australian Customs Service. This model benefits application designers, software developers, Australian Customs Service, and the export traders since it delivers a clear view of the trade and the corresponding software application processes.

Key words: Visual Business Modelling Language (VBML), Speech Act Theory (SAT), Electronic Commerce, Electronic Data Interchange (EDI), traditional EDI, web-based EDI, XML/EDI

1. INTRODUCTION

It is essential that a model of a system is perceived as reflecting a piece of reality and the user's requirement (Bergholtz & Johannesson, 2000). While models help to understand the system by simplifying (Conallen, 1999), they should also capture systems and business details sufficiently.

There have been various modelling languages used to present software architectures, business systems, and an increasing emphasis on speech act theory in this context. We develop a Visual Business Modelling Language (VBML) that can break down the web-based business document information exchange and visually represent it by reflecting the essential user requirements and processes in Australian export trading activities. Using VBML, we built a business model for electronic document exchange between Australian export traders and the Australian Customs Services, using web technology and a traditional EDI (Electronic Data Interchange) network.

In the following section, we investigate some of the features of common modelling languages and their objectives. Then, we examine how Speech Act Theory (SAT) has been integrated into some modelling languages. Although it has been highlighted that SAT can address problems of a range of modelling languages, its categories have not been widely used as components, and they are not visually presented in models. The advantages of using the Visual Business Modelling Language are demonstrated in section 5. In concluding, we expect that VBML may be a valuable tool beyond the context of our case.

2. BUSINESS MODELLING OF BUSINESS APPLICATIONS

Many business models exist to guide businesses to enhance their conduct of commercial activities (Lawrence, 2001). Due to the common use of business applications over internet, intranet and extranet, there is a constant need of business modelling languages. Models help us to understand the system by reducing complexity (Conallen, 1999). It is critical that any proposed model is able to spell out the business requirements and components of system architecture through underlying business-modelling language. Therefore, many existing process description languages and business process languages (being modelling tools) place a great emphasis on business needs and requirements.

Examining process description languages (Johannesson & Perjons, 2000, Swenson, 1993, Guerin, 2001, Pitt, 2001, Scheer, 1999, Weske, 1999), process definition languages (Cass, 2000), and the Unified Modeling Language (D'Sourza, 1999, Tanuan, 1998, Conallen, 1999), shows some common pitfalls. Many languages highlight the importance of consideration of social acts or speech acts in the application design and in the business model. While there is an emphasis on the use of speech act categories in models, there are no visual representations for speech acts in any modelling language. A particular language uses only three speech act elements, namely belief, desire and intention (BDI) (Pitt, 2001). While BDI are critical in most business applications, the same applies to other speech act categories too. Because of such shortfalls, we have examined the types of speech act elements and the presentations of speech act symbols that are related to business activities.

We are testing the capabilities of the proposed components for modelling electronic commerce. Our objective is to represent visually web-based Australian export trade in a model. In section 3 we will present how we apply SAT to the business communication.

3. SPEECH ACT THEORY

As already mentioned above, various modelling languages apply speech act theory (SAT). SAT helps to clarify that messages are not just pieces of data, but have some social effects (Hasselbring & Weigand, 2001). Speech Act Theory is referred to in various disciplines such as philosophy, linguistics, communication, and sociology (Smith, 1990, Tien, 2000). A number of researchers in computer and communication technologies have already considered SAT in the design of applications.

The basic tenet of SAT is that speech acts imply a function of meaning (morpheme) in a communicative sentence. Three basic categories of speech acts are distinguished: A message can be locutionary to deliver a meaning; this act is to say something (e.g. love, hate, desire, etc). The illocutionary message (e.g. warning, convince, persuade, etc) has a force; it informs with a tone, attitude, feeling, motive or intention. The third is a perlocutionary act (e.g. promise, producing consequential effects).

Speech acts can be assertive (statement characterised as either true or false, e.g. The database is used over two networks), directive (get the hearer to do something, e.g. Please change that.), comissive (commits the speaker to some future course of actions, e.g. I promise to be there), expressive (expresses something to do with the speaker's psychological state, e.g. I hate this), declarative (makes the state of affair for the statement, e.g. The project is completed.). These speech acts provide us with the social and pragmatic aspects of communication needed for software architecture design. We apply SAT to communication as follows:

· Assertive: The users state what is true or false in the software application.
E.g. The permit is issued when approved is granted.
In our example of VBML model, we use: *acknowledgment, intention.*

· Directive: The users set a directive or instruct to have something done.
E.g. The multimedia message must contain fonts, colours, data, text, graphics, images, sound and video.
In our example of VBML model, we use: *request*.

· Comissive: The users want the application to achieve some kinds of end results.
E.g. the software must be developed as an inventory system.
In our example of VBML model, we use: *commitment*, *obligation*, *responsibility*, and *promise*.

· Expressive: The users state the cognitive preference of design features such as like/ dislike in the application.
E.g. Software caters for user-friendliness and ease of use with simple keyboard buttons and mouse clicks.
In our example of VBML model, we use: *belief* and *desire*.

· Declarative: The users require the state of work to be demonstrated.
E.g. The software development has to commence next month and end in six months period.
In our example of VBML model, we use: *trust*.

In our research, we focus on the more frequently used actions in general business applications, namely *belief, desire, intention, request, acknowledgment, commitment, obligation, responsibility, promise and trust.* The speech acts should be used in any model in order to cater for communicative, institutional, and deontic notion (Jayaweera et al., 2001). SAT reflects how language, understanding and communication work, and stresses the role of inference and context (Smith, 1990, Kimbrough, 1997). Speech act concepts are thus employed in developing and describing systems for information retrieval and computer-mediated communication (Johannesson & Perjons, 2000, Kimbrough & Moore, 1997, Winograd & Flores, 1987, Hassel, 1998). When deciding how to model something, determining the correct level of abstraction and detail is critical to providing something that will be of benefit to the users of the model (Conallen, 1999).

Considering the social effects qualifies the implementation of SAT as a soft approach in modelling. In contrast to that, most application systems are still built using a hard approach. The hard approach designs a system with the software application detailing the application structure for a particular type of hardware and operating system platform. Adopting a soft approach to supplement the hard approach, the design and development of an application system will capture in the critical business requirements. Therefore, there should also be an emphasis on the soft approach by incorporating speech acts as additional business details into application design and development. The speech acts we are proposing are limited to the generic ones and thus valid for most business applications, especially for electronic commerce activities over the web. Their usefulness is shown by the following examples:

- A user *believes* that a program task is performed to achieve a result.
- A user *desires* an instant response to an e-mail reply.
- A business client has an *intention* to book an air-ticket.
- The vendor *promises* to deliver the service.
- In electronic commerce, pressing the submit button is to *request* for a product with a buyer's *commitment*, *obligation*, or *responsibility* to pay for the product.
- After pressing the submit button, the browser user expects an *acknowledgment* message.
- The customer *trusts* that his *request* for product he sent and his payment *committed* will help him obtain the product finally.

The ten speech act categories are selected due to their anticipated frequency of use in all business application scenarios. The adoption of speech acts into a business model makes the system architecture salient with a more pertinent business requirements and user needs specification.

4. VISUAL BUSINESS MODELLING LANGUAGE

In modelling, the visual representation of actual knowledge on the application structure and business needs is essential; this is particularly true for complex systems. A useful visual language should specify, visualise, construct and document the artefacts of software systems. It should also be used to develop a business model and non-software systems by the systems designer and application developers. In a clear and well-explained model, any hidden facts and ideas will be made explicit with graphical symbols and simple textual notations.

We are therefore developing a Visual Business Modelling Language (VBML). VBML contains the essential graphical symbols for speech act elements (*belief, desire, intention, request, acknowledgment, commitment, obligation, responsibility, promise and trust*) and for process description elements. For simplicity reasons, we allocate to desire and intention one symbol since both acts are too close in semantic social effects. The same applies to commitment, obligation, and responsibility. Therefore, the ten speech acts are presented by seven graphical symbols in VBML. Other than symbols, VBML allows simplified textual notations to explain ideas within a model. The graphical symbols we develop aim at demonstrating both the business process symbols and the essential speech act elements that have not been adopted yet by many modelling languages. All proposed BML symbols are shown in figure 1, followed by an explanation of their semantics.

4.1 Visual Business Modelling Language (VBML) and Its Graphical Symbols

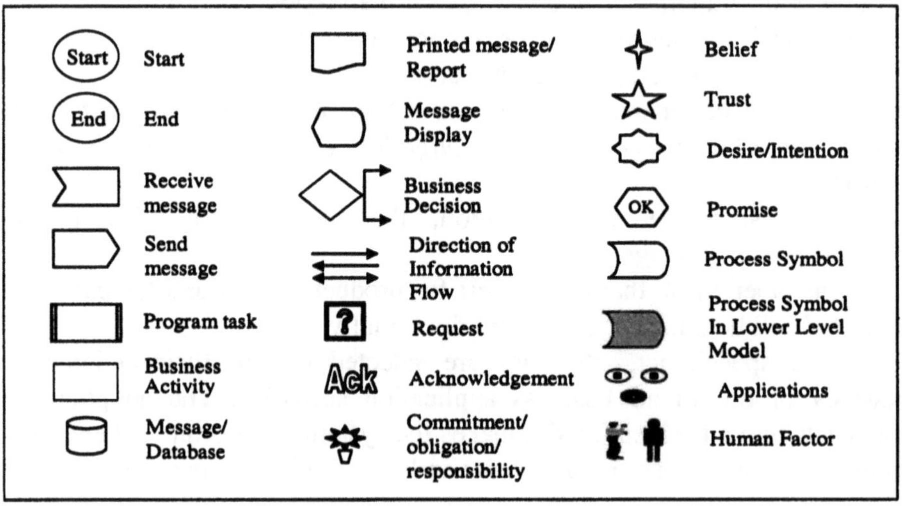

Figure 1. Symbols used in VBML

The symbols in figure 1 are defined as follows:

Start	Indicates the start of any process instance.
End	Describes the end of a message flow of the process instance.
Receive Message	Describes the acceptance of a message from the input queue.
Send Message	Describes the sending of a message.
Program task	It is a predefined software program to perform a designated task.
Business Activity	Describes any business operation(s) to be performed on the process instance.
Message/ Database	This is the database either used in any business process or within a software system.
Printed Message/ Report	It is the output available in a hardcopy information format.
Message Display	It is the output available as softcopy information for display on computer screen.

Business Decision	The business decision is made here based on certain rules.
Direction of Information Flow	There are symbols to show the direction the information flows into the next process or activity.
Request, Acknowledgement, Commitment/obligation/ Responsibility, Belief, Trust, Desire/Intention, Promise	These are the speech acts shown in any related processes, program tasks, or at any point deemed appropriate in the model.
Process Symbol	At a higher level of model, the process symbol is used to indicate some tasks to be performed in a specific process in order to achieve a business activity.
Process Symbol in Lower Level Model	In a lower level model, two process symbols encapsulating one or more software applications are used to elaborate the program tasks needed in order to carry out a process not expanded at a higher level model.
Applications	These are the software applications used in various situations to perform specific program tasks.
Human Factor	Both are symbols showing actors taking part in the business activity or the use of software application.

5. MODELLING OF AN INTERNET BUSINESS APPLICATION WITH SPEECH ACT ELEMENTS – PROCESSING OF AUTHORISATIONS TO EXPORT BY THE AUSTRALIAN CUSTOMS SERVICE

Before the application of any visual aid, it is essential to know the background of application systems, so the use of visual aid can show the functions and application processes effectively. Hence, it is crucial for us to expound the conceptual understanding on the web-based export cargo declaration.

We began the requirements engineering with a case study (Yin, 1994) in the Australian Customs Service Information Centre. Data were obtained by interviewing customs officers, and by collecting government literature, descriptions of work processes and manuals on trade regulations and computer systems architecture. All of the available documentation was subjected to analysis (Weske et al., 1999).

The procedures an export trader has to follow through before the exportation of cargo are explained in figure 2. The web-based Australian export trade procedures involve two essential parties, namely Australian Customs Service (ACS) and export traders.

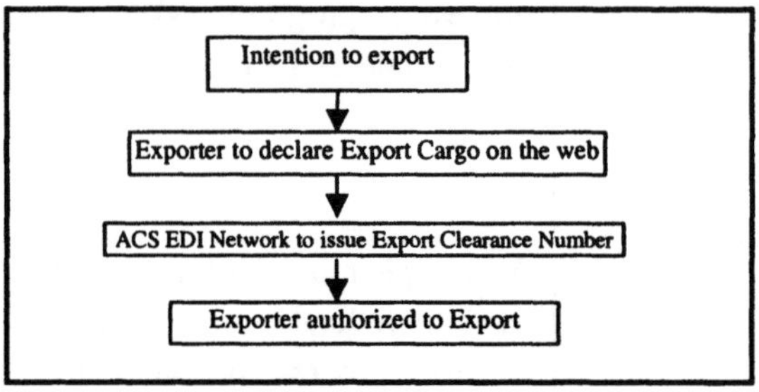

Figure 2. The Procedures an export trader has to follow through before any exportation

Figure 2 shows how an export trader with the *intention* to export has to declare his cargo with ACS as a *request*. Exporters of all goods need to obtain a legal authority (a *promise* from government) to export with an export clearance number from Australian Customs Service before any exportation (a *commitment*, *obligation* and *responsibility* to export).

5.1 Technological Architecture of Australian Export Trade

The Web-based declaration involves the use of a-browser to lodge an export cargo declaration/reporting. The message sent via the web-browser will have to be picked up by a traditional Electronic Data Interchange (EDI) network in ACS for processing. EDI is a form of paperless exchange of business documents over the telecommunication lines and private networks in standardised electronic format between the computer of an organisation and its customers and/or suppliers (Swindells & Henderson, 1998, Ketler et al., 1997, Clarke, 1999).

EDI is used in Australian Customs Service's two computerised EXIT systems for exporting purposes (Australian Customs Service, 1994). EXIT systems are the application systems that process the messages the export traders send via the web-browser. In other words, the Internet front end does not replace EDI (Hasselbring & Weigand, 2001). The web technology XML (eXtensible Markup Language) works together with an existing EDI network. Export traders use web-browser to communicate their message with ACS's EDI network. The community of export traders declares cargo through the web-browser. XML technology produces web-based EDI that is a common format for communication over the web and over the legacy EDI network. The export traders do not have pay to use the EDI network service but pay for Internet service to use the browser.

Using the graphical symbols designed above, we can simply provide a bird-eye's view on the business document processes involved in web-based Australian export trade.

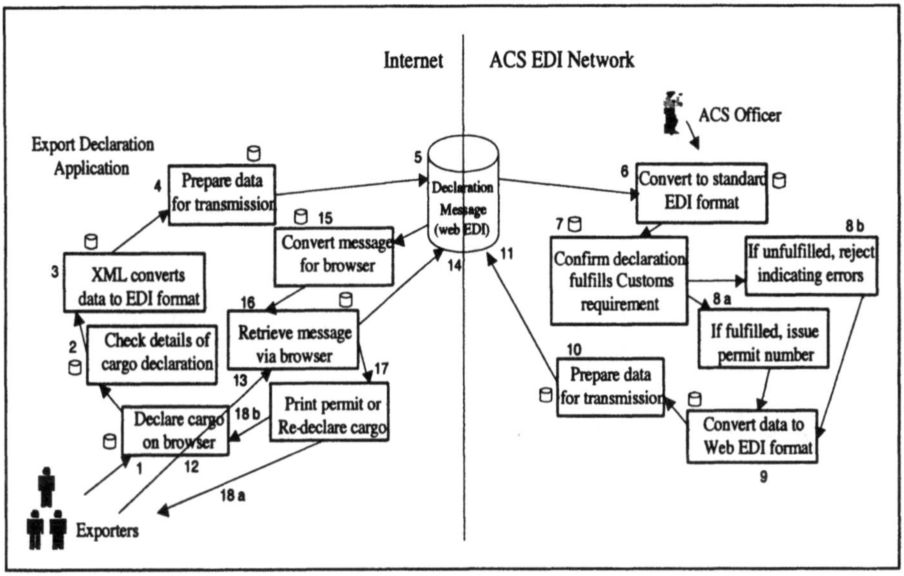

Figure 3. An Overview of Web-based Business Document Exchange in the Australian export trade

The internetworking by connection involving Internet and ACS EDI network is shown in figure 3. The vertical line indicates a data transmission required for the web-based message to be transferred to an EDI network for processing. The two types of human symbols represent both the export traders and the ACS officer handling and overseeing the activities. The message/database symbol represents a common web-based EDI format required for the web technology and the EDI network in ACS. On the left-hand-side of the vertical line, the activities taking place within a web export declaration application are shown. On the right-hand-side of the vertical line, the activities in the application over EXIT systems in the ACS EDI network are shown. The document exchange starts when the exporters use the web-based application to declare a cargo (box 1). Both the exporter and the application program will check the details of the cargo declaration (box 2). With XML, it converts the message into web-based EDI format (box 3). The application will then prepare the data for transmission (box 4). After the message is transmitted (via cylinder 5) into the ACS EDI network, the value-added network will convert such message into the required standard EDI format (box 6) for processing. The EXIT system application will check whether a declaration message contains all information required and fulfils customs regulations (box 7). If fulfilled, customs will issue an export clearance number (box 8a). If unfulfilled, customs will reject the declaration producing an error message (box 8b). Such information together with the original message will be converted into web-based EDI again (box 9). The system will then prepare (box 10) and store the message in the network mailbox (box 11). The exporter will retrieve the returned message over the internet (box 12). The exporter actually accesses the ACS EDI network mailbox picking up the processed message through Internet facility (box 13). When the web export declaration application picks up the returned processed message (box 14), it converts the message (box 15) for display on the browser (box 16). At the point when the message is displayed (box 17), the exporter either can print the issued permit (approval) to export the cargo (arrow 18a); or has to re-declare the cargo providing more details (disapproval hence error message, after arrow 18b). That starts the business document exchange cycle again.

5.2 Speech Acts in Australian Export Trade

We will examine the speech acts elements concerned throughout web-based business documents exchange between ACS and export traders before we can visually present them in our model. Speech act symbols are used in the model to demonstrate the export and ACS requirements on the software systems. With the knowledge of the business requirements from our case study, we have developed a model for web-based application systems.

Figure 4 shows that an exporter initiates an export declaration with a *belief* that the exporter will obtain an export clearance permit for the exportation of cargo. The exporter then submits a cargo declaration *request* to ACS for processing receiving an *acknowledgement*. There is a cargo reporting process in ACS to handle the message. After processing, the exporter will try to retrieve the declaration message with a *belief* that the request is answered. The retrieved message is a sign of *acknowledgement* of the message being received with either an approval or rejection with some error messages. If the reply message is an approval (*promise*), the exporter can print out the export clearance permit *trusting* with a *commitment* to export his physical cargo. Otherwise, the disapproval shown as a form of error message(s) will be displayed on browser. The exporter will now have an *intention* or *desire* to re-declare (*request*) his cargo again with a *belief* that his revised declaration will be reprocessed and issued with a permit.

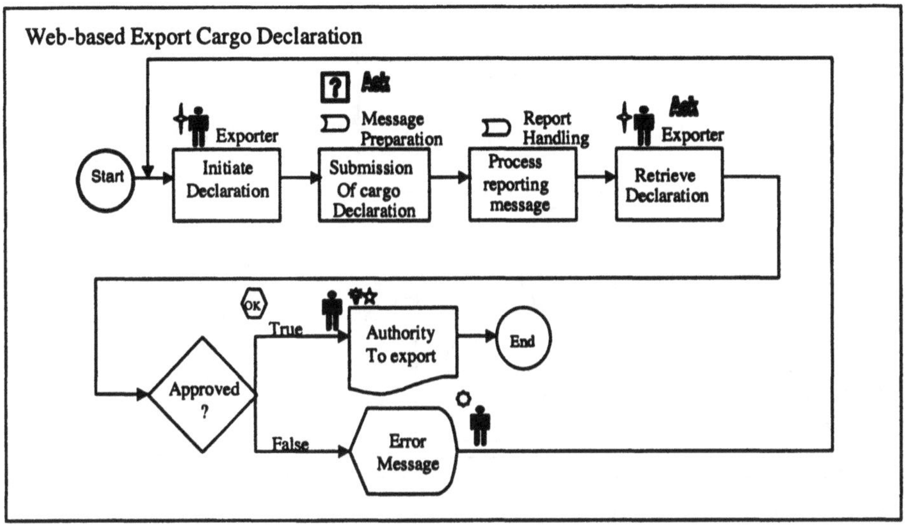

Figure 4. Export Cargo Declaration over the Internet

5.3 A Model with Further Details in Processes Involved in Web-based Australian Export Trading

Notice that there are two process symbols in figure 4 that need to be further illustrated. Therefore, the aims of figure 5 are to pursue the details not covered in figure 4.

We will first examine the details of the first *process* symbol (with the textual notation of message preparation above it) in figure 4. Note that this *process* aims at the submission of a cargo declaration. To show how the submission message can be prepared, we break down the program tasks involved in the export declaration software application. Over the web application, it first obtains the message entered by the exporter. The application will then validate the format of data entered. It also checks whether the data fulfil the general export requirements. The next task is to convert the message into the web EDI format. After conversion, it will send the message out as a *request* for permit over the Internet to the ACS. Once the transmission is performed, the application will prompt out an *acknowledgement* message indicating whether the transmission is done successfully.

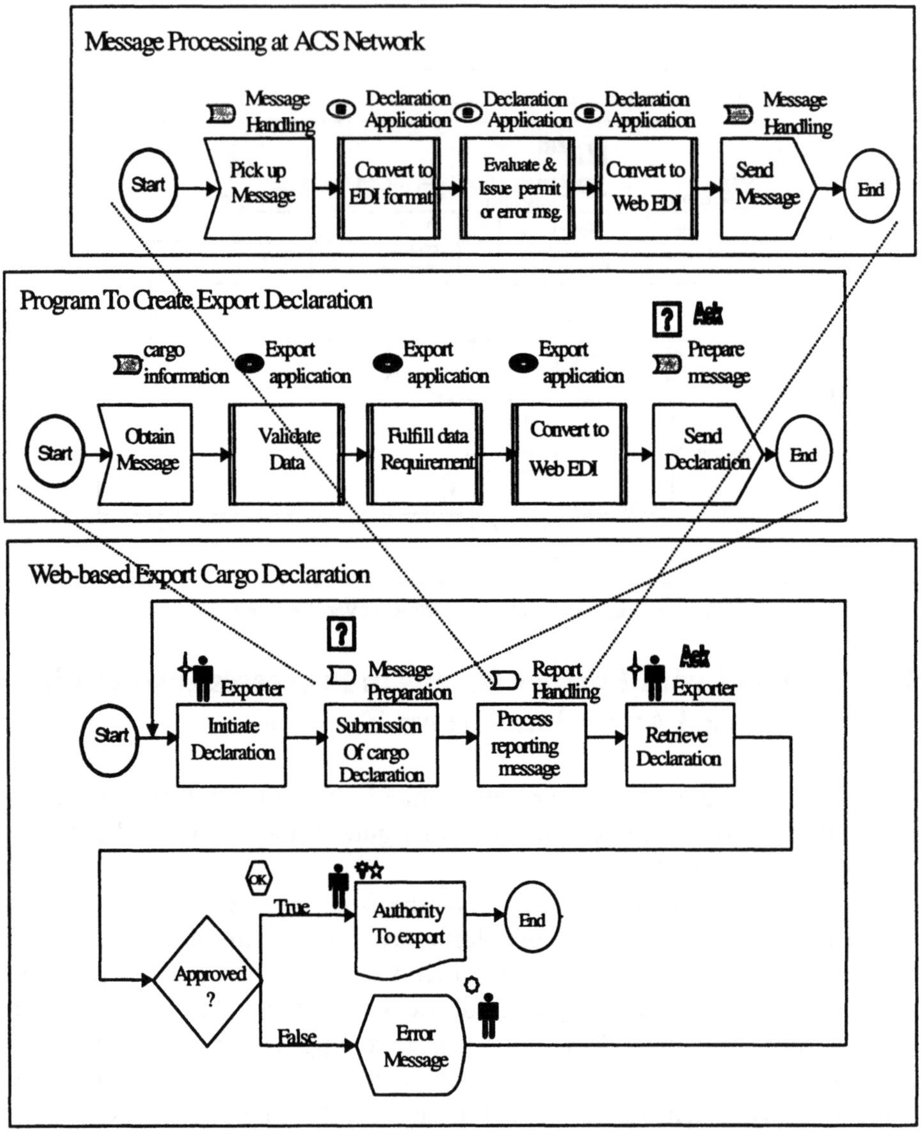

Figure 5. Elaboration of Processes Involved at ACS's End in Australian Export Trade

The details of the second *process* symbol (with the textual notation of report handling above it) in figure 4 are as follows: once the ACS network picks up the message sent over, the EXIT system application will convert the message into the standard EDI format (UN/EDIFACT) suitable for processing in the EDI network. The application will also evaluate the message for information required. It will issue the export clearance number for any message fulfilling the ACS rules and export requirements. Likewise, it will reject any message not fulfilling the rules and requirements producing one or more error messages for information omitted, erroneous, or incomplete in cargo declaration. The message will then be converted into web EDI format. Such a message is sent out from the ACS network and returned to the exporter via internetworking. In conclusion, figure 6 illustrates how various business activities and processes with the required speech acts can be represented visually in a model for Australian export trade.

6. CONCLUSION AND FUTURE DIRECTION

While the previous modelling languages have not described speech act elements and developed corresponding modelling symbols, VBML aims at fixing theses pitfalls. The use of all symbols in VBML allows for a more comprehensive coverage of aspects of requirements in the business model based on it. VBML implies also the proposition of the use of a soft system approach to supplement the traditional hard system approach in modelling. The advantages of the VBML models are that web-application designers, software developers, and business users can have much clearer views of the overall picture, the embedded processes and the application requirements of the integration work done. This has been shown by an application for the web-based Australian export trade.

We envisage that VBML can be further improved and modified. Currently, we regard it as a proposition awaiting more future development work. In addition, it will require more testing to ensure its applicability in other business contexts and to explore its acceptance within the potential VBML user communities.

REFERENCES

Australian Customs Service. (1994). EXIT Procedural Manual. *Canberra, ACT: Australian Customs Service.*

Bergholtz, M., & Johannesson, P. (2000). Validating Conceptual Models – Utilising Analysis Patterns as an Instrument for Explanation Generation. *Paper presented at the 5th International Conference on Applications of Natural Language to Information Systems.*

Cass, A. G., Lerner, B.S., McCall, E.K., Osterweil, L.J., Sutton, S.M., & Wise, A. (2000). Little-JIL/Juliette: A Process Definition Language and Interpreter. *Paper presented at the 22nd International Conference on Software Engineering, Limerick, Ireland.*

Clarke, R. (1999). Electronic Data Interchange (EDI): An Introduction. *Available: http://www.anu.edu.au/people/Roger.Clarke/EC/EDIIntro.htm [2001, 20th April].*

Conallen, J. (1999). Modelling Web Application Architectures with UML. Communications of the ACM, 42*(10), 63-70.*

D'Sourza, D. F., Wills, A.C. (1999). *Objects, Components, and Frameworks with UML: The Catalysis Approach*. Mass.: Addison-Wesley Longman.

Guerin, F., & Pitt, J. (2001). Denotational Semantics for Agent Communication Languages. *Paper presented at the 5fth International Conference on Autonomous Agents, Montreal, Quebec.*

Hassel, L. (1998). Media, Speech Act Theory and Computer Supported Cooperative Work. *Drexel University, U.S.A.*

Hasselbring, W., & Weigand, H. (2001). Languages for Electronic Business Communication: State of the Art. Industrial Management & Data Systems, 101*(5), 217-226.*

Jayaweera, P., Johnnesson, P., & Wohed, P. (2001). From Business Model to Process Pattern in E-Commerce. *Paper presented at the 6th International Workshop on the Language-Action Perspective on Communication Modelling (LAP2001), Montreal, Quebec.*

Johannesson, P., & Perjons, E. (2000). Design Principles for Application Integration. *Paper presented at the 12th Conference on Advanced Information Systems Engineering, Stockholm.*

Johnson, L. (1998). *Meaning and Speech Act Theory.* A Marvin Farber Conference on Law and Institutions in Society, SUNY Buffalo University.

Ketler, K., Willems, J., & Hampton, V. (1997). The EDI Implementation Decision: A Small Business Perspective. *Paper presented at the 1997 Conference on Computer Personnel, San Francisco, CA.*

Kimbrough, S. O., & Moore, S. A. (1997). On Automated Message Processing in Electronic Commerce and Work Support Systems: Speech Act Theory and Expressive Felicity. ACM Transactions on Information Systems, 15*(4), 321-367.*

Lawrence, E., Corbitt, B., Fisher, J., Lawrence, J., & Tidwell, A. (2001). Internet Commerce: Digital Models for Business *(2nd ed.). Brisbane, Australia: Wiley.*

Pitt, J., Kamara, L., & Artikis, A. (2001). Interaction Patterns and Observable Commitments in a Multi-Agent Trading Scenario. *Paper presented at the 5th International Conference on Autonomous Agents, Montreal, Quebec.*

Scheer, A. W. (1999). ARIS- Business Process Modelling. *Berlin: Springer.*

Smith, B. (1990). Towards a History of Speech Act Theory. In A. Burkhardt (Ed.), Speech Acts, Meanings and Intentions: Critical Approaches to the Philosophy of John R. Searle *(pp. 29-61). Berlin, New York: de Gruyter.*

Swenson, K. D. (1993). Visual Support for Reengineering Work Processes. *Paper presented at the Conference on Organizational Computing Systems, Milpitas, CA.*

Swindells, C., & Henderson, K. (1998). Legal Regulation of Electronic Commerce. The Journal of Information, Law and Technology (JILT), *3.(3), Available: http://elj.warwick.ac.uk/jilt/98-93/swindells.html [2001, 20th April]..*

Tanuan, M. (1998). Software Architecture in the Business Software Domain: The Descartes Experience. *Paper presented at the 3rd International Workshop on Software Architecture, Orlando, Florida.*

Tien, L. (2000). Publishing Software as a Speech Act. Berkeley Technology Law Journal, 14*(1), 1-57.*

Weske, M., Goesmann, T., Holten, R., & Striemer, R. (1999). A Reference Model for Workflow Application Development Processes. *Paper presented at the International Joint Conference on Work Activities Coordination and Collaboration, San Francisco, CA.*

Winograd, T., & Flores, F. (1987). *Understanding Computers and Cognition: A New Foundation for Design.* Reading, Mass: Addison-Wesley.

Yin, R. K. (1994). Case Study Research: Design and Methods. *Thousand Oaks, CA: Sage.*

BIOGRAPHIES

Lisa Soon is a research student in Information Technology at the Queensland University of Technology, Australia. Her current research interests include E-Commerce, E-Business, export trading and information management.

Phoebe Y. Chen is currently the Lecturer in the Faculty of Information Technology at the Queensland University of Technology, Brisbane, Australia. She completed her PhD in the field of Information Systems and Computer Science at the University of Queensland. Her research interests include scientific visualization, multimedia, bioinformatics, database, E-Commerce and web-based intelligent systems.

THE METRIC HISTOGRAM: A NEW AND EFFICIENT APPROACH FOR CONTENT-BASED IMAGE RETRIEVAL

Agma J. M. Traina, Caetano Traina Jr., Josiane M. Bueno
Computer Science Department
University of Sao Paulo at Sao Carlos - Brazil
[agma | caetano | josiane]@icmc.sc.usp.br

Paulo M. Azevedo-Marques
Science of Image and Medical Physics Center of the Medical School of Ribeirao Preto
University of Sao Paulo at Ribeirao Preto - Brazil
pmarques@fmrp.usp.br

Abstract This paper presents the *metric histogram*, a new and efficient technique to capture the brightness feature of images, allowing faster retrieval of images based on their content. Histograms provide a fast way to chop down large subsets of images, but are difficult to be indexed in existing data access methods. The proposed metric histograms reduce the dimensionality of the feature vectors leading to faster and more flexible indexing and retrieval processes. A new metric distance function *DM*( ) to measure the dissimilarity between images through their metric histograms is also presented. This paper shows the improvements obtained using the metric histograms over the traditional ones, through experiments for answering similarity queries over two databases containing respectively 500 and 4,247 magnetic resonance medical images. The experiments performed showed that metric histograms are more than 10 times faster than the traditional approach of using histograms and keep the same recovering capacity.

Keywords: content-based image retrieval, feature-based indexing techniques, histograms.

1. INTRODUCTION

The main practice used to accelerate the data retrieval in database management systems is indexing the data through an access method tailored to the domain of the data. The data domains stored in traditional databases - such as numbers and small character strings - have the total ordering property. This property leaded to the development of the current Database Management Systems - DBMS. However, when the data do not have this property, the traditional access methods cannot be used. Data embedded in multi-dimensional domains are examples of information that cannot be directly sorted. Spatial access methods have been developed for such data domains, e.g., the R-tree [1] and its derivatives, and the methods derived from the k-d-tree [2].

Complex data, such images, video, sound, time series and DNA strings, among others do not have implicit order property. That is, these data cannot be sorted using only their raw information, and there is no direct way to create an access method to improve their retrieval over sequentially scanning all of them. In this paper we focus on images. Sequential scanning over a large set of images is impractical due to the high computational cost of comparing two images. There are two usual approaches to search for images in an image database. The first one attaches textual description to each image, and the search process finds the required images through these texts. This is not a good solution, as besides it cannot be automatized, the retrieval depends on the objective of the operator when he or she was describing the image, not on the objective of the query. The second approach uses image processing algorithms to automatically extract characteristics from the images, which are then indexed. This approach is independent of human subjectivity, and is the one adopted in this paper.

Indexing the extracted characteristics is usually done through spatial access methods, where each extracted feature is a dimension. Regarding image histograms, each bin is indexed as a dimension. However, the spatial access methods are efficient up to a limited number of dimensions, in general not larger than 10 or 20. Indexing images through their histograms (usually with 256 bins or more) is highly inefficient. It has been shown [3] that the main factor affecting the efficiency of a multi-dimensional access method is the intrinsic dimensionality of the data set, that is, the number of uncorrelated dimensions. However, this indexing could be done more efficiently if the correlations between close bins were used. Many attempts have been done to find more concise representations of histograms using dimensionality reduction techniques [4] [5]. All these attempts leads to histograms representations with a reduced number of dimensions, but with a pre-defined number of dimensions.

In this paper we consider that histograms of two images can have different numbers of correlations between its bins, so reduced histograms from those images could have distinct number of dimensions. This points out that reduced histograms are in a not spatial domain - this domain does not have a defined number of dimensions, as each reduced histogram has a different number of "reduced bins". However, as we show in this paper, it is possible to define a metric dissimilarity function between any pair of reduced histograms, so this domain turns out to be a metric one. A new class of access methods, applicable to metric domains, has been recently developed. So, our proposed method of histogram reduction leads to a metric representation of the histogram, that can be indexed through a metric access method [6]. As we will show, this approach leads to a very precise retrieval of data, whereas it can be up to 10 times faster than using traditional histograms, even when using the same access method.

The main motivation of this paper is to develop an efficient technique for image retrieval aiming medical applications. The work shown herein is part of the development of a picture archiving and communication systems (PACS) [7], used to integrate the information regarding patients in a hospital. A PACS is a valuable tool helping the physicians when diagnosing. The images of medical exams are stored together with conventional data (text and numbers). Therefore, it is possible to ask both queries regarding the content of images and the usual queries based on textual information.

The remaining of this paper is structured as follows. In the next section, we first give a brief history of spatial and metric access methods, including a concise description of the main techniques for extracting image features aiming their comparison by content. Section 3 introduces metric histograms as well as the *DM* distance function to be used for comparing the new proposed metric histograms. Section 4 presents the experiments performed in order to evaluate the proposed method, regarding precision/recall and time measurements. Section 5 presents the conclusion of this paper.

2. BACKGROUND

Image database management systems rely on efficient access methods to deal with both traditional data (texts, numbers and dates) and image data. The design of efficient access methods has attracted researchers for more than three decades. There are many consolidated access methods for traditional data, such as the B-tree and hash-based indexing access methods. Spatial data have been addressed through the so called Spatial Access Methods - SAMs, which include treelike structures, such as the R-tree [1], R+-tree [8], R*-tree [9], k-d-B-Tree[10], space- filling curves [11], spatial hash files [12], etc. An excellent survey on SAMs is given in [13]. Spatial domains have been widely used to store feature sets from images and other complex data.

The majority of features extracted from images can be seen as multidimensional points in a *n*-dimensional space. This is the case of histograms, moment invariants, Fourier features, and principal component analysis among others. The well-known spatial access methods downgrade the retrieval of objects when the dimension of the objects increases and a sequential scan processing would outperform such methods. Therefore, other access methods which can deal with high-dimensional data sets could be used in order to answer questions on such objects. The X-tree [14] and TV-tree [15] were developed to manage high dimensional data. However, it is necessary to highlight that in some occasions it is not possible to have all the obtained feature vectors with the same number of components (dimensions). Thus, it is not possible to use any SAM. For such situations the Metric Access Methods - MAMs - were developed. In metric domains the only information available is the objects and the distances between them. The distance function is usually provided by a domain expert, who gathers the particularities of the target domain in order to compare objects.

Formally, given three objects, x, y and z pertaining to the domain of objects S, a distance function $d(\ )$ is said to be metric if it satisfies the following three properties:

i. symmetry: $d(x,y) = d(y,x)$,

ii. non-negativity: $0 < d(x,y) < 4$, $x \ \ y$ and $d(x,x) = 0$,

iii. triangle inequality: $d(x,y)$ # $d(x,z) + d(z,y)$

A metric distance function is the foundation to build MAMs, which were developed since the pioneering work of Burkhard and Keller [16]. They are now achieving an efficiency level good enough to be used in practical situations, as is the case of the M-tree [17], the Slim-tree [18] and the Omni-family members [19].

Data in metric domains are retrieved using similarity queries. The two most frequently used similarity queries are defined following.

- ***k-nearest neighbor*** or ***k-NN query***: $kNN=<s_q, k>$, which asks for the k objects that are the closest to a given query object center s_q, with s_q 0S (the object domain). For example, in an image database domain, a typical query could be: "*find the 5 nearest images to image$_1$*".

- ***range query***: $Rq=<s_q, r_q>$, which searches for all the objects whose distance to the query object center s_q is less or equal to the query radius r_q. Using the example previously given, a query could be: "*find all the images that are within 10 units of distance from image$_1$*".

Calculating distances between complex objects are usually expensive operations. Hence, minimizing these calculations is one of the most important aspects to obtain an efficient answer for the queries. MAMs minimize the number of distance calculations taking advantage of the triangular inequality property of metric distance functions, which allows to prune parts of the tree during the answering process. Metric access methods built on the image features have been successfully used to index images and are suited to answer similarity queries [20].

Direct comparison between images can be very costly. Thus, a common approach is to extract features from the images. The main features used to compare images are: color, shape and texture, as well as the spatial relationship between the image objects [21] [22] [23]. Many work has been done in the field of content-based image retrieval aiming to speed up such comparisons [24] [21], as well as proposing new techniques for image comparison, using color histograms [25], shape [26] and texture [27]. The algorithms to extract shapes and textures are very expensive and dependent on the application domain, so it is better to leave them as the last step for separating the images, when the candidate response set was already reduced using the other features. The importance of color or brightness histograms is due to the simplicity of getting and comparing them, operations that are performed in linear time.

3. THE PROPOSED IDEA - METRIC HISTOGRAMS

Images are commonly represented as a set of elements (*pixels*) which are placed on a regular grid. The pixel values are obtained from a quantization process and correspond to the brightness level. Thus, formally an image can be represented by the following notation:

Definition 1: An **image** *A* is a function defined over a two-dimensional range $G = [0,x_0] \times [0,y_0]$ taking values on the set of possible brightness values $V=[0,v_0]$. That is, $A = \{(x,y, v(x,y))/ (x,y)\ 0\ G \text{ and } v\ 0\ V\}$.

Definition 2: The **histogram** $H_A(z)$ of an image *A* provides the frequency of each brightness value *z* in the image. The histogram of an image with *t* brightness levels is represented by an array with *t* elements, called bins.

Definition 3: The **normalized histogram** $NH_A(z)$ of an image *A* provides the frequency of each brightness value *z* in the image, given in percentage. The normalized histogram of an image with *t* brightness levels is also represented by an array with *t* elements.

Obtaining the normalized histogram of images is not a costly operation. The normalized histogram is invariant to geometrical transformations as well as to linear contrast transformations. Normalized histograms allow comparisons of images of any size, so geometric transformations performed on the source images will give the same histogram.

Figure 1 shows an image obtained from magnetic resonance and its associated normalized histogram. This image has a spatial resolution of 512x512 pixels displayed in 256 brightness levels, thus its histogram has 256 bins. Indexing histograms like this one requires indexing arrays with 256 elements or, in terms of indexing structures, dimensions. The distance (or dissimilarity) between two histograms can be measured as the summation of difference between each bin, which is know as the Manhattan distance function or L_1 norm.

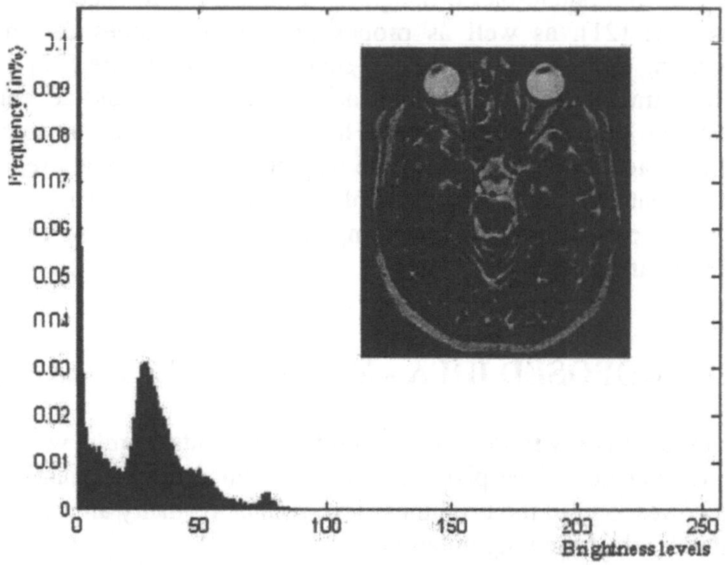

Figure 1 – An MR image and its normalized histogram.

In this work, we assume that the brightness levels are similar to its close levels, so the shape of the histogram can be kept using an approximation of it. Therefore, we propose to represent an approximation of a normalized histogram through a set of line segments. Histograms of different images can be approximated using different number of lines, so the approximation can be optimized to describe each histogram. Thus, these approximations are defined in a metric domain - this domain does not have a number of dimensions defined, as each approximation needs a different number of lines. This leads to the following definition.

Definition 4: A ***Metric histogram*** $MH_A(z)$ of an image A is defined as $M_H(A)=\{N_A, <b_k, h_k> \mid 0 \leq k < N_A\}$, which is a set of N_A buckets b_k, each one with the normalized height h_k.

A normalized histogram is composed by a number of bins. This number depends on the brightness resolution of the image, so it is a fixed number. In a metric histogram, the equivalent to the histogram bin is called a *bucket*. Each bucket corresponds to a line in the approximation. Buckets do not need to be regularly spaced. The number N_A of buckets in a metric histogram depends on the acceptable error in the approximation process and on the image itself. Each bucket k is a pair $<b_k, h_k>$, where b_k is the index of the rightmost bin of the original histogram represented in bucket k, and h_k is the normalized value of the rightmost bin represented in bucket k. Notice that b_0 is always zero. To simplify the notation, we indicate the bucket b_k of the metric histogram of image A as A_{bk}, and the normalized value h_k of the metric histogram of image A as A_{hk}. Figure 3(a) presents the metric histogram of two images A and B, and the components of their metric histograms.

The algorithm used to generate the metric histogram finds the ***control* points**, which are the inflection, minimum and maximum local points on the histogram, in order to create the approximation curve on the normalized

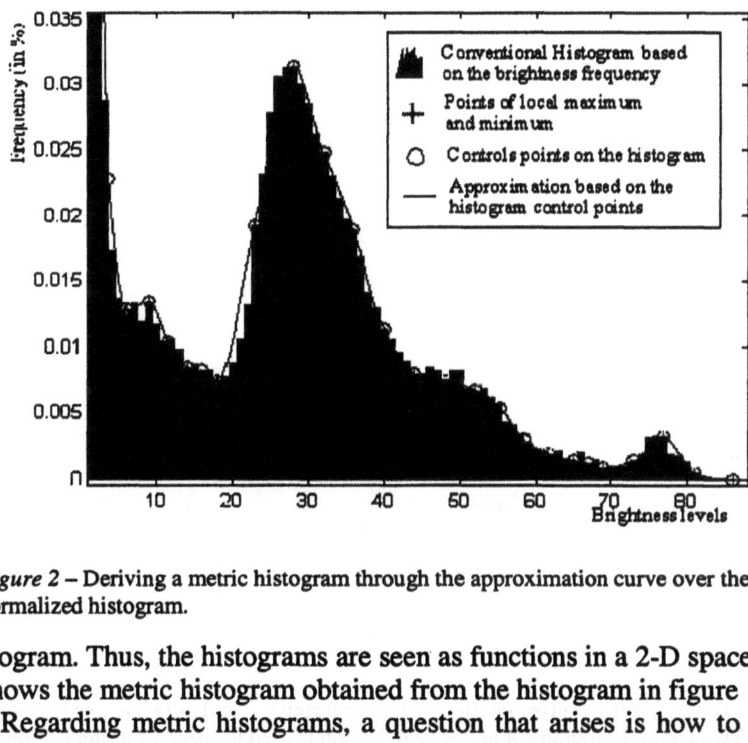

Figure 2 – Deriving a metric histogram through the approximation curve over the normalized histogram.

histogram. Thus, the histograms are seen as functions in a 2-D space. Figure 2 shows the metric histogram obtained from the histogram in figure 1.

Regarding metric histograms, a question that arises is how to compare them, as the number of buckets and the spawning of the buckets from different histograms are variable. That is, the usual distances for histograms, such as Euclidean, Chi-square, Manhattan, Kolmogorov-Smirnov, Kuiper, between others [4] cannot be used. Therefore, we developed a new metric distance function in order to quantify the dissimilarity between metric histograms.

Definition 5: The distance function ***MHD*( )** between two metric histograms is given by the non-overlapping area among the two curves representing the metric histograms, i.e.

$$MHD(M_H(A), M_H(B)) = \int_0^{end\_longest\_M_H} \left| M_H(A,x) - M_H(B,x) \right| dx$$

Figure 3 gives an example of how to calculate the distance between two metric histograms and figure 4 depicts the algorithm developed to calculate this distance function. In figure 3(a) the two histograms are overlapped, and the intersecting points and the ones which limit the buckets are shown. Figures 3(b) to 3(d) show how such points are used to calculate the area inside each region (in the steps of the algorithm in figure 3). Note that the number of steps is greater than or equal to the number of buckets of the histogram with more buckets. This is due to the fact that as the width of the buckets is variable, in some occasions they must be divided in order to

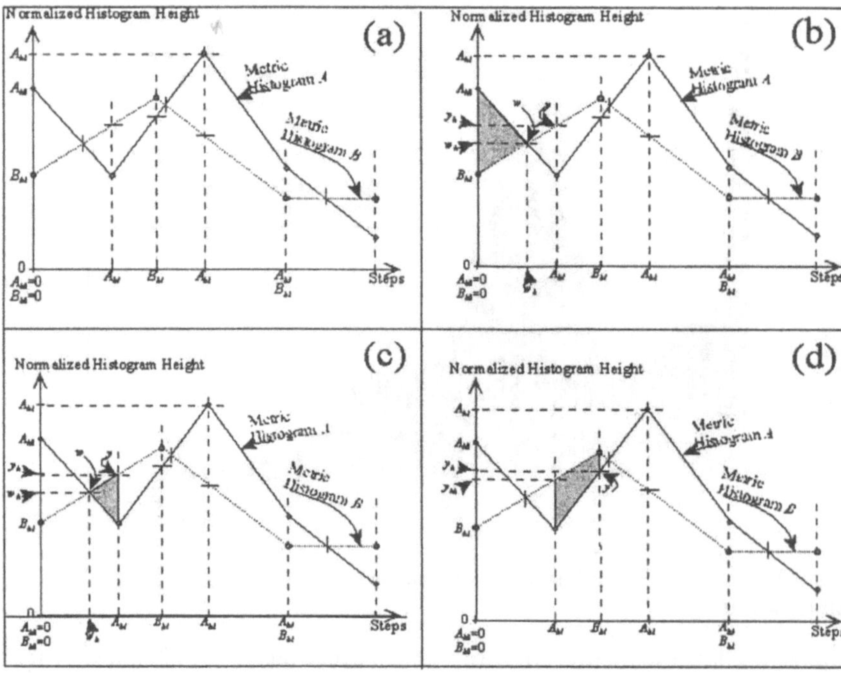

Figure 3 – Distance between two metric histograms through calculating the area between them. (a) Two metric histograms *A* and *B*, and the points used to specify the steps of the algorithm. (b) First step of the algorithm, exemplifying when the two MH intersects each other. (c) Second step of the algorithm. (d) Third step of the algorithm.

obtain the area between the two metric histograms. This is exemplified in figure 3(b). Figures 3(c) and 3(d) shows the next two steps performed to calculate the *MHD*() function, helping to understand how the algorithm works. When one of the metric histograms finishes before the other one, that is, when $N_A < N_B$, the calculation of the distance also stops. It is straightforward to demonstrate that the distance *MHD*( ) is metric.

Ours experiments show that the number of buckets in the metric histogram is much smaller than the number of bins of normalized histograms, coming from 256 bins to 20 - 32 buckets in the metric histogram. It is important to recall that the metric histograms are obtained from normalized histograms. Thus, the following properties hold:

Property 1 - An original image and the same one scaled, translated or rotated will have the same metric histogram.

Property 2 - The metric histograms are curves in the space, thus the metric histograms can be adjusted at its beginning and ending. Therefore, metric histograms are also invariant to the image contrast.

The *MHD* distance function: calculating the distance between two metric histograms
Input: the two metric histograms $M_H(A)$ and $M_H(B)$
Output: the distance between $M_H(A)$ and $M_H(B)$.

set $dist$=0, s=0, a=0, h_a=A_{b0} , h_b=B_{b0} , i=1 and j=1
while there is more steps to compare
  if bucket $A_{bi} < B_{bj}$, then
    calculate the value of B at position A_{bi} as y=(A_{bi}, y_2)
    set bm=A_{bi}, $base$=bm-s, and y_1=A_{hi}
    increment i
  else
    calculate the value of A at position B_{bj} as y=(B_{bj}, y_1)
    set bm=B_{bj}, $base$=bm-s, and y_2= B_{hj}
    increment j
  if line ((a, h_a), (a, h_b)) intersects line ((b_m, y_1), (b_m, y_2)), then
    calculate the intersection w=(w_b, w_h)
    calculate $area_1$= $\left|(w_b - a) * \frac{h_a - h_b}{2}\right|$ and
    $area_2$= $\left|(b_m - w_b) * \frac{y_1 - y_2}{2}\right|$
    add $area_1$ + $area_2$ to $dist$
  else
    calculate $area_1$=$base * \frac{h_a + y_1}{2}$ and
    $area_2$=$base * \frac{h_b + y_2}{2}$
    add $\left|area_1 - area_2\right|$ to $dist$
  set h_a=y_1 and h_b=y_2
  set a=$base$ + a
return $dist$

Figure 4 – Algorithm for calculating the *MHD* distance function.

These two properties highlight that some restrictions of using histograms for image retrieval are overpassed using metric histograms. That is, it becomes invariant to geometric transformations (scale included) and contrast.

4. EXPERIMENTS

We implemented our proposed metric histogram and the distance *MHD*() using the Slim-tree as the metric access method to answer similarity queries. The Slim-tree has been used because it allows the minimization of the overlap between nodes in the structure as well to measure this overlap. So far, only the Slim-tree has these capabilities, which have been shown to be useful when dealing with multi-dimensional and non-dimensional datasets [28], as is our two classes of histograms.

We have used two image databases in the experiments. The first one, named *"MRHead500"*, has 500 human brain images obtained by magnetic resonance tomography (MRT), and the second one, named *"MRVarious4247"*, has 4,247 images from various human body parts also obtained by MRT. Each image has 256 brightness levels and different spatial resolution. We extracted the normalized histogram and generated the metric histogram of each image, creating two sets of features for each database. Each set of features was indexed using the Slim-tree structure (four Slim-trees in the total). The normalized histograms were compared using the Manhattan distance function over the 256-element arrays, and the metric histograms where compared using the *MHD* distance function with the number of buckets varying from 11 to 32.

The main objective of this paper was to define a faster way to pre-select images in a database, which is performed based on the image histograms, to reduce the need of image comparisons when answering similarity queries. To evaluate our proposed method, the experiments compared the set of images resulting from answering nearest-neighbor queries using normalized histograms and metric histograms as well. To this intent, we assumed that the results obtained from the normalized histograms, which is the traditional approach, are the correct ones. The objective was to compare the images retrieved using their metric histogram with the images retrieved using their normalized histogram. We calculated the *precision* and *recall* measurements on the results for each set of images obtained. Precision and recall are parameters commonly used to evaluate information retrieval systems as well as image retrieval systems [4] [29]. Recall indicates the proportion of relevant images in the database which has been retrieved when answering a query. Precision, by the other hand, is the proportion of the retrieved images that are relevant for the query. Formally, let *X* be the set of relevant images for a given query, *Y* be the set of retrieved images and *x*, *y* and *z* be the number of images in the sets $X \cap Y$, $\overline{X} \cap Y$ and $X \cap \overline{Y}$, respectively.

Thus, precision and recall can be expressed through the following conditional probabilities:

$$precision = P(X \mid Y) = \frac{P(X \cap Y)}{P(Y)} = \frac{x}{x+y}$$

$$recall = P(Y \mid X) = \frac{P(Y \cap X)}{P(X)} = \frac{x}{x+z}$$

4.1 Precision and recall measurements

Figures 5 and 6 present the precision and recall curves obtained when asking nearest-neighbor queries for six different numbers of neighbors over the *MRHead500* and *MRVarious4247* databases respectively. The numbers of neighbors refer to portions of the database, varying from 0.5% to 15% of each image database. That is, to ask *k*-NN queries requiring 1% of the database, means to ask NN queries with *k*=5 for the *MRHead500* database, and with *k*=43 for the *MRVarious4247*. The curves present the average value from asking 50 queries for each number of neighbors, with the center image randomly chosen from images in the database. In these experiments, each query is submitted to both Slim-trees, the one indexing the normalized

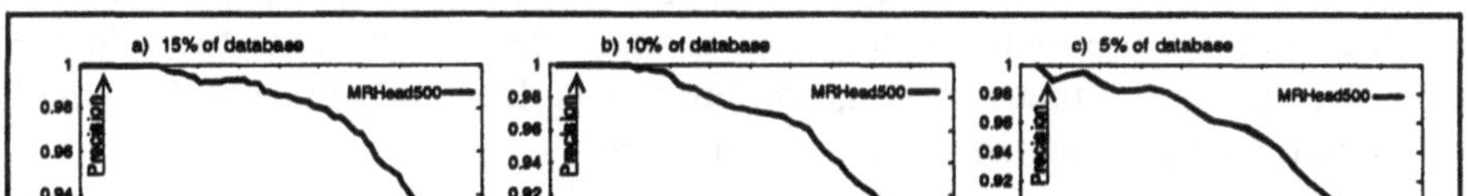

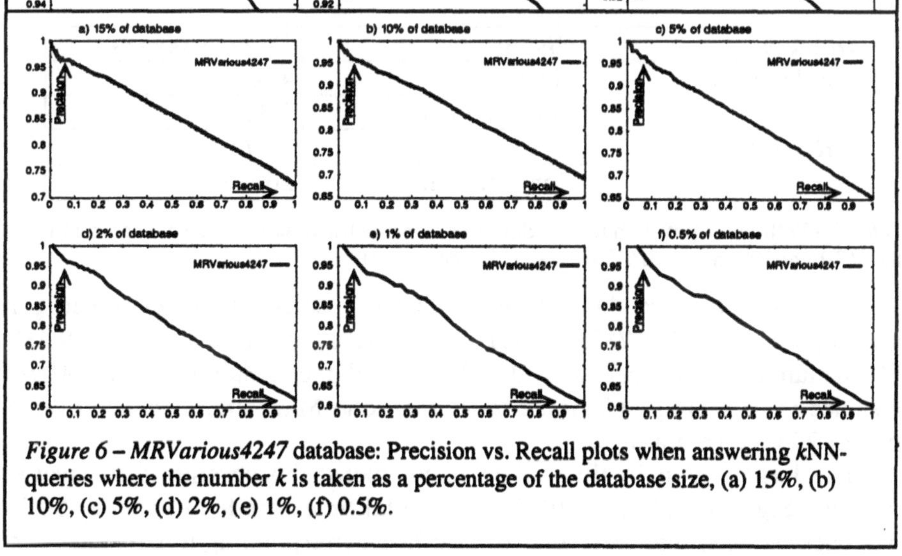

Figure 6 – MRVarious4247 database: Precision vs. Recall plots when answering *k*NN-queries where the number *k* is taken as a percentage of the database size, (a) 15%, (b) 10%, (c) 5%, (d) 2%, (e) 1%, (f) 0.5%.

histogram, and that indexing the metric histogram. Each answer set is sorted by the similarity of each histogram to that of the center of the query. The plots are calculated verifying that increasing numbers of histograms in the answer set of the tree indexed by the metric histogram is present in the answer set of the tree indexed by the normalized histogram. As it can be seen, the retrieval precision is high, always over 60% even for the *MRVarious4247* heterogeneous data set. With respect to the more homogeneous *MRHead500* data set, the results are always better than 70% of precision, even for queries retrieving 0.5% of the database with 100% of recall.

4.2 Timing comparison

Two questions tackled in this section are: (a) How much is the time difference for indexing the image databases through conventional and metric histograms? (b) Is the difference in time relevant when answering queries over the normalized and the metric histograms?

Table 1 reports the wall-clock times for building the Slim-tree in order to index the normalized (conventional) and the metric histograms. It can be seen that it is much faster to build the index over metric histograms (58% faster in the small data set, and 690% faster in the larger data set). The extra time needed to get the approximation over the conventional histograms in order to obtain the metric histograms pays off during the queries. The time needed to create the metric histograms is equivalent to the time to build the index tree using the metric histogram, but this is done only once and is small when comparing to the time to answer queries.

Database	**Histogram**	**Time** (in seconds)
MRHead500	Metric	4.62
	Conventional	7.31
MRVarious4247	Metric	33.76
	Conventional	266.79

Table 1 – Wall-clock time to build the Slim-tree using metric or normalized histograms from the *MRIHead500* and the *MRVárious4247* image data sets.

We also measured the number of distance calculations performed per second, and found 1,289,400 *MHD* distances per second and 269,430 Manhattan distances per second. That is, the calculation of one *MHD* distance is in average 4,7 times faster than one Manhattan distance over a pair of 256-element arrays.

The largest gain in time when using metric histograms is to answer queries. Figures 7(a) and 7(b) show the total times needed to answer 50 *k*-NN queries, when the value of *k* is specified corresponding to percentage of the database. Thus, the numbers are proportional to the database size and the results can be compared to different database sizes. Figure 7(a) shows the times to answer queries on the *MRHead500* database, and figure 7(b) shows the times to answer queries on the *MRVarious4247* database. As it can be seen, the gain ranges from 4 times faster for small *k* (0,5% of the database) to more than 10 times faster for larger portions of the database (15% of the database). All measurements were taken using an Intel Pentium II 450 MHz computer running Windows NT. The software was implemented in Borland C++ language.

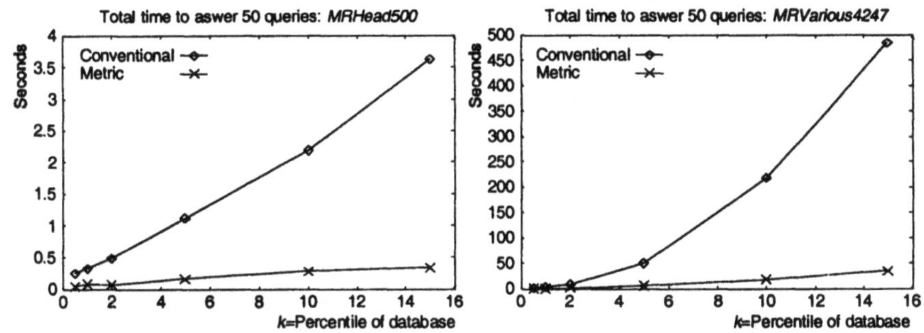

Figure 7 – Total time to answer 50 nearest-neighbor queries for each portion of the data set: 0.5, 1, 2, 5, 10 and 15%, using the conventional and the metric histograms. (a) *MRHead500* data set; (b) *MRVarious4247* data set.

5. CONCLUSIONS

Comparing two images is a very time consuming process. When queries are issued over an image database to retrieve information based on the image content, a filtering process takes place trying to reduce the number of images to be compared. This filtering operation uses features extracted from the images through relatively inexpensive algorithms. One of the features most frequently used in the early filtering stages is based on the image histograms.

The main objective of this paper is to define a faster way to execute the filtering process over an image database based on its histograms. To achieve this target we proposed a new technique, called the "metric histogram". We showed that using this technique the filtering step can be improved, achieving up to 10 times faster image selection for similarity queries. Moreover, the creation of index structures using metric histograms are at least 58% and up to 700% times faster as compared to structures created using the conventional histograms.

Metric histograms are defined in a metric domain, so the parameters that best describes one histogram can be used without compromising the whole set of images. To allow using metric access structures to answer similarity queries, we defined the *MHD*( ) distance function, which complies with the properties of a metric distance function. This function is also a faster way to compare histograms, as it can be executed in average 4,7 times faster than using the Manhattan distance function over 256-element vectors.

Metric histograms also have some very desirable side effects: it allows the retrieval of images in a way that is invariant to scale, rotation and translation of the objects in the image, and is also invariant to the contrast of the image. These effects enable that images similar to the target one, but with different contrast, scale, rotation, etc. can also be obtained without further computational effort.

ACKNOWLEDGMENTS

This research was supported, in part, by the scholarship grant from FAPESP (São Paulo State Research Foundation) number 98/03.209-6, and by CNPq (Brazilian National Research Council) under grants 52.1685/98-6, 860.068/00-7 and 35.0852/94-4. The authors also thank the HCRP (Clinical Hospital of Ribeirao Preto) for providing the data used in this work, and Humberto Razente as well as Fabio Chino for their support in the development of the software used in this work.

REFERENCES

[1] Guttman, A., "*R-Tree : A dynamic Index Structure for Spatial Searching*," in ACM SIGMOD, Boston, MA, 1984.

[2] Bentley, J.L., "*Multidimensional Binary Search Trees Used for Associative Searching*," *Comunications of the ACM*, vol. 18, pp. 509-517, 1975.

[3] Korn, F., Pagel, B.-U., Faloutsos, C., "*On the 'Dimensionality Curse' and the 'Self-Similarity Blessing'*," *IEEE TKDE*, vol. 13, pp. 96-111, 2001.

[4] Brunelli, R. and Mich, O., "*On the Use of Histograms for Image Retrieval*," in IEEE Intl. Conf. on Multimedia Computing and Systems (ICMCS), Florence, Italy, 1999.

[5] Berman, A. and Shapiro, L.G., "*Selecting Good Keys for Triangle-Inequality-Based Pruning Algorithms*," in Intl. Workshop on Content-Based Access of Image and Video Databases (CAIVD '98), Bombay, India, 1998.

[6] Chávez, E., Navarro, G., Baeza-Yates, R., Marroquín, J.L., "*Searching in Metric Spaces*," *to appear in the ACM Computing Surveys*, 2001.

[7] Siegel, E.L. and Kolodner, R.M., *Filmless Radiology*. New York City, NY: Springer Verlag, 1999.

[8] Sellis, T.K., Roussopoulos, N., Faloutsos, C., "*The R+-tree: A Dynamic Index for Multi-dimensional Objects*," in VLDB, Brighton, England, 1987.

[9] Beckmann, N., Kriegel, H.-P., Schneider, R., Seeger, B., "*The R*-tree: An Efficient and Robust Access Method for Points and Rectangles*," in ACM SIGMOD, 1990.

[10] Robinson, J.T., "*The K-D-B-Tree: A Search Structure For Large Multidimensional Dynamic Indexes*," in ACM International Conference on Management of Data - SIGMOD, SIGMOD Conference 1981:, 1981.

[11] Liao, S., Lopez, M.A., Leutenegger, S.T., "*High Dimensional Similarity Search With Space Filling Curves*," in IEEE ICDE, Heidelberg, Germany, 2001.

[12] Samet, H., "Spatial data structures in Modern Database Systems: The Object Model, Interoperability, and Beyond,",, W. Kim, Ed.: Addison-Wesley/ACM Press, 1995, pp. 361-385.

[13] Gaede, V. and Günther, O., "*Multidimensional Access Methods,*" *ACM Computing Surveys*, vol. 30, pp. 170-231, 1998.

[14] Berchtold, S., Keim, D.A., Kriegel, H.-P., "*The X-tree: An Index Structure for High-dimensional data,*" in VLDB, Bombay, India, 1996.

[15] Lin, K.-I.D., Jagadish, H.V., Faloutsos, C., "*The TV-Tree: An Index Structure for High-Dimensional Data,*" *VLDB Journal*, vol. 3, pp. 517-542, 1994.

[16] Burkhard, W.A. and Keller, R.M., "*Some Approaches to Best-Match File Searching,*" *CACM*, vol. 16, pp. 230-236, 1973.

[17] Ciaccia, P., Patella, M., Zezula, P., "*M-tree: An efficient access method for similarity search in metric spaces,*" in VLDB, Athens, Greece, 1997.

[18] Traina, C., Jr., Traina, A.J.M., Seeger, B., Faloutsos, C., "*Slim-Trees: High Performance Metric Trees Minimizing Overlap Between Nodes,*" in Intl. Conf. on Extending Database Technology, Konstanz, Germany, 2000.

[19] Santos, R.F., Filho, Traina, A.J.M., Traina, C., Jr., Faloutsos, C., "*Similarity Search without Tears: The OMNI Family of All-purpose Access Methods,*" in IEEE ICDE, Heidelberg, Germany, 2001.

[20] Bozkaya, T. and Özsoyoglu, Z.M., "*Indexing Large Metric Spaces for Similarity Search Queries,*" *ACM Transactions on Database Systems (TODS)*, vol. 24, pp. 361-404, 1999.

[21] Smeulders, A.W.M., Worring, M., Santini, S., Gupta, A., Jain, R., "*Content-Based Image Retrieval at the End of the Early Years,*" *IEEE Trans. on PAMI*, vol. 22, 2000.

[22] Aslandogan, Y.A. and Yu, C.T., "*Techniques and Systems for Image and Video Retrieval,*" *IEEE TKDE*, vol. 11, pp. 56-63, 1999.

[23] Güntzer, U., Balke, W.-T., Kiessling, W., "*Optimizing Multi-Feature Queries for Image Databases,*" in VLDB, Cairo - Egypt, 2000.

[24] Flickner, M. and alli, e., "*Query by Image and Video Content: The QBIC System,*" *IEEE Computer*, vol. 28, pp. 23-32, 1995.

[25] Pass, G., Zabih, R., Miller, J., "*Comparing Images Using Color Coherence Vector,*" in ACM Multimedia, Boston, MA, 1996.

[26] Tuytelaars, T. and Gool, L.v., "*Content-based Image Retrieval Based on Local Affinely Invariant Regions,*" in Information and Information Systems (Visual'99), 1999.

[27] Gimel'farb, G.L. and Jain, A.K., "*On Retrieving Textured Images from an Image Database,*" *Pattern Recognition*, vol. 29, pp. 1,461-1,483, 1996.

[28] Traina, C., Jr., Traina, A.J.M., Faloutsos, C., Seeger, B., "*Fast Indexing and Visualization of Metric Datasets Using Slim-trees,*" *IEEE TKDE*, vol. to appear, 2002.

[29] Yamamoto, H., Iwasa, H., Yokoya, N., Takemura, H., "*Content-based Similarity Retrieval of Images Based on Spatial Color Distributions,*" in 10th Intl. Conference on Image Analysis and Processing, 1999.

DESIGNING DYNAMIC WEB PAGES IN THE WYSIWYG INTERFACE

David Wolber, Yingfeng Su, Yih-Tsung Chiang
Department of Computer Science, University of San Francisco
wolber,suyi2,chiayi2@usfca.edu

Abstract: WebSheets is a programming in the WYSIWYG interface tool for building dynamic web pages that connect to databases. The system allows designers to "program" by entering query by example (QBE) and spreadsheet formulas into visual components of HTML documents. The system then automatically generates dynamic web pages that can be executed in a browser.

Key words: spreadsheet, programming by example, QBE, dynamic web page

1. INTRODUCTION

The web is becoming more dynamic in that more and more pages display dynamic content, computed from live database data, instead of static text and graphics. Unfortunately, our end-user web development tools, such as Front Page (Microsoft, 2002), only allow a designer to create static web pages. Designers that do not program are excluded from creating dynamic pages without the help of a programmer.

Emerging tools such as XMLC (Lutris, 2002) and WebMacro (WebMacro, 2002) do allow the designer to specify the *presentation* of a dynamic web page. With these tools, the designer uses a WYSIWYG editor to design the layout of the page, entering sample data where the dynamic content will be. The designer then marks these dynamic hotspots in the HTML code. The programmer, working separately, writes code that replaces the hotspots with data computed from a live database data.

Though template tools allow designers to play a role in dynamic web page creation, designers still cannot build a *complete* dynamic web page without the aid of a programmer. Such exclusion from the creative process is especially frustrating to designers savvy enough to use spreadsheets and database management systems. These designers possess all the skills necessary to specify all the elements of many dynamic pages (HTML, formulas, database information), but there are no tools that integrate these elements, so the savvy designer's skills are of no help.

We have designed a prototype of such an integrated system, which we call WebSheets. Our approach, called *programming in the WYSIWYG interface*, is to combine some well-known end-user programming methods, namely spreadsheet formulas, QBE (Zloof, 1977) and Programming by Example (PBE), with a WYSIWYG HTML editor. The dynamic content of a page is specified not with abstract programming or SQL statements, but within the context of the graphical interface (e.g., in table cells). The system then performs the job of the programmer by automatically generating an HTML page and Java servlet based on the designer's specifications.

We have observed a number of designers and experience programmers using the prototype. Our observations suggest that the tool can be used effectively by designers who are not programmers. The feedback we received also suggests that the tool can significantly reduce development time for designers and programmers alike.

While future papers will report on formal usability tests, this paper provides an overview of our approach, including the development process and the code generation. We also compare our approach to those used in Macromedia's Ultradev 4 (Macromedia, 2002), in schema-based, one-click web development systems, and in PBE systems.

2. THE DEVELOPMENT PROCESS

A WebSheets designer begins development by entering text, graphics, and components (e.g., tables) just as if a static page were being developed. The difference comes when the designer right clicks on a visual table in order to map it to a database table.

If a designer wishes to map the visual table to an existing database, a dialog is provided that allows the designer to select the database, table, and the columns to map. If no database exists, the designer can enter a sample row in the visual table, and specify that WebSheets automatically generate a database table. Thus, without knowing anything about database tables or columns, a user can create a dynamic web page and its underlying persistent data.

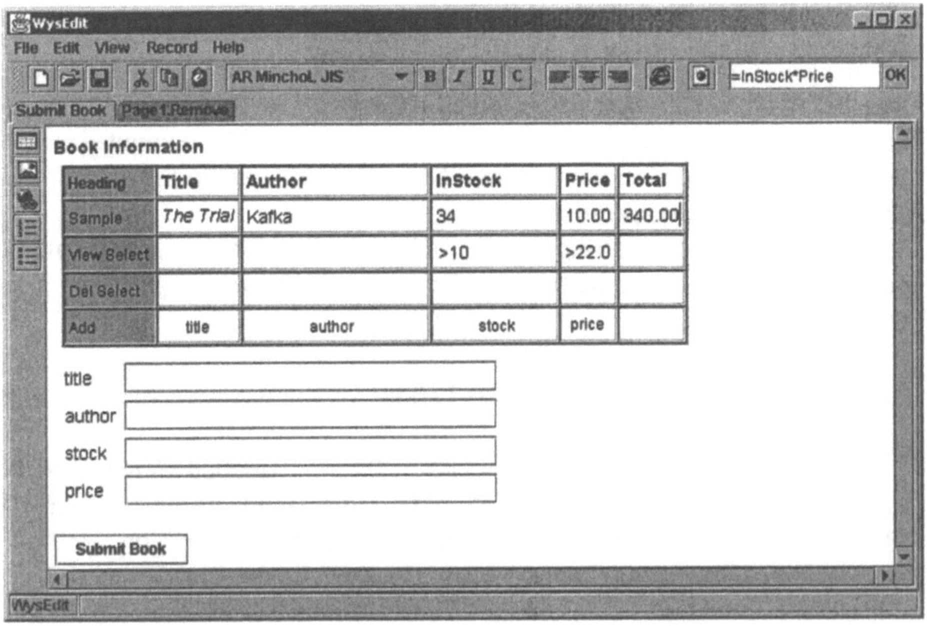

Figure 1. WebSheets Development of a Bookstore page

After the mapping step, the development-time visual table represents both a run-time view and the mapped database table. If the designer runs the dynamic page immediately after the mapping, the resultant web page will display all records of the mapped database table in the visual table. If such a simple web page was required, the designer could just as well have used a *one-click* web front-end system like ASPapp (ASPapp, 2002) WebSheets focus, however, is to allow designers to specify more complicated dynamic pages.

To facilitate this, a mapped visual table appears with one sample row of "live" database data, and four other auxiliary rows, empty except for labels in the left-most column that help guide the designer (see Figure 1).

2.1 PBE Formatting and Formulas

The designer specifies the formatting of all table data by example, that is, by formatting the data in the row labelled "Sample". For instance, in Figure 1, the designer has italicized the title *The Trial.* When the resulting dynamic page is run in a browser, the titles of all rows will appear italicized.

During the mapping phase, the designer can leave some columns of the visual table unmapped (not corresponding to a database column). The designer can enter spreadsheet-like formulas in these columns. For instance, in Figure 1, the designer has entered the formula "=InStock*Price" in the non-mapped column labelled "Total". On entry, formulas are evaluated using the live database data in the other columns of the sample row. This is done only to provide immediate feedback to the user. The computed value (e.g., 340.00) is placed in the cell and the formula appears in the toolbar (as it is in Excel and most spreadsheets).

Just as with the formatting, the formula specified for the sample row is applied to all rows that appear when the resulting dynamic page is run in a browser.

2.2 Specifying Selection with QBE

The designer enters QBE expressions in the row labelled "View Select" to specify the database rows that should be displayed. The advantage of QBE is that the designer can specify complex selection without understanding SQL syntax, as all expressions are entered in the context of table cells. For example, suppose the designer enters expressions in the view select row as in Figure 1. The system automatically builds the query:

SELECT * from BookTable where InStock>10 and Price>22.0

In the resultant dynamic web page, only the selected books will be displayed.

The row labelled "Del Select" is similar to the "View Select" row, but the QBE entered is used to choose which rows are deleted from the database when the page is invoked. If "Kafka" were entered in the Author column of the "Delete Select" row in Figure 1, the following SQL statement would be generated:

DELETE * from BookTable where Author=Kafka

If the "Del Select" row is left blank, no deletions will occur.

2.3 Input Forms

The row labelled "Add" facilitates the specification of input pages in which the end-user enters new records in a table. If the designer enters constant data in this row, a record containing that constant data is entered in the database table each time the page is invoked.

Of course, database operations are often based on something other than constant data. In many dynamic pages, the operations will depend on data entered by the user in an input form.

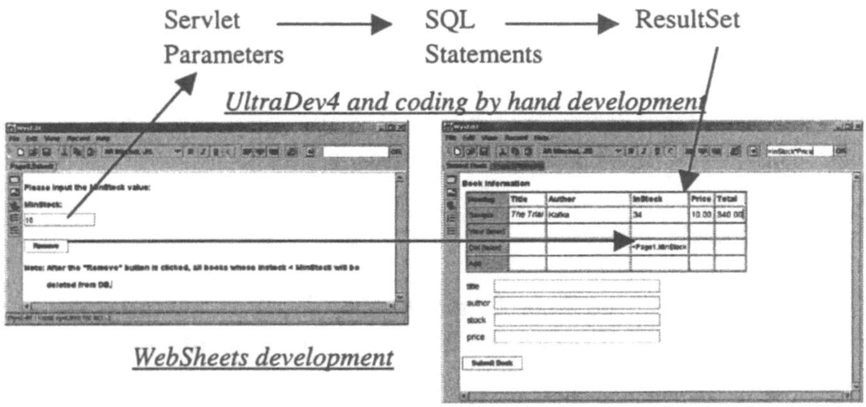

Figure 2. An input form page (left) and a result page (right).

WebSheets allows QBE expressions and spreadsheet formulas to include references to the names of input form data. For instance, in the "Add" row of Figure 1, the designer has entered the names of the input form text boxes (note that the default name of a text component is taken from its label).

At run-time, when the Submit Book button is selected, the values in the text boxes will be used to add a record to the database. After the add operation, the visual table will then be updated using the criteria in the view select row (InStock>10 and Price>22.00).

Formulas and expressions can also refer to input form data from another page in the development environment. The designer just qualifies the component name with the page name, e.g., "page1.MinStock"(See Figure 2).

2.4 Entry Points

A dynamic web page can be invoked from submit actions (e.g., buttons) in other pages as well as itself. For instance, the dynamic page in Figure 1 invokes itself (redraws itself with one new record) when the user selects the Submit Book button. It is also invoked by the Remove button on another page, as shown in Figure 2.

A WebSheets designer maps a button to a page by right-clicking on the button and specifying the name of any open page in the development environment. When a page is specified as a result page of a button, a new tab appears in the result page's development-time window. In the right side page shown in Figure 2, there are two tabs—the one corresponding to the "Submit Book" button in the same page, and the selected "Page1.Remove" tab corresponding to the "Remove:" button in the left-side input page. The designer chooses a tab to specify the actions that should occur when the page is loaded as a result of clicking the button the tab represents. In Figure 1, the designer has chosen the "Submit Book" tab to specify the actions that should occur when the "Submit Book" button is clicked. In Figure 2, the designer has chosen the "Page1.Remove" tab to specify the actions (e.g., a delete) that should occur when Page1's "Remove" button is clicked.

2.5 Code Generation

After completing the specifications, the designer invokes the code generation operation and web pages are created for each editor page open in the development environment. The pages are automatically registered with a server (currently, a WebLogic (BEA 2002) server), so the designer can "run" the pages and immediately see the results in a browser.

Figure 3 illustrates the WebSheets code generation process. From the designer's WYSIWYG specifications, WebSheets generates an HTML template file suitable for use with the Lutris Ehydra XMLC compiler (Lutris 2002). The HTML template contains id tags for all visual components—either the default ids WebSheets assigns when the component is inserted, or the ids the designer has explicitly specified. If this template file were sent directly to a browser, all tables would appear with the headers and the single sample row but without the guide rows (View Select row, etc.).

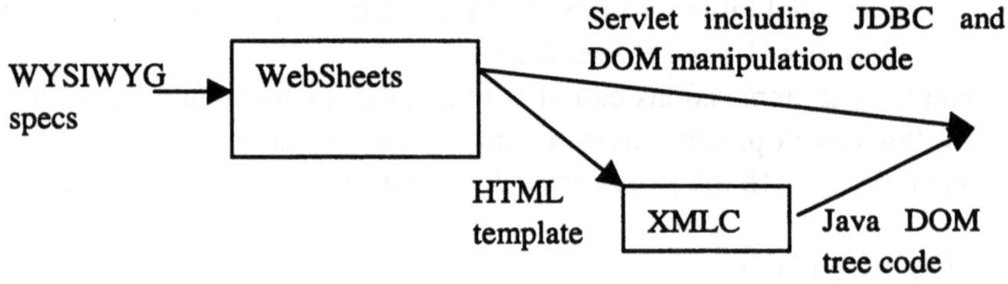

Figure 3. Code Generation in WebSheets

After generating the template file, WebSheets invokes the XMLC compiler. XMLC takes the template HTML file as input and generates Java code representing the page as a Document Object Model (DOM) tree. If this DOM tree were invoked from a servlet, it, too, would display the page with the single sample row specified during development.

Finally, WebSheets generates a Java servlet that manipulates the DOM tree to insert dynamic content. The generated servlet executes the database operations specified in the auxiliary rows of the development-time table, then modifies the DOM tree. This servlet is the key automation of the system, essentially replacing the work that generally requires a programmer.

Following is code from the servlet generated from the Bookstore page of Figure 2:

```
Class BookStoreServlet extends HTTPServlet
 { /...
   public void service(HttpServletRequest req, HttpServletResponse res)
           throws ServletException, IOException {
    If(actionTag.equals("Page1.Remove")) {

     // Access request parameters
     String minStock = req.getParameter("MinStock");
     // Access DOM tree created from HTML templ
     BookListDOM doc = new BookListDOM();
     // Execute specified delete operations using JDBC and SQL Delete statements
     stmt.execute("delete from BOOKS where INSTOCK<" + minStock);
     // Execute the specified Select statement to obtain a resultset.
     rs = stmt.executeQuery(
           "select BOOKS.ISBN, BOOKS.NAME,
           BOOKS.PRICE, BOOKS.INSTOCK from BOOKS );
     // Use DOM manipulation code to:
     while(rs.next()) {
         // Use DOM manipulation code to enter these values in the DOM tree.
           doc.setText_table1_col0(rs.getString(1));
           doc.setText_table1_col1(rs.getString(2));
           doc.setText_table1_col2(rs.getString(3));
           doc.setText_table1_col3(rs.getString(4));
         // Evaluate the spreadsheet formulas of the "expressions"
           doc.setText_table1_col4(String.valueOf(rs.getInt(3) * rs.getInt(4)));
         // Clone the sample row
         tempRow.getParentNode().insertBefore(tempRow.cloneNode(true), tempRow);
     }
     // Remove the sample row
     tempRow.getParentNode().removeChild(tempRow);
     // Write the updated DOM tree to the browser
     out.println(doc.toDocument());
 } else if(actionTag.equals("Submit Book")) {
     // ...
 }
```

Code Listing 1. Generated Servlet Code

Since the designer can specify entry points to a page from various input forms, the generated servlet must handle requests from each of those entry points, each of which may send a different set of request parameters. Thus, the code generator associates a particular action tag with each entry point and inserts the tag in the submit action statement of the invoking servlet. The service method of the invoked servlet (which may be the same as the invoking servlet) checks the action tag value and proceeds dependent on it. In the code of Listing1, two action tags have been specified, one for the button named "Page1.Remove", and one for a button named "Submit Book".

The code for each action tag corresponds to the expressions entered in the corresponding tab in the development time environment. If expressions were entered in the "Add" row, the code will contain SQL INSERT statements (wrapped in JDBC code). If expressions were entered in the select delete row, the code will contain SQL DELETE statements (as in Code Listing 1). The code will always contain a SELECT statement based on the expressions entered in the view select row. If no such expressions exist, the generated SELECT statement will not contain any WHERE clauses (this is the situation in Code Listing 1)

After obtaining a result set of live database data from the SELECT statement, the generated code manipulates the DOM tree to insert the data into the HTML table. The code first clones the sample row of the DOM tree in order to access its formatting. It then adds a row in the DOM tree for each of the rows in the result set, setting the data's formatting as specified in the sample row. As it loops through the rows, the code also evaluates any spreadsheet formulas in expression columns and inserts this dynamic data in the DOM tree node for that column. When all rows have been inserted, the code removes the sample row and writes the updated DOM tree to the browser.

3. RELATED WORK

This section compares the WebSheets approach to those used in related commercial and research systems.

3.1 Commercial Web Development

Macromedia's UltraDev 4 (Macromedia, 2002), the union of Dreamweaver and Cold Fusion, is the commercial system most similar in goals and approach to WebSheets. Like WebSheets, an UltraDev 4 designer can build some dynamic web pages without programming. The systems differ in that UltraDev 4 is more of a visual interface to a *program*, with many dialog boxes and property sheets, whereas WebSheets is more of a programming in the interface system, like a spreadsheet.

Take, for instance, the development of a simple page that allows an end-user to add a record using input form data. In UltraDev 4, the designer creates a ResultSet object that is mapped to the database table. The designer then maps the columns of this ResultSet to columns of the visual table. Next, the UltraDev4 developer chooses the Submit button and maps it to an Add Record operation by choosing it from a list of operations. He then maps the input form's text boxes to the parameters of the page being built. Finally, he maps the page parameters to the parameters of the Add Record operation created earlier. Though performed in a visual manner, the process is similar to the steps a programmer would complete if coding by hand (see the top of Figure 2).

Because database operations are specified within the user interface (e.g., in the "Add" row of a table) the WebSheets designer can avoid thinking in terms of result sets, page parameters, and other programming concepts. The circuitous route of specification, from input form to page parameters to result set to visual table, is also avoided, as the designer can directly specify a mapping between form data and an add record operation by referring directly to the form data in the "Add" row of the table (see the direct link near the bottom of Figure 2).

3.2 Schema-based Code Generators

ASPapp (ASPAPP 2002) is indicative of tools that generate dynamic web pages directly from a database schema. These tools provide an immediate (one-click) web front-end to any existing database. Most provide wizards that allow some specialization of the generated pages. A designer can also edit the generated code after the fact to make layout and other modifications, using whatever tools and editors are available.

Since specialization is facilitated through a wizard in schema-based generation, row selection expressions must be specified outside the context of the interface, with SQL-like statements entered in dialogs. In WebSheets, expressions are specified in the context (a table cell) of the target interface.

WebSheets is also designed so that any component in the interface, e.g., a list box, text area, even raw text, can be mapped to database table columns. The wizard approach of a schema-based system can offer flexibility, but the designer must imagine the user interface components when specifying the system, as opposed to beginning with the interface and mapping it to the persistent data.

3.3 Declarative Definition of Web Sites

Similar to schema-based generators are systems such as Strudel (Fernandez, 1998) that provide an intermediate layer between the raw database and the web site. These systems allow a designer to specify a query that describes the structure of the website to be built. From the query, the system builds a data model, often in XML, which represents the part of the database that the website covers. Various methods are then used to map this model to the actual layout of the web pages.

3.4 Query by Templates

Query by Templates (QBT) (Sengupta, 1997) is a generalization of QBE. Its focus is visual specification of interfaces for XML data instead of database data. The semi-structured nature of XML data leads to a more natural mapping of non-tabular graphical components to the data, so QBT users can specify queries within "components" such as poems.

3.5 Forms/3 Spreadsheets

Forms/3 (Burnett, 2001) is a programming environment based on the spreadsheet. Spreadsheet formulas need not be placed only in cells of a table, but can be entered in any visual component or even as a property of some complex component such as a graphic. Tables need not be of a fixed size, but can contain a variable number of rows and columns.

Like with regular spreadsheets, the data entered in a Forms/3 interface is persistent. But though there is the concept of dynamically sized tables, there is no notion of an underlying store beneath the visible data that the designer manipulates. Thus, it cannot be used to create interfaces to existing databases or to specify traditional database operations.

3.6 Programming by Example

PBE systems are intelligent macro facilities. Instead of just recording a designer's demonstrations and later playing them back, these systems infer a *generalized* program. PBE has been applied successfully in many domains, the results of which have been reported in two books (Cypher et. al., 1993, Lieberman, 2001). It has even been applied to dynamic web page development, but only in the context of building wrapper programs (Kushmerick, 2000, Bauer et. al., 2001), i.e., pages that get data from other already existing web pages.

Led by the first author's previous experience (Wolber, et. al. 2001, Myers et al, 2000), our original idea was to apply PBE to the development of web pages that connect to databases. The system would display the entire "live" database table at development time, instead of a single sample row, thereby making the system more WYSIWYG. Instead of specifying formulas and QBE, as in WebSheets, the designer would demonstrate examples of the database operations using sample data. To specify an Add Record operation, for instance, the designer would add a row to the visual table, then cut and paste data from the input form to the new row. To specify selection criteria, the designer would provide sample rows that fit the criteria, and the system would infer the SQL Select statement. In this manner, abstract variable names would be unnecessary because the designer would work only with sample data.

But after analyzing paper and partial prototypes, we came to the conclusion that the concreteness afforded by PBE was not worth it for our target domain (dynamic web pages that access databases). Users found the manipulations to demonstrate an Add Record operation laborious, compared to just providing an auxiliary add row and allowing the designer to specify what to add in a spreadsheet manner (even if variable names had to be used). Delete and select were also found problematic, as numerous examples were necessary for the system to infer a generalized selection expression. Finally, providing feedback and editing of an inferred program is notorious difficult for PBE systems. With our spreadsheet-like approach, this problem was solved, since the designer can always see the "program" specification directly in the WYSIWYG interface.

For these reasons, we chose to abandon PBE as the basis for WebSheets. In the current prototype, PBE is used only in the sense that formatting and formulas are specified in the sample row and then automatically applied to all rows, and a user can provide a sample row and the system will generate a database table.

4. STATUS AND FUTURE WORK

WebSheets is a research prototype based on a rudimentary HTML editor. The table widget only allows conjunction (AND) expressions to be specified, and spreadsheet formulas are limited to mathematical operators and a small built-in function set. These limitations can easily be fixed. For instance, we are currently implementing a COM connection that will allow any Excel formula to be specified.

The prototype has been completed to the point that our basic approach can be tested. It has been used to create complete web applications such as the Bookstore example illustrated in this paper. Feedback from users has been encouraging—most are amazed at how quickly dynamic web pages can be built.

We have begun to perform extensive usability testing in order to refine the system and verify its usefulness. We also plan to make a more complete WebSheets version publicly available so as to get widespread feedback.

In the next version, we will implement dynamic visual components other than tables. A designer will be able to "program" lists, combo boxes, and sets of text cells in the same manner as tables. We will also design and implement a method for specifying updates to table rows, a capability not covered in the current system.

One direction of future work concerns the specification of relational tables in the WebSheets framework. Currently, a database table will be created from a sample row, but no relations are inferred. We are currently exploring a number of techniques for specifying relations in the WYSIWYG interface, including inferring such relations from multiple sample rows and from analyzing the links between pages.

Following the lead of (Sengupta, 1997), we would also like to explore mapping the designer's visual specifications to XML data, instead of databases, and generating XML data, instead of a table, from sample row(s).

5. CONCLUSION

WebSheets is not completely *programming in the WYSIWYG*. In fact, it is based on a table widget with auxiliary rows that are seen only during development, and not at run-time. However, the auxiliary rows allow database operations (select, add, delete) and formulas to be specified *in the context* of the user interface, that is, in the column-based manner that has long been effective in Spreadsheets and QBE systems.

WebSheets combines this in-context specification with a method for defining interaction, that is, the way a dynamic page should change dependent on how it is invoked. By representing the various invocations of a page with a tabbed window, the designer can separately specify the operations that should occur when the user clicks on, for example, an "Add Record" button and a "View Records" button. Our goal is to refine this basic approach to the point that designers can build complete, customizable and complex dynamic web pages.

REFERENCES

ASPapp,Inc. (2002), http://www.aspapp.com

Bauer, M. Dengler, D., Paul, G., and Meyer, M.(2001) Programming by Demonstration for Information Agents, chapter in Your Wish is my Command, Henry Lieberman, Ed. San Francisco: *Morgan Kaufmann*, 2001

BEA, Inc. (2002)., http://www.bea.com.

Burnett, M. Atwood, J., Djang, R. , Reichwein, J., Gottfried, H. and Yang,S.(2001),Forms/3: A First-order Visual Language to Explore the Boundaries of the Spreadsheet Paradigm, Journal of Functional Programming, 11(2):155-206, *Cambridge University Press.*

Cypher, A. (1993) Watch What I do: Programming By Demonstration, *MIT Press.*

Fernandez, M., Florescu, D, Kang, J., Levy, A., and Suciu, D. (1998) Catching the Boat with Strudel: Experiences with a Web-site Management System, in Proc. of ACM SIGMOD Conference on Management of Data, Seattle, WA. *,ACM.*

Florescu, D., Levy, A., and Mendelzon, A.,(1998)Database Techniques for the World-Wide Web: A Survey, SIGMOD Record, 27(3):59-74, *ACM*..

Kushmerick, N. (2000) Wrapper Induction: Efficiency and Expressiveness, Artificial Intelligence, 118, 2000, pp. 15-66.

Lieberman, H. ed. (2001) Your Wish is My Command: Programming by Example, *Morgan-Kaufmann.*

Lutris, Inc. (2002), http://www.lutris.com/products/index.html

Macromedia (2002), http://www.macromedia.com

Miller, R., Myers, B., (1997), *Creating Dynamic World Wide Web Pages by Demonstration.* Carnegie Mellon University School of Computer Science Technical Report, no. CMU-CS-97-131 and Human Computer Interaction Institute Technical Report, CMU-HCII-97-101.

Microsoft, Inc. (2002), http://www.microsoft.com

Myers, B., McDaniel R., and Wolber, D.,(2000), Intelligence in Demonstrational Interfaces, in Communications of the ACM, March, 2000. vol. 43, no. 3. pp. 82-89, *ACM.*

Sengupta, A. Dillon, A., (1997), Query by Templates: A Generalized Approach for visual query formulation for text dominated databases. In the Conference on Advanced Digital Libraries (ADL '97).

WebMacro (2002), http://www.webmacro.org

Wolber, D., and Myers, B. (2001), "Stimulus-Response PBD: Demonstrating When as Well as What", Your Wish is My Command, Lieberman, H. ed. San Francisco: *Morgan Kaufmann.*

Zloof, M., (1977),"Query-by-Example: A Database Language", IBM Systems J., 21(3), *IBM.*

BIOGRAPHIES

David Wolber is an associate professor in the University of San Francisco's department of computer science. His research interests include recommender systems, programming by demonstration, and visual programming.

Yingfeng Su is completing a Master's degree in computer science at the University of San Francisco.

Yih-Tsung Chiang is completing a Master's degree in computer science at the University of San Francisco.

IMPROVING IMAGE RETRIEVAL WITH SEMANTIC CLASSIFICATION USING RELEVANCE FEEDBACK*

Hong Wu
National Lab of Pattern Recognition
Institute of Automation, Chinese Academy of Sciences
Beijing 100080, China
hwu@nlpr.ia.ac.cn

Mingjing Li, Hong-Jiang Zhang, Wei-Ying Ma
Microsoft Research Asia
49 Zhichun Road
Beijing 100080, China
{mjli, hjzhang, wyma}@microsoft.com

Abstract In this paper, we investigate the combination of image semantic classification with content-based image retrieval. A flexible scheme is proposed to take advantage of image classification, which may be obtained manually or automatically, to enhance image retrieval. In this scheme, a semantic feature vector is composed for an image based on its class membership information, and is combined with low-level features in image retrieval. Relevance feedback techniques are also used to adjust both the semantic feature and low-level features of the query in order to better reflect the user's intention. Experimental results on a collection of 10,000 images with manual classification demonstrate the effectiveness of the proposed method.

Keywords: content-based image retrieval, image classification, relevance feedback, semantic feature, and class membership.

* This work was performed at Microsoft Research Asia.

1. INTRODUCTION

The performance of most current content-based image retrieval (CBIR) systems (e.g. Pentland et al. 1994, Flickner et al. 1995, Smith & Chang 1996) is limited due to the gap between high-level concepts and low-level features, and the subjectivity of human visual perception. One approach to improving this situation is to employ relevance feedback (RF) techniques (Cox et al. 1996, Rui et al. 1998, Rui & Huang 2000). In the relevance feedback process, the system dynamically learns and refines the query and retrieval results to capture the user's intention. However, most of RF methods in CBIR systems are not so effective as in text information retrieval systems, due to the fact that refining low-level features to map semantic content is often difficult. Therefore, some works (e.g. La Cascia et al. 1998, Cox et al. 1997) engaged in incorporating semantic attributes with low-level features in image retrieval.

On the other hand, as image databases get large, a good organization is needed to aid better searching and browsing. Big image collections are often grouped into semantic classes, which may be further organized in a hierarchy. These semantic classes may be constructed manually, as did in most of the image search engines, or automatically using semantic attributes. Some efforts (e.g. Szummer & Picard 1998, Vailaya et al. 1998, Bradshaw 2000) attempted to use low-level features to automatically classify images into semantic classes, such as indoor, outdoor, man-made and natural, etc. WebSeek (Smith & Chang 1997) performs a semi-automatic classification of images on the Web into a hierarchy of subjects by using associated text and filename cues.

A straightforward way to combine image classification with CBIR is to use classes as a filter to restrict the search range, and to reduce both searching time and potential retrieval errors. For example, when performing image search in WebSeek, the user first selects a category through the hierarchy of subjects, browses and selects an image as the query example. Then, the searching process is constrained in that category. In Simplicity (Wang 2000), query image is first classified by the system as one of n predefined semantic classes (indoor-outdoor, objectionable-benign, and graph-photograph), and retrieval is enhanced by narrowing down the searching range to that particular category.

However, this method is not effective in some cases. (1) In some image databases, the number of image categories is large. Although they can be organized in a hierarchy, it is not easy for a common user to find the intended category. So users tend to perform retrievals at a high level in the hierarchy, and the detailed classification is not used. (2) When the user's need does not have apparent relations with these categories, due to the subjectivity and diversity of human perception of image content, it is difficult for the user to make a choice. For example, there are some landscape images categorized as four classes, Asia, Europe, America, Africa, and Oceania. If a user want to find some images of beach, this categorization is not helpful to this query. And automatically constraining the searching range will not work in this case as well. Therefore, using image classes as a filter for image retrieval has a very limited success.

In this paper, a simple but flexible scheme is proposed to integrate semantic classification with low-level features for improving the performance of content-based image retrieval systems. Class membership of an image is used as the semantic feature and is represented as a Boolean vector. Such semantic feature and low-level features are used complementarily to retrieve images. And they are modified simultaneously through a relevance feedback process to better reflect user's perception of image content. This scheme may be considered a practical application of the hidden attribute approach described by Cox et al. (1997). Experimental result shows the effectiveness of the proposed method.

The rest of the paper is organized as follows. The proposed image retrieval scheme is presented in Section 2. The preliminary experimental results are presented in Section 3. Finally, we give discussion and concluding remarks in Section 4.

2. INCORPORATING CLASSIFICATION IN CBIR

Image classification can be regarded as treating a group of images as equivalent. Images within classes are more similar than those across classes in some way. The intuition of using semantic classification in CBIR is like following. If one or more images in a class are relevant to the user's query, other images in the same class are expected to be relevant in some extent as well.

To fully utilize the classification information existing in some image datasets, image classes are treated as pseudo keywords such that many techniques in text information retrieval (Baeza-Yates & Ribeiro 1999) may be deployed. For the sake of simplicity, a Boolean vector is formed for every image with each element corresponds to a class. If the image belongs to a particular class, the corresponding element in the vector is set to 1; it is set to 0 otherwise. This vector can be used as a semantic feature in addition to low-level features in image retrieval. Low-level features (e.g. Pentland et al. 1994, Flickner et al. 1995, Cox et al. 1996, Smith & Chang 1996) are visual statistics of images, and are characterized by feature vectors as well.

There are three main parts in the proposed scheme: semantic feature representation, integration in retrieval, and relevance feedback. We mainly present the details related to the semantic feature in this section.

2.1 Semantic Feature Representation

In our approach, image classes are treated as indexing terms in traditional information retrieval, and each term is assigned a binary weight. Term weight f_{ij} denotes the membership of image i to class j, i.e., $f_{ij}=1$ if $i \in j$, $f_{ij}=0$ if $i \notin j$. The semantic feature of image i is defined as an m-dimensional vector:

$$F_{ih} = (f_{i1}, f_{i2}, \cdots, f_{im})^T \quad (1)$$

where m is the total number of classes. In case that there is a class hierarchy, all high-level classes are also included.

As in text information retrieval, more sophisticated term weighting may be introduced in the feature representation, such as TF*IDF. Then, we get another definition:

$$F_{ih}' = (f_{i1} \times \log(\frac{N}{n_1}), f_{i2} \times \log(\frac{N}{n_2}), \cdots, f_{im} \times \log(\frac{N}{n_m}))^T \quad (2)$$

where N is the total number of images in the database, n_j is the number of images in class j. The new definition implies that classes with more images are less useful in retrieval.

2.2 Retrieval with Classification

In our scheme, the visual similarity and the semantic similarity between two images are calculated separately. The former is based on the low-level features, while the latter is based on the class membership. The overall similarity is the weighted sum of these two similarities, as defined in Equation (3):

$$S(q,i) = \omega * S_h(Q_h, F_{ih}) + (1-\omega) * S_l(Q_l, F_{il}) \quad (3)$$

where q is the query and i is an image in the database, S_h and S_l are their semantic and visual similarities, respectively. Q_h and F_{ih} are semantic features of query and image i respectively, while Q_l and F_{il} are low-level features. ω is the semantic weight, subject to $0 \le \omega \le 1$.

The semantic similarity between the query and an image is calculated by the cosine of the angle between these two vectors:

$$S_h(Q_h, F_{ih}) = \frac{Q_h \bullet F_{ih}}{\|Q_h\| \cdot \|F_{ih}\|} \tag{4}$$

To compute the visual similarity, distance between the query and an image is first calculated by diagonally weighted Euclidean distance based on the low-level feature:

$$D(Q_l, F_{il}) = \sqrt{(F_{il} - Q_l)^T \Lambda (F_{il} - Q_l)} \tag{5}$$

$\Lambda = diag(w_1, \ldots, w_n)$, each diagonal element model the different importance of corresponding element of the low-level feature. The distance is further converted to visual similarity, which monotonously decreases as the distance increases. The similarity is normalized to the interval between 0 and 1.

2.3 Relevance Feedback

Relevance Feedback (RF) is an interactive learning technique, first introduced in text information retrieval. During retrieval, the user is asked to give feedbacks regarding the relevance of current outputs of the system, and the system learns from the feedbacks and refines the query to better capture the user's intention. In our scheme, different RF algorithms are adopted for semantic feature and low-level features respectively in the same relevance feedback process.

Initially, the semantic feature of the query is not available if the query example is new to the system, thus all elements in the vector are set to 0. On the other hand, if the example is from the database, its semantic feature vector may be used directly. However, it is not necessarily consistent with the user's intention. Therefore, relevance feedback is deployed to iteratively refine the semantic feature vector of the query in order to better reflect the user's intention.

Here, we adopt the Rocchio formula (Baeza-Yates & Ribeiro 1999) to refine the semantic feature of the query:

$$Q' = \alpha Q + \beta \frac{\sum Q^+}{n^+} - \gamma \frac{\sum Q^-}{n^-} \tag{6}$$

where Q is the original query, Q^+ is the set of positive (relevant) examples, n^+ is the number of positive examples, while Q^- and n^- are that of negative (irrelevant) examples respectively, Q' is the updated query. This procedure automatically re-weights query terms by adding the weights from the actual occurrence of those query terms in the positive samples, and subtracting the weights of those terms occurring in negative samples. Query is also expanded using the term weights from the positive and negative samples. After updating, the semantic feature of query is no longer a Boolean vector. In our experiments, the query is treated as a positive example. So the parameters are set as $\alpha = 0$, $\beta = 1$, and $\gamma = 0.5$, to limit the effects of negative feedback. Actually, no negative weights are used in the updated query, i.e., a term weight is set to zero if it is negative. After relevance feedback, the class containing more positive examples and less negative examples will be assigned a larger weight, and more images from this class will be retrieved hopefully.

For relevance feedback on the low-level features, a simpler version of the general relevance feedback framework proposed by Rui & Huang (2000) was implemented in our system. The low-level feature vector of query (Q_l in Equation (5)) is updated to the average of features of all the relevant images. The weight of *i*-th element of low-level feature (w_i in Equation (5)) is set to inverse of σ_i^2, the variance of *i*-th element of all relevant low-level features.

3. EXPERIMENTAL RESULTS

In this section, we will compare the performance of the system adopting our scheme with that only based on low-level features. And further, to investigate the application of our scheme with different classification, we designed two experiments. In the first experiment, the classification in the Corel data set is used, which was constructed manually by domain specialists. In the second experiment, the classification was made automatically using feature-based classification algorithms.

3.1 System Implementation

We integrated the proposed scheme into a prototype CBIR system, which adopts the query by example (QBE) mode. During the retrieval, the user only marks the retrieved images as relevant or irrelevant. There are six kinds of low level visual features used in the system: 256-dimensional color histogram in HSV space, first and second color moments in Lab space, 64-dimensional color coherence vector in LUV space, MRSAR texture feature, Tamura coarseness feature, and Tamura directionality. Their effectiveness has been proven in previous works (Liu et al. 2000, Lu et al. 2000). When classification is used in retrieval, the semantic feature vector is defined by Equation (1).

3.2 Experimental Design

The image database we used consists of more than 10,000 images from the Corel dataset. It is a large and heterogeneous image set. Domain professionals classified all images in the dataset into semantic categories, each of which contains 100 images. Originally, there are 101 categories in the database. We merged some categories that share the same semantic meaning, such that each merged category depicts a distinct semantic topic. For example, category *Castles* in Disk07 and category *Castle II* in Disk08 are merged into one category, *Castle*. After that, we got a total of 79 categories.

We designed an automatic feedback scheme in the experiments. First, some query images are selected, and the ground truth is determined for each query image. After that, a reproducible relevance feedback for every query can be simulated based on the ground truth and the retrieval results of the system. At each iteration of the feedback, the system scans the first 30 retrieved images, and labels 3 irrelevant examples and at most 3 relevant examples, not including previous labelled images. Then the system uses these labelled examples and that from previous iterations to conduct relevance feedback.

Precision-scope curve is used to evaluate the image retrieval performance. Scope specifies the number of images returned to the user. Precision is defined as the percentage of retrieved images that are actually relevant. Results with and without classification information are referred to as "Class" and "Orig" respectively.

3.3 Result Using Manual Classification

In this experiment, all 79 categories in the database are used as classification information. Thus, a 79-dimensional vector is formed for each image as the semantic feature.

We selected 200 image examples as the query set. Most images are from the database, but 4 images are not. Then we collected judgments from 7 subjects as the ground truth. For every query example, each subject was required to scan the whole image set, and label all relevant ones based on his/her subjective judgment. In fact, the subjects selected different and varying numbers of relevant images for each query image. Therefore, the retrieval precision was calculated for each subject separately and averaged finally, as if there were 1,400 different queries.

The result of this experiment is presented in Figure 1, where "rf" stands for relevance feedback, the digit before it stands for the number of iterations in feedback. The semantic weight is set to 0.2 in case that classification is used. The result shows that the proposed method can improve the performance in this experiment. P(20) of "Orig" without relevance feedback is 0.16. After the second iteration of relevance feedback, P(20) of "Orig" is 0.27, while that of "Class" is 0.54.

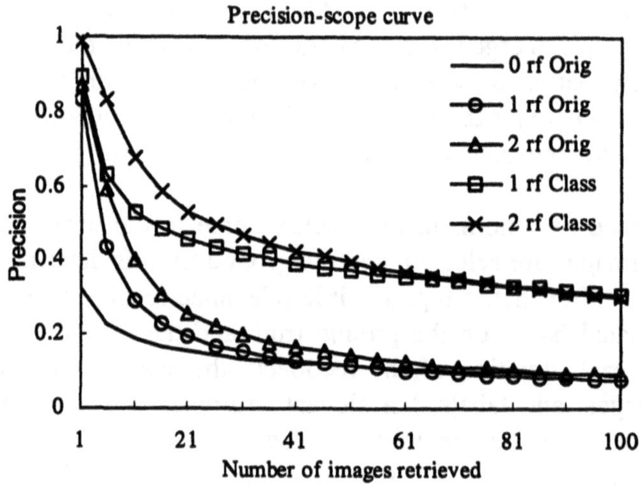

Figure 1. Average precision for the first two iterations.

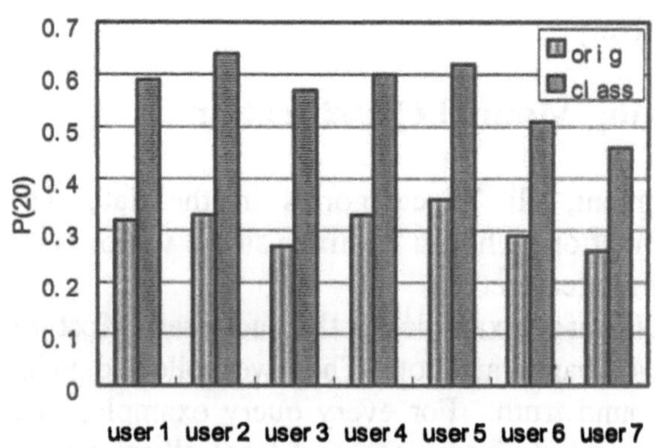

Figure 2. P(20) of different users.

Figure 2 illustrates the improvement of P(20) for different users. We can see that our approach makes obvious improvement for all 7 users. After investigating the data in detail, we also got some valuable observation. If most of the ground truth images of a query distribute in 1 or 2 categories, our method tends to make a greater improvement in precision. On the contrary, if the distribution is dispersive, our method tends to make a smaller improvement, or even make a little drop. In other words, if there is a good agreement between the user's intention and the image classification, our method will likely make improvement. Because the classification in Corel dataset was performed by domain professionals, it might match the perception of a common user very well. So much improvement is observed in the experiment.

3.4 Relationship between the Improvement and the Nature of Classification

Due to the subjectivity of human visual perception, certain classification can not satisfy all the different users and uses of images. This is why, in the above experiment, some queries of the total 1,400 queries are not consistent with the classification, although it was performed by domain professionals. To figure out how the nature of classification affects the efficiency of our approach. We did some quantitative analysis of the relationship between the performance improvement and the agreement between the classification and the user's perception. The improvement of the performance is measured in terms of the difference of P(20) after 2 iterations of relevance feedback, based on the method using classification and the original method only using low-level features. The classification and user's intention can be regard as two partitions of the image set. For a given classification, the partition is $\Theta_C = \{\theta_{C_1}, \ldots, \theta_{C_M}\}$, where M is the number of classes. The user's intention can also be considered as a classification, which classifies images into two classes, either relevant or irrelevant. And the corresponding partition is $\Theta_U = \{\theta_R, \theta_I\}$. The images in the same subset of a partition are regarded to be similar, the images from different subset dissimilar. The agreement between a classification and a user's intention is measured based on their agreement on the similarity or dissimilarity of image pairs. Inspired by Squire and Pun (1998), the agreement measure is defined as:

$$S(\Theta_C, \Theta_U) = \frac{2}{N(N-1)} \sum_{i=1}^{N-1} \sum_{j=i+1}^{N} X_{ij}(\Theta_C, \Theta_U) \tag{7}$$

where N is the number of relevant images in the database, i.e., only the relevant images are used in computing the agreement. This is because the similarity between the irrelevant images is hard to judge. $X_{ij}(\Theta_C,\Theta_U)$ is a binary variable which is 1 when relevant images i and j are in the same class of Θ_C. The value of S is between 0 and 1.

The agreement measure of all queries is quantified into 10 degrees, and the precision improvement is averaged for the queries belonging to the same degree. The precision is that of top 20 images at the 2nd iteration of relevance feedback. The analysis is based on the results of the experiment described in section 3.3. The relationship between the improvement and the agreement is illustrated as following.

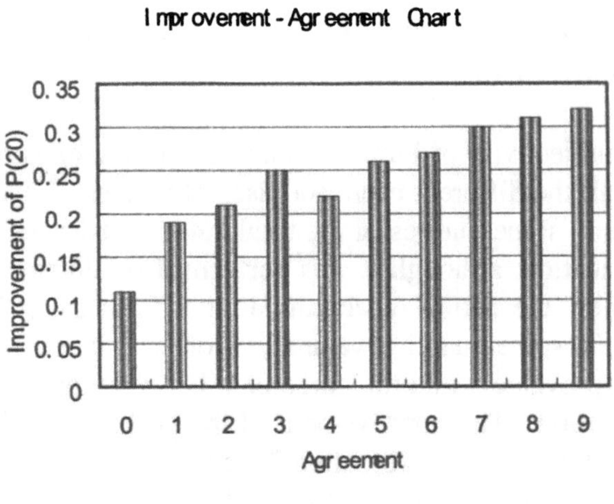

Figure 3. The relationship between improvement and agreement

From figure 3, we can find that more agreement between the classification and the user's perception, more improvement on the precision of the corresponding queries. Note that the agreement is based on statistics. The user's perception does not necessarily have explicit relation with the classification. For example, there is no explicit relation between the beach images and the categories of Asia, Europe, America, Africa, and Oceania. However, if most beach images are distributed in one or two categories, our approach will take advantage of this information and improve image retrieval accuracy.

3.5 Result Using Automatic Classification

In this experiment, we tested our method when using automatic image classification. Two SVM classifiers were trained to classify the images into semantic classes. Images were first classified to indoor or outdoor and outdoor images were further classified to man-made or natural. This method achieved an accuracy of 91.6% for indoor vs. outdoor classification, while 93% for man-made vs. natural classification. It is comparable to other classification algorithms (Szummer & Picard 1998, Vailaya et al. 1998).

In this experiment, we chose 30 out of 79 categories, totally 4,400 images. The criterion of selecting these 30 categories is mainly to guarantee the accuracy of image classification, and exclude those images unrelated to the classification, such as images of "flag", or "marble".

The classification made by domain professionals was not used in composing the semantic feature, but as the ground truth. That is, a retrieved image was considered a match if it belongs to the same category of the query image. The automatic classification was used to form a 4-dimensional semantic feature vector for each image. The semantic weight is set to 0.1. We tested 220 sample images chosen randomly from these 30 categories. To evaluate the performance, we averaged the precision over all queries. P(20) of "Orig" without relevance feedback is 0.28. After 2 iteration of relevance feedback, P(20) of "Orig" is 0.48, while P(20) of "Class" is 0.52. The improvement is small.

After analyzing the data, we found that the observation in the previous experiment still holds. Since the automatic classification is very coarse, too many images are located in one or two classes, and many queries from these classes can get less benefit from our scheme, and the performance also suffer from misclassification and inconsistency between some users' intention and the automatic classification.

4. DISCUSSIONS AND CONCLUSIONS

In this paper, we have proposed a flexible scheme to effectively combine the semantic classification with content-based image retrieval. Our approach automatically detects the correlation between the user's intention and the classification and takes advantage of it. Although any kind of semantic classification can be used, the advantage brought by our method does depend on the nature of the classification. If the classification conforms with the consensus of the users' intention well, an apparent improvement of the overall performance may be achieved. Experimental results on a large heterogeneous image collection with manual classification show that the proposed method is effective.

We may further refine this method in the future. In Section 2, a fixed weight is used to combine the semantic feature and low-level features. Dynamic adjustment of the weight may make the approach more flexible. Furthermore, we may take account of the relationship between classes in image retrieval. In practice, this method may be used together with the traditional methods that use image classes as a filter.

ACKNOWLEDGMENTS

We thank Zhong Su, Fang Qian and Xiaofei He for constructive feedback.

REFERENCES

Bradshaw B. (2000) Semantic Based Image Retrieval: A Probabilistic Approach. Proc. ACM Multimedia, Los Angeles, California.

Baeza-Yates R. and Ribeiro B., editors. (1999) Modern Information Retrieval. Addison Wesley.

La Cascia M., Sethi S., and Sclaroff S. (1998) Combining textual and visual cues for content-based image retrieval on the World Wide Web. In Proc. IEEE Workshop on Content-based Access of Image and Video Libraries, Santa Barbara, CA.

Cox I. J., Miller M. L., Omohundro S., and Yianilos P. (1996) PicHunter: Bayesian Relevance Feedback for Image Retrieval. In Int. Conf. on Pattern Recognition, Vienna, Austria.

Cox I. J., Ghosn J., Miller M. L., Papathomas T. V., and Yianilos P. N. (1997) Hidden annotation in content based image retrieval. In Proc. IEEE Workshop on Content-Based Access of Image and Video Libraries, pages 76-81.

Flickner M., Sawhney H., Niblack W., Ashley J., Huang Q., and Dom B. et al, (1995) Query by Image and Video Content: The QBIC System. IEEE Computer, 28(9).

Liu W., Sun Y., Zhang H.J. (2000) MiAlbum—A System for Home Photo Management Using the Semi-Automatic Image Annotation Approach. Proc. ACM MULTIMEDIA 2000, Los Angeles, California.

Lu Y., Hu Ch., Zhu X., Zhang H.J., Yang Q. (2000) A Unified Semantics and Feature Based Image Retrieval Technique Using Relevance Feedback. Proc. ACM MULTIMEDIA 2000, Los Angeles, California.

Pentland A., Picard R., and Sclaroff S. (1994) Photobook: Tools for Content-based Manipulation of Image Databases. In Proc. of the SPIE Conference on Storage and Retrieval of Image and Video Databases II, pages 34--47.

Rui Y., Huang T. S., Ortega M., Mehrotra S. (1998) Relevance feedback: A power tool in interactive content-based image retrieval. IEEE Trans. on Circuits and Systems for Video Technology, 8(5).

Rui Y. and Huang T. S. (2000) Optimizing Learning In Image Retrieval. Proc. of IEEE Int. Conf. on Computer Vision and Pattern Recognition (CVPR), Hilton Head, SC.

Smith J. R. and Chang S. –F. (1996) Visualseek: a fully automated content-based image query system. In Proc. of ACM Multimedia 96, pages 87--98, Boston MA USA.
Smith J. R., Chang S. –F. (1997) Visually Searching the Web for Content. IEEE Multimedia Magazine, Vol. 4 No. 3, pp. 12-20.
Squire D. M. and Pun T. (1998) Assessing agreement between human and machine clusterings of image databases. Pattern Recognition, Vol. 31, No. 12.
Szummer M. and Picard R. W. (1998) Indoor-Outdoor Image Classification. IEEE Int. Workshop on Content-based Access of Image and Video Databases.
Wang J. Z. (2000) SIMPLIcity: A region-based image retrieval system for picture libraries and biomedical image databases. *Proc. ACM Multimedia, Los Angeles, California.*
Vailaya A., Jain A., and Zhang H.J. (1998) On Image Classification: City Image vs. Landscapes. *Pattern Recognition, Vol. 31, No. 12, pp. 1921-1936.*

BIOGRAPHIES

Hong Wu received his B.S. degree in computer science in 1993 from University of Science and Technology of China, and is now a Ph.D. candidate in National Lab. of Pattern Recognition at Institute of Automation, Chinese Academy of Sciences. His research interests include image processing, machine learning, and information retrieval, with a focus on content-based image retrieval.

Mingjing Li received his B.S. in electrical engineering from University of Science and Technology of China in 1989, and Ph.D. in Pattern Recognition from Institute of Automation, Chinese Academy of Sciences in 1995. He joined Microsoft Research Asia in July 1999. His research interests include handwriting recognition, statistical language modeling, search engine, and multimedia information retrieval.

Hong-Jiang Zhang received his B.S. from Zhengzhou University, China in 1982, and Ph.D. from the Technical University of Denmark in 1991, both in electrical engineering. His research interests include video and image analysis and processing, content-based image/video/audio retrieval, media compression and streaming, computer vision and their applications in consumer and enterprise markets. He has published over 120 articles in the above area. He is a senior member of IEEE, also serves on the editorial boards of 5 professional journals and a dozen committees of various international conferences.

Wei-Ying Ma received the B.S. degree in electrical engineering from the national Tsing-Hua University in Taiwan, and the M.S. and Ph.D. degrees in electrical and computer engineering from the University of California at Santa Barbara. From June 1997 to March 2001 he was a researcher in the Hewlett-Packard Laboratories at Palo Alto. He is currently a research manager of Media Management Group in Microsoft Research Asia. He is an associate editor for the Journal of Multimedia Tools and Applications, and has served on organizing and program committees of many international conferences.

ORAL-QUERY-BY-SKETCH: AN XML-BASED FRAMEWORK FOR SPEECH ACCESS TO IMAGE DATABASES

Shiow-yang Wu
Department of Computer Science and Information Engineering
National Dong Hwa University
Hualien, Taiwan, R. O. C.
showyang@csie.ndhu.edu.tw

Wen-Shen Chen
Department of Computer Science
and Communication Engineering
Dahan Institute of Technology
Hualien, Taiwan, R. O. C.
tedc@ms01.dahan.edu.tw

Abstract We propose an XML-based framework for speech access to multiple image databases without the need for keyboard or pen-based input. The key idea is to orally command the system in drawing an abstract sketch of the target images using simple graphical objects. We define an oral language for image description and query control named SpeechQuel. The abstract sketch is represented in W3C SVG format while all other query constraints are represented using a device and system independent XML language called SpeechQuelX. This facilitates content-based access to multiple and/or heterogeneous image databases with a single query. Preliminary implementation result successfully demonstrates the feasibility and efficiency of our approach.

1. INTRODUCTION

Among all the potential applications of multimedia access, many situations demand easy and hand-free operation to query information from heterogeneous data sources. In such cases, speech accessing methods are the most convenient and promising approach. For disable users, speech access may be the only acceptable method. We propose an XML-based framework (entitled Oral-Query-by-Sketch) for integrated speech access to multiple image databases without the need for keyboard or pen-based input. The key idea is to orally construct an abstract sketch of the target image(s) using simple graphical objects. An image description and query control oral language called SpeechQuel is defined to command the system in drawing such an abstract sample for querying the image databases by content. To facilitate unified access to multiple and/or heterogeneous image databases, all query constraints are represented using a simple and system independent XML language named SpeechQuelX while the abstract sketch in W3C Scalable Vector Graphics (SVG) format respectively. A new image database can be added into the access range with a simple SpeechQuelX/SVG to native query format translator. This can be done in a straightforward manner with the XSLT technology and any standard SVG to acceptable graphic format convertor. Preliminary implementation result successfully demonstrates the feasibility and efficiency of our approach. As a summary, the main contributions of this paper are:

- The Oral-Query-by-Sketch framework for accessing image data sources based on orally constructed abstract sketches.
- An XML-based approach for unified access to multiple and/or heterogeneous image databases.
- An oral language SpeechQuel for sketch description and query control.
- A device and system independent XML language SpeechQuelX to represent the image queries.
- The application of XSLT technology for translating SpeechQuelX queries into native image database query constraints.
- Several useful criteria for empirically evaluating the effectiveness of query by example image retrieval methods.
- Techniques for integrating off-the-shelf speech recognition interfaces with multiple image databases from different vendors.

The rest of the paper is organized as follows. Section 2 provides a background survey of related issues and research work. Section 3 presents our framework and system architecture. Section 4 describes the SpeechQuel language and the associated SpeechQuelX representation format. In Section 5, we report a preliminary implementation of our framework and propose several useful criteria for empirical evaluation and performance comparison of related content-based image retrieval methods. The evaluation results demonstrate the feasibility and performance of our framework. Section 6 concludes the paper.

2. RELATED WORK

The development of image retrieval techniques can be traced back to 1970's where the main idea was to employ text-based retrieval on human annotation of images [2]. With major difficulties such as vast amount of labor required as well as the annotation impreciseness due to human perception subjectivity, these techniques are still useful for processing text-based information associated with images. Content-based image retrieval techniques emerge since the early 1990's [1, 9]. These techniques explore content-based features such as color [12], shape[12], and texture[7] for more accurate and efficient access. Since then, a number of content-based image retrieval systems such as QBIC[4] and MARS[5] have been developed and their performance reported. Among all the previous work, only a limited number of projects were reported on speech based access to document database[11], let alone image data sources. There were a number of systems along the line of query-by-sketch [10, 8, 13]. However, most (if not all) of them were based on hand-drawn sketches. The Oral-Query-by-Sketch approach reported here is unique in that we provide a framework for speech access to image sources based on orally described abstract sketches composed of elementary graphical objects. This is not only useful for normal usage but also well suited for situations that demand hand-free access such as in mobile environments or for disable users. Furthermore, we employed XML technologies[3] and the SVG format[6] to facilitate unified access to multiple image databases using the same user interface and query. A special effort was also placed on the smooth integration of off-the-shelf speech interfaces and image retrieval systems from different vendors.

3. SYSTEM FRAMEWORK AND ARCHITECTURE

The Oral-Query-by-Sketch framework and system architecture were designed with several criteria in mind. First of all, we want to enable hand-free and speech access to multiple(possibly heterogeneous) image sources. This calls for a simple yet effective oral language for image queries and the accompanied system architecture for integrating the speech interface with different sources. The goal is especially challenging for the nature of the targets. On text based information, there are many speech to text systems available for spoken language access. For image information, however, content-based retrieval techniques are much more desirable. It is unclear how to seamlessly integrate speech interface into such techniques for even a single database, let alone multiple or even heterogeneous sources. Furthermore, many existing content-based retrieval methods require several rounds of image selection and feedback process to reach the final target. This is in general not desirable or even unacceptable in the intended situations such as mobile environments or for disable users. There is clearly a need for far more simple yet precise content-based access methods.

Our solution to these challenges is the framework and architecture as depicted in Figure 1, a deliberately designed oral language SpeechQuel for image query, as well as an XML-based representation method to cope with heterogeneity. The key ideas are as follows:

- The user employs the image description and query control language SpeechQuel to orally command the system in drawing an abstract sketch of the target image(s) using simple graphical objects.
- The speech input is processed by an off-the-shelf speech recognition software and converted into text-based SpeechQuel commands.
- The system follows the commands in drawing and displaying the abstract sample image. User can construct the sample from a template library or from scratch. User can also refine the sample interactively with visual properties editing commands. Query constraints and nonvisual properties can be specified easily as well. Details of the SpeechQuel language will be discussed in the next section.
- The internal representation of the sketch is divided into two parts. The image itself is represented using the standard SVG format. All other information are represented using an XML language named SpeechQuelX. These include all other query conditions and nonvisual property settings.
- For each image information source, such as an image database, a corresponding query generator is needed to convert the SpeechQuelX/SVG representation of the sketch image and query conditions into native query format for the retrieval of images that are similar to the sample. With the use of XML and standard SVG representations, the query generator can be easily constructed using XSLT and standard SVG conversion technologies.
- Query results from different sources are combined and send back to the user. If the results contain the target image(s), the process ends with a success. Otherwise the user can provide feedback and/or refinement of the sample to start another round of image retrieval.

Orally constructing an abstract sketch using simple graphical objects for content-based access is probably the most distinctive feature of our framework. The system architecture is also designed to be highly modular in the sense that the speech interface as well as the image databases can be basically any exiting and/or off-the-shelf packages or systems. A new image source can be added into the access range as long as it supports a standard SVG to acceptable graphic format convertor and a simple SpeechQuelX to native query format translator. Since SVG is a widely supported W3C format, and SpeechQuelX is a simple

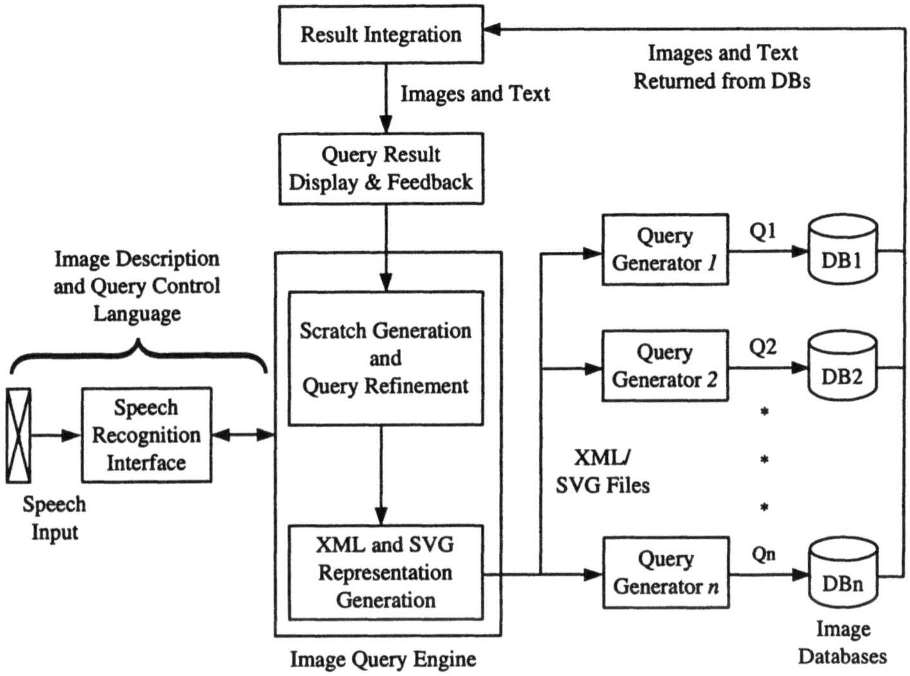

Figure 1. The Oral-Query-by-Sketch system architecture.

XML language, building such a convertor or translator is a rather straightforward task. In fact, we provided a simple function in the prototype system to convert an SVG file into JPEG format, and employed the XSLT technology to specify the automatic translators for all the image databases we tested without any difficulty. The key benefit of using the SpeechQuelX/SVG intermediate format is to cope with the potential heterogeneity of different image sources. It also facilitates independent technology and/or system improvement of individual module without affecting the others.

Another key characteristic of our framework is that, by using abstract sample image as the starting point, all image databases we tested were able to quickly retrieve the target images within one or two rounds. This significantly reduced the number of images required to be transmitted between the user and the image servers in comparison with the normal retrieval methods. This characteristic not only reduces the response time significantly but also makes our techniques well suited for bandwidth limited access such as in mobile environments.

4. THE SPEECHQUEL LANGUAGE

Drawing a desired image with oral commands is far from easy. We were first inspired by the technique of hand drawing crime suspect based on witness

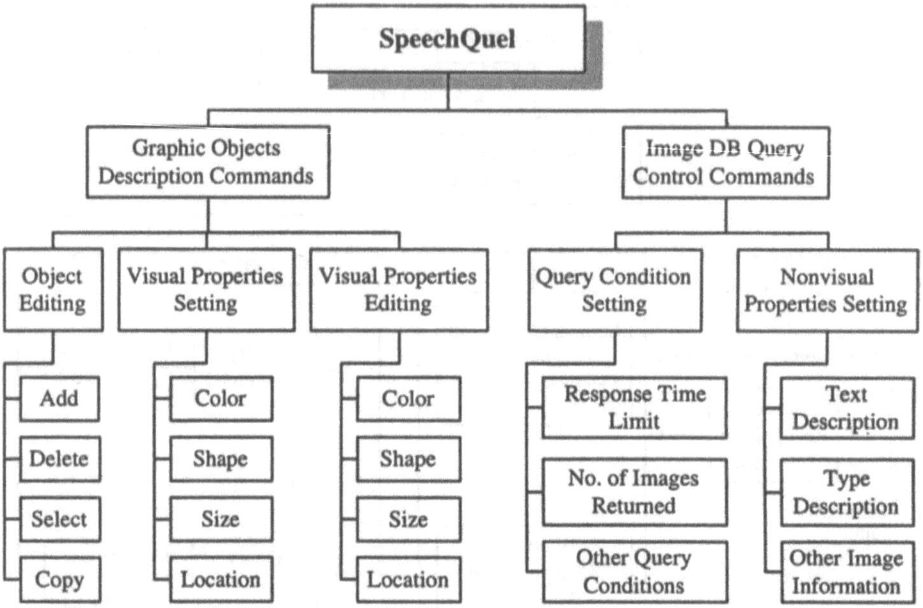

Figure 2. The SpeechQuel Language.

description. The pursue of image details is soon abandoned since it is quickly becoming clear that there is no way to define an oral command language that can cover even the modest level of details. Even with such a language, the user is probably unwilling to learn and remember all the commands for describing image details. Besides, describing such an image may take a considerably long period of time. The key point is that our purpose is to quickly retrieve the target image(s), rather than coming up with a fine drawing. For content-based retrieval, we may not need all the details. Therefore we came up with the idea of composing an abstract sketch using simple graphical objects such as circles, triangles, squares, etc. The whole idea is materialized in the language SpeechQuel(Figure 2).

The SpeechQuel language commands are divided into two categories:

- Graphical objects description commands: These are commands for drawing and editing the sample image based on the composition of elementary graphical objects such as circles, squares, triangles, etc.
- Image database query control commands: These are commands for setting the query constraints such as the response time limit, as well as specifying other nonvisual properties.

An important design consideration here is to come up with a natural and minimal set of oral commands that are versatile enough to compose the sample image user desired. We provide graphical object creation and editing commands to add, select, delete, copy, remove objects. Visual properties such as color, shape, size, and location can be specified or modified with corresponding properties setting/editting commands. There are also commands for moving selected objects, enlarging or reducing object size, as well as saving completed sample images as templates.

To allow finer control over the image retrieval process, another set of commands is provided for setting query constraints and nonvisual properties. The user can specify the response time limit to get whatever result the system retrieved so far. The number of images transmitted between the DBs and the user can be specified to reduce the bandwidth requirement. Users are also allowed to enter text-based information which can sometimes provide indispensable hints in identifying the target images.

We reemphasize the important idea of specifying an abstract sample instead of a detail image. As will be presented in Section 5, with proper shape and color, a simple image can be very efficient in helping the underlying database systems quickly retrieve the target image(s).

Once the abstract sketch is completed, it is represented using an XML/SVG format. The image itself is coded in W3C SVG format for better interoperability. All other information are represented with the XML language SpeechQuelX. The language is designed with tags for most of the commonly used query control commands/settings of existing content-based image databases. We also add some less commonly used query constraints for mobile users such as the response time limit and the maximum number of images allowed to be transmitted between the databases and the user.

The actual retrieval of the images is facilitated by a query generator which simply converts the SpeechQuelX/SVG representation into native query format. A new query generator must be constructed for adding a new image database with different query format into the access range. As stated earlier, however, constructing such a translator is a rather straightforward task with the help of standard XSLT and SVG technologies.

We demonstrate the entire process by going through a sample session in retrieving an image of two kitties. The target and the abstract sketch are shown in Figure 3. The abstract sketch is constructed using SpeechQuel commands as follows (originally in Mandarin and translated into English).

1 "Background color"_"Green"

2 "Add Object"

3 "Shape"_"Ellipse", "Color"_"Brown", "Size"_"Medium",
"Location"_"Center"

4 "Copy Object"_"One"

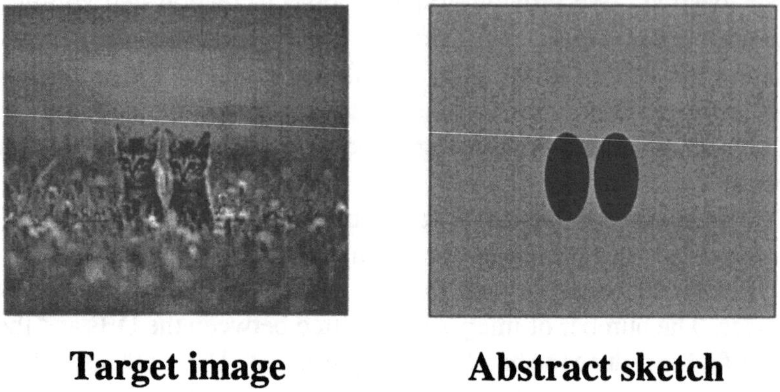

Figure 3. A target image and the abstract sketch for its retrieval.

Note that when a command such as "Copy Object" is issued, the system will number all available objects for selecting the target. The "one" in the last command denotes the selection of the first object on the list for copying.

With the just constructed abstract sketch, we can further instruct the system to search a target database and return a specified number, say 5, of closely matched images. The query conditions and the abstract sketch are transformed into SpeechQuelX/SVG representation respectively as in Figure 4. The SpeechQuelX/SVG files are sent to the corresponding query generator of the target image database. The resulting query for the IBM QBIC image database is shown in Figure 5. The QBIC database will do a search with the abstract sketch as sample and return 5 images as required.

As a closing remark for this section, a SpeechQuel user does not need to construct every abstract sample from scratch. We have designed a group of commands to import a template from a sample library as well as adding a completed sample into the template library. The user can invoke a template as a starting point or even superimpose one template on top of a half-finished sample or another template. This makes the job of orally constructing the abstract sample a lot easier than describing everything from scratch. Also note that the templates are saved as SVG text files, not with the images themselves. It therefore takes up only a small portion of the disk space.

5. IMPLEMENTATION AND EVALUATION

In our prototype system, we used the Mandarin-to-text software of the Applied Speech Technologies Inc.(`http://www.speech.com.tw`) as the speech interface. For the image database systems, we employed the QBIC[4] and a locally developed system for their readily accessibility. To evaluate our techniques upon different types of image content, we collected three different image

```
<?xml version="1.0" encoding="BIG5"?>
<ImageDB>
  <Random flag="true" />
  <KeyWord flag="true" keyword="Cats" />
  <Text flag="false" />
  <Color flag="false" weight="0" />
  <Texture flag="false" weight="0" />
  <Shape flag="true" weight="0" />
  <FileNoLimit No="5" />
  <SampleFileName name="sample.jpg" />
</ImageDB>

<?xml version="1.0"?>
<svg width="400" height="200">
<g>
  <rect x="0" y="0" width="401" height="401"
    style="fill:rgb(0,200,0);" transform="rotate(0)" />
  <ellipse cx="214" cy="104" rx="20" ry="13"
    style="fill:rgb(57,57,57);" transform="rotate(90)" />
  <ellipse cx="184" cy="104" rx="20" ry="13"
    style="fill:rgb(57,57,57);" transform="rotate(90)" />
</g>
</svg>
```

Figure 4. The SpeechQuelX representation of the query constraints and the SVG representation of the abstract sketch.

```
<?xml version="1.0" encoding="BIG5"?>
<qbic>
  <parameter> -r </parameter>
  <parameter> -T "Cats" </parameter>
  <parameter> -i "sample.jpg" </parameter>
  <parameter> -n 5</parameter>
  <parameter> -f QbDrawFeatureClass </parameter>
</qbic>
```

Figure 5. The transformed query constraints for the QBIC database.

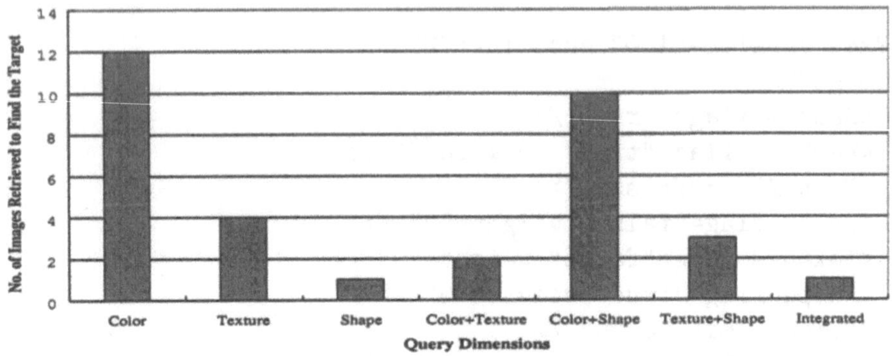

Figure 6. Flowers DB Search Effectiveness.

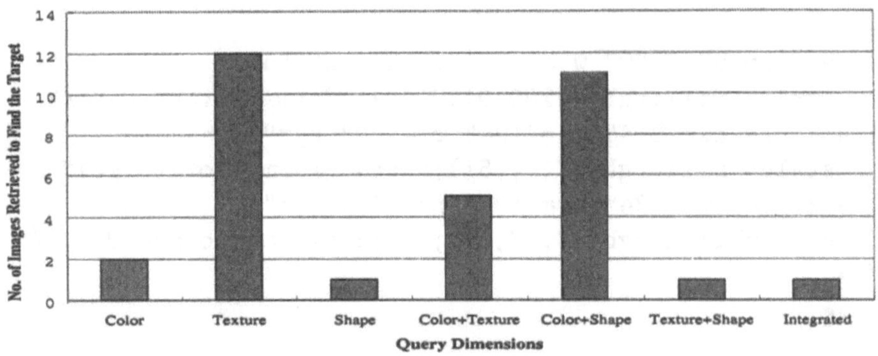

Figure 7. Snoopy DB Search Effectiveness.

databases: a flowers gallery, a collection of cat images, and a database of Snoopy cartoon(referred to as **Flowers, Cats,** and **Snoopy** respectively).

5.1. Search Effectiveness

In the first set of experiments, we pick an intended target image from each database and use the SpeechQuel language to orally command the system in drawing an abstract sample of the target. We then instruct the system to search the target based on different features such as color, shape, texture, as well as the combination of these query dimensions. The effectiveness of the search is measured by the number of images required for each database to find the target. The results are presented in Figure 6 for the Flowers gallery, Figure 7 for the Snoopy Cartoon collection, and Figure 8 for the Cats database.

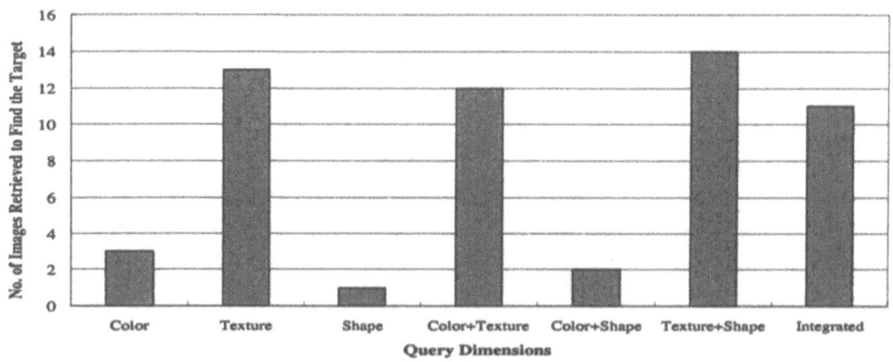

Figure 8. Cats DB Search Effectiveness.

It can be observed that different query dimensions have considerably varying effects on three types of image content. For example, query by color is quite effective for both **Snoopy** and **Cats** but fails rather miserably on **Flowers.**This coincides with our expectation since orally discriminating different flowers on color alone is far more difficult than Snoopy and Cats images that are already quite distinctive in their color feature. Among all the dimensions, query by shape consistently outperforms all the others including combination of different features. This is the natural result of our use of simple graphical objects to compose the abstract sketch. It is much more easier to describe the desired image with an abstract sample that mimics the shape of the target than with other features such as texture.

5.2. Abstract Sample vs Random Samples

A commonly used retrieval method for many content-based image databases is to provide a set of random samples to start the search. The user then interactively selects an image that is closest to the target as feedback and get another set of similar images in return. The process continues until the intended target image is finally retrieved. It normally takes several rounds of retrieval and feedback to get to the target. One of the most distinctive feature of our approach is to use an abstract image as the starting point. It is therefore our goal in this set of experiments to compare our approach with random sampling.

To make things in favor of random sampling, we use the target image itself as the seed and retrieve a fixed number of similar images(say 3) using various query dimensions. The random sampling process is considered a success as soon as it finds ANY image that falls in the group. It doesn't have to find the exact target image itself. This also reduces the effect of selecting the wrong feedback images which is rather subjective in the first place.

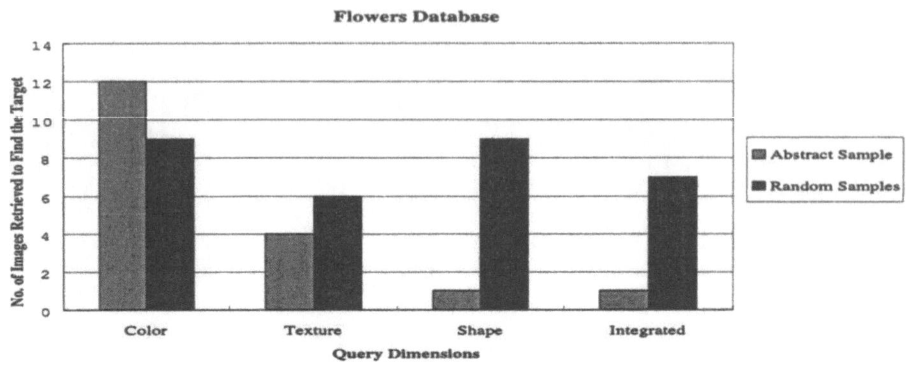

Figure 9. Abstract Sample vs Random Samples - Flowers.

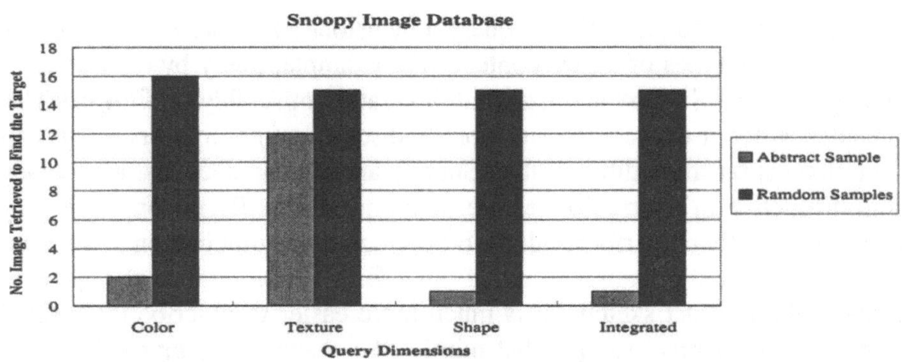

Figure 10. Abstract Sample vs Random Samples - Snoopy.

The results of the experiments are presented in Figure 9, Figure 10 and Figure 11. We can see that the abstract sample approach is superior on all three types of images and almost all query dimensions. The only exception is query by color on Flowers which is again not surprising for the difficulty of orally discriminating flowers by color alone. Also note that query by shape is again the most effective and consistent query dimension.

5.3. Expert vs Naive Users

As stated earlier, the effectiveness of the traditional interactive retrieval method dependents heavily on the user of picking the most appropriate query dimension(s) and making the right feedback choice(s). This is not an easy job for a naive user who may not have any knowledge about content-based image retrieval. Our approach is much more user friendly in that even a naive user

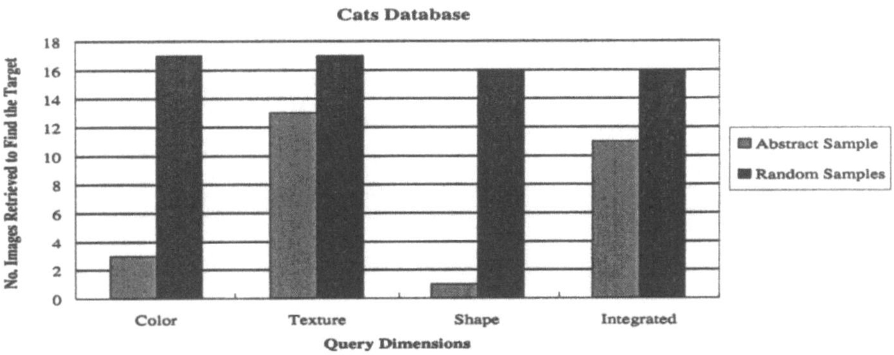

Figure 11. Abstract Sample vs Random Samples - Cats.

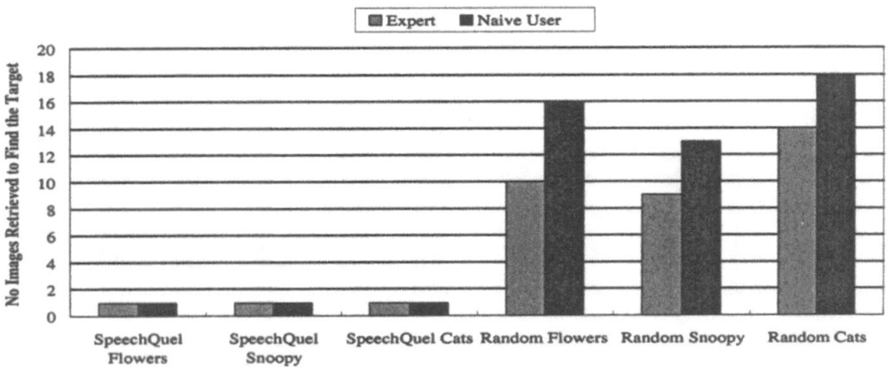

Figure 12. Expert vs Naive Users.

can describe an abstract sample that is equally effective as an expert. For the purpose of verifying our claim, we have conducted a set of experiments to compare the performance of expert vs. naive users using both SpeechQuel and the traditional interactive approach. The result (Figure 12) is very encouraging. While experts consistently outperform naive users using traditional method, both are equally effective using our approach. This is a clear indication that Oral-Query-by-Sketch is a quite natural and easy to learn method that successfully raises the performance of naive users to a higher level that is comparable to that of the experts.

5.4. Search Efficiency and Translation Overhead

In this set of experiments, we intended to measure the system efficiency in terms of search time as well as the percentage of time used for data transfor-

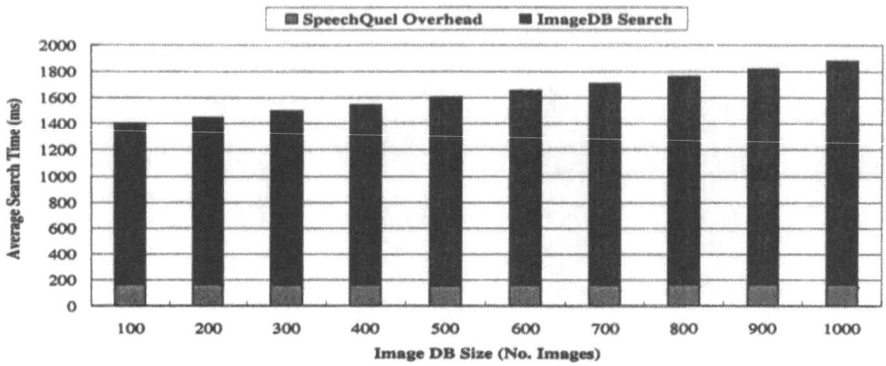

Figure 13. Search efficiency and translation overhead - query by shape.

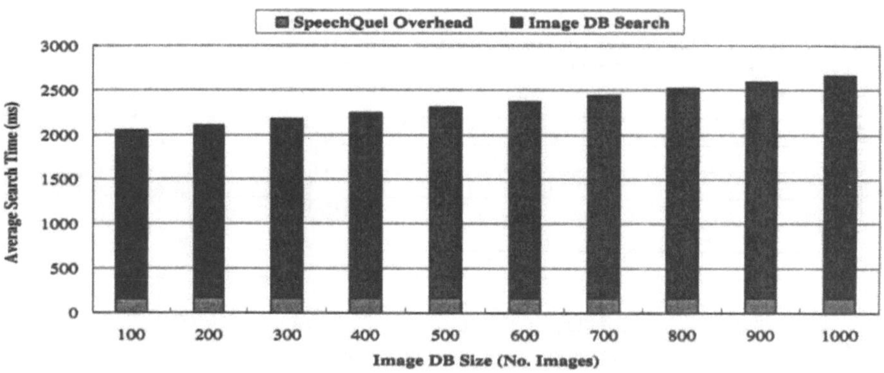

Figure 14. Search efficiency and translation overhead - query by color, shape and texture.

mation. To be an effective technique, the translation overhead must be kept to a minima. We measured the system response time with database size ranging from 100 to 1000 images using both query by shape and by the combination of color, shape and texture. The result is again quite encouraging as presented in Figure 13 and Figure 14. We can see that, the total search time increases linearly with database size which is not surprising. What's more interesting is that the translation overhead takes up a small and fixed amount of cost that is independent of the size of the database and the query dimension of choice. This is highly desirable for a speech access method both in normal usage and in demanding situations such as mobile environments.

As a summary, the Oral-Query-by-Sketch framework enables speech access to image databases with high precision and low overhead. The benefits of hand-free access, low image transmission requirement and low overhead also make it highly suitable for disable users or for mobile multimedia access.

6. CONCLUSIONS AND FUTURE WORK

We have proposed and implemented the Oral-Query-by-Sketch framework for integrated access to multiple image databases. The use of abstract sketch and speech access make it especially useful for situations that demand hand-free operations. Empirical results successfully demonstrate not only the feasibility but also the effectiveness of our approach. We plan to extend and migrate our prototype system onto a PDA and wireless communication platform. There is also a need to construct a rich template library to help the user in constructing the abstract sample. We are also evaluating the possibility of automatically constructing a set of templates from a given image source. Since the abstract sketch described by the user is typically quite different from the target image, there is a potential benefit of developing effective matching criteria and content-based image retrieval methods to explore the similarity on an abstract level.

References

[1] Y. Aslandogan and C. Yu. Techniques and systems for image and video retrieval. *IEEE Transactions on Knowledge and Data Engineering*, 11(1):56–63, January/February 1999.

[2] S.-K. Chang and A. Hsu. Image information systems: Where do we go from here? *IEEE Trans. on Knowledge and Data Eng.*, 4(5):431–442, Oct. 1992.

[3] D. Connolly. Extensible markup language (xml). w3c (mit, inria, keio), 1999. Available at: http://www.w3.org/XML/.

[4] M. Flickner, H. Sawhney, W. Niblack, J. Ashley, and Q. H. et al. Query by image and video content: The qbic system. *IEEE Computers*, 28(9):23–32, Sept. 1995.

[5] T. S. Huang, S. Mehrotra, and K. Ramchandran. Multimedia analysis and retrieval system (MARS) project. Proc. 33rd Annual Clinic on Library Application of Data Processing - Digital Image Access and Tetrieval, 1996.

[6] C. Lilley. Scalable vector graphics (svg). w3c (mit, inria, keio), 2000. Available at: http://www.w3.org/Images/SVG/Overview.html.

[7] W. Y. Ma and B. S. Manjunath. A comparison of wavelet transform features for texture image annotation. In *Proc. IEEE Int. Conf. On Image Proc.*, 1995.

[8] S. Muller, S. Eickeler, and G. Rigoll. Multimedia database retrieval using hand-drawn sketches. In *ICDAR '99. Proceedings of the Fifth International Conference on Document Analysis and Recognition*, pages 289–292, 1999.

[9] Y. Rui, T. Huang, and S. Chang. Image retrieval: current techniques, promising directions and open issues. *Journal of Visual Communication and Image Representation*, 10(4):39–62, Apr. 1999.

[10] E. D. Sciascio and M. Mongiello. Query by sketch and relevance feedback for content-based image retrieval over the web. *Journal of Visual Languages and Computing*, 10(6):565–584, 1999.

[11] F. Smith, B. Peters, D. Crookes, and G. Philip. Speech access to a document database system. In *Proc COMAD'89, Hyderabad, India*, Nov. 1989.

[12] J. Wang, W.-J. Yang, and R. Acharya. Color clustering techniques for color-content-based image retrieval from image databases. In *Proc. IEEE Conf. on Multimedia Comput. and Syss*, 1997.

[13] Y. Zhong and A. K. Jain. Object localization using color, texture and shape. *Pattern Recognition*, 33(4):671–684, Apr 2000.

QUERYING VIDEO DATA BY SPATIO-TEMPORAL RELATIONSHIPS OF MOVING OBJECT TRACES

Chikashi Yajima† Yoshihiro Nakanishi† Katsumi Tanaka††

†*Division of Computer and Systems Engineering, Graduate School of Science and Technology, Kobe University. 1-1, Rokkodai, Nada, Kobe, Hyogo 657-8501, Japan*

{yajima, nakanisi} @db.cs.kobe-u.ac.jp

††*Department of Social Informatics, Graduate School of Informatics, Kyoto University. Yoshida Honmachi, Sakyo, Kyoto 606-8501, Japan*

ktanaka@i.kyoto-u.ac.jp

Abstract We propose a query method that allows viewers to search video data based on the spatio-temporal relationships of moving objects using a simple and intuitive mode of input. In order to make a query, for example, of a certain segment or style of play in sports footage, it is necessary to express the complex movements of objects in an intuitive manner. In the proposed method, the user inputs this information as an object trajectory using a mouse or pen via a GUI. The usability of our proposed method is evaluated using a prototype query system with four main function; video query based on object speed, spatially absolute or relative query based on object movement, querying of movements of multiple moving objects specifying the spatio-temporal relationships among objects by expressing each object's trace on a *timeline* or *multi-canvas*, and providing a non-linear viewing experience by allowing the user to control playback by drawing object traces directly on the video screen while watching the video.

Keywords: video data, spatio-temporal, direct specification, moving object, trace

1. INTRODUCTION

Recently, much attention has been given to retrieving and delivering video data because of the rapid advances in digital video technologies. In order to retrieve video data, it is necessary to attach indices of meta data to the contents of the video data. For example, meta data can be automatically computed from video as feature vectors or manually inserted by annotators as keyword indices. The user can use this meta data in order to retrieve video intervals. However, it should be noted that there are events that cannot be expressed by keywords. For example, as there is a limited vocabulary to represent movement, it is impossible to retrieve a scene that satisfies the following request: "I want to see images of a player moving *in this way*." In this paper, we consider how video data for multiple moving objects can be queried.

In order to make that query, it is necessary to be able to express an object's complex movements or the spatio-temporal relationships between objects. To define such a query language that can describe various movements, the continuously changing positions of multiple moving objects have to be described. However, the query language seems to be so complex that users might not easily be able to make that query.

We propose a method for querying video intervals by drawing moving object traces with a mouse or a pen via a graphical user interface (GUI). This method is intuitive in that it does not require special background knowledge or training. The user draws traces and then uses the traces to search for video intervals that capture similar object movements. In order to verify the usability of our proposed method, we constructed a prototype. The prototype has the following four main functions; querying video images with consideration of an object's speed to some extent,

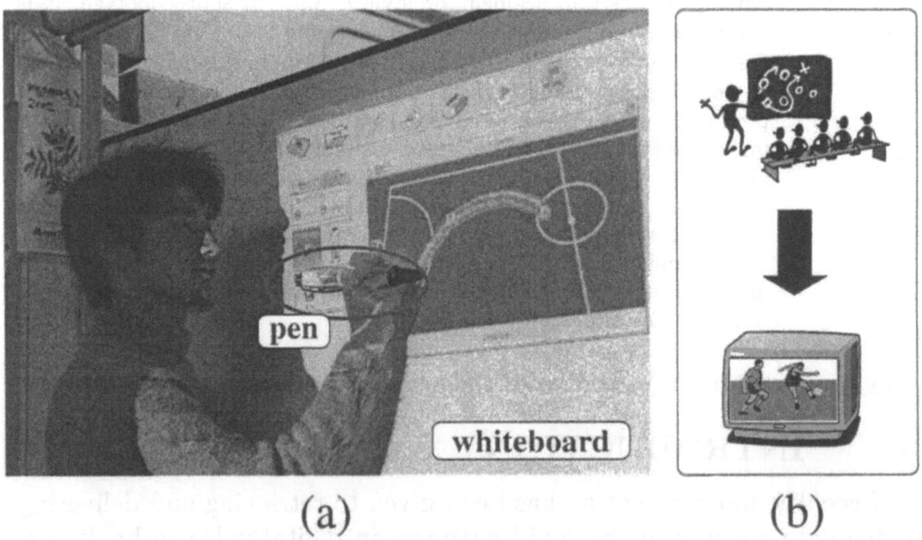

Figure 1 (a) Demonstration of our prototype (b) An example of assumed application

spatially absolute or relative querying of an object's movement, querying of movements of multiple moving objects specifying spatio-temporal relationships among objects by expressing each object's trace on a *timeline* or *multi-canvas*, and controlling playback to provide a non-linear television experience by drawing moving object traces directly on a video image while watching a video.

Figure 1(a) shows a demonstration of the prototype we developed. The prototype allows us to make queries by drawing moving object traces with a pen on a whiteboard. For video database systems that contain a time-series of positional data of captured objects, our approach has several applications. One is a type of video on demand (VOD) application, in which the user can easily specify his favorite scenes by drawing traces. The other is a type of analysis application that is used for sport video data (See Figure 1(b)). Hereafter, we assume that video data contains time-series data indicating the positions of moving objects as meta data. Due to recent advances in positioning systems, this data can be generated by using small GPS-based sensors.

The paper is organized as follows. Section 2 provides a survey on related work. In Section 3 and 4 we discuss the method for querying video intervals based on the spatio-temporal relationships of moving object traces. In Section 5 we describe a query based on drawing of moving object traces directly onto a video screen while watching a video. Finally, we conclude this paper in Section 6.

2. RELATED WORK

There is growing interest in querying the large resources of digital video data. Allen laid the foundation for multiple research studies on time intervals (Allen, 1983). He showed that there are 13 distinct temporal relationships that can exist between two arbitrary time intervals. In our work, we propose a method to query video intervals by querying the movements of multiple moving objects. Here, it is necessary to specify not only the temporal relationships but the spatial relationships as well. We therefore propose a *timeline* that can specify both the 13 temporal relationships and the spatial relationships.

Generally, the most well-known method of querying video data is by using keywords. Previous work (Oomoto and Tanaka, 1993) (Hwang and Subrahmanian, 1996) emphasized the annotation model in order to efficiently retrieve video intervals indexed by a set of keywords. The Informedia project (Wactlar et al., 1996) uses the full-text information retrieval system for queries based on keywords for video databases. However, our prototype does not assume the existence of such keywords.

Meta data and queries in our work are a time-series of position and drawn moving object traces respectively. This is because the vocabulary to express complex movements or relationships between multiple objects is very limited.

We consider that our work is divided into two fields. The first field is, as mentioned before, video databases. The second is moving object databases related to spatio-temporal databases. Other researchers are engaging in moving object databases that support the spatial objects with continuously changing position (Forlizzi et al., 2000) (Nabil et al., 1997). Forlizzi et al. define a discrete data model that is described as a collection of data types and operations which can be plugged in as attribute types into any DBMS data model to obtain a complete model and query language. This model also implements the abstract model of the work by (Güting et al., 2000).

Next, we compare the work by (Erwig et al., 1999)(Erwig and Schneider, 2000) which is similar to ours. They also have the same motivation of formulating queries by the visual specification of movements. They proposed a visual interface in order to specify predicates to be used in queries on spatio-temporal databases. The intersections of a trace with another object's trace is translated into a sequence of predicates, which can represent, for example, *disjoint, meet, equal, inside*, and so on. These predicates are mainly based on the variety of events between moving objects, and they are only interested in specifying topological relationships and need only information about relative positions of objects with respect to each other. In our work, however, we need information about absolute positions of objects for retrieval. This information can be obtained due to recent advances in positioning systems. It should be noted that we have different ways of specifying spatio-temporal relationships of multiple moving objects: they put emphasis on the predicates to represent abstract relationships and not discrete positional relationships between objects by translating visual notation into a sequence of predicates. We emphasize the specification of the discrete temporally changing positional relationships by using our proposed method (see Section 4).

3. QUERYING INDIVIDUAL MOVING OBJECT'S MOVEMENT

The snapshot of our prototype is shown in Figure 2. We chose soccer as a subject because it represents video data that captures multiple moving objects. We explain our proposed approach using this prototype. The main component of this prototype is the *canvas* on which the user

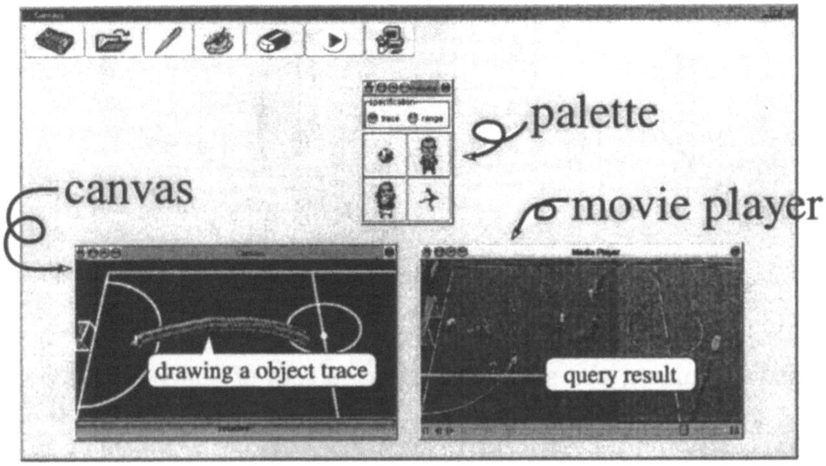

Figure 2 Snapshot of our prototype

draws a moving object trace. The prototype has a palette by which a user can specify what is the moving object of interest.

We explain a way to query by drawing a moving object trace. Figure 2 shows that by drawing a trace, a user can search for video intervals that capture object movements similar to the drawn trace query. With our prototype, the query process is described as follows:

1) On the palette, the user selects an object of his or her interest.

2) On the *canvas*, the user draws a trace of the specified object.

3) The user pushes a button to retrieve the desired video intervals.

Figure 2 shows that a ball trace drawn on the *canvas* is used as the query, and the query result is played by the movie player.

In order to retrieve video intervals, conventional time-series matching is done between the time-series data of the moving object's positions and the data of the drawn trace on the *canvas.* We use the Dynamic Time Warping (DTW) method (Berndt and Clifford, 1996)(Yi et.al., 1998). DTW is suitable for matching voices, audio frequencies and medical signals. This method can compute the distance between two time-series even if the lengths of the two series are different. Figure 3(a) shows how DTW works.

We explain in detail how a set of desired intervals can be acquired by using DTW to apply two-dimensional time-series data. S is the time-series data given by the drawn trace, and T is the moving object's

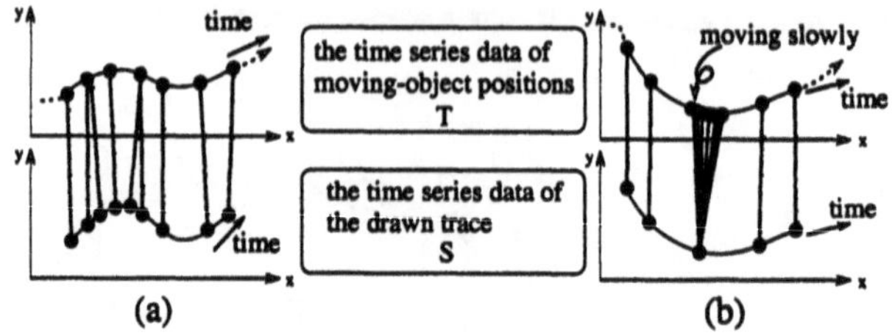

Figure 3 Dynamic Time Warping

position. Assuming there are two discrete sets of time-series data, S and T, which are given as follows: $S = s_0 s_1 \ldots s_i \ldots s_{I-1}$ and $T = t_0 t_1 \ldots t_j \ldots t_{J-1}$, where s_i and t_j are the ith and j^{th} factors of S and T respectively, and I and J are the lengths of S and T, respectively. Given the two time-series S and T, DTW creates a matching matrix $M[i,j]$, using the difference between the two sets, $d(i,j)$, by the following formulas.

$$
\begin{aligned}
d(i,j) &= \mid s_i - t_j \mid \\
M[0,j] &= d(0,j) \quad (0 \leq j \leq J-1) \\
M[i,0] &= d(i,0) + M[i-1,0] \quad (1 \leq i \leq I-1) \\
M[i,j] &= d(i,j) + min\{M[i-1,j], M[i-1,j-1], M[i,j-1]\} \\
&\qquad (1 \leq i \leq I-1 \ , \ 1 \leq j \leq J-1)
\end{aligned}
$$

Next, we define the procedure $Q(T_s, T_e)$ that requires two arguments, T_s and T_e, as follows:

(1) We define the following value as e:

$$min \ \{ \ M[I-1, T_s], \ M[I-1, T_s+1], \ \ldots, \ M[I-1, T_e] \ \}$$

If e is more than a certain threshold, the calculation by function $Q(T_s, T_e)$ stops.

(2) We define a t_e that satisfies the equality between $M[I-1, t_e]$ and e. We define a t_s that is calculated by tracing the calculation process from $M[I-1, t_e]$ to $M[0, t_s]$.

(3) An interval that is yielded by the starting time t_s and the ending time t_e is regarded as one of the answers.

(4) We calculate the following two formulas, $Q(T_s, t_s - 1)$ and $Q(t_e + 1, T_e)$. That is, the procedure Q has a recursive structure.

By using the defined procedure, we calculate a set of desired intervals. Calculating $Q(0, J-1)$ recursively makes it possible to retrieve a set of video intervals.

The reason why we use the DTW is that the time axes are different in the two time-series: one is a hand-drawn trace and the other is the moving object's positional data. Although the lengths of the two time-series are different, the DTW makes it possible to compute their pattern distance by normalizing the time-axis. However, a problem arises in querying the velocity and acceleration of the object's movement. This is especially obvious when the object's movement is slow. Since the DTW makes the two time-series datasets correspond in a way that minimizes their pattern distance, a particular point sometimes corresponds to an arbitrary number of points, as shown in Figure 3(b). That is, there is no limitation in the number of points in one time-series data that corresponds to a point in another time-series data. This leads to the problem: we cannot distinguish the speeds of the two time-series datasets. In order to resolve this, we limit the number of points that can correspond to a particular point, which makes it possible to protect the time-axis from extreme expansion and contraction.

In this way, we can distinguish fast movements from slower movements *to some extent.* The reason why we say *to some extent* is that the described algorithm is insufficient in treating the object's speed and acceleration. It is difficult to set a threshold value for the number of points that can correspond to a particular point because drawing speed (that is, the length of the two time-series) generally differs from one person to another if more than one person tries to make the same query. This problem will be the subject of future work, at which time we will consider a way to dynamically set the threshold value described above.

4. SPECIFYING THE SPATIO-TEMPORAL RELATIONSHIPS OF MULTIPLE MOVING OBJECTS

4.1. TIMELINE

In order to formulate a query by drawing traces of the movements of multiple objects, it is necessary to be able to specify the spatio-temporal relationships of these objects. In order to make this specification, we propose the usage of a *timeline.* Figure 4 shows an example for specifying the spatio-temporal relationships between two traces:

1) On the *canvas*, the user draws traces of multiple object (See Figure 4(1)).

2) On the *timeline*, the user specifies the intended relationships by dragging the rows of the *timeline* while watching the bottom row (See Figure 4(2)).

The bottom row of the *timeline* represents the spatial relationships of multiple moving objects in a specific temporal relationship.

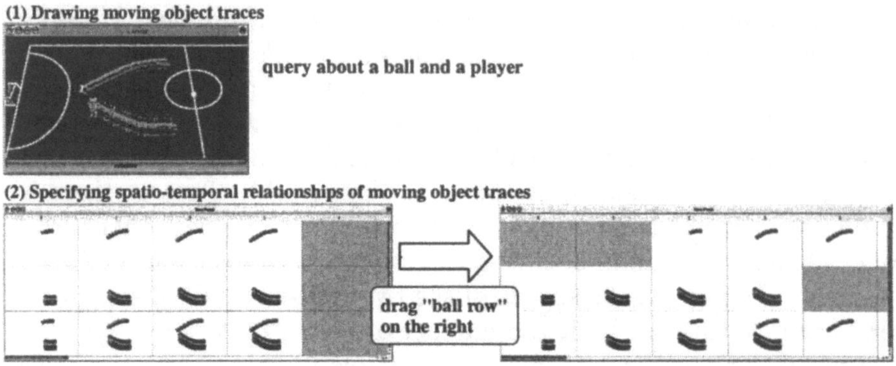

Figure 4 Specifying spatio-temporal relationships of multiple moving objects by using a timeline

4.2. SPATIALLY RELATIVE QUERIES AND MULTI-CANVAS

4.2.1 Spatially Relative Queries. We propose a spatially relative query. A spatially relative query means a query to retrieve object movements whose *shape* is similar to a given trace but independent of the position of the trace. The other method, described in Section 3, is called a spatially absolute query. The difference between the two is whether or not the position of the trace is considered. (See Figure 5).

The retrieval process is described as follows: (1) Find the minimum rectangle that includes the drawn trace. This rectangle is known as the template. (2) Employ the "template matching" method. As shown in Figure 6, this is the raster scanning of the given template from the edge of the field. (3) At each point while scanning, the DTW is applied.

The above method, however, requires a very large number of calculations because the whole field is scanned. In order to modify this method, we employ the following technique: if template matching shows a low level of similarity in a certain local domain, the nearby domain is also given a low level of similarity. By employing this technique, any domain

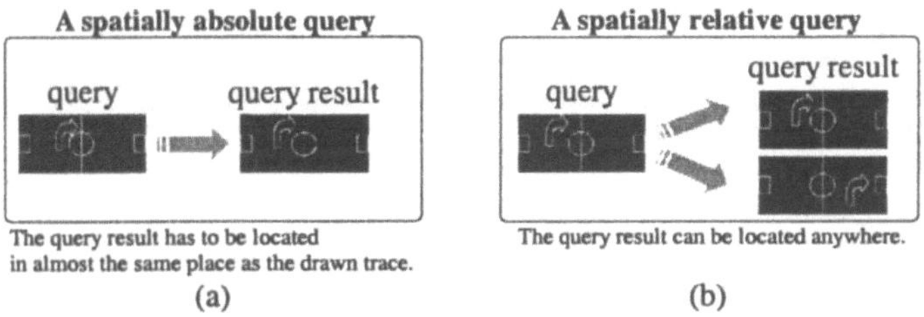

Figure 5 A spatially (a) absolute and (b) relative query

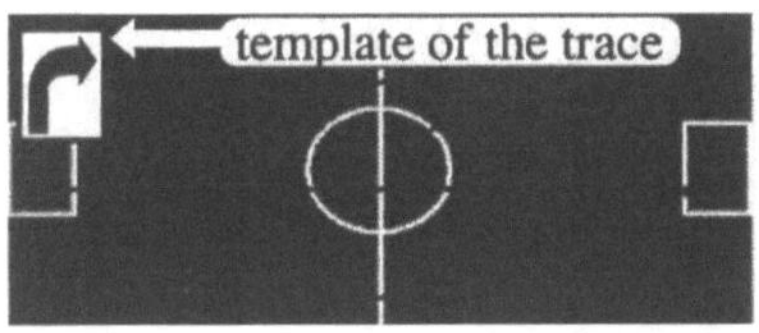

Figure 6 Template matching

that is expected to have the low similarity according to the DTW can be trimmed, and the comparative number of calculations can be reduced.

4.2.2 Multi-Canvas. Let us apply a spatially relative query to multiple moving objects. In order to formulate such a query, it is necessary to provide a user interface that can easily specify spatial and temporal relationships. To do this, we introduce the *multi-canvas*, which can specify the spatio-temporal relationships of multiple moving objects by using multiple *canvases* that are spatially distributed. Figure 7 shows the spatio-temporal relationships of multiple moving objects. Our prototype provides a button that the user can select to make a new *canvas* appear. The user can then freely drag each *canvas* to change its position. By changing the positions of the *canvases* either vertically or horizontally within a *multi-canvas*, it is possible to change a query without having to redraw the traces.

The query shown by Figure 7(a) can be represented by one *canvas*. This query can be interpreted as two traces that are temporally synchronous and spatially absolute (that is, the position of the trace is considered), and produces the same query in Figure 4 but without a *timeline*.

In order to specify the spatial relationships of multiple moving objects by using the *multi-canvas*, we propose to place the *canvases* vertically. We emphasize that the *canvas* whose background is undefined gives a

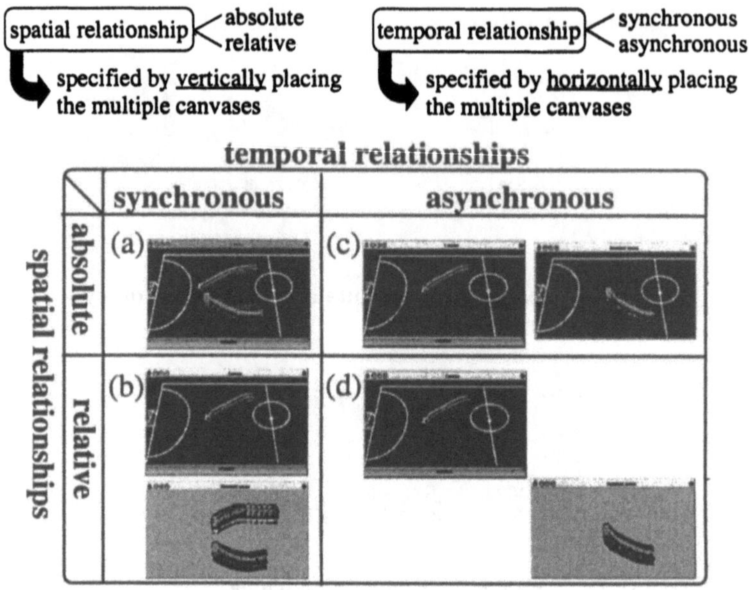

Figure 7 Specifying spatio-temporal relationships by using a multi-canvas

spatially relative query. The query shown by Figure 7(b) represents a spatially absolute query for the ball in the upper *canvas* and a spatially relative query for the two players in the lower *canvas.* The interval given by the movements of the ball and the two players has to be synchronous. There are spatially absolute relationships between the two players because they are drawn on the same *canvas.* If the two players do not have spatially absolute relationships between them, another *canvas* has to be used. That is, three *canvases* have to be placed in one vertical line.

In order to specify the temporal relationships of multiple moving objects by using the *multi-canvas*, the horizontal axis of *canvases* is used. That is, the horizontal positions of the *canvases* by nature signify the temporal relationship of video. The *canvas* placed on the right corresponds to the video interval that takes place after the interval of the *canvas* placed on the left. If the *canvases* are not placed horizontally such as in Figure 7(a) and (b), the interval given by each object's movement has to be synchronous. However, *canvases* can be placed horizontally in the number of asynchronous relationships.

Figure 7(c) and (d) both show the following movement: a ball moves first, then a player moves. The difference between Figure 7(c) and (d) is whether a spatially relative query is given for the player. The focus here is that, by dragging only the canvas containing the player in Figure

7(c) below, the query will have the exact same meaning as the query in Figure 7(d). Also, the *canvas* whose background is undefined gives a spatially relative query. Dragging the *canvas* changes the background automatically.

4.3. COMPARISON BETWEEN THE TIMELINE AND THE MULTI-CANVAS

In this subsection, we compare the *timeline* mentioned in Section 4.1 with the *multi-canvas* mentioned in Section 4.2. More than one *timeline* is can be used to specify the spatio-temporal relationships of multiple moving objects and to give a spatially relative query; however, the query in this case is a complicated procedure. There are two reason for this and the comparison between the *timeline* and the *multi-canvas.* First, the advantage of a *timeline* is that it can specify the temporal relationships of multiple moving objects precisely and in detail. On the other hand, a query by a *multi-canvas* can specify the temporal relationships only as synchronous or asynchronous. In other words, the *timeline* regards time as contiguous instants, and the *multi-canvas* regards time as roughly contiguous intervals. Thus, the *timeline* is preferred when a detailed specification of temporal relationships is desired. Second, given a spatially relative query, more than one *timeline* has to be used, and the query becomes complicated because of the detailed specification. On the other hand, a query by a *multi-canvas* cannot specify spatio-temporal relationships in detail, but it is easier to handle. Thus, the *multi-canvas* is preferred when a simple query formulation is desired.

5. QUERY BY DIRECTLY DRAWING ON A VIDEO SCREEN

Television watching is changing because of the rapid advances in digital broadcasting, which makes it possible to watch television in both real time and also by watching past videos in storage. Moreover, we will be able to watch television in a non-linear way, which will make it possible to acquire more detailed or related information while watching. In this section, we propose a way of querying video data by directly drawing on a video screen while watching the video.

As shown in Figure 8, we can consider the following example in a soccer video game. A certain player, receives the pass, gets a shot at the goal, but fails to score. While watching this or any other soccer program, we often think of what would have happened **if** the player had passed the ball to a nearby player instead. At that time a query that considers

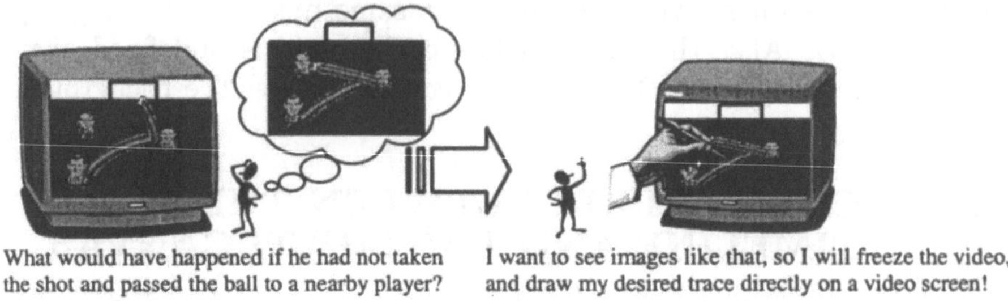

Figure 8 Concept of a query by directly drawing on a video screen

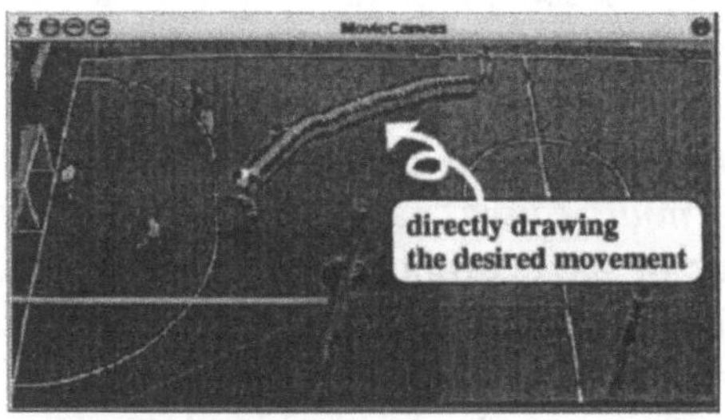

Figure 9 Query by directly drawing on a video screen

a different movement can be generated. The answer to this query has to be a past video scene that is similar to the current situation.

As shown in Figure 9, our query formulation process is described as follows:

1) The moment a desired query is issued while watching a video, the video is frozen.

2) The user draws the desired movement on the still image.

3) The user presses a button to retrieve the desired video intervals.

The formulated query requires two types of information for processing: (1) the drawn trace on the still image, and (2) the positions of the moving objects at the moment the video is frozen. The positions of all moving objects can be acquired at the specified moment because our targeted video data has the time-series data, which indicates the positions of the moving objects as meta data. Also, when drawing a trace, the user clicks the captured object on the still image; consequently, the system can specify which object is selected without using the palette mentioned in Figure 2.

The algorithm of retrieving video intervals is described as follows:

1) We use m to denote the number of all objects appearing in the still image and t_f to denote the time the video is frozen. For objects $o_1, o_2, \ldots, o_m$, let us denote the set of their positions at time t by $P(t) = \{p_1(t), p_2(t), \ldots, p_m(t)\}$.

2) For a specified (drawn) trace, retrieve a set of (past) video scenes, each of which contains the movement of a specified object that is similar to the trace. Let us denote the set of starting times of each answer video scene by $T = \{t_1, t_2, \ldots, t_n\}$.

3) Given two sequences, $P(t_f)$ and $P(t_k)$, where $t_k \in T$, the Euclidean distance between the two is calculated for each t_k. The smaller the Euclidean distance, the bigger the similarity value between times t_f and t_k. If the calculated distance value is less than a certain threshold value, the interval which has the starting time at t_k become the answer (See Figure 10).

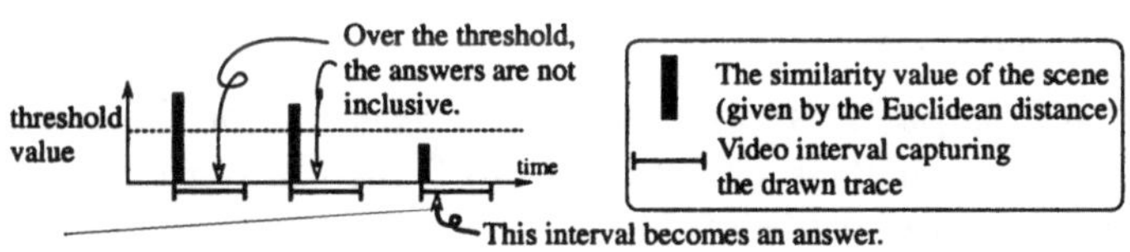

Figure 10 Retrieving video intervals by directly drawing on a video screen

Next, we consider a method to modify the query result in an incremental manner. That is, we propose to combine the query on the *canvas* and the query on the still image in order to obtain more precise answers in a incremental way. As shown in Figure 11, the query on the still

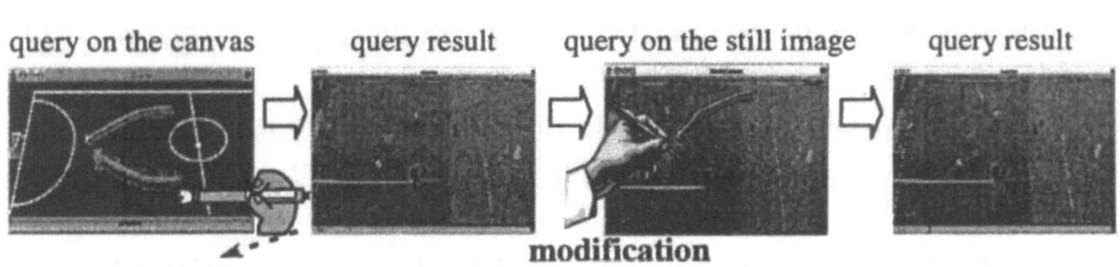

Figure 11 Modification of the query result

image is used to modify the query result from a previous query on the *canvas*.

This method has two advantages. First, as shown in Figure 11, modification of the query result allows the user to acquire a more precise set of video intervals. Second, the user gives a query on the *canvas* in an abstract manner. Then, adding the modification on the still image of the answer video allows the user to be able to give a more definite query.

6. CONCLUSION

We have presented a user interface to query video data that captures multiple moving objects by hand-drawn traces. Using the interface developed in our research allows the user to query video intervals intuitively and easily by specifying the spatio-temporal relationships of multiple moving objects. In order to acquire a qualitative evaluation of our proposal, we asked several people to test our developed prototype after we taught them how to use it. Their summarized comments include that it is an intuitive and easy way of query formulation and it is possible for end users to issue a query for moving objects without having a specialized knowledge.

Acknowledgments

This research is partly supported by the research for the grant of Scientific Research (12680416 and 13224054) form Ministry of Education, Science, Sports and Culture of Japan.

References

J.F.Allen. (1983) "Maintaining Knowledge about Temporal Intervals", *Communications of the ACM, 26(11):832-843, 1983.*

E. Oomoto and K. Tanaka. (1993) "OVID: Design and Implementation of a Video-Object Database System", *IEEE Transactions on Knowledge and Data Engineering, 5(4):551-563, August, 1993.*

E.J. Hwang and Y.S. Subrahmanian. (1996) "Querying Video Libraries", *Journal of Visual Communications and Image Representation, 7(1):44-60, March, 1996.*

H. Wactlar, T. Kanade, M. Smith, and S. Stevens. (1996) "Inteligent Access to Digital Video: Informedia Project", *IEEE Computer, 29(5):46-52.*

L. Forlizzi, R.H. Güting, E. Nardelli, and M. Schneider. (2000) "A Data Model and Data Structure for Moving Objects Databases", *SIGMOD Record, 29(2):319-330,June 2000.*

M. Nabil, A.H.H. Ngu, and J. Shepherd. (1997) "Modeling Moving Objects in Multimedia Database", *The 5th Conference on Database Systems for Advanced Applications, Melbourne, Australia, 1997.*

M. Erwig, R.H. Güting, M. Schneider, and M. Vazirgiannis. (1999) "Spatio-Temporal Data Types: An Approach to Modeling and Querying Moving Objects in Databases", *GeoInformatica, 3(3):269-296, 1999.*

R.H. Güting, M.H. Böhlen, M. Erwig, C.S. Jensen, N.A. Lorentzos, M.Schneider, and M. Vazirgiannis. (2000) "A Foundation for Representing and Querying Moving Objects", *ACM Transaction on Database Systems, 25(1), 2000.*

M. Erwig and M. Schneider. (2000) "Query-By-Trace: Visual Predicate Specification in Spatio-Temporal Databases", *The 5th IFIP Conference on Visual Database Systems (VDB5), 2000.*

D.J.Berndt and J.Clifford. (1996) "Finding Patterns in Time Series: A Dynamic Programming Approach", *Advances in Knowledge Discovery and Data Mining, pp.229-248, 1996.*

B. Yi, H.V. Jagadish, and C. Faloulsos. (1998) "Efficient Retrieval of Similar Time Sequences Under Time Warping", *The 14th International Conference on Data Engineering (ICDE'98), pp.201–208, IEEE Computer Society Press, Feb. 1998.*

Biographies

Chikashi Yajima is currently a graduate student of the Department of Computer and Systems Engineering at Kobe University. He received his B.E. in Computer Science from Kobe University in 2001. His research interests include multimedia databases.

Yoshihiro Nakanishi is currently a graduate student of the Department of Computer and Systems Engineering at Kobe University. He received his B.E. in Computer Science from Kobe University in 2000. His research interests include multimedia databases.

Katsumi Tanaka received his B.E., M.E., and Ph.D. degrees in Information Science from Kyoto University in 1974, 1976, and 1981, respectively. In 1986, he joined the Department of Instrumentation Engineering at Kobe University as an associate professor. In 1994, he became a professor of the Department of Computer & Systems Engineering and the Division of Intelligence Science (Information and Media Sciences, later), Graduate School of Science & Technology at Kobe University. Since 2001, he has been a professor of the Department of Social Informatics, Graduate School of Informatics at Kyoto University. His interests include object-oriented databases, historical database models, hypermedia systems, and multimedia information systems. Dr. Tanaka is a member of the ACM, IEEE Computer Society, and the Information Processing Society of Japan (IPSJ).

MULTI-VIEW COMBINED VISUAL SIMILARITY RETRIEVAL FOR FACE DATABASE

Yongsheng Gao and Maylor K. H. Leung
School of Computer Engineering
Nanyang Technological University, Singapore 639798
asysgao@ntu.edu.sg, asmkleung@ntu.edu.sg

Abstract This work proposed a new multi-view combined visual similarity retrieval approach for face database. The search and retrieval employ a novel facial corner coding and matching approach, which delivers fast searching speed for database retrieval. The experimental results demonstrate that the facial corners can be a useful identity feature for human face database retrieval. The profile view of a face provides a complementary structure of the face that is not seen in the frontal view. The proposed multi-view modified Hausdorff distance combines the facial corners of multiple views and achieved an improved accuracy. This technique is not limited to two view combined retrieval but a generic approach for multiple view combined similarity retrieval.

Keywords: Visual similarity, image retrieval, multi-view fusion.

1. INTRODUCTION

Most of the current studies of human face database retrieval focus on frontal faces [1-14]. Little attention has been paid to multiple view combined face database retrievals. In mug shots face searching and retrieval for law enforcement, the face profile view is another important source of identity features for the retrieval of faces. The profile view of a face provides a complementary structure of the face that is not seen in the frontal view. The retrieval system combining both frontal and profile views of faces can improve the system accuracy. And it would be more foolproof because it is difficult to fool the profile face identification by a mask or make-up.

This work proposed a new multi-view combined visual similarity retrieval approach for face database. The search and retrieval employ a novel facial corner coding and matching approach, which delivers fast searching speed for database retrieval. Unlike other face profile matching techniques that make use of the profile silhouette only, this method integrates the outline and interior facial parts in the profile matching. The proposed multi-view modified Hausdorff distance fuses the frontal and profile view faces to achieve an improved system performance. The technique is not limited to two view combined retrieval but a generic approach for multiple view combined similarity retrieval. This study is believed to be the first piece of work for multi-view combined visual similarity retrieval of face database and investigating the facial corners for human face matching.

In the following, a facial corner feature extraction and matching method is presented in Section 2. In Section 3, the combined image similarity retrieval of multiple views using corners is presented. A multi-view modified Hausdorff distance is proposed and described in detail. Encouraging experimental results are reported in Sections 4. Finally, the paper is concluded in Section 5.

2. FACIAL CORNER EXTRACTION AND MATCHING

Corners and vertices represent a class of information in image analysis. These features can be used to identify rigid objects in the scene, for example, for stereoscopic matching, geometrical calibration, due to their accuracy and less ambiguous locations. However, for non-rigid objects with smooth surfaces, such as human faces, it remains an unexplored question whether corners or dominant points can be used for identification and how well they perform. This work is believed the first attempt to apply corner coding and matching on human face retrieval.

2.1 Facial Corner Detection

Edges are the most fundamental features of objects in the 3D world. The edges in an image reflect large local intensity changes that are caused by the geometrical structure of the object, the characteristics of surface reflectance of the object, and viewing direction. Edge detection is an important technique in computer vision and pattern recognition systems since the edges usually correspond to some important properties of objects, such as object shape and boundary.

Edge extraction has been studied most extensively, and many reliable algorithms have been proposed and implemented [15-26]. A popular scheme for edge detection is to find the extrema in the blurred spatial derivates of the intensity images. The idea of blurred Laplacian filtering is extensively elaborated by Marr *et al.* [15, 16]. The Canny edge detection algorithm [20] is considered a "standard method" used by many researchers. Based on the assumption that intensity edges are ideal step edges corrupted by Gaussian noise, the Canny edge detector uses linear filtering with a Gaussian kernel to smooth noise and then computes the edge strength and direction for each pixel in the smoothed image. The edge detection algorithms proposed by Chen and Yang [21], Nevatia *et al.* [22], Nalwa *et al.* [23], Iverson *et al.* [24], Bergholm [25] and Rothwell *et al.* [26] are only a few examples from a large volume of these algorithms that had been presented to the vision community. The continuing development of edge detectors is producing increasingly complex edge detection algorithms. However, the increased sophistication of newer algorithms is not producing a commensurate improvement in performance [17] since the early algorithms of Roberts [18] and Sobel [19]. M. D. Heath *et al.* [27, 28] had investigated the performance of different edge detectors. They compared the edge detectors based on experimental psychology and statistics, in which humans rated the outputs of low level vision algorithms. One of their clear results is that "no one single edge detector was best overall; for any given image it is difficult to predict which edge detector will be best" [28].

The proposed face retrieval method using facial corners does not rely on any specific edge detector. It is a general method that any edge detector can be used. In this study, an edge detector based on the algorithm of Nevatia [22] is used followed by a thinning process to generate one pixel wide edge curves.

To generate facial corners, the dynamic two strip algorithm (Dyn2S) [30] is utilized to detect dominant points on the facial edge curves. In Dyn2S algorithm, a strip is fitted to the left and right of each point on the curve, and the points inside each strip are approximated as a straight line. The orientation and width of the strip are adjusted automatically. Longer and narrower strips are favored. A measure of "merit" based on the strips lengths and widths, and the angle between the strips is calculated. This merit provides an objective evaluation of the prominent strength of each point. The results of applying these processes on the frontal and profile faces are illustrated in Figure 1.

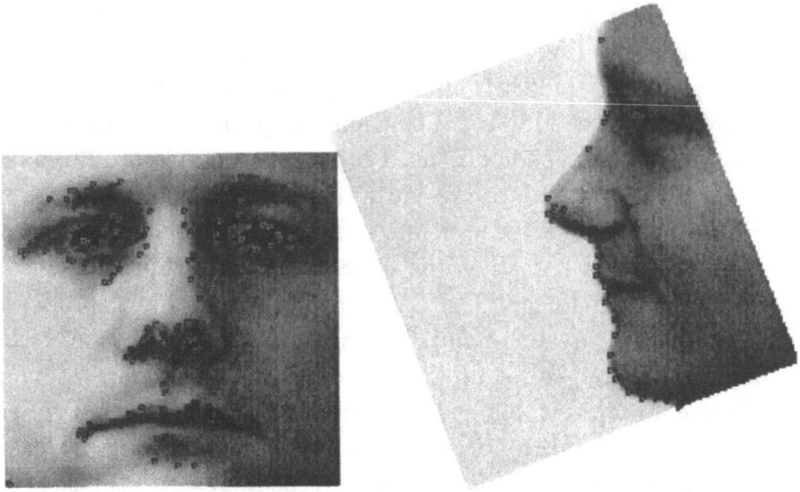

Figure 1 Facial corners extracted from frontal and side view faces.

2.2 Corner Matching

The Hausdorff distance is a shape comparison metric based on binary images. It is a distance defined between two point sets. Unlike most shape comparison methods that build a one-to-one correspondence between a model and a query image, the Hausdorff distance can be calculated without explicit point correspondence. Huttenlocher *et al.* [31] argued that the Hausdorff distance for binary image matching is more tolerant to perturbations in the locations of points than binary correlation techniques since it measures proximity rather than exact superposition. Takács [29] used Hausdorff distance to measure the similarity of two binary frontal face images, and achieved 92% accuracy in identifying the input. He argued that the process of face recognition might start at a much earlier stage and edge images could be used for fast screening of faces without the involvement of high-level cognitive functions. Here, we extend the Hausdorff distance measure from binary image matching to facial corner point matching in order to further reduce the computational time to cater for the high speed requirement in image database retrieval.

Given two finite facial corner point sets $M = \{ m_1 , m_2 , ..., m_k \}$ (representing a model in the database) and $T = \{ t_1 , t_2 , ..., t_n \}$ (representing a query image), the Hausdorff distance is defined as

$$H(M,T) = \max(h(M,T), h(T,M)) \quad (1)$$

where

$$h(M,T) = \max_{m_i \in M} \min_{t_j \in T} \left\| m_i - t_j \right\| \tag{2}$$

and $\| m_i - t_j \|$ is Euclidean norm between the points m_i and t_j. The function *h(M,T)* is called the directed Hausdorff distance from *M* to *T*. It identifies the point $m_i \in M$ that is the farthest from any point of *T* and measures the distance from m_i to its nearest neighbor in *T*. The Hausdorff distance *H(M,T)* is the maximum of *h(M,T)* and *h(T,M)*. Thus, it measures the degree of mismatch between two sets by measuring the distance of the point of *M* that is farthest from any point of *T* and vise versa.

The Hausdorff distance defined as (1) and (2) is very sensitive to outlier points. A few outlier points, even only a single one, can perturb the distance greatly, though the two objects might be very similar. Dubuisson and Jain [32] investigated 24 forms of different Hausdorff distance measures and indicated that a Modified Hausdorff Distance (MHD) measure has the best performance. The directed MHD is defined as

$$h(M,T) = \frac{1}{p} \sum_{m_i \in M} \min_{t_j \in T} \left\| m_i - t_j \right\| \tag{3}$$

where *p* is the number of points in *M*. The definition of the undirected MHD is the same as (1). The MHD is robust to outlier points that might result from segmentation errors. In this study, a new multi-view modified Hausdorff distance (MVMHD) is proposed for the combined image similarity retrieval of multiple views for human face databases.

3. COMBINATION OF MULTIPLE VIEWS

Let $M = \{M^1, M^2, \cdots, M^n\}$ be an object model in the database, which is composed of *n* views from *n* specific viewing angles, and $T = \{T^1, T^2, \cdots, T^n\}$ be a query object composed of *n* views of the same viewing angles as in the model. Define $M^1 = \{m_1^1, m_2^1, \cdots, m_{p_1}^1\}$, $M^2 = \{m_1^2, m_2^2, \cdots, m_{p_2}^2\}, \ldots, M^n = \{m_1^n, m_2^n, \cdots, m_{p_n}^n\}$ to be *n* point sets representing *n* model views of object *M* in the database and $T^1 = \{t_1^1, t_2^1, \cdots, t_{q_1}^1\}$, $T^2 = \{t_1^2, t_2^2, \cdots, t_{q_2}^2\}, \ldots, T^n = \{t_1^n, t_2^n, \cdots, t_{q_n}^n\}$ to be *n* point sets representing *n* views of a query object *T* from the same viewing angles as in the model *M*. $p_1, p_2, \ldots, p_n$ and $q_1, q_2, \ldots, q_n$ are point numbers in model and query views, respectively. A multi-view modified Hausdorff distance (MVMHD) is defined as the distance between the model image set *M* and the query image set *T*:

$$H_{MVMHD}(M,T) = \max(h_{MVMHD}(M,T), h_{MVMHD}(T,M)) \quad (4)$$

The directed MVMHDs from *M* to *T* and from *T* to *M* are defined as (5) and (6).

$$h_{MVMHD}(M,T) = \frac{1}{\sum_{k=1}^{n} N_{M^k}} \sum_{k=1}^{n} \sum_{m_i^k \in M^k} \min_{t_j^k \in T^k} \left\| m_i^k - t_j^k \right\| \quad (5)$$

$$h_{MVMHD}(T,M) = \frac{1}{\sum_{k=1}^{n} N_{T^k}} \sum_{k=1}^{n} \sum_{t_i^k \in T^k} \min_{m_j^k \in M^k} \left\| t_i^k - m_j^k \right\| \quad (6)$$

where the superscript k stands for the kth view of the model set M or the query set T, and n is the number of views in representing an object. For a point $m_i^k \in M^k$ in kth view of the model M, $h_{MVMHD}(M,T)$ identifies its nearest neighbor point in the kth view T^k of T and measures the distance from m_i^k to the identified point. All the points in each view of M contribute equally to the calculation of the directed MVMHD.

4. EXPERIMENTAL RESULTS

A face database [33] of 30 persons with 2 frontal and 2 profile views per person from the University of Bern was used to test the capability of the proposed MVMHD approach on multi-view combined face image retrieval. Each image has the size of 512 × 342 pixels with 256 gray levels, and with variations of the head position, size and contrast. One profile and one frontal face images of all individuals were used as queries while the others were used as models. Though there are 30 pairs of models and queries, one can have 60 retrieval experiments (one query is matched against 30 models in each retrieval experiment) if the roles of models and queries are interchanged. Sample sets of the frontal and profile faces are shown in Figure 2.

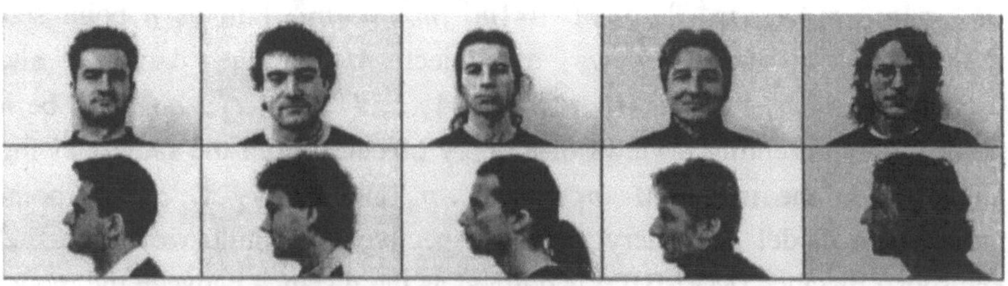

Figure 2 Example sets of frontal and profile view faces in the database.

In order to remove the influences of hair, neck, and other foreign objects such as the collar of shirts, the face retrieval process should be restricted to the personal identity area with eyebrows, eyes, nose, mouth, and chin only. For this purpose, an automatic profile location algorithm is employed to detect the nose tip and chin points. The distance between these two points was used as a reference to normalize image size, align face position and crop facial area. An example of the profile cropping process is illustrated in Figure 3. For the frontal faces, the eye locations are detected for normalization, alignment and cropping.

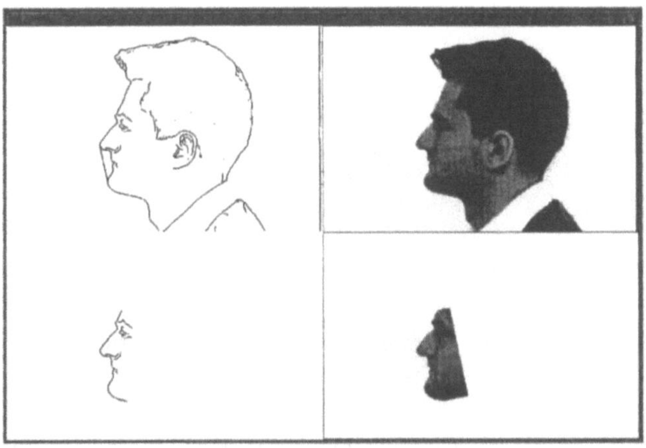

Figure 3 **Illustration of profile face cropping.**

A prototypical multi-view combined face retrieval system using the proposed MVMHD method was implemented (Figure 4). The experimental results of combined similarity retrieval of frontal and profile views are summarized in Table 1 together with the retrieval accuracy using single frontal view and profile view. The proposed facial corner matching can correctly retrieve 96.67% of frontal view faces and 90% of profile view faces. The combined retrieval on facial corner features using the multi-view modified Hausdorff distance improved the system performance up to 100%. These results show that the facial corners can be a useful identity feature for human face retrieval, which delivers fast searching speed. And the combined retrieval of multiple views using the proposed MVMHD demonstrated a better system performance.

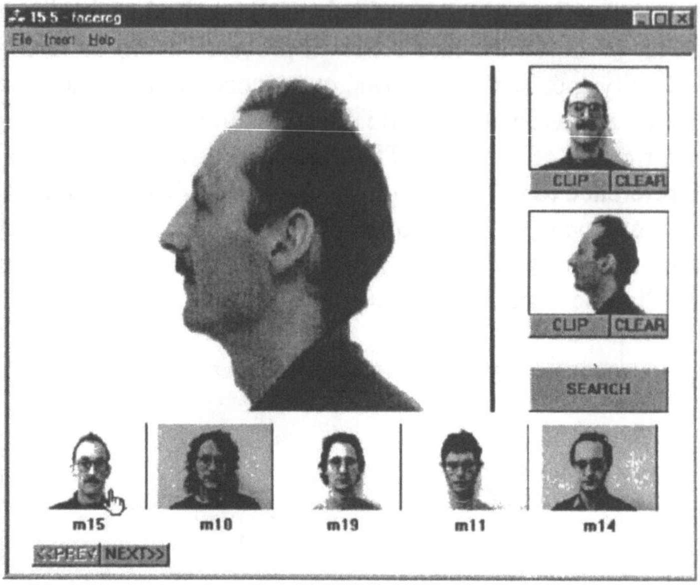

Figure 4 An example of multi-view combined face database search and retrieval result. The frontal and profile views in the right windows are query views. The images at the bottom are five best matched individuals (the leftmost is the best match) retrieved from the model database.

Table 1 The retrieval results of single view (frontal and side view) and combined views.

	Single view		Combined views
	Frontal view	Side view	
Retrieval accuracy	96.67%	90.00%	100%
Average distance of all matches	5.87	9.16	6.57
Average distance of correct matches	3.18	3.99	3.34

5. CONCLUSION

So far, no single face matching method can guarantee 100% accuracy. However, a face retrieval system that integrates the matching of frontal and profile faces could achieve better accuracy. This study is believed to be the first piece of work for multi-view combined visual similarity retrieval of face database and investigating the facial corners for human face matching. The experimental results demonstrate that the facial corners can be a useful identity feature for human face database retrieval, which delivers fast searching speed. The profile view of a face provides a complementary structure of the face that is not seen in the frontal view. The proposed multi-view modified Hausdorff distance combines the facial corners of multiple views and achieved an improved accuracy. This system would be more foolproof because it is difficult to mislead the profile face identification by a mask or make-up.

REFERENCES

[1] M. Turk and A. Pentland, "Eigenfaces for Recognition", Journal of Cognitive Neuroscience, Vol. 3, pp. 71-86, 1991.

[2] A. Pentland, B. Moghaddam and T. Starner, "View-based and Modular Eigenspaces for Face Recognition", Proc. IEEE Computer Soc. Conf. On Computer Vision and Pattern Recognition, pp. 84-91, 1994.

[3] S. Lawrence, C. L. Giles, A. C. Tsoi and A. D. Back, "Face Recognition: A Convolutional Neural-Network Approach", IEEE Transaction on Neural Networks, Vol. 8, pp. 98-113, 1997.

[4] S. H. Lin, S. Y. Kung and L. J. Lin, "Face Recognition/Detection by Probabilistic Decision-Based Neural Network", IEEE Transaction on Neural Networks, Vol. 8, pp. 114-132, 1997.

[5] S. Y. Kung and J. S. Taur, "Decision-based neural networks with signal/image classification applications", IEEE Transaction on Neural Networks, Vol. 6, pp. 170-181, 1995.

[6] M. Lades, J. C. Vorbrüggen,, J. Buhmann, J. Lange, C. von der Malsburg, R. P. Würtz and M. Konen, "Distortion Invariant Object Recognition in the Dynamic Link Architecture", IEEE Transaction on Computers, Vol. 42, pp. 300-311, 1993.

[7] L. Wiskott and C. von der Malsburg, "Recognizing Faces by Dynamic Link Matching", Neuroimage 4, pp. S14-S18, 1996.

[8] F. Samaria and F. Fallside, "Face Identification and Feature Extraction using hidden markov models", G. Vernazza, editor, Image Processing: Theory and Application, Elsevier, 1993.

[9] Y. Kaya and K. Kobayashi, "A Basic Study on Human Face Recognition", Frontiers of Pattern Recognition, S. Watanabe, Ed. pp. 265, 1972.

[10] R. Bruneli and T. Poggio, "Face Recognition: Features versus Templates", IEEE Transactions on Pattern Analysis and Machine Intelligence, Vol. 15, pp. 1042-1052, 1993.

[11] I. J. Cox, J. Ghosn and P. N. Yianios, "Feature-based face recognition using mixture-distance", Computer Vision and Pattern Recognition, Piscataway, NJ: IEEE Press, 1996.

[12] B. S. Manjunath, R. Chellappa and C. von der Malsburg, "A feature based approach to face recognition", Proc. IEEE Computer soc. Conf. on Computer Vision and Patt. Recog., pp. 373-378, 1992.

[13] M. Bichsel, "Strategies of Robust Object Recognition for Identification of Human Faces", Ph.D. thesis, Eidgenossischen Technischen Hochschule, Zurich, 1991.

[14] C. L. Kotropoulos, A. Tefas and I. Pitas, "Frontal Face Authentication Using Discriminating Grids with Morphological Feature Vectors", IEEE Transactions on Multimedia, Vol. 2, pp. 14-26, 2000.

[15] D. Marr, "Vision: A Computational Investigation into the Human Representation and Processing of Visual Information" W. H. Freeman, San Francisco, CA., 1981.

[16] D. Marr and E. C. Hildreth, "Theory of Edge Detection", Proc. Royal Soc. of London, Vol. B207, pp. 187-217, 1980.

[17] K. L. Boyer and S. Sarkar, "Assessing the State of the Art in Edge Detection:1992" SPIE, Application of Artificial Intelligence X: Machine Vision and Robotics, Vol. 1708, pp. 353-362, 1992.

[18] L. G. Roberts, "Machine Perception of Three-Dimensional Solids", Optical and Electro-Optical Information Processing, J. T. Tippett *et al.* eds., pp. 159-197, Cambridge Mass.: MIT Press, 1965.

[19] I. E. Sobel, "Cameral Model and Machine Perception", PhD thesis, Stanford Univ., 1970.

[20] J. Canny, "A Computational Approach to Edge Detection", IEEE Transaction on PAMI, Vol. 8, pp. 679-698, 1986.

[21] G. Chen, and Y. H. Yang, "Edge Detection by Regularized Cubic B-Spline Fitting", IEEE Transactions on Systems, Man and Cybernetics, Vol. 25, pp. 636–643, 1995.

[22] R. Nevatia and K. R. Babu, "Linear Feature Extraction and Description", Computer Graphics and Image Processing, Vol. 13, pp. 257-269, 1980.

[23] V. S. Nalwa and T. O. Binford, "On Detecting Edges", IEEE Transaction on PAMI, Vol. 8, pp. 699-714, 1986.

[24] L. A. Iverson and S. W. Zucker, "Logical/Linear Operators for Image Curves", IEEE Transactions on PAMI, Vol. 17, pp. 982-996, 1995.

[25] F. Bergholm, "Edge Focusing", IEEE Transactions on PAMI, Vol. 9, pp. 726-741, 1987.

[26] C. A. Rothwell, J. L. Mundy, W. Hoffman and V. D. Nguyen, "Driving Vision by Topology", Int'l Symp. Computer Vision, pp. 395-400, Coral Gables, Fla., Nov. 1995.

[27] M. D. Heath, S. Sarkar, T. Sanocki and K. W. Bowyer, "A Robust Visual Method for Assessing the Relative Performance of Edge-Detection Algorithms", IEEE Transactions on PAMI, Vol. 19, pp. 1338-1359, 1997.

[28] M. D. Heath, S. Sarkar, T. Sanocki and K. W. Bowyer, "Comparison of Edge Detectors: A Methodology and Initial Study", Computer Vision and Image Understanding, Vol. 69, pp. 38-54, 1998.

[29] B. Takács, "Comparing Face Images using the Modified Hausdorff Distance", Pattern Recognition, Vol. 31, pp. 1873-1881, 1998.

[30] M. K. H. Leung and Y. H. Yang, "Dynamic two-strip algorithm in curve fitting", Pattern Recognition, Vol. 23, pp. 69-79, 1990.
[31] D. P. Huttenlocher, G. A. Klanderman and W. J. Rucklidge, "Comparing Images Using the Hausdorff Distance", IEEE Transactions on Pattern Analysis and Machine Intelligence, Vol. 15, pp. 850-863, 1993.
[32] M. P. Dubuisson and A. K. Jain, "A Modified Hausdorff Distance for Object Matching", Proceedings 12th International Conference on Pattern Recognition, Jerusalem, Israel, pp. 566-568, 1994.
[33] Bern University face database. ftp://iamftp.unibe.ch/pub/Images/FaceImages/

BIOGRAPHIES

Yongsheng Gao received the BSc and MSc degrees in Electronic Engineering from Zhejiang University, China, in 1985 and 1988 respectively, and his PhD degree in Computer Engineering from Nanyang Technological University, Singapore. Currently, He is an assistant professor with Nanyang Technological University. His research interests include computer vision, pattern recognition and face recognition.

Maylor K.H. Leung received the BSc degree in physics from the National Taiwan University in 1979, and the BSc, MSc and PhD degrees in computer science from the University of Saskatchewan, Canada, in 1983, 1985 and 1992 respectively. Currently, Dr. Leung is an associate professor with Nanyang Technological University, Singapore. His research interests include structural pattern processing, face recognition, motion analysis and string processing.

DVQ: A DTD-DRIVEN VISUAL QUERY INTERFACE FOR XML DATABASE SYSTEMS

Long Zhang, Shihui Zheng, Aoying Zhou
Computer Science & Engineering Department
Fudan University, Shanghai, China
{lzhang0, shzheng0, ayzhou}@fudan.edu.cn

Hongjun Lu
Computer Science Department
Hong Kong University of Science & Technology, Hong Kong, China
luhj@cs.ust.hk

Abstract XML has been recognized as a promising language for data exchange over the Internet. A number of query languages have been proposed for querying XML data. Most of those languages are path-expression based. One difficulty in forming path-expression based queries is that users have to know the structure of XML data against which the queries are issued. In this paper, we describe a DTD-driven visual query interface for XML database systems. With such interface, a user can easily form path-expression based queries by clicking elements in the DTD tree displayed on the screen and supplying conditions if necessary. The interface and the query generation process are described in detail.

Keywords: XML, DTD, visual query, path expressions

1. INTRODUCTION

The Extensible Markup Language (XML) is an emerging standard for data representation and exchange on the Internet. There is a consensus among the researchers that XML is as an easy-to-write, easy-to-parse language to exchange data in a variety of applications on the Internet. Currently, most business data is stored in relational or object-relational systems. It will continue to be so since the matured relational technology provides excellent queriability, scalability and availability. It becomes a natural choice to store XML documents in relational systems to make use of such advantages and hopefully ease the difficulties in integrating XML documents into other applications. Large amount of research work has been conducted to study issues related to storing XML documents using relational database management systems (Shanmugasundaram et al., 1999; Deutsch et al., 1999; Shanmugasundaram et al., 2000; Manolescu et al., 2001). Storing an XML document into a relational database system requires to map the document into relational tables. In other words, a relational schema must be defined. Yoshikawa and Amagasa categorize such XML-Relation mapping into two categories: *structure-mapping-based* approach and *model-mapping-based* approach (Yoshikawa and Amagasa, 2001). The structure-mapping-based approach generates a relational schema from an XML document based on its logical structure described by its DTD (Document Type Descriptor). The model-mapping-based approach generates a relational schema for an XML document based on its representation model (e.g. trees) without understanding its logical structure.

To query XML data, several XML query languages were proposed including LOREL (Abiteboul et al., 1997), XML-QL (Deutsch et al., 1998), XPath (Clark and DeRose, 1999) and XQuery (Chamberlin et al., 2001). Although those query languages differ from each other in ways of expressing queries, one of the common features of XML queries is that they are mainly path expression based, which is rather different from set-oriented relational query languages, such as SQL.

Compared to querying relational database using SQL, querying XML data is more difficult from the users' viewpoint since users need to know the structure of the data. When XML data is stored in relational systems, this becomes much more difficult, especially when structure-mapping based approach is used for schema mapping as the original structure may not be well reflected by the relational schema. While storage of XML and related query processing techniques received well attention, the efforts in providing users with facilities to ease the difficulty of writing path-expression based XML query are very limited. The DataGuide (Goldman and Widom, 1997; Goldman and Widom, 1998) interface in Lore system can generate simple LOREL (Abiteboul et al., 1997) queries by exploring the DataGuide of semi-structured data. But it can only specify simple path expressions, and set conjunctive conditions on only a unique path. Both the BBQ (Munro et al., 2000) visual interface of MIX and EquiX (Cohen et al., 1999) interface display the DTD structure of XML data to facilitate user to browse and formulate query. But they cannot construct arbitrary regular path expressions and complex constraint conditions too.

In this paper we present DVQ, a DTD-driven visual query interface for an XML-Relational database system VXMLR (Zhou et al., 2001). VXMLR adopts a structure-mapping based approach to map XML data into relational tables managed by a commercial RDBMS. Its query interface, DVQ, displays the structure of the stored XML data on the screen. By simple clicking the nodes in the DTD structure and entering related conditions, a user can easily form path expressions. DVQ then generates the path expression based queries automatically. The query results are represented by XSLT and delivered to users through DVQ. With DVQ, VXMLR users navigate the nested structure of the stored XML data, form query and browse the result documents through DVQ seamlessly. The unique features of DVQ include the following.

- It provides users with a graphical interface so that complex queries can be formed by users' simple GUI actions. Not only XML experts, but also ordinary users can specify query without the knowledge of the XML query languages.
- It is powerful enough to specify regular path expressions with wildcards and any complicate conditions with conjunction, disjunction and negation. At the same time, the WYSWYG (What You See is What You Get) feature of DVQ makes query formulation rather straightforward.
- In addition to enter queries, DVQ also provides facilities for users to navigate through the XML structure and to view the intermediate results of the major steps in query processing.
- It is a separate module running at the client side and driven by DTD of original XML data. That is, it is independent on the underlying XML-relational mapping schema. So, it is a portable module that can be used in any XML database system.

The remainder of this paper is organized as follows. In Section 2, we introduce some background information. In Section 3, we describe the architecture of DVQ. Section 4 describes how DVQ forms path expressions with set constraint conditions using examples. In Section 5, we present DVQ's function of monitoring XML query execution and displaying the query results. Finally, conclusions are presented in Section 6.

2. BACKGROUND INFORMATION

In this section, we introduce some background information about XML data and XML queries.

2.1. A DTD Sample

Unlike HTML documents where their structures are usually unknown, the data type definition (DTD) of an XML document describes the nested relationships between data elements in the document. A DTD example is shown in Figure 1, and we will use it as running example in the following discussion.

The DTD in Figure 1 describes XML documents about the information of laboratories. There are two basic constructs in XML documents, element and attributes, indicated by !ELEMENT and !ATTLIST, respectively. Elements in XML documents can be nested. Each document has a unique root element, which is labinformation in our example. It contains three sub-elements, labname, project, and member. Character * after project indicates that a laboratory element instance can have zero or more projects. + indicates that a laboratory element instance may have one or more members. Each member element has a unique ID attribute, and sub-elements name, email, URL, publication and project. The sign ? after URL indicates that this element is optional, that is, a member instance may not have a URL. The contents of an element is denoted by #PCDATA. The other portion of the DTD can be interpreted in a similar way. Note that member and project are defined recursively. That is, a member element can have project as sub-element, and vice versa.

```
<!ELEMENT labinformation (labname, project*,member+)>
<!ELEMENT member (name,email,URL?, publication*,project*)>
<!ELEMENT project (projtitle,introduction?,member*)>
<!ATTLIST member ID ID #IMPLIED>
<!ELEMENT publication (title,author*,year)>
<!ELEMENT labname (#PCDATA)>
<!ELEMENT projtitle (#PCDATA)>
<!ELEMENT name (lastname?,firstname)>
<!ELEMENT lastname (#PCDATA)>
<!ELEMENT firstname (#PCDATA)>
<!ELEMENT email (#PCDATA)>
<!ELEMENT URL (#PCDATA)>
<!ELEMENT introduction (#PCDATA)>
<!ELEMENT author (name)>
<!ELEMENT year (#PCDATA)>
```

Figure 1. A Sample DTD.

2.2. Path Expressions

We can see from the DTD example that data elements in an XML document are nested to form a tree structure (a graph with IDREF). Figure 2 depicts an example document and its graphical representation, data graph. With such a structure, we can represent an element by the path from the root of the tree to the element. If we adopt the dot notation to denote the parent-child relationship, the path for a members name can be expressed as project.member.name, for example. In general, the path expressions can be more complex. If r, r_1, and r_2 are elements or attributes, a path expression has the form the root of

$r = (r)* \mid (r)+ \mid (r)? \mid r_1.r_2 \mid (r_1|r_2) \mid \# \mid name$

Where *, +, ? mean 0 or more, 1 or more, and 0 or 1, occurrences, respectively. Concatenation $r_1.r_2$ is used to form a path from r_1 to r_2.

Alternation " | " stands for disjunction. Wildcard "#" denotes arbitrary occurrences of any regular expressions. We distinguish two types of path expressions: simple path expression (SPE) and regular path expression (RPE). Simple path expressions are path expressions that consist of only element or attribute names such as `labinformation.project.member.name`. Regular path expressions are path expressions that contain regular operators. For example, `#.(project.member)*.name` is a RPE.

```
<project>
  <projname>XML</projname>
  <member ID="&3">
    <name>Zhou Aoying</name>
    <email>ayzhou@fudan.edu.cn</email>
    <publication author="Zhou">
      <title>A Algorithm ...</title>
      <year>Journal of ...</year>
    </publication>
    ...
  </member>
  <member ID="&24">
    <name>Zengping Tian</name>
    <project>
      <projname>clustering</projname>
    </project>
  </member>
</project>
```

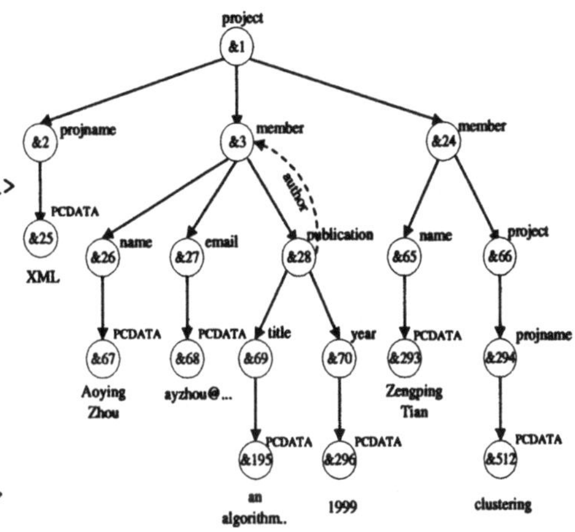

Figure 2. An XML document and its data graph.

2.3. VXMLR: A Visual XML-Relational Database System

The detailed description of VXMLR is out of the scope of this paper. To illustrate the context where DVQ works, we depict the architecture of VXMLR as shown in Figure 3. In VXMLR, XML documents are stored in a relational database system, managed by a relational DBMS. An input XML document is first parsed into a DOM tree. At the same time, the DTD for the document is extracted. The document tree is then mapped to relational tables and stored in the database. User issue queries through DVQ, the visual interface. Those queries are then transformed into SQL statements ready to submit to the underlying relational DBMS. To generate efficient SQL statements from path expression based queries, VXMLR maintains some statistics of data and a path directory. Both the statistics and the path directory are used in the query rewriting process to reduce the number of SQL statements and simplify join conditions. The query results returned from DBMS are constructed and expressed using XSL, which are then delivered to the user through DVQ.

3. DVQ: THE VISUAL QUERY INTERFACE

VXMLR system was implemented on the top of Microsoft SQL Server. The server side program is implemented in C++. The client side program, i.e., the visual query interface, which runs on a browser, is written in Java. Figure 4 shows the reference architecture of DVQ.

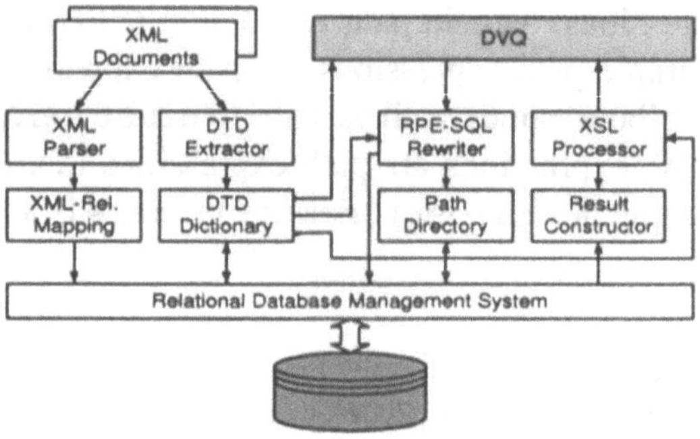

Figure 3. Reference architecture of VXMLR.

The portion upper the dashed line is the client side of VXMLR, while the below portion is the server side. The system works as following: at first, once a DTD descriptor is selected by user, the *DTD Sender* transfers the encoded DTD information to DVQ by way of *CGI*. Next, the *DTD Receiver* at the client side receives the decoded DTD and the *DTD Tree Generator* parses it into hierarchical structure, which then is displayed in *Query Interface*. Once user has constructed the query and clicked the *Submit* button, The *Query Generator* module generates path expression query automatically. The *Query Sender* module then sends the generated query to server. At the server side, the *Query Receiver* decodes the query and submits it to the *Query Engine* of VXMLR. The *Query Engine* translates the query into efficient SQL statements, which is then executed by the underlying RDBMS. VXMLR *Query Engine* constructs the result document using the result relational tables returned by RDBMS. Finally, the result document is represented by the *XSL Processor* and transferred to the browser for displaying.

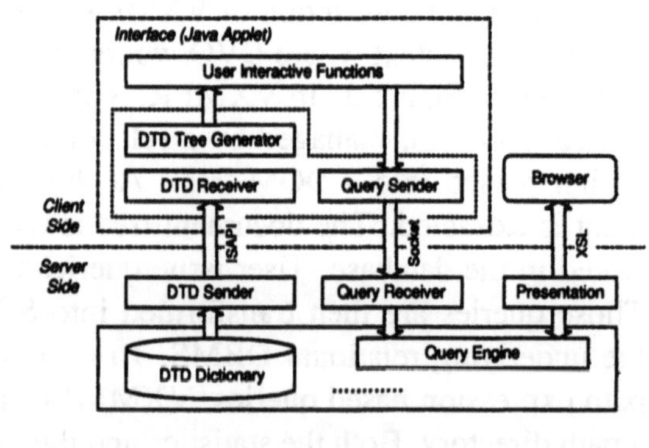

Figure 4. The reference architecture of DVQ.

Figure 5 is the screen dump (main window) of DVQ interface. It consists of two panels and some buttons. The left panel displays the DTD structure of XML data to be queried. What shown is the sample DTD in Figure 1 as a hierarchical directory, where elements and attributes are represented by their names, preceded with a diamond or a dot, respectively. Sub-elements or attributes are expressed as the children of their parent node. User can click the icon before an element to explore or collapse its subtree. Recall that `project` and `member` are defined recursively, which is represented by "`project-member`" and "`member-project`" in the DTD panel. The DTD panel provides an easy way for user to navigate the nested structure of the stored XML data conforming to the DTD. To the right of the DTD panel is two tabbed panels, *Selection*

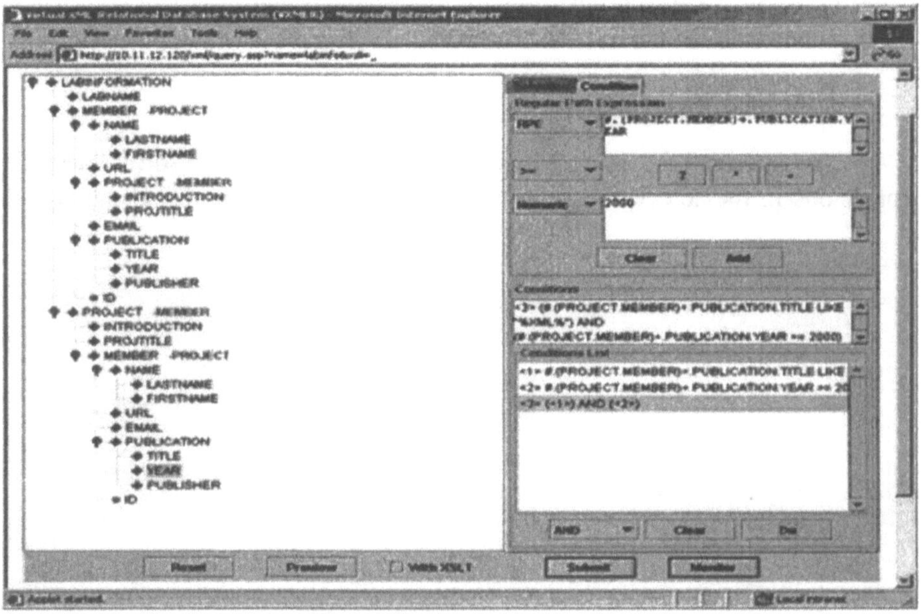

Figure 5. The DVQ interface.

and *Condition*. The *Selection* panel is used to form the target items (i.e. a list of path expression) to be retrieved. The *Condition* panel is for user entering the conditions that the retrieved items must satisfy. The basic components of both panels are path expression.

At the bottom of the main window are four buttons and a check box. The leftmost is the *Reset* button, which lets user to clear up the constructed items in the *Selection* and *Condition* panels. The *Preview* button brings up a dialog that displays the generated query for user to preview. To the right of the *Preview* button is a XSLT check box, which indicates the query result will be returned as plain XML file or XML page expressed by XSL. To the right of the XSLT check box is the *Submit* button, which triggers the query to be submitted to the VXMLR server for executing. When the right most *Monitor* button is pushed, an XML page will displayed that shows the elapsed time and query statements in each step of query processing.

4. VISUAL QUERY FORMATION

A user query session in VXMLR consists of four steps: First, browses the DTD structure and forms the output items by clicking nodes in the DTD structure and set constraints through the *Condition* panel. Second, after a user completes the specifications of the output items and constraints, a query in the form of path expressions is generated. Third, the generated query is submitted to the VXMLR server for executing. Finally, the result is returned from VXMLR server to the interface for user to browse.

4.1. Form Path Expressions

We first introduce the *Selection* panel and then show how to formulate path expressions in the select part of a query. Figure 6 shows the DTD panel and

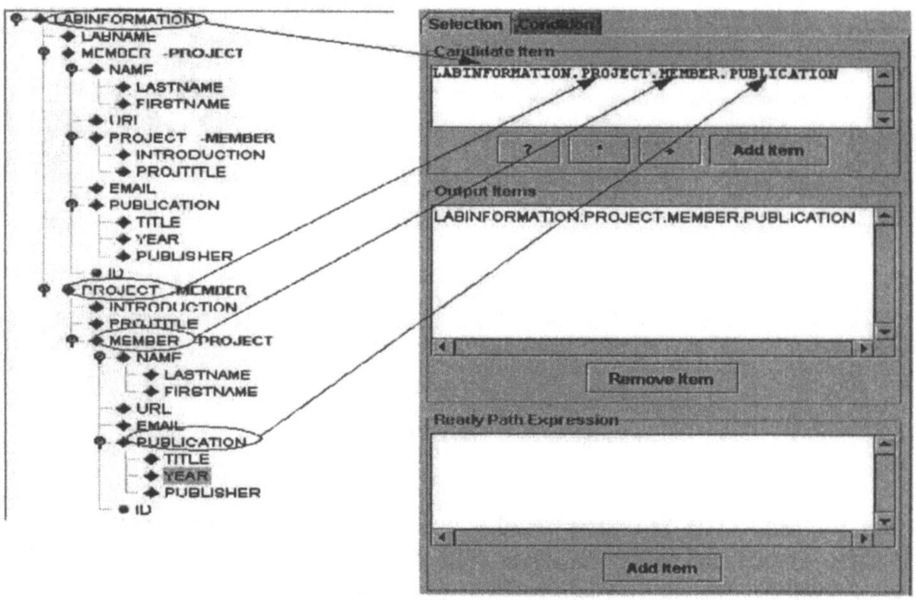

Figure 6. Specifying simple path expression by SELECT panel.

Selection panel. The *Selection* panel consists of three text boxes, *Candidate Item*, *Output Items*, and *Ready Path Expression*, and some buttons. The first text box on the top of *Selection* panel, *Candidate Item*, is used for showing the path expression being constructed. There are four buttons under the *Candidate Item* text box. The first three buttons are regular operator buttons labelled with "?", "*", and "+" respectively, which trigger those regular operators been added to the current path expression shown in the select text box. To the right of the regular operator buttons is the *Add Item* button, which brings up the path expression in the *Candidate Item* text box added into the *Output Items* text box under those buttons.

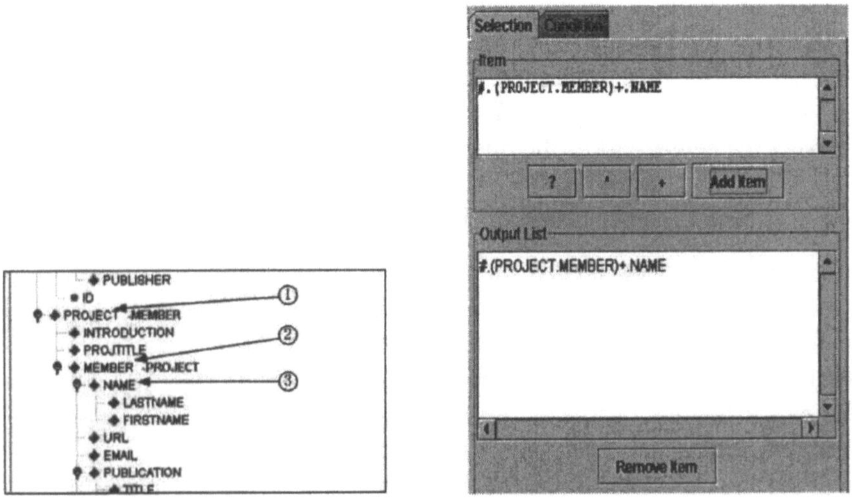

(1) (2)

Figure 7. Example for specifying regular path expressions by DTD panel (1) and SELECTION panel (2).

Now, we show by example how to form simple path expressions. A simple path expression is constructed in a natural way by clicking the nodes in the DTD panel following top-down links. Clicking a node and its children starting from the root triggers the name of the clicked nodes appended into the *Candidate Item* text box consecutively. Figure 6 shows that user clicks the nodes `labinformation,project`, `member` and `publication` consecutively. The generated path expression is SPE,

```
labinformation.project.member.publication
```

which is displayed in the *Condition Item* text box.

If the first clicked element is not the root element, or not the child of the element in the tail of the current path expression, then there is at least one element between the tail of the current path and the clicked element. A "#" operator is inserted before it automatically. For example, as shown in Figure 7(1) step one, user clicks the `project` element first followed by element `member` and `name` element. The first clicked element, `project`, is not the root. Those actions form a regular path expression `#.project.member.name`.

User can also insert the regular operators manually by first highlighting a segment in the path expression followed by clicking the corresponding operator button. The operator is then added on the path segment automatically. In Figure 7(2), highlighting path segment project.member followed by clicking "+" button forms a regular path expression `#.(project.member)+.name`.

Now user clicks the *Add Item* button. It triggers the current path expression in the *Candidate Item* text box appended to the *Output* text box. User can specifies target items and add them into the output items continuously.

Alternatively, user can also use the *Remove Item* button under the *Output* text box to remove one or more path expressions from the *Output Item* text box. At last, the path expressions in the *Output Item* text box will be used to construct the select part of the query.

4.2. Set Constraints on Output Items

Constraints can be placed on the paths in output items by *Condition* panel. Figure 8 shows the *Condition* panel, it consists of three text boxes, three pop-menus and several buttons. Same as the *Selection* panel, the *Path Expression* text box on the top of the *Condition* panel and the three regular operator buttons under it are for user to form path expressions, on which constraints are then replaced. The below part of the *Condition* panel is two text boxes labelled with "Conditions" and "Condition List", which let the user to combine multiple constraints to form complex conditions.

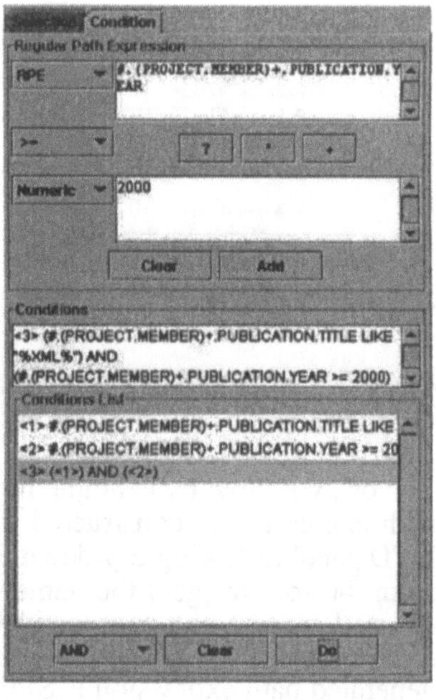

Figure 8. Forming constraints with CONDITION panel.

To the left of the "?" operator button is the comparator popup menu, which consists of a set of basic comparators ("=", ">", ">=", "<", "<=", "*LIKE*", "*IN*"). Below the comparator popup menu is the *Type* popup menu, which indicates the type of the expression. The type of an expression can be a numeric, a string, a Boolean, or a path expression. In VXMLR, each element is stored as an attribute with string type in relational database. The comparator and type popup menus enable user to flexibly treat an element as other types. For example, user can specify a comparison between target element "`year`" with an integer "2000". In VXMLR, the comparison is implemented by casting the attribute in the relation as a numeric type. To the right of the *Type* popup menu is the *Expression* text box. User can use it to input an expression, which forms a condition comparing the path expression in the *Path Expression* text box with an expression, or input another path expression by clicking the nodes in the DTD panel, which form a condition that joins two paths. In Figure 8 , user first forms this path expression "`#.(project.member)+.publication.year`" in the *Path Expression* text box by clicking the corresponding elements and "+" button. Next, user selects the comparator ">=" and "NUMERIC" type, and inputs an integer values "2000" in the *Expression* text box. Finally, the following constraint condition

```
#.(project.member)+.publication.year>=2000
```

is formed. At this point, user can click the "ADD" button under the *Expression* text box to add the above condition into the *Condition List* text box or withdraw the formed condition by clicking the *Clear* button under the expression text box. In the *Condition List* text box in Figure 8, the condition has been added into the *Condition* text box.

DVQ is powerful enough to construct arbitrary complex conditions with "AND", "OR" and "NOT" predicates. Figure 8 also shows how to form complex conditions using the *Predicate* popup menu at the bottom of the *Condition* panel. User first highlights the two conditions have been added to the *Condition* text box, then selects the "AND" predicate from the *Predicate* popup menu. Those actions bring up the two conditions in the *Condition* text box are connected by "AND" predicate and the following conjunctive condition,

```
#.(project.member)+.publication.title LIKE '%XML%'
AND #.(project.member)+.publication.year>=2000
```

is formed. Continuing to add expressions and predicates, arbitrary nested complex condition composed of conjunction, disjunction and negation can be composed also. The generated conditions are simultaneously displayed in the *Conditions* text box above the *Condition List* text box. To the right of the predicate popup menu of the two buttons are labelled with "Clear" and "Add", which bring up the conditions in the *Condition* text box are cleared or added into the where part of the formed query.

4.3. Executing Query and Browsing Result

After a user specifies the path expression and the related conditions as shown in Figure 7 (2) and Figure 8, DVQ will form the query automatically. User can preview the generated query by clicking the *Preview* button in the right part of the main window.

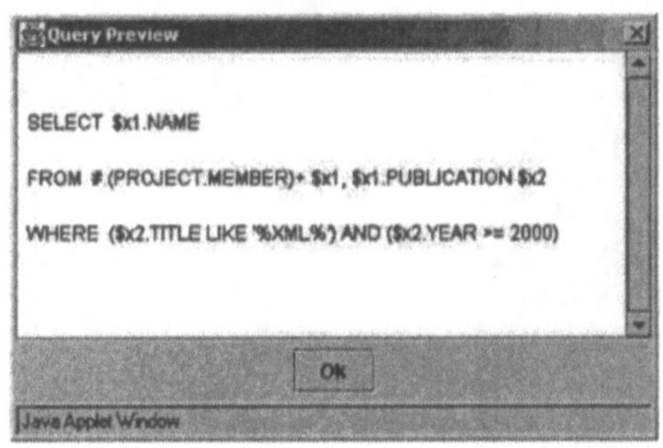

Figure 9. The preview dialog box displaying the generated query.

Figure 9 shows the dialog triggered by the click action, which displays the generated query. Note that variables are added into the queries. DVQ converts the query into the forms of Figure 9 automatically. We just sketch out the main idea for conversion and do not go into the details for query conversion here: the query generator first finds all of the path prefixes of those path expression appearing in the output items and constraint conditions, next, assigns each common path prefix a variable and place those common prefixes in the FROM clause. Then replaces all common prefixes with variable in all of those path expressions. Finally, states the constraints in the WHERE clause and puts the retrieved items in the SELECT clause. For our example, `#.(project.member)+` and `publication` are two common prefixes, which are assigned variables $x1 and $x2 respectively. The SELECT clause consists of the target item $x1.member.name and WHERE clause consists of "`$x2.title LIKE ' %XML%'and $x2.year>=2000`".

The generated query can be submitted to the VXMLR sever by click the *Submit* button. Then the query session enters into the third step: VXMLR server translates the query into SQL statements and submits it to RDBMS, then transforms the results into XML documents. If the XSLT check box is selected, then the XSLT sheet of the document is also returned. Finally, the result document is displayed in the browser and delivered to user. For example, the following query,

```
Select $x1
From sigmod.issue.articale.article $x1
Where $x1.initialpage>=100 and $x1.initialpage<=200
```

retrieves the articles with initial page above 100 in SIGMOD RECORD, and the result document represented by XSLT is shown in Figure 10.

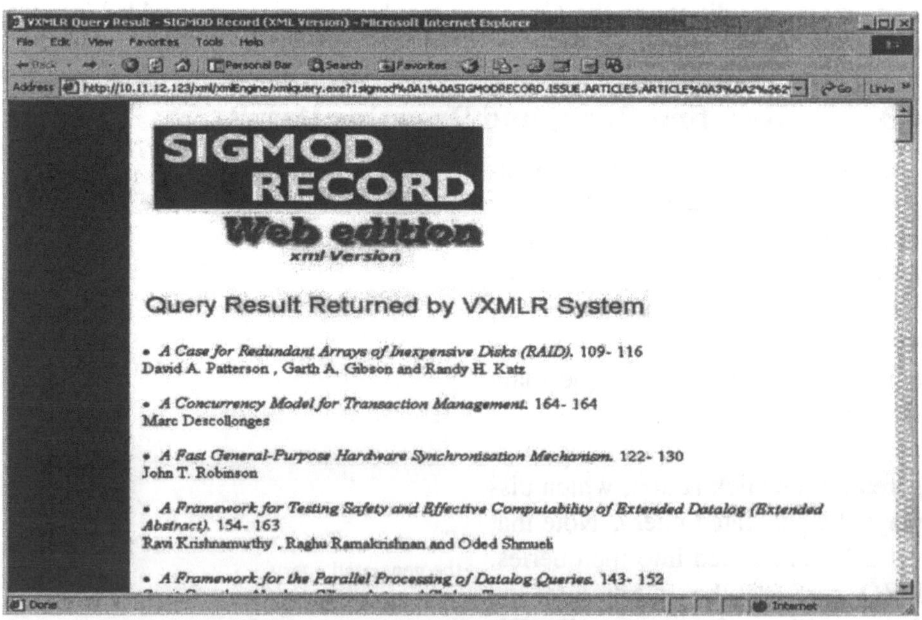

Figure 10. The result document represented by XSL.

5. MONITORING FACILITY

Querying XML data stored in relational systems is a relatively complex process. The user formed path expression queries have to be translated into SQL statements first. When the user query is a regular expression query, it needs to be transformed to simple path expression queries first. With the monitoring facility of DVQ, user can view the results of those intermediate results, in addition to time used for each step.

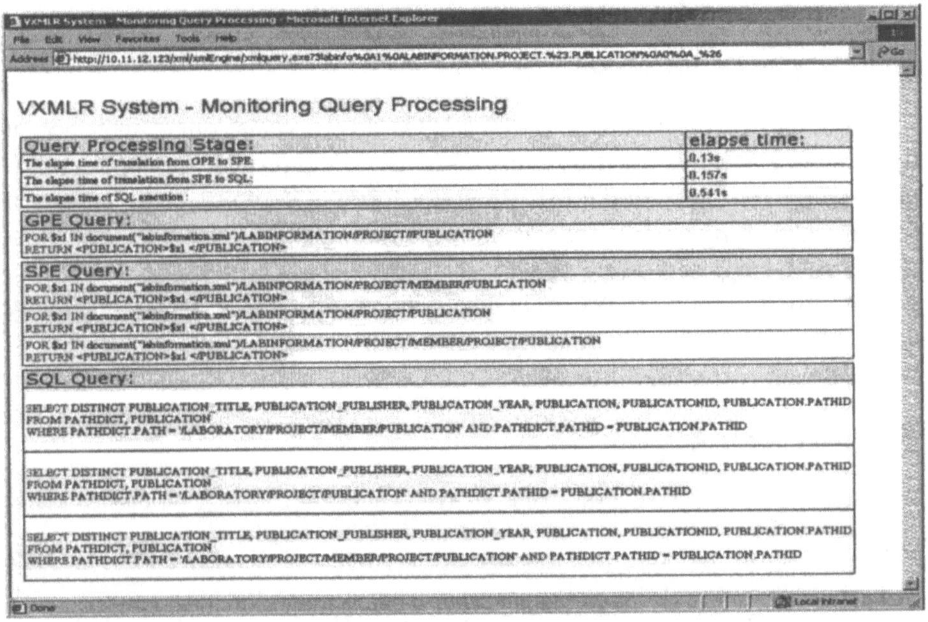

Figure 11. Browing query translation

Figure 11 shows a screen dump of execution of a query that selects all of the publications reachable from the project node via zero or more edges. That is,

```
select labinformation.project.#.publication
```

It can be seen that DVQ displays the following information: the elapsed time of each main query processing stage and their results, the original regular path expression query, the corresponding simple path expression queries, and the SQL statements executed by the underlying DBMS.

For the example shown in Figure 11, the original RPE query is expanded to three simple path expressions.

```
select labinformation.project.member.publication
union select labinformation.project.publication
union select labinformation.project.member.project.publication.
```

A simple path expression can be straightforwardly translated into joins between parent element and child element in SQL statement. With the path directory that materializes the paths from the root to elements existing in the data, a simple path expression can be translated into a rather simple SQL query. For example, SPE query

```
select labinformation.project.member.publication
```

is translated into the following SQL statement.

```
select labinformation.project.member.publication
from PathDirectory, publication
where PathDirectory.path="abinformation.project.member.publication"
and PathDirectory.pathid=publication.pathid
```

6. CONCLUSIONS

In this paper, we presented DVQ, a DTD-driven visual query interface of a prototype XML databases system, VXMLR. DVQ provides users a graphical interface for navigating XML structure, forming complex path expression queries, submitting queries for execution, browsing query results and monitoring the main steps of a query session.

The current version of DVQ only displays one DTD, and user can only query single document. We are extending this version so that users can query across related documents with different DTDs.

REFERENCES

S. Abiteboul, D. Quass, J. Mchugh, and et al. The Lore Query Language for Semistructured Data, *International Journal on Digital Libraries, 1(1): 68-88, April 1997.*

J. Clark and S. DeRose. XML path language (XPath), *W3C Recommendation 16 Nov. 1999, http://www.w3.org/TR/xpath, 1999.*

D. Chamberlin, D. Florescu, J. Robie, J. Simeon, and et. al. XQuery: A query Language for XML, Technical report, *World Wide Web Consortium, Feb. 2001. Available from http://www.w3.org/TR/xquery.*

Michael J. Carey, Laura M. Haas, Vivekananda Maganty, John H. Williams: PESTO : An Integrated Query/Browser for Object Databases, *Proceedings of the Twenty-Second International Conference on Very Large Data Bases, 1996, 203-214.*

S. Cohen, Y. Kanza, Y. Kogan, W. Nutt, Y. Sagiv, A. Serebrenik. EquiX Easy Querying in XML Databases, *WebDB 1999: 43-48.*

A. Deutsch, M. Fernandez, D. Florescu, and et al. XML-QL: A Query Language for XML, *W3C Note, 1998. Available: http://www.w3.org/TR/1998/NOTE-xml-ql-19980819/*

A. Deutsch, M. Fernandez, D. Suciu. Storing Semistructured Data with STORED, *Proceedings of the 28th SIGMOD International Conference on Management of Data, May 1999.*

Mary F. Fernandez, A. Morishima, D. Suciu. Efficient Evaluation of XML Middle-ware Queries, *Proceedings of the International Conference on Management of Data, Santa Barbara, California. Jun. 2001.*

R. Goldman and J. Widom. DataGuides: Enabling Query Formulation and Optimization in Semistructured Databases, *Proceedings of the 23rd International Conference on Very Large Data Bases, Athens, Greece, August 1997, 436-445.*

R. Goldman and J. Widom. Interactive Query and Search in Semistructured Databases, *International Workshop on the Web and Databases, Valencia, Spain, Mar. 1998.*

I. Manolescu, D. Florescu, D. Kossmann. Answering XML queries on heterogeneous data sources, *Proceedings of the International Conference on Very Large Data Bases, Roma, Italy, Sept. 2001.*

A. Marian, S. Abiteboul, G. Cobena, L. Mignet. Change-Centric Management of Versions in an XML Warehouse, *Proceedings of the 23rd International Conference on Very Large Data Bases, Roma, Italy, Sept. 2001.*

J. McHugh, S. Abiteboul, R. Goldman, D. Quass, and J. Widom. Lore: A Database Management System for Semistructured Data, *SIGMOD Record, 26(3): 54-66, Sept. 1997.*

A. Mendelzon, G. Mihaila, T. Milo. Querying the World Wide Web, *Int. J. on Digital Libraries, 1(1): 54-67. 1997.*

K. Munroe, Y. Papakonstantinou. BBQ: A Visual Interface for Browsing and Querying XML, *Proceedings of the Fifth IFIP Working Conference on Visual Database Systems, 2000.*

B. Nguyen, S. Abiteboul, G. Cobena, M. Preda. Monitoring XML Data on the Web, *Proceedings of the International Conference on Management of Data, Santa Barbara, California. June 2001.*

J. Robie, J. Lapp, and D. Schach. XML Query Language (XQL), Available from *http://www.w3.org/TandS/QL/QL98/pp/xql.html, Dec. 1998.*

J. Shanmugasundaram, J. Kiernan, E. J. Shekita, and et.al. Querying XML views of relational data, *Proceedings of the International Conference on Very Large Data Bases, Roma, Italy, Sept. 2001.*

J. Shanmugasundaram, E. J. Shekita, R. Barr, and et.al. Efficiently Publishing Relational Data as XML Documents, *Proceedings of the International Conference on Very Large Data Bases, Cairo, Egypt, September 2000, 65-76.*

J. Shanmugasundaram, K. Tufte, C. Zhang, and et. al. Relational Databases for Querying XML Documents: Limitations and Opportunities, *Proceedings of the International Conference on Very Large Data Bases Edinburgh, Scotland, 1999.*

M. YoshiKawa and T. Amagasa. XRel: A path-based approach to storage and retrieval of XML documents using relational databases, *ACM Transactions on Internet Technology, Volume 1, Number 1, 2001.*

P. Veltri, S. Cluet, D. Vodislav. Views in a large scale XML repository, *Proceedings of the International Conference on Very Large Data Bases, Roma, Italy, Sept. 2001.*

A. Zhou, H. Lu, S. Zheng. and et. al. VXMLR: A Visual XML-Relational Database System, *Proceedings of the International Conference on Very Large Data Bases, (Demonstration), Roma, Italy, Sept. 2001.*

MODELLING AND INDEXING OF FUZZY COMPLEX SHAPES

Jinglan Zhang, Binh Pham and Phoebe Chen
Faculty of Information Technology
Queensland University of Technology
GPO Box 2434 Brisbane QLD 4001 Australia
(jinglan.zhang, b.pham, p.chen)@qut.edu.au

Abstract: At the conceptual stage of design, designers have only vague ideas of initial shapes that they gradually refine. A tool that supports conceptual design should capture such imprecise features but current CAD systems that are based on precise geometry and topology information cannot satisfy this requirement. This paper presents the representation, construction and display approaches for fuzzy complex shapes. We also discuss techniques for indexing and retrieving of fuzzy shapes in an object relational database with a fuzzy processing module.

Key words: Fuzzy shape, Fuzzy solid modelling, Fuzzy CAD system, and Fuzzy database.

1. INTRODUCTION

Design, especially in the conceptual stage, is intrinsically imprecise because of designers' vague thinking and incomplete initial information. The tools that support conceptual design should be human-oriented and able to capture such imprecise features. However, current Computer-Aided Design (CAD) systems that are based on precise geometry cannot satisfy this requirement. Although the parameteric and feature-based modelling approaches (Shah and Mäntylä 1995) have made current CAD systems more flexible and meaningful, they still cannot cater for the imprecise characteristics of human because of the underlying precise representation. Since people have the ability to qualitatively identify, describe, and analyse shapes and spatial relationships by a natural language, it is desirable to use words which are related to shape, position or orientation to specify shape and spatial relationship in top-down conceptual design stage. Fuzzy set theory (Zadeh and Kacprzyk 1999) is able to deal with linguistic terms, therefore is a promising approach for simulating human behaviour in describing, locating and reasoning process in shape design. Hence, we chose this approach to address the imprecise design problem in a solid modelling system. A fuzzy model can describe a system qualitatively using linguistic words whereas these words are associated to fuzzy quantities represented by fuzzy sets. So, fuzzy modelling is both a qualitative and quantitative scheme.

The applications of fuzzy sets in geometric modelling area are relatively new and most of existing work concentrates on fuzzy modelling of two-dimensional geometric objects (Anile et al. 2000; Buckley and Eslami 1997a; Buckley and Eslami 1997b; Martin 1994; Pham 2001; Rosenfeld 1998). We aim to investigate techniques for applying fuzzy theory into solid modelling systems, hence, we introduced the concept of a fuzzy shape as a set of shapes that looks similar yet slightly different. For example, the term *very sharp shape* with *squarish* traverse section potentially refers to a set of shapes from an object that looks like a pyramid to an exact pyramid (Figure 1(a)). A fuzzy component (fuzzy part or simple fuzzy shapes) is defined as a family of shapes which are represented by a set of parameters with fuzzy values. A fuzzy complex shape is the combination of any fuzzy parts under crisp or fuzzy spatial information through Boolean operations.

In previous papers, we have investigated the representation, specification, optimisation and management approaches of fuzzy components (Pham and Zhang 2000; Zhang et al. 2001; Zhang et al. 2002a; Zhang et al. 2002b). Although the superquadric model has relatively wide geometric coverage, its representation ability is still limited since it uses only one equation to represent shapes. Hence, a mechanism for creating complex shapes must be provided. This paper focuses on the construction of fuzzy complex shapes based on descriptive terms that are related to shape, spatial location and orientation, and the indexing and retrieving of fuzzy complex shapes in a fuzzy database. This paper is organised as follows. Section 2 describes the geometric representation of fuzzy complex shapes. The construction of fuzzy complex shapes based on Boolean operations is discussed in section 3. Section 4 gives an overview of the conceptual modelling of the fuzzy database for the management of fuzzy complex shapes. Section 5 discusses the indexing and retrieving of fuzzy complex shapes in a fuzzy database implemented in the framework of object relational database. Finally, the conclusions and future work are presented in the last section.

2. REPRESENTATION OF FUZZY COMPLEX SHAPES

Existing solid modelling methods, such as Constructive Solid Geometry (CSG) and Boundary Representation (B-Rep) (Mäntylä 1988), are based on precise representation of geometric objects, such as vertices, edges, surfaces as well as the exact topology relationship between them. These methods are good at supporting detail design where all design details must be represented exactly yet they are very weak to support conceptual design that is qualitative and uncertain. Qualitative models such as *geons* (Dickinson et al. 1993) cannot provide sufficient quantitative information that is required for shape specification and manipulation in CAD system. Superquadric models proposed by Barr (Barr 1981) use several shape parameters to quantitatively define a shape, yet each shape parameter is related to one quality of the shape such as squareness/roundness and size. Hence superquadrics is both quantitative and qualitative. Such a property makes superquadrics the ideal candidate for bridging qualitative conceptual shape design and quantitative detail design. It also makes it possible to introduce fuzzy set approach into CAD systems where fuzzy sets are used to represent design intents. We therefore choose superquadrics as the basic representation for 3D shape components, where a shape is represented by a set of shape descriptors and a set of shape parameters (Pham and Zhang 2000).

2.1 Representation of fuzzy primitives

Fuzzy primitives (or fuzzy shape components, simple shapes) refer to fuzzy shapes that can be represented by superquadrics directly. The detailed parameters and equations of superquadrics can be found in (Barr 1981; Barr 1984; Pham and Zhang 2000) and here we give only an abstract representation:

$$\mathrm{SQ} = F(\varepsilon_1, \varepsilon_2, a_1, a_2, a_3, k_x, k_y, k_v, t), \quad (1)$$

where SQ is a superquadric shape, F is the function relating all these parameters; ε_1 and ε_2 are shape parameters which control the shape roundness and squareness along north-south direction and west-east direction respectively; a_1 is the overall size; a_2 and a_3 are ratio parameters which represent the ratio of the lengths of a shape along y and z axes to the length along x axis, and a_2 and a_3 control the relative dimension of the two cross sections of a superquadric shape; k_x and k_y control the tapering property; k_v controls the bending property; and t controls the twisting property. This representation is superellipsoids (Barr 1981) with deformation parameters and we still call them superquadrics for simplicity. When these parameters take fuzzy values, in particular, fuzzy real numbers, the resultant shape is a fuzzy shape which has many shape elements with variable membership degrees. Figure 1(b) shows a *slightly bent* fuzzy superquaic shape with round traverse section, where the membership degrees vary from 1.0 to 0.6.

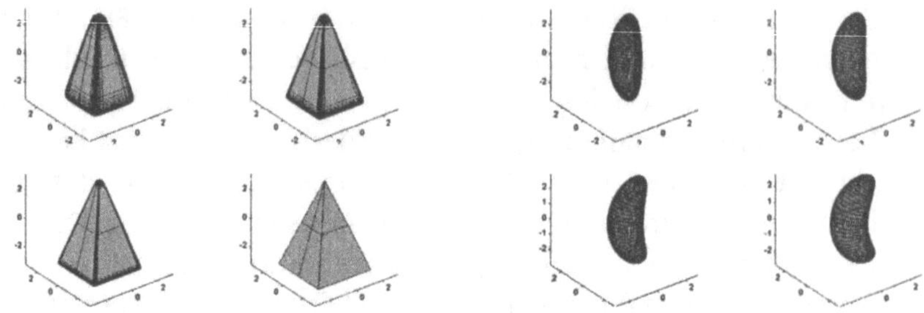

(a) Typical shape elements of a very sharp with squarish traverse section fuzzy shape.

(b) Typical shapes of a *slightly bent* with round *traverse section* fuzzy shape.

Figure 1. Elemental fuzzy shapes

Complex shapes can be generated by combining simple shapes through transformation (including translation, rotation, and scaling) and Boolean operations (intersection, union, difference) (Mäntylä 1988). We now discuss the representation of fuzzy complex shapes and their construction.

2.2 Representation of fuzzy spatial information

To support vague conceptual design, an effective method for specifying and reasoning of spatial relationship between objects is crucial to efficiently construct assemblies. Spatial information such as distance and orientation can be crisp, interval or fuzzy. We focus on the specification of spatial information using fuzzy sets because crisp and interval spatial information are special cases of fuzzy spatial information. We first define a set of spatial description words and then define fuzzy quantities associated with them.

Fuzzy representation of directions

In user interface level, we use words related to the *primary directions* along the three axes X, Y, and Z and *secondary directions* described according to their locations in XY, XZ, and YZ planes to describe directions. Primary directions include:

Primary Directions = {*Left, Right, Front, Back, Top, Bottom*},
and secondary directions include:

Secondary Directions = {*Top Right, Top Back, Top Left, Top Front, Bottom Right, Bottom Back, Bottom Left, Bottom Front, Right Front, Right Back, Left Front, Left Back*}.

The eight directions in the horizontal plane (XZ) can be represented by a circular neighbouring structure (Hernández 1994). We use the trapezoidal and triangular shape of membership functions to represent the fuzzy set values of directions as they are easy to manage. As the directions in each plane vary between 0° and 360°, the value range is fixed for any directions. We use 0° to 360° (beta angle) in XZ plane and 0° to 180° in YZ plane (gamma angle) (Figure 2) to describe directions because the product of these two intervals covers all directions in the three dimensional Euclidean space. Hence, we can equally partition the direction space into overlapped fuzzy regions, where the number of fuzzy sets are determined by the number of directions we aim to describe. We take eight directions in XZ plane and four directions in YZ plane as these are the mostly used directions in daily life.

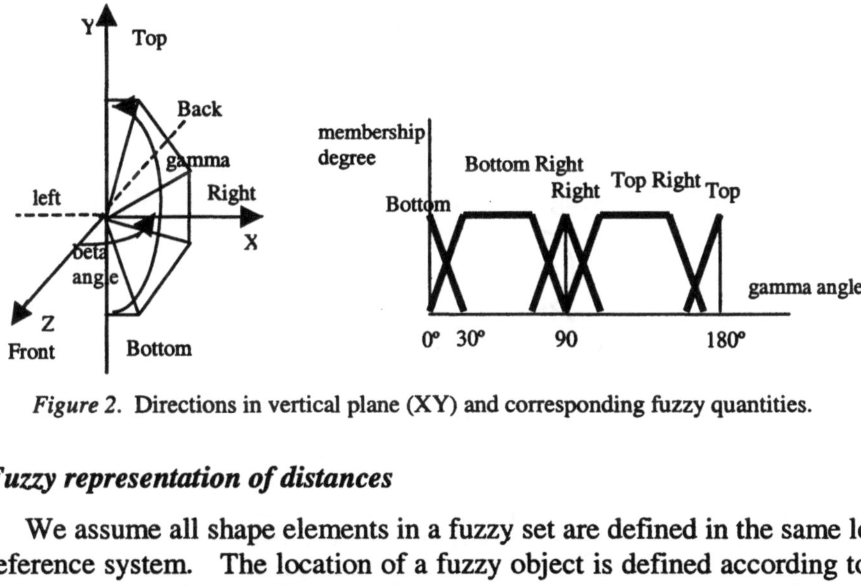

Figure 2. Directions in vertical plane (XY) and corresponding fuzzy quantities.

Fuzzy representation of distances

We assume all shape elements in a fuzzy set are defined in the same local reference system. The location of a fuzzy object is defined according to its reference point in a global coordinate system and a global transformation matrix can be formed for each shape components. Locations defined according to an existing object can be converted to the global coordinate system. Although distance can be specified linguistically such as *very close*, the domain of distance can hardly be fixed, hence it is very difficult to construct fuzzy sets for each word related to distance description. We therefore seek for the representation of fuzzy distance using fuzzy numbers, where each number is a fuzzy triangular norm. Since the orientations and distances are specified using fuzzy sets, the transformation matrix is also a fuzzy set. Take the translation transformation matrix for example. Assume that we move an object right about 3 units, up about 2 units, and forward about 4 units, then the transformation of the object will be:

$$X = X + \tilde{3}, \quad Y = Y + \tilde{2}, \quad Z = Z + \tilde{4},$$

where $\tilde{2}, \tilde{3}$, and $\tilde{4}$ are fuzzy triangular numbers with centre point at the real number of 2, 3, and 4.

2.3 Representation of fuzzy complex shape

A complex solid can be constructed using a graph model such as B-Rep or a Boolean model such as CSG. Since a superquadric model has no representation of vertices and edges, we use Boolean operations to compose complex objects from simple components. After a Boolean operation, the resultant shape becomes another shape component and can be submitted to further Boolean operations. This constructive approach, called Constructive Solid Geometry (CSG), uses a CSG tree to represent the construction process and the structure of a complex shape. In the CSG tree, each leaf node is a superquadric shape component along with its transformation matrix while each branch node is a Boolean set operation, including union (+), intersection (*), and subtraction (-) (Figure 3). Since the CSG model can be described in concise text language, it supports the top-down design process and is suitable for introducing fuzzy theory into complex shape design.

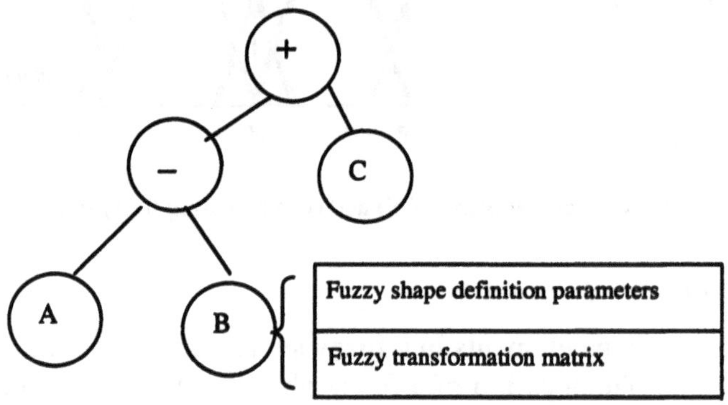

Figure 3. CSG representation of a composite shape

3. CONSTRUCTION OF FUZZY COMPLEX SHAPES

Once we know the size, position and orientation of two objects that have the same dimension (e.g. either 2D or 3D), we can perform Boolean operations on them to compose a complex shape. We discuss the Boolean set operations of crisp superquadric shapes first, then move to the discussion of Boolean operations on fuzzy shapes.

3.1 Boolean operations of crisp superquadric shapes

In CSG models, Boolean set operations are essentially the point set membership classification problem (or boundary classification) which determines if a given point *in* or *out* of a given solid and separates a whole space into two half spaces (Mäntylä 1988). The point set classification consists of two parts: the point set classification against each primitive in the CSG model and the combination of all classification results. If a primitive is composed of many half spaces, the point set classification against a primitive includes the classification against each half space and the final recombination. Since superquadrics uses only one analytic equation to define whether a point belongs to an object, it is also a kind of half-space modelling approach. Hence, we can apply the point set classification approaches for other CSG models to superquadric models.

As a superquadric primitive has only one half space, the point set classification is conceptually easier than other types of half spaces. However, superquadrics are higher-order analytic representation of geometric shapes, the calculation of the intersection points of two superquadric shapes cannot be based on the analytic calculation of two surfaces. Instead, they can only be obtained by numeric methods which discretise a solid into many units of basic shapes such as cubes. We therefore convert the superquadric shape representation to regular, exhaustive space enumeration where the interested space is partitioned into equal interval distance along x, y, and z directions. Boolean operations are then performed based on the point-set classification of all points in the space against each superquadric shape.

This hybrid model based on CSG and space enumeration uses pure half-space concept for Boolean operations. The exhaustive enumeration approach is simple, general, but needs huge memory consumption and is only approximate. We employ this model for testing the methods for performing Boolean operations on fuzzy objects which will be discussed in the next subsection. The union and difference operations of two crisp shapes, a rectangular prism and a double pyramid, are calculated using this model (Figure 4).

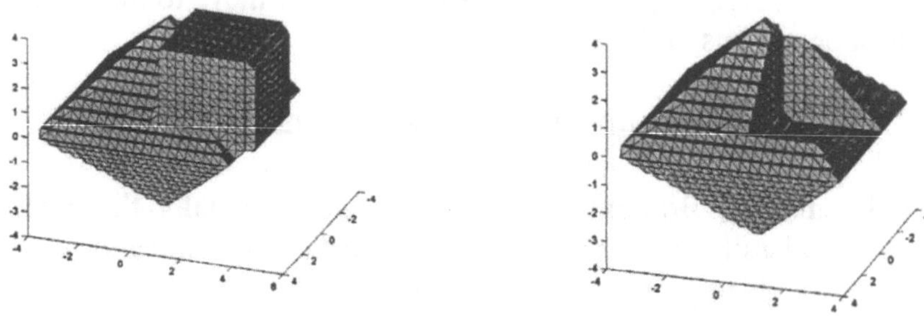

Figure 4. Union and difference operation of two crisp superquadric shapes.

3.2 Boolean operations of fuzzy superquadric shapes

A fuzzy shape is a set of crisp shapes controlled by fuzzy shape parameters (Figure 1). As the boundary of a fuzzy shape is not a crisp boundary but a boundary zone, the point set membership classification for Boolean operation cannot be performed using the conventional approach based on crisp half-space. One approach to solve this problem is to use the family of alpha-cuts representation of fuzzy sets and the interval principles (Klir and Yuan 1995). The family of alpha-cuts of a fuzzy set (Figure 5), which are fuzzy subsets with the membership grades of all elements equal to or greater than the value alpha, can uniquely represent a fuzzy set (Klir and Yuan 1995). Each alpha-cut can be represented by the two endpoints of this alpha level. Similarly, a fuzzy shape, which is a fuzzy set of shape elements, can be represented by its boundary shape elements in all alpha-levels. Each alpha-cut of a fuzzy shape includes an interval of crisp shapes between the two boundary shapes of this level. For example, a fuzzy circle with fixed centre location and fuzzy radius, can be represented by its lower and upper boundary circles at one alpha level (Figure 6(a)). The Boolean operations of two fuzzy shapes can therefore be mapped to the Boolean operations of the boundary shapes at each alpha-level. For each alpha level, only the boundary shapes are calculated and used for set operations. The resultant fuzzy shape is all shape elements between these boundary shapes at each alpha level. Using this approach, the set operations of fuzzy shapes are mapped to traditional Boolean operations of crisp objects.

The result of the set operation of two real number fuzzy sets is also a real number fuzzy set (Figure 5). The results of Boolean operations of two fuzzy shapes *A* and *B* are also fuzzy shapes. Assume $p=(p_1,p_2,\cdots,p_n)$, $n=9$, are shape parameters of a superquadric shape *S*(*p*), then the alpha-cut of fuzzy shape *A* is:

$$A(\alpha) = \{S(p) \mid p_i \in P_i(\alpha), i = 1 \cdots 9, \alpha \in [0,1]\}, \tag{2}$$

where P_i is the fuzzy value of parameter p_i. The membership degree of a crisp shape to a fuzzy set (shape) is the minimum of its membership degrees of all its parameters to the corresponding fuzzy values.

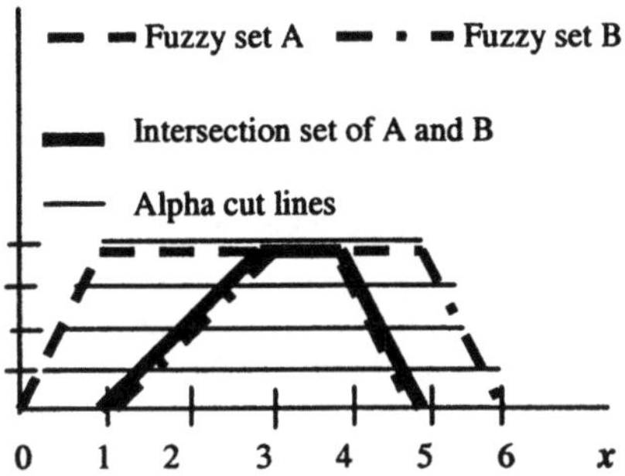

Figure 5. Fuzzy set intersection based on family of alpha–cuts.

According to the interval arithmetic principle and the family of alpha-cuts representation of fuzzy sets, the set operations of the two fuzzy shapes A and B, denoted by $A \circ B$, can be represented as:

$$A \circ B(\alpha) = \{a \circ b \mid a \in A(\alpha), b \in B(\alpha)\}. \tag{3}$$

Replacing each interval using their two end points, we can derive the following equation for calculating the interval of $A \circ B$:

$$\begin{aligned} &[A \circ B(\alpha)^- \quad A \circ B(\alpha)^+] = [\\ &\min\{a \circ b : a \in \{A(\alpha)^-, A(\alpha)^+\}, b \in \{B(\alpha)^-, B(\alpha)^+\}, \\ &\max\{a \circ b : a \in \{A(\alpha)^-, A(\alpha)^+\}, b \in \{B(\alpha)^-, B(\alpha)^+\}], \end{aligned} \tag{4}$$

where $A(\alpha)^-$ and $A(\alpha)^+$ represent the lower and upper bound of an interval for an alpha level of a fuzzy set A. The corresponding notions for set B and $A \circ B$ have the same meaning.

Since a shape has many parameters and each parameter has two boundary values at each alpha level, the boundary shapes of each alpha level are all shapes formed by the combination of all these boundary values. The two boundary shapes that participate in the set operation are selected according to their spatial occupancy (volume). The resultant boundary shapes of a set operation at an alpha level are again selected according to their spatial occupancy. The result of set operations of two fuzzy shapes is a new fuzzy complex shape and can attend further set operations. We take the union of two fuzzy circles as an example to show how the method based on the family of alpha-cuts works. Assume two fuzzy circles A and B are bounded, closed, and regular point set. They are located in their precise location and their radii take fuzzy values. At each alpha level, the radius for each circle has two lower and upper boundary values and thus defines two crisp circles denoted by A_L, A_U, B_L, and B_U (Figure 6(a)). The resultant fuzzy shape of the union operation on these two fuzzy shapes is bounded by four crisp shapes: A_LB_L, A_LB_U, A_UB_U (Figure 6(b)), and A_UB_L (Figure 6(c)). The resultant shapes, A_UB_U and A_LB_L, are selected as the boundary shapes for the union of the two fuzzy shapes at the corresponding alpha level because they have the minimum and maximum areas.

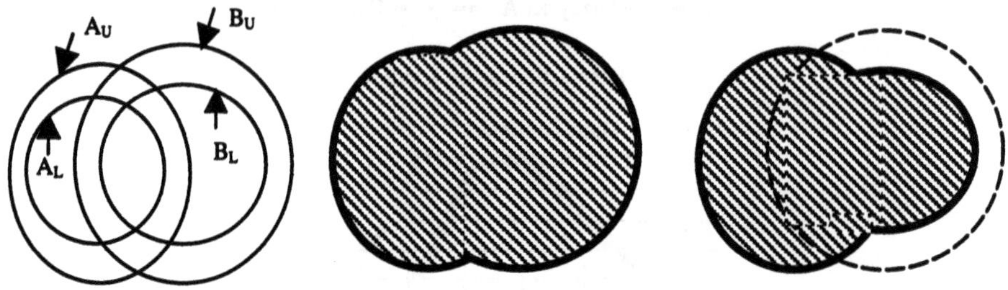

(a) Two fuzzy circles bounded by their boundary circles at an alpha level.

(b) Union of the two upper boundary circles (A_UB_U).

(c) Union of the an upper circle and a lower circle (A_UB_L).

Figure 6. Union of two fuzzy circles at one alpha level. (Dashed lines for reference only).

4. CONCEPTUAL MODEL OF THE FUZZY SHAPE DATABASE

A Solid Modeling (SM) system contains the geometry and topology information of modelled objects as well as a large amount of non-geometric information such as material properties. We focus on the management of geometry and topology information.

In our system, a fuzzy shape component is represented by a set of linguistic descriptors and a set of parameters with fuzzy values. A complex shape (or assembly) consists of shape components and subassemblies which are the combination of a group of components and/or other subassemblies. The order and the way in which shape components and/or subassemblies are assembled is modelled in a CSG tree (Figure 3). A CSG tree can be stored in different levels where leaf nodes and sub-trees can be used many times.

We use the CSG model as the main modeller for structural representation and the regular space enumeration model as the secondary modeller for Boolean operations and the calculations of geometric properties. The CSG model is internally converted into space enumeration. These two models coexist to avoid the conversion effort and support quick display. When the CSG model changes, the corresponding space enumeration model should be upgraded associatively. We focus on shapes that were created by a set of Boolean operations on a set of predefined fuzzy shape components according to specified fuzzy spatial information. As the dataset for the space enumeration model is very large, it is calculated after the construction process and only the dataset for the resultant shape is stored.

Relational database management systems (RDBMS), which use tables as basic units, are very popular because of their simple structure, quick response time, and firm foundation on relational mathematics. Hence, many existing SM systems have interfaces to one or more RDBMS such as ORACLE (LaCourse 1995). As a RDBMS uses flat tables to represent data, it meets difficulties in handling large assemblies because of the complex semantics associated with 3D models and complex nested entities. An object-oriented database management system (OODBMS), which is a collection of data and methods, can capture the complex semantics and structures, but it has no firm theory foundation and no easy-to-use query language. Object relational database systems (ORDBMS), a hybrid of RDBMS and OODBMS, can handle complex data and still can use the knowledge and experience obtained from RDBMS (Connolly et al. 1999). We therefore chose the ORDBMS to construct the shape database and developed a fuzzy processing module for handling fuzzy values. We call this shape database a fuzzy database because the attribute values are fuzzy and the query processing is based on fuzzy theory. The basic structure of an assembly database, including the entities and attributes as well as relationships between tables are shown in Figure 7. The Descriptors, Parameters, and Transformation matrix take complex array structure and have fuzzy values. A fuzzy set is treated as an object with data and corresponding methods for processing the data.

5. INDEXING AND QUERY OF FUZZY SHAPES

A CAD database allows the attachment of attributes to a solid object and uses these attributes to retrieve objects. Indexing is the task aimed at finding a set of attributes which can identify an object in a relation. In the fuzzy shape database, every shape has a unique, system-generated identification code and is employed as the primary key to support quick searching. Database users often want to retrieve data based on one or more values which are not the primary key. Hence, secondary keys need to be specified to index shapes for different searching purposes. The combination of shape name and version is usually employed as an alternative index. Hence, we also provide this index to conform to the general systems. As conventional CAD systems are based on exact geometric information and qualitative information is not readily available, higher-level semantic shape searching is almost impossible. However, in the fuzzy solid modelling system, fuzzy shape components are specified using a set of linguistic words such as *very round* or *extremely bent*. This set of shape descriptors can be used to index shape and support semantic-based shape query and retrieval. We therefore derive a set of descriptors from the characteristics of superquadrics, including *squarness, roundness, bevelness, pinchness, bendness, taperness,* and *twistness,* to index shape components (Zhang et al. 2002b).

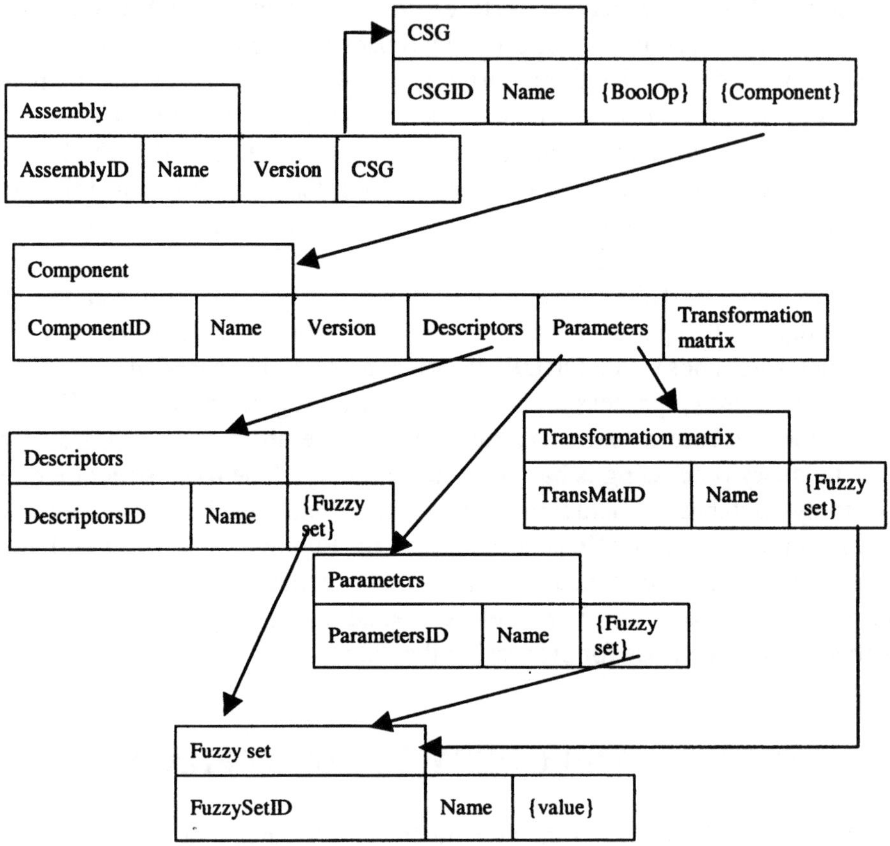

Figure 7. Database structure for fuzzy shapes

In a conventional database, a data item is self-indexed. For example, the query "find people whose salary is over $2000" can always find the satisfied people if suitable tuples exist. Hence, users just need to specify attributes for indexing and do not need specify a special measure to evaluate the index. However, in a fuzzy database, an attribute may take a fuzzy value and it cannot index itself because a fuzzy set is a range value with different membership degrees. Hence, a measure determining whether a fuzzy datum satisfy a fuzzy condition must be defined. We use the *similarity measure* which is the minimum ratio of the cardinal (area) of the intersection of two fuzzy sets to their own cardinals. Once we define this measure, we can perform a fuzzy query such as "find a slightly bent shape" from a set of shapes having the attribute bendness and taking fuzzy values. If the attribute value is crisp, the similarity measure degenerates to the membership degree to which the crisp value belongs to the condition fuzzy set.

A complex shape is the result of Boolean combinations over fuzzy shape components but the properties of the original components may be eliminated after Boolean operations. Therefore, we cannot query a complex shape by descriptors directly. However, a complex shape is maintained by a CSG tree, including a set of components and their corresponding transformation matrices. So, we can query a complex shape according to its construction process. Although the same object may have many different construction processes and hence have many different CSG models, one CSG model corresponds to only one solid shape. In addition, experienced designers tend to use a set of rules (experiences) to guide the construction process, hence, for the same complex shape, different designers will have the same construction process in many cases. The support of CSG-based query is therefore desirable. CSG model is concise and can be represented using text such as "C = A + B". Such a property along with the linguistic description of shape components and spatial information make it possible to formulate a query using words. For example, the query "find a shape which is the union of a very bent cylinder and a very sharp pyramid" can be performed.

The CSG-based searching is essentially a graph matching problem. Graph matching techniques, such as the Labelled Graph Matching (LGM) which finds the optimal correspondence between two graphs (Shams and Brady 2001) or the Largest Common Subgraph detection (LCSG) which finds the largest collection of objects with the same relationship in both images (Shearer et al. 2001), have been applied mostly to image processing area. As the CSG tree representation of a complex shape is also a graph, these techniques can also be used to support structure-based object searching. To support the graph matching in an SM database, we first translate the text-based query into a CSG tree, then we can use the approach proposed by Shearer et al (Shearer et al. 2001) to find the largest common subgraph of the condition CSG and a datum CSG. As the shape component and the transformation matrices contain fuzzy data, this matching process will also use the similarity measure of fuzzy sets to calculate the similarity of two CSG trees. The detailed equation for calculating the similarity of two graph without fuzzy data can be found in (Shearer et al. 2001). The similarity calculation of two CSG trees with fuzzy shape components and fuzzy transformation matrices needs to calculate the similarity of two fuzzy components or two fuzzy numbers and corresponding algorithms can be found in (Zhang et al. 2002b). This CSG-based index can find complex shapes according to their construction process, spatial information and shape components. The similarity calculation of two CSG graphs can also be weighted and the weightings of these three factors can be predefined.

A query interface which supports flexible, uncertain understanding can better grasp a designer's thinking and will be easier to be accepted. Hence, the CSG-based shape indexing and the natural language-based query will be very helpful and complementary to the conventional shape indexing and query approaches.

6. CONCLUSIONS AND FUTURE WORK

The fuzzy representation of shapes, distance, and orientation as well as the set operations on fuzzy complex shapes based on the technique of family of alpha-cuts make it possible for a solid modelling system to handle imprecise information. The fuzzy database model, which is implemented within the framework of an object relational database with the incorporation of a fuzzy processing module, makes it possible to manage fuzzy shapes. However, fuzzy computation is time consuming because of the higher order of superquadrics and the large amount of data processing for fuzzy sets.

The construction of fuzzy complex shapes based on the family of alpha-cuts approach has been tested in a prototype system. A prototype system for the management of fuzzy components has been constructed. Hence, future work includes extending the fuzzy database to cater for the management of fuzzy complex shapes, refining and optimising the proposed approach and investigating new approaches for fuzzy shape design and management.

REFERENCES

Anile, A. M., Falcidieno, B., Gallo, G., Spagnuolo, M., and Spinello, S. (2000). "Modeling Uncertain Data With Fuzzy B-Splines." *Fuzzy Sets and Systems*, 113, 397-410.

Barr, A. H. (1981). "Superquadrics and Angle-preserving Transformations." *IEEE Computer Graphics & Appl.*, 1, 11-23.

Barr, A. H. (1984). "Global and Local Deformations of Solid Primitives." *Computer Graphics*, 18(3), 21-30.

Buckley, J. J., and Eslami, E. (1997a). "Fuzzy Plane Geometry II: Circles and Polygons." *Fuzzy Sets and Systems*, 87(1), 79-85.

Buckley, J. J., and Eslami, E. (1997b). "Fuzzy Plane Geometry I: Points and Lines." *Fuzzy Sets and Systems*, 86, 179-187.

Connolly, T. M., Begg, C., and Strachan, A. (1999). *Database Systems*, ADDISON-WESLEY, England.

Dickinson, S., Biederman, I., Pentland, A., Eklundh, J.-O., Bergevin, R., and Munck-Faiwood, R. (1993). "The Use of Geons for Generic 3-D Object Recognition, ." Proc. *Intl. Joint Conf. on Artificial Intelligence (IJCAI)*, Chambery, France, 1693-1699.

Hernández, D. (1994). *Qualitative representation of spatial knowledge*, Springer-Verlag, Berlin ; New York.

Klir, G., and Yuan, B. (1995). *Fuzzy Sets and Fuzzy Logic*, Prentice Hall, New Jersey.

LaCourse, D. E. (1995). *Handbook of solid modeling*, McGraw-Hill, New York.
Mäntylä, M. (1988). *An Introduction to Solid Modeling*, Computer Science Press, Inc., U.S.A.
Martin, R. R. (1994). "Modelling inexact shapes with fuzzy sets." Proc. of CSG'94, J. R. Woodwark, ed., Information Geometers Ltd., Winchester, 73-98.
Pham, B. (2001). "Representation of Fuzzy Shapes." Proc. of International Workshop on Visual Form 4, C. Arcelli, ed., Springer-Verlag Berlin Heidelberg, LNCS, 2059, 239-248.
Pham, B., and Zhang, J. (2000). "A Fuzzy Shape Specification System to Support Design for Aesthetics." Soft Computing in Measurement and Information Acquisition, L. Reznik, ed., Physica-Verlag, Heidelberg, in print.
Rosenfeld, A. (1998). "Fuzzy geometry: An updated overview." *Information Sciences*, 110, 127-133.
Shah, J. J., and Mäntylä, M. (1995). *Parametric and Feature-Based CAD/CAM*, John Wiley & Sons, Inc., NY, U.S.A.
Shams, L. B., and Brady, M. J. (2001). "Graph matching vs mutual information maximization for object detection." *Neural Networks*, 14, 345-354.
Shearer, K., Bunke, H., and Venkatesh, S. (2001). "Video indexing and similarity retrieval by largest common subgraph detection using decision trees." *Pattern Recognition*, 34, 1075-1091.
Zadeh, L. A., and Kacprzyk, J. (1999). "Computing with Words in Information/Intelligent Systems 1: Foundations." Studies in Fuzziness and Soft Computing, L. A. Zadeh and J. Kacprzyk, eds., Physica-Verlag Heidelberg.
Zhang, J., Pham, B., and Chen, P. (2001). "Fuzzy Genetic Algorithms Based on Level Interval Algorithm." Proc. of the 10th IEEE Intl. Conf. on Fuzzy Systems, Melbourne, Australia.
Zhang, J., Pham, B., and Chen, P. (2002a). "A Fuzzy Genetic Algorithm for Creative Shape Design." Proc. of the Fourth International Symposium on Tools and Methods of Competitive Engineering (TMCE 2002), accepted, Wuhan, China.
Zhang, J., Pham, B., and Chen, P. (2002b). "Indexing and Retrieval of Fuzzy Shapes." Fuzzy Logic: A Framework for the New Millennium, V. Dimitrov and V. Korotkich, eds., Physica-Verlag, Heidelberg, 240-250.

BIOGRAPHIES

Jinglan Zhang is a PhD student in Information Technology at the Queensland University of Technology, Australia. She received her BS and MS degrees in CAD/CAM from Beijing University of Aeronautics and Astronautics, China. Her current research interests include applications of fuzzy logic and evolutionary computation in CAD systems.

Binh Pham is currently the Professor and Director of Research in the Faculty of Information Technology at the Queensland University of Technology, Brisbane, Australia. Her research interests include computer graphics, multimedia, CAD, image analysis, and intelligent systems.

Phoebe Y. Chen is currently the Lecturer in the Faculty of Information Technology at the Queensland University of Technology, Brisbane, Australia. She completed her PhD in the field of Information Systems and Computer Science at the University of Queensland. Her research interests include scientific visualization, multimedia, bioinformatics, database technologies and web-based intelligent systems.

Author Index

MIX
Papier aus verantwortungsvollen Quellen
Paper from responsible sources
FSC® C105338

If you have any concerns about our products,
you can contact us on
ProductSafety@springernature.com

In case Publisher is established outside the EU,
the EU authorized representative is:
Springer Nature Customer Service Center GmbH
Europaplatz 3, 69115 Heidelberg, Germany

Printed by Libri Plureos GmbH
in Hamburg, Germany